£37.50

JUDGE WITHOUT JURY

Judge Without Jury

Diplock Trials in the Adversary System

JOHN JACKSON

and

SEAN DORAN

CLARENDON PRESS · OXFORD
1995

Oxford University Press, Walton Street, Oxford OX2 6DP
Oxford New York
Athens Auckland Bangkok Bombay
Calcutta Cape Town Dar es Salaam Delhi
Florence Hong Kong Istanbul Karachi
Kuala Lumpur Madras Madrid Melbourne
Mexico City Nairobi Paris Singapore
Taipei Tokyo Toronto
and associated companies in
Berlin Ibadan

Oxford is a trade mark of Oxford University Press

Published in the United States
by Oxford University Press Inc., New York

British Library Cataloguing in Publication Data
Data available

Library of Congress Cataloging in Publication Data
Jackson, John.
Judge without jury: Diplock trials in the adversary system/John
Jackson and Sean Doran.
p. cm.—(Oxford monographs on criminal law and criminal
justice)
Includes bibliographical references and index.
1. Criminal procedure—Northern Ireland. 2. Jury—Northern
Ireland. I. Doran, Seán. II. Title. III. Series.
KDE550.J313 1995
345.416'05—dc20
[344.16055] 95–2377
ISBN 0–19–825889–5

1 3 5 7 9 10 8 6 4 2

Typeset by Cambrian Typesetters Frimley, Surrey
Printed in Great Britain
on acid-free paper by
Bookcraft Ltd., Midsomer Norton, Avon

To Kathy, Jane and Alex.
J. J.

To my father.
S. D.

General Editor's Introduction

At a time when the merits of jury trial are under discussion in many jurisdictions, this major comparative study of jury and non-jury trials is particularly welcome. Its empirical foundations lie in the system in Northern Ireland, where jury trials and judge-only trials have been conducted in different categories of criminal case for some years. Based on observation of trials and on interviews with key actors, including judges and counsel, the study also makes some comparisons with other jurisdictions in which judge-only trials take place. It advances the debate about trial by jury in criminal cases in several ways. Often that debate is conducted without any exploration of alternative modes of trial: this study delves deep into one such alternative. Often that debate involves assumptions about the effect of judge-only trials on the accusatorial or inquisitorial nature of proceedings: this study discusses what the main implications are, and argues that consideration of the procedural aspects should not be neglected when taking decisions on the nature of the tribunal. In this study the authors raise the debate about the criminal trial to a new level.

Andrew Ashworth
London
1995

Preface

Of all the departures from the normal legal process occasioned by Northern Ireland's troubled recent past, the system of trial without jury in Diplock courts must rank as the most significant. Just as the institution of the jury is frequently characterised as the hallmark of a stable legal system, the denial of jury trial to persons charged with offences related to the troubles has often been viewed as a symbol of the instability of an emergency legal regime.

When the Diplock trial system was introduced in 1973 on the recommendation of Lord Diplock as part of a package of measures designed to deal more effectively with the growing threat of political violence, few would have predicted its enduring for over two decades. Yet when we began to examine Diplock trials in the late eighties, they had become an established feature of Northern Ireland's criminal justice system, dealing with around one-third of all serious criminal cases in the jurisdiction. With no end to violence in sight at that point in time, the Diplock era seemed set to continue indefinitely. At the time of writing now, however, our project having been completed, the political scene has been transformed and the Diplock trial system no longer carries that same air of permanence. Violence has given way to a period of peace and calls are being made for the dismantling of the entire emergency regime, including the Diplock courts.

It is therefore a particularly apposite time to evaluate the Diplock trial system and this is one purpose of the book. Beyond this objective, however, we have sought to consider more broadly the effect that the withdrawal of the jury produces on the adversarial trial process. Although the trial of serious cases without a jury is often perceived as alien to our legal culture, it is a growing phenomenon throughout the common law world. Yet given the centrality of the jury to the development of the rules and practices of the criminal trial, it is difficult to imagine that the character of that trial remains unchanged in the jury's absence. One might expect, for example, that the new found judicial role as the ultimate decision-maker would tempt judges to adopt a more interventionist or 'inquisitorial' stance during the trial. In addition, it might be thought that judges lack the 'freshness' of approach which the jury imports to the criminal process and may therefore develop an intolerance to defence arguments heard repeatedly over time. The conduct of counsel could also be expected to alter in the changed setting of the non-jury trial. If the character of the proceedings *is* affected in these ways, then we must consider whether the removal of the jury needs to be accompanied by a thorough rethinking of the trial process rather than resting on the assumption that our existing trial structure can simply accommodate such fundamental change.

These issues lie at the heart of the book, with the Diplock trial serving as their backdrop. A lasting peace may signal the end of the Diplock regime, and many would greet its departure with relief, as the passing of one of the most prominent images of the Northern Ireland troubles. But even if the courts are consigned to the basement of Northern Ireland's chequered past, there are wider lessons to be drawn from the Diplock experience of judging without jury. This book aims to extract these lessons.

John Jackson and Sean Doran
Belfast
March 1995

Acknowledgements

In the setting up and conduct of the research project which led to this book and in the course of writing the book itself, we have been fortunate to receive assistance, encouragement and support from many quarters. First thanks must go to the Leverhulme Trust for funding the research project over a period of two and a half years (1989–92). The grant received enabled us primarily to employ a research associate throughout the fieldwork phase of the project. Our research associate, Adele Watters, deserves much praise for her patient and thorough observation of trials and her meticulous attention to detail in the compilation of the results of the study. Without Adele's assistance, the authors would no doubt have struggled in vain to overcome their ingrained lawyers' resistance to the discipline of statistical analysis.

A study of participants in the trial process would be much impeded in the absence of their co-operation. We acknowledge gratefully, therefore, the co-operation of the Lord Chief Justice of Northern Ireland, who gave permission for notes to be taken, for transcripts to be made of court proceedings and for interviews to be conducted with judges. Thanks are also due to those judges and members of the Bar who agreed to be interviewed by us and who gave up their time to talk to us. These interviews were conducted on the understanding that anonymity would be guaranteed and we have endeavoured to meet this understanding. Staff of the Northern Ireland Court Service and the Statistics and Research Branch of the Criminal Justice Policy Division, Northern Ireland Office, are also to be thanked for their assistance, particularly in supplying us with any statistical information which we requested.

Throughout the writing of the book, we called upon various readers to subject our work to early critical scrutiny. They did so willingly and their comments played an important part in our shaping of the final product. Special thanks are due in this regard to Neil Duxbury and Joanna Shapland. From the early stages of the project to its completion, their advice, encouragement and copious comments on draft chapters were truly invaluable to us.

We would also like to thank the following for their comments on draft chapters of the book: Ron Allen, Andrew Ashworth, Derek Beyleveld, Dennis Boyd, Craig Callen, Colm Campbell, Matthew Campbell, Brice Dickson, John Finn, Eliahu Harnon, Tim Jones, Maria Leitner, Ken Lidstone, David Nelken, Mike Seigel, William Twining, and Martin Wasik.

For their help and encouragement in getting the project off to a good start, thanks are due to Des Greer, Reid Hastie and Peter Tillers. Also to His Honour Judge Bentley, Yvonne Jacobs, and Rick Lempert, for providing us with materials and ideas at different stages of the project.

There were several occasions on which either one or both of us gave an airing to the ideas emerging from our work in progress. The participants at the following seminars and conferences are thanked for their encouragement and comments: staff seminar, Faculty of Law, University of Manchester, December 1989; staff seminars, Faculty of Law, Queen's University, Belfast, May 1990 and May 1991; postgraduate seminar, Faculty of Law, University of Sheffield, February 1994; International Seminar on Evidence and Litigation, Cardozo Law School, New York, March 1990; Reform of Evidence Conference, organised by the Society for the Reform of Criminal Law, Vancouver, August 1992; Rights of the Accused Conference, Jerusalem, December 1993; United Kingdom Association of Law and Philosophy Conference, Glasgow, March 1994.

We are grateful to the following for giving us their permission to cite and quote from unpublished work: Ron Allen, Sir Louis Blom-Cooper, Mirjan Damaska and Joanna Shapland.

Considerable assistance was also given to us by staff at the law libraries of Queen's University, Belfast, Manchester University and Sheffield University. We are grateful too for the secretarial assistance given to us at those institutions. Particular thanks to Sarah Tiffany at Manchester for her work on the presentation of the tables in the book.

Sean is indebted to the Faculty of Law at Manchester for a valuable period of study leave in Michaelmas Term 1991.

Credit is due also to the staff at Oxford University Press for their work in the editing and production of the book.

Finally, we would like to pay tribute to our families and friends for their support and their patience in sticking with us throughout this lengthy project. Many thanks.

The largest single factor in administration of law after all is the personality of the judge.

Leon Green, *Judge and Jury*

Contents

Table of Cases

Table of Statutes

1

Introduction

There is no more potent symbol of the common law tradition than the jury. From fictional portrayals of the legal process in action to popular accounts of notable cases, the jury is typically presented as the fulcrum of the adversary trial system. Legal scholarship too has concentrated considerable attention on the institution of the jury, both on the mechanics of this method of trial and on the broader issue of the desirability of lay participation in the administration of justice. In the words of one author, the orthodox literature in the field of evidence has tended 'to treat the contested jury trial as the paradigm case of all trials.'[1]

There are, however, several ironic facets of such 'jury-centredness' which have provided much of the stimulus for this book. First, the actual part played by the jury in the legal process is much more limited than its popular depiction would suggest. Although the jury is viewed by most as the *ideal* mode of conducting trials according to adversarial tenets, its practical influence has for many years been in steady decline. Juries have virtually disappeared from civil proceedings and they are now called upon infrequently in coroners' courts.[2] Further, magistrates' courts, which process the bulk of criminal cases, are being entrusted with an ever-expanding range of offences deemed suitable for summary trial.[3]

Secondly, in many Commonwealth and other common law jurisdictions, even the jury's traditionally sacred domain of the serious criminal trial has yielded to other forms of tribunal.[4] In several African countries and in India, for example, trial by judge and assessors has become the norm. In Singapore the trial of serious criminal cases is conducted by a judge sitting alone and in Israel criminal cases are tried by a judge alone or in the most serious cases by

---

[1] Twining (1990), 157.

[2] For discussion of the limited circumstances in which the jury is used in civil trials, see Spencer (1989), 394–6.

[3] The ability of defendants to elect for trial by jury has been eroded since the recommendation of the James Committee (1975) that a number of offences be transferred to the sole jurisdiction of magistrates. See section 15 of the Criminal Law Act 1977 and sections 37 and 39 of the Criminal Justice Act 1988. Note also the recommendation of the Royal Commission on Criminal Justice that the accused's right to elect for jury trial in 'either way' offences be abolished: see note 17 below and accompanying text.

[4] For discussion of the jury in other common law countries, see Cornish (1968), 15–18; Enright and Morton (1990), 141–6.

a panel of three judges. More strikingly, in the United States and Canada, which (the former in particular) many would cite as the jury's most secure territory and which do remain closely wedded to the jury ideal, it is possible for an accused to opt for trial by judge alone in all but the most serious cases.[5] Lastly, and central to the present work, there are some jurisdictions which have preserved jury trial in the normal run of cases, but which have been driven by certain exigencies to abandon it for limited categories of cases. Thus, cases connected with the emergency situation in Northern Ireland are dealt with by a judge sitting alone in a Diplock court,[6] while in the Republic of Ireland trials with terrorist connotations are handled by the Special Criminal Court, composed of a panel of three judges.[7]

The third source of irony is the obdurate public support of the jury in the face of the most caustic criticism from within and without the legal fraternity. On one hand, it is claimed that 'society is undergoing a major crisis of confidence in the jury system,'[8] and it is certainly more acceptable in the nineties to question the jury's efficacy than in the days when Lord Devlin and others were most eloquently extolling its virtues.[9] The perception of the jury as a varied group of individuals who import a collective civilian common sense to the legal process, and who are thereby well equipped to hand down decisions on factual matters in dispute, is now frequently condemned as idealistic and unreal.[10] Specific concerns about high acquittal rates,[11] jury 'nobbling',[12] the cost of conducting trials[13] and the complexity of certain trials such as those involving serious fraud[14] have tended to chip away at the credibility accorded to the jury's decision-making prowess. The fact that eminent legal personae, such as Lord Hailsham and Lord Roskill, have added their voices to the sceptical lobby has fortified the view that the jury is an institution under threat.

On the other hand, commitment to the principle of trial by jury remains strong and any call for its abolition or modification invariably meets with a robust rejoinder in its defence.[15] The uncovering of a number of serious miscarriages of justice in England and Wales prompted the establishment in 1991 of a Royal Commission on Criminal Justice to make a critical

---

[5] For a brief historical account of the right to waive jury trial in the United States, see Kalven and Zeisel (1966), 22–4.

[6] The name derives from the Commission, chaired by Lord Diplock in 1972, which proposed the adoption of non-jury courts in trials arising out of the emergency.

[7] For discussion, see Robinson (1974), (1980); Ryan and Magee (1983), 377–90; Jackson (1986), 66–7; Walker and Hogan (1989), 227–44.

[8] Enright and Morton (1990), 1.   [9] See Devlin (1956).

[10] See, for example, Darbyshire (1991).   [11] See Mark (1973).

[12] See Spencer (1989), 259; Enright and Morton (1990), 70–4, 148–9.

[13] James Report (1975): see note 3 above.

[14] Roskill Report (1986).

[15] See letters responding to Darbyshire (1991) in Criminal Law Review [1992] 387–9.

evaluation of many facets of the English criminal justice system. Interestingly, the jury was not mentioned in the Commission's terms of reference,[16] but one of the Commission's most controversial recommendations was a proposal to abolish the defendant's right to elect for jury trial in so-called either-way offences (that is, offences which are triable either in the Crown Court or in the magistrates' court).[17] This proposal provoked an immediate outcry and, in contrast to many other of the Commission's recommendations, it was not endorsed by the Government.[18]

A number of points may be made in defence of the jury, but perhaps one of the most telling is the way in which it can act as a link between the community of professional participants who operate within the criminal justice system (for example, the police, court administrators, probation officers, prosecutors, lawyers, and judges) and the community outside who are, of course, affected by crime and the criminal justice system but who have little voice within it. As one writer has graphically put it, the jury system injects 'lay acid' into the legal system.[19] One of the most significant features to be highlighted by studies of the criminal process made in the last 30 years is the fact that structural changes within criminal justice have been geared towards 'crime control' rather than 'due process', to use Packer's famous dichotomy.[20] The 'crime control model' is a system dedicated to apprehending and convicting the guilty as speedily as possible by putting a premium on the fact-finding endeavours of the police rather than on formal trial procedures. The system, analogous to a conveyor belt production line, is to be contrasted with the 'due process model' which stresses the possibility of error and the freedom of the individual by erecting an obstacle course of formal, adversary processes before individuals can be convicted. This is not to say that all professional participants within the system are steeped in a crime control ideology. The problem is that these participants can easily be sucked into a system of conviction. In their study of defendants in the criminal court system of England and Wales, Bottoms and McClean saw a divergence not so much between crime control and due process, as between what they called a 'liberal bureaucratic' model, which gives some recognition to the protection of defendants but which still emphasizes

---

[16] For the Commission's terms of reference, see p. iii of its report.

[17] See recommendation 114 of the report.

[18] For comment on the reaction to the proposal, see Maher (1994). The recommendation is officially 'under consideration', but the government has announced that it is considering alternative means of retaining in the magistrates' courts cases which are 'most appropriately dealt with there', including the reclassification of offences, and mechanisms allowing magistrates to retain jurisdiction in more cases. See *Interim Government Response to the Royal Commission on Criminal Justice* (Feb. 1994).

[19] Bankowski (1988), 20.

[20] Packer (1964). See, for example, in this country, Bottoms and McClean (1976); McBarnet (1981); McConville and Baldwin (1981); McConville, Sanders, and Leng (1991).

quantitative output, and a due process model, which emphasizes above all quality control at the expense of quantitative output.[21] Although there were similarities in the value systems underlying these two models, in practice the liberal bureaucratic model offered much stronger support to the aims of the crime control model than to those of the due process model. The jury system can be viewed as counter-balancing this liberal bureaucratic system in those cases which are eventually contested in the Crown Court, and as upholding due process values at least to the extent that defendants are assured of an independent external scrutiny of the merits of the prosecution case. Of course, jury trial is in practice an infrequent phenomenon. Nonetheless, its very existence symbolizes adherence to due process.[22]

In her renowned analysis of the criminal process, however, McBarnet was sceptical about the extent to which the jury system contributes to due process.[23] Throughout her study she distinguished between the ideology and the substance of the law, between the rhetoric of due process and the practice and structure of criminal justice. The rhetoric of due process suggests that it is the common sense of juries that decides the verdict, but the reality of criminal justice practice is that trial by jury is a rare event, and that when it does occur the jury's decision is critically affected by rules of evidence, case law, advocacy, and the role of the judge. A more recent study has given support to this view by concluding that the police, who are steeped in an overtly crime control professional culture and ideology, occupy a pivotal position in the process (in spite of the presence of the Crown Prosecution Service) because they control who is charged with what offences, and they control the information relevant to the charge.[24] Others have also concluded that conviction and sentencing are fundamentally influenced by the police.[25] The participants who work within the court system (apparently the jury included) can normally do little other than endorse the constructions of guilt made by the police, because they do not have the means to do otherwise.

One problem with evaluating the jury system in the United Kingdom is that researchers are forbidden from examining what goes on in the jury room, with the result that we know very little about how juries actually operate.[26] Some jury research was conducted in the 1970s, mainly comparing real jury verdicts with the verdicts of mock or shadow juries and

---

[21] Bottoms and McClean (1976), 226–32.
[22] See Chan, Duff, Findlay, and Howarth (1990), 92.   [23] McBarnet (1981).
[24] McConville, Sanders, and Leng (1991).
[25] See Chambliss and Seidman (1971); Ericson and Baranek (1982).
[26] The prohibition is contained in section 8 of the Contempt of Court Act 1981. The Royal Commission on Criminal Justice recommended that section 8 should be amended to enable research to be conducted into juries' reasons for their verdicts. See recommendation 1 of the report.

with the views of professional participants.[27] Research conducted for the Royal Commission on Criminal Justice examined juror perceptions of jury service.[28] Whether the continuing faith in the jury system is warranted, it should be recognized that the system can act as an obstacle to the implementation of reforms at other stages of the criminal process, both before and after trial. Some, including the Home Secretary who established the Royal Commission on Criminal Justice, called for the Commission to review the suitability of the entire adversary system and suggested that it give serious consideration to the alternative, 'inquisitorial' systems favoured in continental Europe. The reforms canvassed by the Commission included the establishment of some form of pre-trial judicial examination along the lines of the *juge d'instruction* in France and the establishment of an independent forensic science service accountable to the courts. The jury poses no direct obstacle to these reforms. Indeed, proof-taking in serious cases in France is in the hands of a career judge before trial, and yet lay adjudicators sitting with professional judges decide the ultimate verdict in the *cour d'assises*.[29] The jury system nevertheless provides a justification for regarding the oral adversarial trial as the centrepiece of criminal justice in common law systems, and such a system questions the need for more formal pre-trial procedures. The argument runs as follows: so long as defendants have the right to their day in court with counsel to argue their case before an independent lay community of peers, what need is there to overhaul pre-trial procedures?[30] The role of the jury can also be seen as an impediment to the creation of effective appellate procedures at the culmination of the criminal process. For one thing, the general verdict delivered by the jury is arguably less pervious to effective review than a reasoned judgment. Another problem is that an appellate court may be reluctant to interfere with a jury verdict in any event, because to override its verdict is to question the value of trial by jury. The English Court of Appeal has been notoriously reluctant to interfere with jury verdicts for this very reason.[31]

A final and arguably most telling irony of the focus on jury trial is that,

---

[27] See Zander (1974); McCabe and Purves (1972), (1974); Baldwin and McConville (1979). For a review of the state of jury research in the United Kingdom, see McCabe (1988); Jackson (1990c).

[28] See Zander (1992). See also Jackson, Kilpatrick and Harvey (1991).

[29] See Pradel (1994), 114; Munday (1993).

[30] This attitude seems prevalent among defendants and defence lawyers, who appear to believe that what happens in court is much more significant than what happens in the police station. See McConville, Sanders, and Leng (1991), 171–2.

[31] 'Since justice is as much concerned with the conviction of the guilty as the acquittal of the innocent, and the task of convicting the guilty belongs constitutionally to the jury, not to us, the role of the Criminal Division of the Court of Appeal is necessarily limited.' (*R v McIlkenny and others* [1992] 2 All ER 417, 425.) See also Justice (1989), para. 4.17 and Nobles, Schiff, and Shaldon (1993).

while the general jury debate has never ceased to attract new and
worthwhile contributions,[32] there is one fundamental area in which the
debate remains relatively uninformed. In contrast to the flourishing body of
literature on the merits and demerits of jury trial, relatively little attention
has been given to the operation of alternative decision-making mechanisms.[33] Despite the wide-ranging nature of its terms of reference the Royal
Commission did not consider radical structural changes. Its solution to the
resource problem, as it saw it, of large numbers of persons electing for trial
in the Crown Court was to abolish the right of election in either-way cases
rather than to look critically at the existing modes of trial and consider
alternative means (short of jury trial) of disposing of middle-range offences
which might prove more acceptable than trial in the magistrates' court.[34]
Even those who have been fundamentally critical of jury trial have tended
neither to offer detailed advice on the construction of a replacement, nor to
study in depth the workings of other trial structures which are already in
place. There have been a number of academic studies of the work of
magistrates' courts.[35] Such studies however, while valuable in themselves,
are not truly pertinent to the jury debate as they are confined to the trial of
less serious cases, presided over in the main by lay magistrates rather than
professional judges.[36] To borrow from McBarnet, trial at summary level is
geared to the ideology of triviality, while the Crown Court trial is geared in
its ideology to the structures of legality.[37] We are concerned with this upper
tier of the criminal justice system and, in particular, the implications of the
removal of what many would regard as its cornerstone, the jury.

On the one hand, there may be fears that the withdrawal of the jury would
further exacerbate the tendency towards conviction which has been the
hallmark of the pre-trial and summary processes, and that the kind of
bureaucratic case management which characterizes those processes would

---

[32] For a collection of essays which offer a useful introduction to the present state of the jury
debate, see Findlay and Duff (1988).

[33] There is a burgeoning literature on alternative dispute resolution, but this has mainly
been confined to civil cases. See the special issue of the Modern Law Review devoted to the
W. G. Hart legal workshop on 'Dispute Resolution: Civil Justice and its Alternatives' (1993)
56 Modern Law Review 277–470 (May issue).

[34] See generally Jackson (1994).

[35] See, for example, Carlen (1976); Bankowski, Hutton, and McManus (1987). In the light
of its proposal to abolish the right of election in either-way offences, which on the
Commission's own reckoning would have increased the work-load of the magistrates' courts
quite considerably, the Royal Commission was criticized for not enquiring into the quality of
justice in the magistrates' courts: see McConville and Bridges (1994), 24–6; Jackson (1994),
259–60.

[36] Although it should be noted that stipendiaries sit frequently in magistrates' courts: for
figures, see H.C. Debs., Vol. 200, cols. 419–20, 11 Dec. 1991. Further, it is worth observing
that in Northern Ireland summary trials are conducted before a legally qualified resident
magistrate: see Dickson (1993), 23–4.

[37] See McBarnet (1981), ch 7.

infect the Crown Court trial. Judges may then be forced to abandon the umpireal neutrality which they must affect before the jury, in favour of the active expedition of contested cases through the system. This in turn would put further pressure on defence lawyers to negotiate pleas out of court. On the other hand, such a shift need not necessarily occur. Much may depend on the extent to which the rules governing trial procedures are changed to accommodate more active intervention by the judge. There is, however, now a considerable body of literature highlighting the gap that often exists in the criminal process between the 'law in the books' and the 'law in action', and which suggests that formal changes may not be necessary to effect changes in practice.[38] Apart from this, McBarnet's work urges us to look closely at the rules of evidence and procedure. It may be that these rules do not in fact oblige judges to affect the umpireal role nearly as much as they are assumed to do in the adversarial trial. Looking beyond the rules, it has been argued recently that criminal justice research in the last 30 years has tended to over-concentrate on both the formal and informal structures of the criminal process and has given insufficient attention to the ideology of the actors in the system.[39] These actors are, of course, influenced by the institutional environment in which they find themselves. But they bring their own values, beliefs, and attitudes to this environment. While these are in part shaped by the working environment, they are also shaped by the actors' education, training, and professional ethos. Judges, as a particularly powerful élite, may be supposed to have developed a very strong sense of what their role should be in the criminal justice system. It does not therefore follow that when the fact-finding functions of the jury are transferred to judges in a jury-less trial, they will necessarily abandon the umpireal role which they supposedly adopt in the jury context. In practice, however, it remains the case that judges have been given a new responsibility, and they may be inclined to pursue a more active investigative approach within this new context than they might otherwise have done, in which case the trial will lose some of its adversarial character.

As well as raising questions about changes in the judge's umpireal role in the trial, the accretion of fact-finding responsibilities to the judge raises the question of whether this will alter counsel's mode of presenting cases in court. Counsel may be not only more constrained in the *manner* in which they are able to present cases; the *substance* of the cases presented may also change. Many observers now view the task of advocacy in the trial as one of presenting a plausible story to the trier of fact.[40] Advocates do more than present bits of evidence to the court; they have to organize the evidence

---

[38] Research suggests, for example, that legal doctrine is rarely invoked by police and prosecutors when deciding whether to charge or in negotiating pleas: see Roshier and Teff (1980), ch 3.   [39] Rutherford (1993), 2.
[40] See for example Bennett and Feldman (1981); Binder and Bergman (1984).

around a version of what happened, and this involves interpretation of the evidence. But the kind of stories that appeal to judges may be quite different from those which appeal to juries. Stories presented before juries may, for example, seek to present the defendant's actions in a particularly merit-orious or unmeritorious light. Judges, on the other hand, may be more interested in whether the evidence adds up to a plausible and coherent picture of guilt. This raises the question of whether judges adopt a different approach to fact-finding than juries and whether this has an effect on the trial *outcome* as well as the trial *process*. Although considerable attention has been given, mostly in the United States, to the way in which juries approach the task of fact finding, there is much less literature on how judges approach the same task.

In this book we hope to shed some light on these questions, and we focus chiefly on the judicial role in non-jury trials. It is our contention that an analysis of the role of participants in the criminal process helps to illuminate the interplay between those actors and their working environment.[41] A study of this kind needs a specific context. The one forum where serious criminal offences are tried without a jury in the United Kingdom is in Northern Ireland. Northern Ireland's 'troubles', as they came to be known euphemistically, generated a host of problems both for government and for the administration of justice.[42] One of these was how to deal effectively with political violence without sacrificing long-standing principles such as the 'rule of law' and the right to a fair trial. At the time of the British Government's assumption of direct control over Northern Ireland's affairs in 1972,[43] one of its first tasks was to re-evaluate the effectiveness of the normal criminal justice process in the light of the escalation of political violence which took place at that time. The previous measure adopted to stem the flow of violence had merely contributed to an intensification of the 'troubles'. This was the use of internment, the detention of suspects without trial, introduced by the Stormont Government in 1971 under powers contained in the Civil Authorities (Special Powers) Act (Northern Ireland) 1922. The Diplock Commission was appointed in October 1972, specific-ally to 'consider whether changes should be made in the administration of justice in order to deal more effectively with terrorism without using internment under the Special Powers Act.'[44]

The Commission's report will be discussed more fully in the next chapter,

---

[41] For a recent study of the role of barristers in the process, see Morison and Leith (1992).

[42] For a discussion of the constitutional problems, see Hadfield (1992).

[43] For the history of Northern Ireland under its own 'home rule', see Buckland (1981); Bardon (1992).

[44] H.C. Debs., Vol. 855, col. 276, 17 Apr. 1973 (William Whitelaw, then Secretary of State for Northern Ireland).

but the recommendation that certain offences should henceforth be tried in the ordinary courts but without a jury stood out at the time as the most drastic departure from the normal criminal process, and has proved one of the most enduring of the wide-ranging emergency measures then also recommended. Now that political events have pointed towards the possibility of a peaceful future for Northern Ireland, with the announcement in 1994 of a ceasefire by republican and loyalist paramilitary groups, the time may be approaching for the revision of the government's emergency strategy. The restoration of jury trial for all indictable offences in Northern Ireland is, however, unlikely in the near future and even if the emergency method of trial were to be discontinued, this would probably be achieved by a gradual phasing out of Diplock trials, rather than by an immediate return to jury trial of all cases.

Of the many legacies of Lord Diplock's legal career,[45] the 'Diplock courts', as this system of trial by judge alone in emergency cases has come to be known, must rank as one of the most significant. The term 'Diplock court' is, however, misleading in so far as it suggests a special criminal court in a special courthouse where special judges deal with special kinds of cases. In fact the single judge trials are heard in Belfast Crown Court, in the same courthouse in Crumlin Road where ordinary Crown Court jury trials continue to be held, and they are presided over by High Court and county court judges who also conduct normal court business in Northern Ireland.[46] It is these 'Diplock trials' which provide the context for our study.

Reference has been made to the enduring appeal of the jury even in the face of mounting pressure for reform. It is then all the more remarkable how swiftly and cleanly the Diplock Commission managed to cut a swathe through the tradition of jury trial in serious criminal cases. It has been pointed out that only seven of the Report's 119 paragraphs deal with the jury issue.[47] Thus, the Commission's radical proposal to exclude the jury from trials arising from the emergency situation in Northern Ireland was (significantly) not accompanied by a thorough investigation of how the adversarial structure of the trial might change when the sole responsibility for decision-making was handed to a judge sitting alone in the Crown Court. Interestingly, the Commission did allude briefly to the singular nature of the adversary framework in its dismissal of the idea of trial by a plurality of judges:

Our oral adversarial system of procedure is ill-adapted to the collegiate conduct of a trial of fact. In criminal proceedings, in particular, immediate rulings on

---

[45] For comment on the contributions made by Lord Diplock in the course of his career to the development of substantive areas of administrative law and the law of contract respectively, see Wilberforce (1986) and Dickson (1989).

[46] The composition of the Northern Ireland judiciary is discussed in Chapter Two.

[47] Greer and White (1986), 3.

admissibility and other matters of procedure have constantly to be made by the single judge when sitting with a jury. It would gravely inconvenience the progress of the trial and diminish the value of oral examination and cross-examination as a means of eliciting the truth, if a plurality of judges had to consult together, albeit briefly, before each ruling was made.[48]

The implication that the adversary trial *is* suited to the single judge format is supported only by the preceding brief observation: 'Non-jury trials in civil actions are always conducted by a single judge alone.' But the analogy with civil trials is open to question, given the clear divergence between evidential and procedural rules in criminal and civil litigation over the past century or more.[49] If the analogy were so clearly tenable, then one might enquire why the demise of the jury in ordinary criminal cases has not been more readily and enthusiastically contemplated.

In an early survey of cases tried in Diplock courts, Boyle, Hadden, and Hillyard touched upon the issue of how the shape and character of the criminal trial might change in the absence of the jury:

The elimination of the jury did reduce the scope for the traditional skills of advocacy and cross-examination, and led to more direct discussion between counsel and judges on the basis of the written statements. There was also an increase in the extent to which the judges themselves sought to take a direct part in the elucidation of the truth by questioning witnesses and counsel. The overall effect was to replace the more theatrical aspects of the traditional jury trial as a contest between the two sides with a more sober search for truth, and to emphasise the extent to which the trial process had become a 'closed-shop' in the hands of a small group of professional lawyers.[50]

The primary concern of the authors of that survey was to analyse statistical trends and the general operation of Diplock courts; the above comments were in a sense peripheral to their main findings. The issues raised in this passage are nonetheless of great significance to the perceived lacuna in the jury debate to which we have drawn attention. The central aim of this book is to investigate in some depth these patterns of qualitative change in the trial process.

More specifically, we address the question of how judges actually approach the fact-finding task, which has been traditionally outside their remit. Does this additional burden alter their essentially 'umpireal role' in the conduct of the trial? Are the rules of evidence and procedure adhered to as scrupulously as in jury trials, given that their development has been so

---

[48] Diplock Report, para. 39. And see also the Gardiner Report, para. 31. Baker 'doubted' the procedural difficulties, except for delay, but went on to reject three-judge courts on other grounds: see generally Baker Report, paras. 109–29.

[49] See Zuckerman (1989) ch 1, in which the author advances the case for treating the rules of evidence in criminal cases as discrete.

[50] Boyle, Hadden, and Hillyard (1975), 99.

deeply affected by the jury's presence?[51] Does the advocate take a different approach to his or her task when faced with a professional judge rather than a jury? How does the jury's absence affect the appellate process? Finally, and more fundamentally, has the absence of the jury occasioned a shift away from our traditional adversarial mode of trial? Essentially, our study aims to test in a systematic fashion by reference to a number of trials whether the Diplock procedure has actually shed some of the hallmarks of the conventional adversarial trial in favour of a more inquisitorial procedure.

The Diplock system permits direct comparison between jury trials and trials by judge alone of similar types of offence in the same jurisdiction. In the first place, the same judges preside over both forms of trial, the Diplock trial now being a normal aspect of a Northern Ireland judge's work-load.[52] Offences tried in Diplock courts are known as 'scheduled offences' as they are listed in a schedule to the legislation which governs the Diplock trial process.[53] The offences are all those which may have a terrorist connection, such as murder, manslaughter, riot, most non-fatal offences against the person, robbery, aggravated burglary, arson, offences involving firearms and explosives, and membership of proscribed organizations. Cases involving such offences may be 'descheduled' by the Attorney-General in his discretion if there is no actual connection with the emergency situation. However, certain offences (notably robbery and aggravated burglary involving a firearm or explosive) *cannot* be descheduled. Defendants in cases of this nature with no terrorist connection, who therefore should be entitled to trial by jury, are tried by Diplock courts due to this quirk in the system of allocation.[54] In addition, the difference between certain 'ordinary' robbery cases and those sent for trial by a Diplock court may not always be significant. So, in terms of the judicial personae, the type of offence, and the type of offender, Diplock trials may be compared with jury trials to check for any divergence in procedure which may have developed between the two.

A further feature of Diplock trials which facilitates comparative analysis stems from the Diplock Commission's apparent acceptance that the transition to trial by judge alone did not require any major upheaval of the adversarial trial structure. The introduction of Diplock courts was achieved with the minimum of alteration to the formal rules of procedure governing the conduct of the trial. Only three changes are worthy of mention: the

---

[51] For discussion of the relationship between the development of rules of evidence and the institution of the jury, see Thayer (1898); Morgan (1937); Nokes (1956).

[52] See Doran and Jackson (1992), 35.

[53] Northern Ireland (Emergency Provisions) Act 1991, Schedule 1.

[54] For a critical examination of the workings of the scheduling system, see Jackson and Doran (1992a).

requirement that the judge provide a reasoned judgment in support of a decision to convict,[55] the provision of an automatic right of appeal against conviction, sentence, or both,[56] and the change in the rules governing the admissibility of confessions.[57] Although the *formal* procedures are virtually identical in each mode of trial, it may be possible to uncover *informal* shifts in the character of the trial which can be attributed directly to the fact that the jury is absent from the Diplock arena.

In Chapter Two, we examine the history and operation of the Diplock system, the controversy surrounding its introduction, and the crises which it has faced in over 20 years of operation. In that context, it is also hoped to explore more fully the questions which the absence of the jury provokes and which the present work seeks to address. In Chapter Three, we construct a theoretical framework for our study by describing two ideal models of proof—an adversarial or contest model and an inquisitorial or inquest model—which claim to encompass the essential elements of the criminal process of proof. Between the two ideal types there is a spectrum on which it ought to be possible to locate any particular trial format. The remainder of the book is devoted to more focused assessment of whether the absence of the jury has caused the Diplock trial to veer away from the contest model and towards the inquest model.

In Chapter Four we explain the methods which we have used to carry out this exercise. In brief, we observed 43 Diplock and jury trials in Belfast Crown Court from 1989 to 1991, we conducted interviews with several judges and members of the Bar who work in Diplock courts, and we studied in depth the transcribed judgments and summings-up from the cases in our sample. The next three chapters concentrate on specific aspects of practice at trial and in them we seek to investigate shifts in the character of the trial at the level of the particular.

Chapter Five begins with a discussion of the judge's traditional umpireal role and moves on to consider whether this role is compromised in Diplock trials. The main focus of the chapter is upon judges' approaches to the enforcement of the rules of evidence and procedure, and the extent to which judges permit counsel to develop factual issues in the respective forms of trial. Chapter Six examines the particular issue of judicial questioning during the oral testimony of witnesses at trial and the effect which such questioning has on the criminal process as a whole. The obvious question to be asked in the context of our survey is whether judges tend to be more interventionist in Diplock trials than when a jury is present. In Chapter

---

[55] Northern Ireland (Emergency Provisions) Act 1991, section 10(5).

[56] *Ibid.*, section 10(6).

[57] For a full discussion of the history and development of the emergency rule on confessions, see Chapter Two.

Seven, we discuss further the changing nature of the judicial role in the light of the conclusions reached in the two previous chapters and in the light of other determinants of judicial control, such as the extent to which judges asked to see witnesses and the degree to which judges discussed the evidence with counsel. This chapter will draw particularly on comments by judges and counsel about how they perceive the differences between the two modes of trials, as well as on our observation of trials.

Chapter Eight involves an examination of how judges reach decisions of fact in Diplock trials and makes a comparison between judicial and lay approaches towards evidence. Chapter Nine then considers the formal judgments that must be delivered in Diplock trials and a study is made of such judgments and the role of the summing-up in jury trials. In a sense, these could be described as two different forms of judicial input in the criminal decision-making process. The chapter concludes by considering the appeals process and discusses the Court of Appeal's power to interfere with Diplock judgments and the extent to which it is (and ought to be) prepared to do so, as compared with its handling of jury verdicts.

In the final chapter, we return to the general issue of whether the Diplock court has changed the character of the traditional adversarial criminal trial. We examine the effect on the criminal process as a whole in Northern Ireland and the broader implications of the withdrawal of the jury from an adversarial process.

From a constitutional perspective, Northern Ireland has been described as a kind of laboratory in which the strengths and weaknesses of different models of practice may be gauged.[58] This notion has both negative and constructive elements. On the minus side, the cynic would claim with some justification that Northern Ireland has too often been viewed as a testing ground for innovation which would not readily be accepted by those elsewhere. The modification of the right to silence in criminal cases is perhaps the most pertinent recent example of this approach.[59] On the positive side, however, the relatively small size of the jurisdiction renders scrutiny of existing legal rules and practices more manageable. In the Diplock court a form of trial is practised which many in the United Kingdom would find alien and unacceptable, and yet which has subsisted for over 20 years within the same broad legal tradition. The attempt to superimpose extraordinary and alien features onto the conventional legal system—the substitution of the jury by professional judges, the modification

---

[58] See McCrudden (1989), 297; Lee (1990), 118–20. For discussion of the challenges which the problems of Northern Ireland pose to law, see Livingstone (1990).

[59] Under the Criminal Evidence (Northern Ireland) Order 1988. The government's proposal to extend the provisions of this Order to England and Wales in the Criminal Justice and Public Order Bill 1994 encountered much more opposition than the original Northern Ireland Order. For further discussion, see Chapter Two.

of the right of silence—also provides a useful context in which to study the way in which the legal system copes with sudden change, and provides a useful backdrop against which to evaluate which elements of our conventional legal culture are 'sacred' and 'untouchable', and which of them may be sacrificed.

One distinguished commentator has remarked that on occasions 'legal systems are subjected to unconventional pressures that may have the effect of uncovering previously unconsidered implications of our indigenous systems.'[60] This study has been undertaken in that spirit. Frequent reference has been made in this chapter to the two sides of the jury debate. The Diplock process too has had its critics and supporters. It is interesting that these groups are not commensurate with each other. A jury defender may yet accept the Diplock system as necessary in the circumstances which have prevailed in Northern Ireland. Conversely, few critics of the jury would advocate wholesale adoption of the Diplock method of trial.[61] We have attempted to set about this task from the perspective of none of the above camps. Rather than attacking the Diplock court on the basis of faith in the jury, or defending it through an expression of faith in the judiciary, we have tried to extract whatever lessons have been yielded by the practical workings of a system of trial by judge alone.

---

[60] Allen (1992), 9.

[61] Although note the view of Blom-Cooper that 'we should not lightly dismiss the contention that trial by judge alone is not the monstrous intrusion into a fundamental right, but in fact provides a model for a modern system of criminal trial and a rational system of justice' (1991), 16.

2

The Diplock Context

There is a simple paradox which has attached to the operation of the Diplock court system since its inception in 1973. The idea of trying serious criminal cases without a jury is anathema to many educated within the common law tradition. To others, the system is undesirable but essential in the difficult circumstances which prevail in Northern Ireland. Others still have had no reservations about the removal of the jury from cases with 'terrorist' connections. Common to these reactions, however, is the realization that the introduction of trial by judge alone marked a departure from the realms of normal criminal procedure. Yet as we have noted, the transition to non-jury trials was unaccompanied by substantial formal modification to the traditional adversarial system of trial. This tension, between the general understanding of the Diplock court as something out of the ordinary and its cloak of legal normality, is central to this book. Our main task is to ascertain whether the formal retention of the adversarial trial structure masks a shift in practice towards a more inquisitorial form of procedure. In this chapter the background to our study is presented through a discussion of the history and development of Diplock courts, the rules which govern their operation, and the controversies which have surrounded this system of trial.

THE INTRODUCTION OF DIPLOCK COURTS

[C]risis stimulates the articulation of what are normally inarticulate premises and attitudes. Nearly everyone hopes that the legislative provisions recommended by the Diplock Commission will have a short life; but it seems likely that its analysis of the preconditions of criminal process in our system will deserve close attention for a long time to come. Small comfort for the people of Northern Ireland.[1]

Within this early reaction in 1973 to the recommendations contained in the Diplock Report, one senses both scepticism about the proposals and resignation to the fact that their impact would prove considerably more than transient. After more than twenty years, during which the Diplock regime has progressed from the status of an innovative and temporary

---

[1] Twining (1973), 407.

legislative scheme to become an institution with a sense of permanence, dealing on average with around a third of all trials on indictment in Northern Ireland until the cessation of paramilitary violence, it is possible to cast a critical eye over the Diplock legacy by examining the practice of the court system which it spawned. It is interesting to note that one of the most forceful objections to the Diplock recommendations has been based on the removal of the jury from terrorist trials in Northern Ireland was effected without proper investigation of how the alternative system might function and without adequate evidence to substantiate the justifications presented for the change.

In its report, presented to Parliament in December 1972, the Diplock Commission identified several problems facing ordinary criminal courts in handling offences of a terrorist nature. First, witnesses who might have been in a position to testify for the prosecution were subject to intimidation by terrorist organizations and were thereby deterred from giving evidence.[2] Secondly, the Commission concluded that the threat of intimidation extended also to jurors, 'though not to the same extent.'[3] Hence the oft-quoted observation that a 'frightened juror is a bad juror even though his own safety and that of his family may not actually be at risk.'[4] Thirdly, the Commission pointed to the danger of perverse verdicts by partisan juries; the property qualifications for jury service which existed at the time were more widely met by Protestants than by Catholics and the rights of stand-by and challenge were exercised so as to accentuate Protestant representation on juries. This gave rise to the fear that there had been instances in which Loyalist defendants in particular had been 'unjustly acquitted.'[5] Diplock noted that the danger of perverse convictions could 'in practice be averted by the judge, though only at the risk of his assuming to himself the role of decider of fact', but the danger of perverse acquittal could not be countered in this way.[6] Finally, the operation of evidential rules on the admissibility of confessions and on proof of possession of firearms rendered the prosecution's task in securing convictions in terrorist cases an unduly onerous one.[7]

Leaving aside the intimidation of witnesses and the evidential constraints for the present, it was the twin problems of juror intimidation and perverse acquittal which formed the central justification for the suspension of jury trial in cases arising out of or connected with the emergency situation. The

---

[2] Diplock Report, para. 7.   [3] *Ibid.*, para. 36.   [4] *Ibid.*

[5] The Diplock Report itself is less specific on this point (see paras. 36–7) than the Attorney-General (Sir Peter Rawlinson) during the parliamentary debates on the Emergency Provisions (Northern Ireland) Bill. He identified a number of cases in which acquittal appeared contrary to the evidence: H.C. Debs., Vol. 855, cols. 381–2, 17 Apr. 1973.

[6] Diplock Report, para. 37. Boyle, Hadden, and Hillyard provided support for this assessment: (1975), 90–3. See too Law Officers' Department (1974). For a more sceptical view, see Greer and White (1986), 38.

[7] Diplock Report, para. 59.

Commission's advancement of these reasons did not go unchallenged. During the parliamentary debates on the Northern Ireland (Emergency Provisions) Bill 1973, the legislation which was constructed on the basis of the Report,[8] and in subsequent academic commentary,[9] the Commission's conclusions were attacked on the grounds of lack of supporting empirical evidence.

In a forcefully argued call for the abolition of Diplock courts and qualified restoration of jury trial, Greer and White expressed several reservations about the evidence presented for both the perverse acquittals and the intimidation claim.[10] While accepting that the studies carried out subsequent to the Diplock Report offered some empirical evidence to support the perverse acquittals argument, they dismissed it as 'fairly weak and inconclusive.'[11] Most significantly, they pointed to the possible distortion of any comparative analysis of trials involving Protestant and Catholic defendants in the 1969–73 period, due to internment:

virtually all Loyalists suspected of involvement in political violence whom the authorities wanted to punish were brought before a court. On the other hand, it could be argued, that those Nationalists against whom the evidence was weak, were interned leaving only those against whom there was a case supported by particularly compelling evidence to face a judge and jury. When considering jury verdicts in the 1969–1973 period, therefore, it is not entirely clear that like is being compared with like. Cases in which the prosecution evidence was weak may account for at least some of the so-called 'perverse' acquittals of Loyalists.[12]

In any event, they argued, the problem of partisan acquittals would best have been countered by the increased democratization of eligibility for jury service and randomization of methods of selecting and empanelling jurors, changes which (ironically) the Juries (Northern Ireland) Order 1974 went some way to achieving in cases other than those tried by judge alone in Diplock courts.[13]

As for the argument concerning juror intimidation, the authors described the evidence in support of it as 'anecdotal and sketchy'[14] and, while the phenomenon may well have existed, its extent was never shown conclusively, or even convincingly, to justify the step which Diplock proposed. Objections to the Diplock recommendations on the basis of the lack of solid evidence were bolstered by the detached manner of the Commission's investigations: 'Almost all the evidence was heard in London, but our

---

[8] See for example the view of Mr Gerard Fitt, then Member of Parliament for West Belfast: 'As Hon. Members on both sides of the House have said, the Diplock Report contains no reference to any case in which the jury brought in a perverse verdict.' (H.C. Debs., Vol. 855, col. 327, 17 Apr. 1973.)   [9] See, for example, Twining (1973), 413.
[10] Greer and White (1986), ch 4.
[11] *Ibid.*, 52. For the studies mentioned, see references in note 6 above.
[12] *Ibid.*, 45.   [13] See Greer and White (1986), 39, 59–60.
[14] *Ibid.*, 52. (See generally 46–52.)

Chairman made two visits to Northern Ireland, each lasting two days during which he met members of the security forces on the ground.'[15] The authors of an important early study of the Diplock system were quick to stress the impression which this detachment cast over the Diplock proposals:

All these recommendations were based almost exclusively on the views of the prosecuting authorities and the security forces. No evidence was received either from the Northern Ireland judges or those practising in the courts, or from the public and their representatives. This in itself was perhaps the best indication of the extent to which the Diplock Committee saw its task as one of remedying certain loopholes and inadequacies in the security system rather than of improving the standards of justice being achieved in the courts.[16]

The fact that the Report recommended the continuation of detention without trial alongside the new court procedures, because intimidation so often rendered cross-examination of witnesses impracticable, added further weight to the critics' attack in view of the potent legal and political objections to the system of internment which 'struck at the very root of public conceptions of justice according to law.'[17] The fact that internment was eventually phased out in 1975 certainly altered the setting in which Diplock courts operate, but this does not detract from the force of the above criticism aimed at the Diplock Report itself.[18]

The arguments for and against the introduction of trial by judge alone are still of interest and significance (although it is the intimidation point alone which has been presented as the enduring rationale for Diplock courts),[19] but as stated before, any continuing discussion must acknowledge that over twenty years of practice in Diplock courts have elapsed. While we do not suggest that the rationale for the Diplock system is no longer open to challenge, we will focus on how Diplock trials have been and are conducted in practice.

The Northern Ireland (Emergency Provisions) Act 1973 gave legislative expression to much of what Lord Diplock recommended,[20] and in August 1973 a new era in the administration of criminal justice in Northern Ireland commenced. In the ensuing years, the government established a series of

---

[15] Diplock Report, para. 4.

[16] Boyle, Hadden, and Hillyard (1975), 95.   [17] *Ibid.*

[18] Note that, although the use of internment was suspended in 1975, the mechanism for its revival remains on the statute book: see the Northern Ireland (Emergency Provisions) Act 1991, section 34. Calls for its reintroduction have been frequently made, particularly from the ranks of Unionist politicians. For the opposing stances of Opposition and Government on whether the power should remain on the statute book, see the debates preceding the 1991 Act: H.C. Debs., Vol. 181, col. 39 (Mr Kevin McNamara); cols. 102–3 (Mr John Cope, Minister of State, Northern Ireland).

[19] See the Baker Report, para. 107. See also Hunter (1987), 28.

[20] In the event, the suspension of jury trial was approved in the Committee of the whole House of Commons by a single vote: see Dickson (1992b), 592.

reviews to re-examine and reassess the legislative provisions. In particular, the procedures were reviewed by a Committee under the chairmanship of Lord Gardiner in 1975, by Sir George Baker in 1984, and by Viscount Colville in 1990.[21] However, the emergency scheme recommended by Lord Diplock has remained intact, although the legislation has been revised on a number of occasions and additional emergency powers introduced. The governing legislation is now the Northern Ireland (Emergency Provisions) Act 1991[22] (hereafter 'the 1991 Act'), section 10 of which provides the basis for the trial of cases in the jury's absence. Section 10(1) reads simply: 'A trial on indictment of a scheduled offence shall be conducted by the court without a jury.' All Diplock trials have taken place in the Crumlin Road courthouse, Belfast, where our survey was based, although provision has been made for trials to be held outside Belfast on the direction of the Lord Chancellor.[23]

From 1973 until the present, well over 10,000 defendants have passed through Diplock courts, the average annual figure having decreased from over 1,000 in the early years to a level of over 400 in each year from 1991 to 1993.

SCHEDULED OFFENCES

No discussion of the operation of Diplock trials would be complete without an explanation of how cases actually fall to be dealt with by the system.[24] The term 'scheduled offence' derives from the fact that offences deemed appropriate for trial by judge alone are listed in Schedule 1 to the 1991 Act.[25] The list of offences is accompanied by a set of Notes which qualify the circumstances in which these offences are sent for trial in Diplock courts. Before looking at the relationship between the Notes and the main body of the Schedule, it is worth noting the types of case which are deemed suitable for trial without jury.

---

[21] Cited throughout the text as the Gardiner Report (1975), the Baker Report (1984) and Colville (1990). The next major review of the legislation will be conducted by John Rowe QC. For full references, see Bibliography (Official Reports).

[22] The 1973 Act was amended by the Emergency Provisions Act of 1975 and a consolidating statute was passed in 1978, which was amended in turn in 1987. The 1991 Act replaces the 1978 and 1987 Acts completely, incorporates some of the provisions of the Prevention of Terrorism Act 1989 applying only to Northern Ireland, and introduces a number of new offences and security forces' powers. The Act has to be renewed annually by order of the Secretary of State and will expire after five years (section 69). See, generally, Dickson (1992b).

[23] Section 9 of the 1991 Act.

[24] For a full discussion and critical assessment of the workings of the scheduling system, see Jackson and Doran (1992a). The present section is based largely on that article.

[25] Certain scheduled offences may be tried summarily, but the disposal of such cases by magistrates is rare. See *Spratt v Doherty* [1983] NI 136; Walker and Hogan (1989), 102.

The list has been amended several times since the introduction of the Diplock system.[26] At present, it includes the common law offences of murder, manslaughter, riot, kidnapping, false imprisonment, and assault occasioning actual bodily harm. The list also includes several statutory offences, such as wounding with intent and causing grievous bodily harm, robbery and aggravated burglary, and arson and aggravated criminal damage. Naturally, many offences involving firearms, explosives, and petrol bombs and the offence of membership of a proscribed organization are also incorporated. The 1991 Act added a fluid category of cases to the Schedule, namely any offence which an officer of the Royal Ulster Constabulary (not below the rank of superintendent) certifies is charged in consequence of a terrorist funds investigation.[27] Finally, the Schedule incorporates participatory offences, and attempt or conspiracy to commit one of the offences listed, as well as the related offences of assisting offenders and failing to give information.[28] An important supplementary provision to the Schedule is found in section 2(2) of the Act, which states that where someone is charged with a non-scheduled offence as well as a scheduled one, both offences will be treated as scheduled for the purposes of the Act. At the time of the passing of the original Emergency Provisions Act in 1973, the government gave an assurance that a non-scheduled offence would only be included in the indictment where it arose out of the same incident as the scheduled one.[29] The foregoing list is not exhaustive, but it gives a reasonable impression of the range of offences which the Schedule encompasses.

An immediate observation is that they are all capable of being committed in connection with the emergency situation. Indeed, some of the offences listed are deemed to be scheduled offences only where the manner of their performance immediately suggests such a connection. Thus, according to Note 3 to the Schedule, robbery and aggravated burglary are regarded as scheduled offences only where it is charged that 'an explosive, firearm, imitation firearm or weapon of offence' was used to carry out the offence.[30]

Obviously, however, such a connection will not exist in all cases. Therefore, built into the legislative scheme is a mechanism designed to redirect to jury trial cases outside the scope of the Diplock system. The key

---

[26] The Secretary of State is given power to amend the Schedule by Order (a power now contained in section 1(3) of the 1991 Act). Amendments have also been effected under miscellaneous statutes. The 1991 Act has brought together all the offences previously contained in the Schedule, with minor amendments and additions.

[27] The provisions governing such investigations are section 57 and Schedule 5 of the 1991 Act.

[28] Under sections 4 and 5 (respectively) of the Criminal Law Act (Northern Ireland) 1967.

[29] H.C. Debs, Standing Comm. B, 1972–3, Vol. 2, col. 218, 22 May 1973 (Solicitor-General).

[30] Or where the offence was committed in relation to or by means of nuclear material within the meaning of the Nuclear Material (Offences) Act 1983.

figure in this process is the Attorney-General. By Note 1 to the Schedule, he is given a discretion to certify that any scheduled offence which is subject to that Note is not to be treated as a scheduled offence and is therefore to be dealt with by jury trial. This certification power does not extend to *all* offences listed in the Schedule. For example, the offences of robbery and aggravated burglary, when allegedly committed in the circumstances mentioned above, and offences under the Prevention of Terrorism Act, are not capable of being descheduled.

There are no formally prescribed criteria governing the exercise of the discretion, but it has been revealed that the pivotal (albeit broadly framed) question is whether a particular case is 'connected with the emergency'. If so, then the discretion will not be exercised.[31] During the debates on the Northern Ireland (Emergency Provisions) Bill 1987, the Attorney-General gave perhaps the most revealing insight to date on the approach adopted in the task of 'descheduling' or 'certifying out'. Responding to proposed clauses which would have specified grounds for the exercise of his discretion, he noted:

That exercise must rest on a subjective assessment, but at least the decision will not be prejudicial. For example, when a defendant appears in an ordinary Crown court, it will be because I have specifically decided that the offence has no terrorist connections. It could be summed up in a sentence—although I do not have the phrase exactly right—by saying that the offence should be causally, not coincidentally, connected with terrorism.[32]

He then proceeded to explain that he attempts to reach a decision in each case within 24 hours, as the decision on bail depends on whether the case falls within the emergency or non-emergency stream.[33] The decision is aided by a note about each case supplied by the Director of Public Prosecutions for Northern Ireland[34] and compiled by someone of the rank of at least assistant director. The Attorney-General stressed the need for 'hard evidence' before he would refuse to certify out, as opposed to 'gossip or talk from the Royal Ulster Constabulary'. The courts would be unlikely to review his decision in the absence of bad faith.[35]

The available statistics reveal that the Attorney-General frequently

---

[31] See H.C. Debs., Vol. 114, cols. 336–9, 8 Apr. 1987, for an explanation by the Attorney-General of his role in the filtering process.

[32] *Ibid.*, col. 338.

[33] The limitations on the power to grant bail in scheduled cases are specified in section 3 of the 1991 Act. Most significantly, bail may only be granted by a High Court judge (or judge of the Court of Appeal).

[34] The office of Director of Public Prosecutions for Northern Ireland was created under the Prosecution of Offences (Northern Ireland) Order 1972. For discussion, see Jackson, Kilpatrick, and Harvey (1991), 167–72.

[35] See Walker and Hogan (1989), 128 (footnote 9).

accedes to applications to certify offences out of the Schedule. Table 2.1 gives figures for the period 1987–93:[36]

TABLE 2.1 *Scheduled offences certified out by the Attorney-General, 1987–1993*

	1987	1988	1989	1990	1991	1992	1993
Total number of offences for which application made	894	1019	1198	984	1045	1108	853
Number of persons involved	509	484	578	530	531	533	459
Number of offences for which application granted	519	552	622	508	619	619	572
Percentage of offences for which application granted	58%	54%	52%	52%	59%	56%	67%

An application may be made by one individual charged with a single offence or with a number of offences, or by a number of persons charged with the same offence. The statistics published since 1987 are more revealing than those previously issued which showed only the total number of *applications* made and granted and thus concealed the number of persons and offences involved. It should be noted, however, that the more recent figures do not in themselves enable a full analysis of the descheduling power because it does not specify those cases where successful applications have been made in respect of some offences but not others. The granting of a certificate in such cases will have little significance, as the accused will still be tried without a jury, by virtue of section 2(2) of the 1991 Act (above).

The scheduling system has been criticized mainly on the ground that it operates in such a way as to send too many 'ordinary' cases for trial without jury. This point was made most forcefully by Walsh, whose survey of 111 cases tried in Diplock courts in 1982 suggested that around 40 per cent of the alleged offences had no observable connection with the emergency situation.[37] The offence of robbery was the most prominent in this category: as we have seen, all armed robbery cases *must* be tried by Diplock courts. Walsh, however, claimed that several of the cases were capable of being descheduled but that background information about the suspect supplied by the police may have swayed the decision against jury trial. The Attorney-General obviously had such criticism in mind when he mentioned

---

[36] Source: Northern Ireland Information Service, *Northern Ireland (Emergency Provisions) Acts: Annual Statistics 1993* (1994).

[37] Walsh (1983), 16, 59–60, 80–2.

the need for 'hard evidence' before refusing to certify out (above) and the figure of 40 per cent has been doubted by the Government.[38]

Although one may argue over the exact number of ordinary cases tried in Diplock courts, this unfortunate feature of the system will remain so long as offences such as armed robbery and aggravated burglary cannot be scheduled out.[39] Several proposals have been made as to how the system should be changed to ensure that the Diplock process is used exclusively for the trial of offences which are genuinely connected to the emergency situation. In broad terms, these proposals fall into two categories. The first approach is to widen the range of offences capable of being tried by jury, either by taking some offences out of the Schedule or by making more offences subject to the power to deschedule. The second type of proposal is to change to a system of certifying *in*, rather than certifying out. Detailed consideration of the options would be beyond the scope of the present work, but as we have argued elsewhere,[40] the case for reform is strong on two counts: first, in view of the fact that ordinary defendants are routinely denied the right to jury trial because of the vagaries of the scheduling system as opposed to the nature of their alleged offence; and secondly, in the light of evidence that the normal system of trial by jury is working satisfactorily in Northern Ireland.

For the present, however, it is worth recalling a point made in Chapter One. This is that, despite its negative aspects, the scheduling system provides a significant dimension to our survey in that it enables certain comparisons to be made. First, cases with and without a terrorist element tried by Diplock courts may be examined in parallel. Also, there may be cases unconnected with terrorism of robbery and armed robbery which do not differ markedly from each other, but which are subject to different forms of trial. We shall now consider in some detail the distinctive aspects of the Diplock mode of trial.

MECHANICS OF TRIAL

Section 10(2) of the Northern Ireland (Emergency Provisions) Act 1991 reads as follows:

---

[38] H.C. Debs., Vol.107, col. 1118, 16 Dec. 1986 (Mr Scott).

[39] The power to deschedule was augmented by the Northern Ireland (Emergency Provisions) Act 1978 (Amendment) Order 1986 (the provisions of which are now incorporated in the 1991 Act). The Order allowed the Attorney-General to certify out certain offences which had previously been incapable of being descheduled (such as false imprisonment and kidnapping). Significantly, however, the Baker Report's recommendation that armed robbery and aggravated burglary should be treated in this way (see paras. 130–51) was not followed.

[40] See, generally, Jackson and Doran (1992a).

The court trying a scheduled offence on indictment under this section shall have all the powers, authorities and jurisdiction which the court would have had if it had been sitting with a jury, including power to determine any question and to make any finding which would, apart from this section, be required to be determined or made by a jury, and references in any enactment to a jury or the verdict or finding of a jury shall be construed accordingly in relation to a trial under this section.

This provision is the legal backdrop to the paradox described at the beginning of the present chapter. A fundamental component of the criminal trial process is removed, but the process itself remains intact and continues functioning as before. The fact-finding role of the jury passes to the judge who must now act in a dual capacity as master of law and arbiter of fact. As already indicated, the way in which judges approach this novel role affords in itself an interesting focus of analysis. At this point, however, it is worth noting that the move to non-jury trial was not accomplished entirely without modification of the ordinary criminal process. First, a judge must give a reasoned judgment in support of a conviction.[41] Secondly, his decision is subject to an automatic right of appeal against conviction and sentence.[42] Thirdly, he is given a power to withdraw from a case in which he has ruled a confession inadmissible on the *voir dire*.[43] And fourthly, although not *formally* altered, the *voir dire* itself has in reality changed in character. In addition, the evidential rules on confessions have been altered in scheduled cases,[44] an issue which has remained controversial since the introduction of the Diplock system. We shall examine the matter of confessions in due course, and we concentrate for the present on the above procedural modifications.

(a) The written judgment

The requirement that a judge produce a judgment stating the reasons for a conviction is ostensibly an important measure of compensation for the jury's absence.[45] Indeed, as a matter of practice, reasons are normally also

---

[41] Northern Ireland (Emergency Provisions) Act 1991, section 10(5).

[42] *Ibid.*, section 10(6).

[43] *Ibid.*, section 11(2). The *voir dire* or 'trial within a trial' is the procedure used to determine whether evidence is admissible, where this determination cannot be made without prior findings of fact. A dispute over the circumstances in which a confession was obtained is the most common reason for holding a *voir dire*. In a jury trial, due to the obvious risk of prejudice, the judge determines the issue on the *voir dire* in the absence of the jury. For discussion see Boyd (1982).

[44] Section 11 of the 1991 Act. The new confessions rule was first contained in section 6 of the 1973 Act and later (with minor modifications) in section 8 of the 1978 Act: see Greer (1980). Section 8 was in turn substituted by section 5A of the 1987 Act: see Jackson (1988b), 249–52. Section 11 of the 1991 Act adheres to the 1987 changes.

[45] Note that a judge must also deliver a reasoned judgment in civil cases, setting out his findings of fact and conclusions as to liability. In the context of serious criminal cases, however, the Diplock judge's responsibility in this regard is unique in this jurisdiction.

given for acquittals (it will be seen that this occurred in several of the cases in our survey). A verdict of guilty or not guilty in bare form is widely viewed as worthy of respect when handed down by the lay tribunal, but the equivalent decision by a single individual in a position of peculiar power requires a more detailed and more overt justification. In essence, the written judgment[46] is designed to fulfil the role played in the ordinary criminal trial by both the judge's summing-up to the jury and the jury's verdict itself. It must, therefore, expound the legal issues involved in the case as well as determining the factual matters in dispute. Much criticism has been directed at this element of the Diplock trial, on the ground that 'the wearing of two hats' here is most visible and consequently prone to the appearance of absurdity. For example, a judge's note that he has 'warned himself' as to the dangers of convicting on the uncorroborated evidence of an accomplice is not only somewhat unusual,[47] but lacks the solemnity of such an exhortation to the jury, for whom the warning was primarily devised.[48]

Whether a written judgment can ever truly compensate for the absence of the summing-up in the criminal trial is a matter which has not been satisfactorily investigated in the past. Our analysis of the judgments in the cases which make up our survey can throw further light on the divergence between the two forms of trial. Moreover, the judgments themselves offer an important insight into how judges generally approach the fact-finding task. Some guidance on the compilation of a written judgment has been handed down by the Court of Appeal in Northern Ireland,[49] but it is of considerable interest to study how individual judges go about the task, and generally how the nature of the case affects the degree of detailed analysis in which judges see fit to engage. Most significantly, perhaps, it is the judgment which provides the raw material for a potential appeal against a Diplock court decision. Given the automatic right of appeal which exists, does this concentrate the judge's mind to an appreciably greater extent than in his preparation of a summing-up to the jury? We shall return to these issues in Chapter Nine.

(b) The right of appeal

The automatic right of appeal has in itself given rise to an interesting debate. On one view, it provides an essential safeguard against wrongful conviction

---

[46] Although the term 'written judgment' is widely used in practice and in the present work, the judge's decision is not always available in recorded form. Unless reported, a judgment will only be written up formally for the purposes of an appeal.

[47] The point has been well made by several observers: see Boyle, Hadden, and Hillyard (1975), 98; Greer and White (1986), 18.

[48] See Doran (1991a).

[49] See for example *R v Thompson* [1977] NI 74.

by a single judge and removes from the Diplock trial that sense of finality which ought not to attach to the decision of one individual, given the potential seriousness of its consequences. An extension of this view has on occasions been used to support the arguments against proposals for three-judge courts replacing trial by a single judge: what further advantage, it has been asked, could a three-judge panel import when an accused already has automatic access to three judges on appeal?[50] This confidence in the effectiveness of the Diplock appeal structure is not, however, universal and it can be demonstrated that the automatic right of appeal has had a less dramatic impact on the rate of success of appeals in Diplock trials than one might expect.[51]

The debate on the degree of protection afforded by the automatic right of appeal will also be considered in Chapter Nine. At this point it is worth noting that, although the present work is primarily concerned with the effect of the removal of the jury on the trial process, the Diplock appellate system is of interest in several respects beyond the statistical picture. As noted in Chapter One, the Court of Appeal in England has until recently shown itself remarkably cautious in its approach to appeals on matters of fact, a trait which had no small impact on the decision to establish the Royal Commission on Criminal Justice. It is tempting to enquire, therefore, whether the Northern Ireland Court of Appeal is (or indeed *ought* to be) more willing to carry out an extensive review of findings of fact in Diplock cases, particularly since those findings are presented in fully reasoned form. It would be instructive to consider whether successful Diplock appeals are typically based on the way in which the trial judge has approached (or 'directed himself on') the law, or on his handling of the facts, or whether they are based more broadly on a genuine doubt about the guilt of the accused. A comprehensive analysis of all Court of Appeal judgments in Diplock cases would be required to provide a definitive answer to such an inquiry. Such a project, although in theory worthwhile, would not be wholly feasible. Unfortunately, not all Court of Appeal judgments are published and, in any event, decisions are not usually based purely on law or fact, but on an amalgam of the two.

(c) The judge's power to withdraw

The next departure from normal procedure in Diplock courts has also caused division of opinion. Under Section 11(2)(iii) of the 1991 Act, a judge

---

[50] See the argument in the Baker Report, para. 119. And see Editorial (1987) 137 New Law Journal 819–20: the point was apparently made by a working party of the Anglo-Irish Ulster Conference, which examined the three-judge courts issue at the end of 1986.

[51] See Chapter Nine, page 281. For further discussion, see Jackson and Doran (1992b), 276–7.

who has ruled a confession inadmissible may 'direct that the trial . . . be restarted before a differently constituted court (before which the statement in question shall be inadmissible)'. In theory, this power represents an important safeguard for an accused who has argued successfully that a statement made by him ought to be excluded. When a judge, acting in his capacity as arbiter of law at the *voir dire* (or in the course of the trial proper) decrees a confession inadmissible, it may be argued that his role as trier of fact will be undermined by his having had access to such prejudicial material.[52] In the normal trial, of course, the jury is excluded from the proceedings on the *voir dire*. The provision in section 11(2), while not obliging a judge to step down in the circumstances mentioned, at least empowers him to withdraw when he deems it appropriate. It should be noted that a judge also has a general common law discretion to discharge the jury and to order that the case be tried before a differently constituted jury, if inadmissible or prejudicial material has 'leaked out' in the course of the trial, or if some other irregularity has occurred,[53] and that discretion extends also to the Diplock context, entitling a judge to direct that the trial be recommenced before a different judge.[54] Interestingly, in some Diplock cases inadmissible material has been removed from the committal papers by means of preliminary editing by a different judge.[55]

As for the differences in opinion about the statutory power, these relate both to its discretionary nature and to the frequency of its use. The Standing Advisory Commission on Human Rights in Northern Ireland has in the past advocated a mandatory rule whereby a case would have to be recommenced before a different judge if a confession statement is ruled out under section 11.[56] There is some force in the argument that it is artificial to give judges a *discretion* about whether to withdraw since arguably the judge who is most prejudiced by the evidence is likely to be least inclined to step down. Viscount Colville, however, in his review of emergency legislation, rejected the proposal for mandatory withdrawal, noting that judges often deal with prejudicial material other than confessions, and pointing to the increase in time and cost which such a move would entail. He did, though, 'favour the use of a pretrial review to determine the issue wherever possible and some more public indication when such a review will be held.'[57]

---

[52] For judicial comment on the difficulties faced by a judge who has heard an inadmissible confession, see *R v Foxford* [1974] NI 181, at 212–13, *per* Lord Lowry LCJ.

[53] See *Archbold*, paras. 4-250–1.

[54] Note *dicta* in *R v Fletcher* [1983] 1 NIJB, 5–6.

[55] Baker Report, para. 54.

[56] *Tenth Report of the Standing Advisory Commission on Human Rights: Report for 1983–84* (1985), 73; *Fourteenth Report of the Standing Advisory Commission on Human Rights: Report for 1987–89* (1989), 103–4.

[57] Colville (1990), para 10.8.7.

There is as yet no statistical evidence available on the frequency of use of the power to withdraw,[58] but academic observations on its exercise have ranged from 'the judge often steps down'[59] to '[u]nfortunately this procedure is rarely used.'[60] The issue of how frequently judges avail themselves of this procedure is significant. It might be a revealing indicator, for example, of how different judges approach their fact-finding responsibilities. Do some regard themselves as impervious to the potentially prejudicial impact of inadmissible material, and able to divorce the fact-finding role completely from such influences? Do others adopt a 'jury-wise' stance and proceed more cautiously in the face of excluded evidence, taking the withdrawal option more regularly? Or perhaps the nature of the circumstances, as opposed to the personality of the judge, is the deciding factor in the majority of cases.

(d) The voir dire

At this point, having considered the judge's formal powers after his decision on the admissibility of a confession, it is appropriate to look more closely at the general nature of the *voir dire* in the Diplock process. At this phase of the trial the dichotomy between the normal and the extraordinary is most sharply depicted in the Diplock context. Take, for example, the following observation: 'The absence of a jury has often had little impact. Most defendants plead guilty, and disputed cases usually revolve around confessions or statements whose admissibility is initially determined even in jury trials by the judge alone.'[61]

Beneath the surface, however, the *voir dire* in a Diplock trial may be shown to bear at least three crucial distinguishing features. First, the fact that the judge himself is also the arbiter of fact at the trial proper (ignoring, for the present, his power to withdraw) endows the *voir dire* with heightened significance. A failed challenge to a confession's admissibility to a judge in an ordinary trial may be followed by an equally enthusiastic challenge to its weight before the jury. In a Diplock trial, the challenge to reliability before the same judge is an altogether different prospect.[62] In fact, this is a situation in which the formal preservation of the ordinary trial structure is essentially negated in practice, as the twin issues of admissibility and weight are frequently dealt with at the same time by the

---

[58] In his 1990 report, Viscount Colville hoped that research results on the issue 'may . . . be available in the autumn' (para. 10.4), but to the best of the authors' knowledge no such results have yet been published.   [59] Walker and Hogan (1989), 110.

[60] Walsh (1983), 99, endorsed by Greer and White (1986), 17.

[61] Walker and Hogan (1989), 103.

[62] On this point, see Jackson (1983a), 13; Greer (1980), 233–6; Greer and White (1986), 17; Korff (1984), 65–6.

judge. Thus, while the issues remain theoretically distinct,[63] it is inevitable that this distinction will become blurred on a practical level. In reality, a failed challenge to the admissibility of a confession is less likely in a Diplock trial to be followed by a judge finding that the confession is false than in a jury setting. This merger of admissibility and weight may have implications throughout the law of evidence, but obviously it is at the *voir dire* stage that its effect is most significant.

A further point is that the evidential rules on confessions in respect of scheduled cases are different and affect the conduct of the *voir dire* in Diplock trials; the defence must establish a *prima facie* case that the confession was wrongly obtained. These rules will be discussed in detail in the next section, as will the third significant aspect of the *voir dire* in Diplock cases. This is that the confession is probably the single most important item of evidence in the context of scheduled cases. As we shall see, this itself has formed the basis of one of the most cogent critical attacks on the Diplock court system. In summary, the *voir dire* is of a different order in Diplock cases despite its formal position as the normal mechanism for determining the admissibility of confessions.

THE ASSAULT ON DIPLOCK COURTS

Although few changes have been made to the Diplock system since 1973, the criticism which greeted its introduction has not receded. It has, however, taken a quite different form from the criticism which has recently beset the English system of criminal justice. We have already noted that in England the criminal justice process and the appeal system have on occasions recently fallen short of public expectation. The uncovering of serious miscarriages of justice in the cases (among others) of the Guildford Four, the Birmingham Six, the Maguire family, Stefan Kiszko, and the Cardiff Three, as well as mounting pressure to reopen other convictions which have caused public concern, created much of the impetus for the Royal Commission's wide-ranging review of the administration of criminal justice. By contrast, the term 'miscarriage of justice' is not one which has figured prominently in the course of the ongoing debate on Diplock courts.[64] We shall later review allegations of specific miscarriages of justice in the Diplock courts, but until recently doubts over individual decisions have been overshadowed by a more general questioning of the fairness of Diplock proceedings.

The same comment could be applied to accusations of bias directed against judges involved in Diplock cases. There have been isolated

---

[63] See *R v Brophy* [1982] AC 476, discussed in detail in Chapter Three.

[64] For discussion of what actually constitutes a 'miscarriage of justice', see Greer (1994).

suggestions of general bias, but they have tended to be inadequately supported[65] (although it is conceded that bias is a trait which is very difficult to substantiate in any context). More generally, the composition of the bench in Northern Ireland has been criticized as not properly representing the population. In the early 1970s and before, the judiciary was identified as being drawn from the Protestant Unionist majority.[66] It would appear, however, that in recent years the composition of the Bench has been brought more closely into line with the balance of religious persuasion in society, although regrettably a statistical breakdown of the religious background of the judges is not officially available. In their follow-up survey of emergency law in Northern Ireland, published in 1980, Boyle, Hadden, and Hillyard compared Diplock courts favourably with pre-1973 jury trials of terrorist suspects, on the specific matter of partisanship:

The elimination of discrimination has been achieved both by the assertion of independent control over the prosecution process and by the suspension of jury trial. The pattern of outcomes and sentencing in Diplock courts does not provide any evidence of systematic bias on the part of the judges against Republican defendants.[67]

This relatively optimistic conclusion was, however, qualified in two important respects, each of which remains significant. First, although judges in Diplock courts could not be generally accused of partisanship, it remained possible that they had become 'case-hardened', a phenomenon which Boyle, Hadden, and Hillyard had earlier described as 'a measure of acclimatization on the part of judges sitting in Diplock trials and an increasing readiness to accept the evidence of the police and security forces in preference to that of the defence.'[68]

The second point is that such a tendency may have been accentuated due to the predominance of the confession as a source of evidence in Diplock cases. In the circumstances which have prevailed in Northern Ireland, and most particularly in the context of terrorist-type offences, the prosecuting authorities would have had extremely limited success if relying solely on civilian witnesses to establish a case against accused persons. In the first place, such witnesses simply have not existed in many cases and, secondly, there has been

---

[65] See for example Jennings and Wolchover (1984), 659; Walsh (1983), 102–4 (admitting that the evidence was not such that definite conclusions could be made, but that there was some indication that Protestants may be more leniently treated than Catholics in relation to charging and sentencing).

[66] See the discussion in Boyle, Hadden, and Hillyard (1975), 12–13.

[67] (1980a), 86. The 'assertion of independent control over the prosecution process' was effected in 1972, when the office of Director of Public Prosecutions for Northern Ireland was created.

[68] (1975), 98. See also the Baker Report, para. 122. For a broader perspective on 'case-hardening', see Damaska (1973), 538–9.

an understandable reluctance to become involved in trials involving suspected members of proscribed organizations.[69] The inculpatory statement by the accused has, therefore, been the most important feature of the prosecution armoury in a large number of Diplock trials. This became even more evident after 1975, when internment ceased to be used by the authorities and pressure on the police to obtain confessions from terrorist suspects increased. The shift in emphasis had its own costs, as allegations of ill-treatment of those held in detention centres escalated, provoking wide-spread concern and culminating in an official inquiry (by the Bennett Committee in 1979) into police interrogation procedures in Northern Ireland. Past estimates have suggested that the confession forms the mainstay of the prosecution case in around 80 per cent of Diplock cases.[70] Concern at this situation has been neatly expressed as follows:

The paradoxical result is that, while the judges have become the unchallenged masters in their own courts, the issues put before them are largely predetermined, so they are left with a residual confirmatory role. Whether this shift in power from courts to police is acceptable depends on the nature both of the special policing powers . . . and the special evidential rules . . .[71]

These comments introduce another important dimension to the debate on Diplock courts: the relationship between the trial process and the broader package of emergency measures introduced in Northern Ireland since 1973. A full examination of the special police and army powers contained in the emergency provisions legislation would be beyond the scope of the present work.[72] While the use of such powers plays a significant part in determining the nature and number of cases brought before Diplock courts, it does not have an immediate bearing on the actual workings of the trial, which is the primary focus of our analysis. The main advantage of the approach we have adopted is that it offers a concentrated insight into one aspect of the actual practice of administration of criminal justice. However, it is important to bear in mind that the trial does not operate in isolation from the earlier phases of the criminal process. Indeed, it is the exceptional pre-trial procedures and the impact of these on the trial itself which have caused

---

[69] Following a recommendation of the Diplock Committee (see para. 97 of the Report), section 5 of the Northern Ireland (Emergency Provisions) Act 1973 provided that a statement signed by a person made in the presence of a constable could be admitted if the person was dead or unable to attend due to bodily or mental condition, was outside Northern Ireland in circumstances where it was not practicable to secure his return, or could not be found in spite of reasonable efforts. The provision was, however, hardly used and was repealed by section 7 of the Emergency Provisions Act 1975. See Boyle, Hadden, and Hillyard (1975), 104–5; Walker and Hogan (1989), 109–10.

[70] See Bennett Report, para. 30; Boyle, Hadden, and Hillyard (1980a), 44.

[71] Walker and Hogan (1989), 109.

[72] For a useful survey of the emergency package see Dickson (1992b).

some to challenge the central claim made by the Diplock Commission, that the emergency trial procedures which it recommended complied with the minimum standards for a fair trial under Article 6 of the European Convention on Human Rights and Fundamental Freedoms.[73] Specifically, it has been argued that the cumulative effect of the 'stop and search' powers, wide powers of arrest, seven-day detention, questionable interrogation practices, weak restrictions on the admissibility of confessions, and non-jury courts is to produce a system of criminal justice significantly weighted against the accused.[74]

When we consider the special evidential rules introduced by the emergency legislation, the linkage between pre-trial procedures and the trial itself is obvious. Most notably, the special rule governing the admissibility of confessions in scheduled cases must feature in any discussion of the Diplock court process. The relationship between the admissibility rule and the acceptable boundaries of police behaviour during interrogation has previously brought the Diplock court into considerable controversy. Although the courts themselves and recent legislative changes have alleviated concern to some extent, it would be wrong to treat the issue as dead, particularly if the confession continues to play such a key part in Diplock trials.

On a somewhat different but related note, the statutory encroachments upon the right to silence in Northern Ireland,[75] although applying to jury cases as well, have also tended to place the Diplock trial under the spotlight. Giving to the tribunal of fact the power to draw inferences from the accused's silence is a radical break with common law tradition, which is anathema to many defenders of the rights of the accused. Although the changes to the confessions rule and the modification of the right of silence would probably have caused concern in their own right, the fact that they were implemented in the setting of a non-jury trial system, where that common law tradition had already been infringed, has arguably intensified this concern.

In the context of the critical assault on Diplock courts, however, all of the above issues pale in significance alongside the one phenomenon which marked the Diplock court's blackest phase. This was the use of 'super-grasses' to obtain bulk convictions of suspected terrorist offenders in the first half of the 1980s. Here the trial process itself came under direct scrutiny. Before reviewing this period of controversy, let us examine in more

---

[73] Diplock Report, para. 14.

[74] See Hunt and Dickson (1983). For further discussion of Diplock courts in the context of human rights challenges, see Jackson and Doran (1993), 508–10.

[75] See the Criminal Evidence (Northern Ireland) Order 1988. For commentary on the operation of the Order see Jackson (1991); Justice (1994).

detail some matters of concern mentioned before, namely, the 'case-hardening' thesis, the significance of confessions, and the rules governing their reception. The contribution of our own study to the issues under discussion will be noted as we proceed.

(a) Case-hardening

The argument that judges in Diplock courts were in danger of becoming case-hardened was first advanced by Boyle, Hadden, and Hillyard following their survey of cases tried by judge alone during the first seven months of the operation of Diplock courts.[76] The same authors returned to the topic in their follow-up survey of the outcomes of all Diplock cases from 1973 to 1979.[77] The figures pointed to a significant decline in the effective acquittal rate in contested cases in Diplock courts, from over 50 per cent in 1973 to around 35 per cent in 1979. The 'effective', as opposed to 'apparent', acquittal rate is calculated on the basis that a defendant who refused to recognize the court (technically a not guilty plea) was in essence pleading guilty to all charges against him. As this stance was adopted much more frequently in the earlier years of the survey, the effective acquittal rate in these years is considerably higher than a bare analysis of statistics would suggest. The authors of that study accepted that the trend of declining acquittal rates was not necessarily attributable to case-hardening alone, and also that the official explanation, of 'greater care by the prosecuting authorities in the selection and preparation of cases', could not be discounted. However, they then analysed statistics which showed that the rate of acquittal in contested jury trials in Northern Ireland had risen from 38 per cent in 1974 to a peak of 61 per cent in 1977 and levelling off at 59 per cent in 1978 and 1979. These figures led them to the following conclusion:

This increase in the acquittal rate in jury trials is of some significance in assessing the possible explanations for the decline in the acquittal rate in Diplock trials. The Director of Public Prosecutions is responsible for preparing cases for both forms of trial, and it is reasonable to assume that similar care is taken and similar standards are applied in all cases. It follows that it is reasonable to eliminate differences in prosecution practice as an explanation for the declining acquittal rate in Diplock trials.[78]

Nonetheless, as the authors conceded, the absence of an 'ideal acquittal rate' renders definite conclusions from the statistics impossible and the authors were duly cautious in advancing the case-hardening thesis.

Certain observers found Boyle, Hadden, and Hillyard's arguments on

[76] See Boyle, Hadden, and Hillyard (1975), 98.
[77] Boyle, Hadden, and Hillyard (1980a), 59–62.   [78] *Ibid.*, 61–2.

case-hardening convincing and have sought to update the statistical picture which they presented,[79] but official reaction to the survey was less than enthusiastic. Most notably, the Baker Report bluntly accepted that greater care by the prosecuting authorities was the factor which had caused the acquittal rate to dip. Citing the figures on acquittal from 1973 to 1983, but not incorporating refusals to recognize the court as effective pleas of guilty, Baker concluded: 'I do not believe the figures prove or even tend to prove anything.'[80] He also urged adherents to the case-hardening view to accept that a rise in the acquittal rate in 1981 and 1982 (to around 35 per cent, from an average of around 20 per cent between 1975 and 1980) 'heralds a new era'. In an earlier passage, Baker stated his opinion, based on conversations with Northern Ireland judges, that 'the danger is well recognised and I am convinced that each one is continually thinking of the possibility and warning himself against leaning or even appearing to lean to the prosecution or against the defence.'[81] Another observer added that the acquittal rates in Diplock cases are not dissimilar to those indicated by research into jury trials in England where the prosecution case depended on confession evidence.[82]

The observations in the Baker Report do have a certain ring of complacency and do not fully answer the case-hardening argument, which is worthy of further consideration. Admittedly, more recent statistics (albeit with no reference to the non-recognition factor, which is in any case now much less significant) show that the acquittal rate has been rather higher in recent years than in the 1970s. This is illustrated by Table 2.2,[83] which demonstrates that the rate of defence success in contested Diplock cases has been running at an average of around 45 per cent since 1984. What the Table also shows clearly, however, is that the aquittal rate still falls short of that in jury trial, in spite of misleading official pronouncements to the contrary.[84]

---

[79] Walsh (1983), 94, 97–8; Greer and White (1986), 22–3.

[80] Baker Report, para. 124.					[81] *Ibid.*, para. 123.

[82] Bonner (1985), 143 (referring to Baldwin and McConville, *Confessions in Crown Court Trials*, RCCP, Research Study No. 5, 1980).

[83] There are two main sources of statistics on the outcomes of Diplock trials in Northern Ireland: *Judicial Statistics for Northern Ireland*, issued by the Northern Ireland Court Service (which also contains figures for non-jury trials), and *Northern Ireland (Emergency Provisions) Acts: Annual Statistics*, prepared by the Statistics and Research Branch, Criminal Justice Policy Division, Northern Ireland Office and issued quarterly through the Northern Ireland Information Service. Statistics on the outcomes of both Diplock and jury trials for the period 1984–93 may also be found in *Commentary on the Northern Ireland Crime Statistics 1993* (1994), Belfast: HMSO. The statistics presented in Table 2.2 are computed from Tables 4.7 and 4.9 of the *Commentary*.

[84] At the Committee stage on the 1991 Act, Lord Belstead, Minister responsible for law and order in Northern Ireland, said that the acquittal rate in Diplock cases was 'the same as in ordinary courts'. (H.L. Debs., Vol. 528, col. 1368, 13 May 1991.) Quoted by Dickson (1992b), 609.

TABLE 2.2 *Pleas and acquittal rates in jury and Diplock trials, 1984–1993*

| | Jury trial | | | | | | | | | |
Year	1984	1985	1986	1987	1988	1989	1990	1991	1992	1993
Persons proceeded against	1121	1333	1263	1210	971	911	952	919	891	826
Pleaded guilty	926	1090	1101	1056	783	767	716	717	673	584
Pleaded not guilty	195	243	162	154	188	144	236	202	218	242
Pleaded not guilty, found guilty	99	115	78	79	97	53	100	104	108	125
Pleaded not guilty, found not guilty	96	128	84	75	91	91	136	98	110	117
% pleading not guilty, found not guilty	49%	53%	52%	49%	48%	63%	58%	49%	50%	48%

| | Diplock trial | | | | | | | | | |
Year	1984	1985	1986	1987	1988	1989	1990	1991	1992	1993
Persons proceeded against	507	698	596	713	515	456	470	423	413	447
Pleaded guilty	426	552	528	634	442	373	386	343	301	328
Pleaded not guilty	81	146	68	79	73	83	84	80	112	119
Pleaded not guilty, found guilty	38	73	39	46	45	41	54	45	53	85
Pleaded not guilty, found not guilty	43	73	29	33	28	42	30	35	59	34
% pleading not guilty, found not guilty	53%	50%	43%	42%	38%	51%	36%	43%	53%	29%

Although the general disquiet over the possibility that judges have become case-hardened may have subsided in recent years,[85] it is submitted that there are certain aspects of the issue which have not been satisfactorily explored. All commentators agree that the presence of other variables renders definite conclusions inadvisable. Moreover, it could be argued that the 'statistical approach' to the issue is in one sense misleading in that it fails to highlight the way in which *individual* judges go about their task. It is surely more valid to analyse the approach of individual judges to particular cases than to attempt an immediate generalization based on acquittal rates.

Thus, in our observation of trials, our analysis of their judgments, and our interviews with counsel and judges, we considered whether judges in Diplock trials—either individually or collectively—are inclined to deal with certain items or types of evidence in a routine manner and others more meticulously. Could it be that the requirement to prepare a reasoned judgment has forced judges to be completely scrupulous in their acceptance or rejection of defence and prosecution 'stories', or has the judgment itself come to assume a rather standardised form? If the latter, can this be attributed to case-hardening as we understand it or does it perhaps represent another (perhaps less worrying) form of acclimatization? Given the limited number of cases in our sample, and also the elusive nature of the concept of case-hardening, we could not claim a conclusive view on the issue. However, our contention remains that any proper investigation into this matter must involve the kind of contextual analysis which we have attempted. Only in this way can flesh be added to the bare bones of statistical breakdown.

(b) Confessions

As stated, the altering of the rule on admissibility of confessions in scheduled cases led to a vigorous debate on the propriety of police practices during the interrogation of suspects. In its Report the Diplock Commission expressed concern that the common law principle that a confession must be voluntary to be admissible was operating as a hindrance to the course of justice and was forcing the authorities 'to resort to detention in a significant number of cases which could otherwise be dealt with both effectively and fairly by trial in a court of law'.[86] The Commission was also critical of the Northern Ireland courts (arguably unfairly[87]) for their strict application of the common law rule in particular cases.[88] The Commission therefore,

---

[85] Although see Committee on the Administration of Justice (1992), 28.
[86] Diplock Report, para. 87.   [87] See Greer (1973).
[88] See para. 83. The decisions which caused the Commission particular concern were *R v Gargan* [1972] NIJB (May); *R v Flynn and Leonard* [1972] NIJB (May).

while taking care to avoid any suggestion that it condoned the more extreme forms of interrogation which had been practised in Northern Ireland in the earliest phase of the troubles, proposed a new test of admissibility based on the terms of Article 3 of the European Convention on Human Rights. The change found expression in section 6 of the Northern Ireland (Emergency Provisions) Act 1973 and later in section 8 of the 1978 Act, the latter provision differing only in respect of its non-application to summary trials.[89]

This provision was in turn substituted by a provision in the Northern Ireland (Emergency Provisions) Act 1987 (now section 11 of the 1991 Act), which changed the admissibility rule in a more significant respect. In its earlier form, the section provided that where the prosecution proposed to introduce a statement made by the accused and where *prima facie* evidence was adduced that he had been subjected to torture or to inhuman or degrading treatment in order to induce him to make the statement, then the court should reject the statement unless the prosecution satisfied it that the statement had not been obtained by one or more of those methods. The courts' interpretation of the section prior to its revision in 1987 has been considered in detail elsewhere.[90] For present purposes, it is worth outlining some broad themes which ran through their approach to the provision.

First, the courts recognized that there was clearly a gap between the test in section 8 and the common law test of voluntariness. For example, the holding out of hopes of advantage or threats of prejudice, which would cause a statement to be excluded at common law, would not necessarily breach the emergency standard. Moreover, the statutory test required some form of deliberate conduct on the part of the interrogator 'in order to' make the accused confess, while at common law the effect upon the accused's mind alone could be the decisive factor.[91] Secondly, the Northern Ireland Court of Appeal adopted a firm stance in relation to the use by interrogators of personal violence. In one decision, the Court found it 'difficult in practice to envisage any form of physical violence which is relevant to the interrogation of a suspect in custody and which, if it had occurred, could at the same time leave a court satisfied beyond reasonable doubt in relation to the issue for decision' under the section.[92] This decision allayed to some extent the concern caused by an earlier ruling in which a Diplock court had appeared to accept that the section left room for 'a moderate degree of physical maltreatment' to be exerted upon a suspect to obtain a confession.[93]

[89] For a comprehensive discussion of the section see Greer (1980).
[90] See Greer (1980); Jackson (1983a), 146–55.
[91] For a case which illustrates the gap see *R v McAllister*, unreported, Mar. 1988: confession ruled out by judge in trial by jury, the police having interrogated the accused on the assumption that they were dealing with a scheduled offence (see Colville (1990), para. 10.5.5.3).   [92] *R v O'Halloran* [1979] NI 45 (per Lowry LCJ, 47).
[93] *R v McCormick and Others* [1977] NI 105 (per McGonigal J, 111).

Thirdly, and perhaps most significantly, the courts were prepared to recognize a discretion to exclude confessions which were strictly admissible under the statutory provision. The discretion was given its broadest expression in an early decision, in which the court noted that conduct and circumstances relevant to the voluntariness of a confession could form the basis of the courts' exercise of its discretion in scheduled cases.[94] Absence of voluntariness, however, would not automatically warrant exclusion, as this would effectively controvert the will of Parliament in enacting the statutory provision. This point was stressed in later decisions in which the courts warned against attempts to reinstate the old common law rules by way of the discretion.[95] On the frequency of the exercise of the discretion, the Baker Report noted in 1984: 'In recent years few confessions have been excluded. It is impossible to be certain in every case whether they were rejected in the exercise of the judge's discretion but certainly 40%–45% were.'[96]

The discretion has now been given a statutory footing,[97] section 11(3) providing that the court may exclude a statement 'if it appears to the court that it is appropriate to do so in order to avoid unfairness to the accused or otherwise in the interests of justice'. It has been noted that, given the courts' prior willingness to use the discretion, the new sub-section is unlikely to have a dramatic impact.[98] The new provision also adds 'any violence or the threat of violence (whether or not amounting to torture)' to the range of conduct which renders a confession inadmissible (as now contained in section 11(2)(b)). Again, as the use of violence does seem to have been construed by the courts as almost invariably infringing the previous statutory prohibition on torture or inhuman or degrading treatment, the change might not be so significant as first appearances would suggest. Nonetheless, the express prohibition on actual or threatened violence can only be viewed as a positive step towards eliminating any remaining trace of uncertainty over the limits of the previous exclusionary rule. This is so in spite of Baker's reservations over the addition of threats of violence to the clause.[99]

Recent legislative developments in the non-emergency field in Northern Ireland have lent weight to another line of attack on the confessions rule.

---

[94] *R v Tohill* [1974] NIJB (Mar.). Also *R v Corey* [1979] NI 49 (the decision itself dates from 1973).

[95] See for example *R v McCormick* [1977] NI 105, 114; *R v Milne* [1978] NI 110, 116. And, more recently, *R v Dillon* [1984] NI 292; *R v Howell and Others* [1987] 5 NIJB.

[96] Baker Report, para. 198.

[97] Both the Baker Report (para. 200) and the Gardiner Report (paras. 46–50) had applauded the courts' use of the discretion and recommended its incorporation in the statutory provision.   [98] Jackson (1988b), 251.

[99] See the Baker Report, para. 200.

The Police and Criminal Evidence (Northern Ireland) Order 1989, which mirrors the English Act of 1984, allows a confession to be admitted unless it was (or may have been) made (a) by oppression, or (b) as a consequence of anything said or done which was likely in the circumstances to render it unreliable (Article 74). It has been argued that the Order has narrowed the gap between section 8 and the ordinary law to such an extent that the emergency test may be abandoned, restoring to normality the rules governing the admissibility of confessions in scheduled cases. Interestingly, Colville rejected this proposal (albeit provisionally) on the substantive ground that the police would, when interrogating suspects, be 'set afloat on a sea abounding in reefs and shoals'. Colville referred to the confused state of the English authorities on section 76 of the Police and Criminal Evidence Act 1984, the equivalent to Article 74: 'By contrast, it is by now relatively clear what may and may not be done during police interrogation, in order to safeguard admissibility under section 8 of any confession obtained; and I would be surprised if the RUC were content at this stage to be governed solely by the PACE Order.'[100]

With respect, the arguments are not entirely convincing. Uncertainty over the precise scope and rationale of the PACE provision is not surprising, given its relatively young age and, in any event, the 'reefs and shoals' have to be faced in ordinary cases. The clarity of the emergency provision is, as we have seen, debatable and it has never been customary to offer the police a conclusive say in the formulation of rules of evidence. It is submitted that the adoption of the PACE provision in scheduled cases would be a positive development. No doubt critics of the emergency framework will continue to argue that such a course be taken. Ironically, this could minimize the identification of the institution of the Diplock court with the controversy surrounding evidence of confessions. Assuming a consistent application of the same test in Diplock and jury trials, the focus would be upon judicial performance in this area generally rather than in Diplock trials alone.

The foregoing summary of the modified test for the admissibility of confessions in scheduled cases and the courts' response to it may at first appear incongruous in the context of a discussion of the critical assault on Diplock courts. From one angle, the Northern Ireland courts may be applauded on their refusal to allow the lower standard of acceptable conduct by interrogators to serve as a pretext for maltreatment of suspects. In particular, the development of the judicial discretion, albeit with some caution in the face of Parliament's stated will, played an important part in ensuring that the new test was not completely distanced from its common law counterpart. Nevertheless, any departure from the norm in respect of the rules governing admissibility of confessions is likely to attract censure,

---

[100] Colville (1990), para. 10.5.7.4. See also para. 10.5.

not only towards its particular form, but towards the system within which that departure is practised.

There is no doubt that the changes in the admissibility test contributed to the prominent role of confessions in the Diplock process, a concern which has already been mentioned. A related issue is the relationship between the high incidence of evidence of confession and the number of guilty pleas before Diplock courts. This is another area in which a purely statistical analysis may fail to produce an accurate picture. Walsh's survey of cases offered the statistic that 93 per cent of the guilty pleas in scheduled cases followed an alleged confession. Given the lower admissibility test in scheduled cases, Walsh viewed the link between confession and plea as causal. Other observers, however, do not accept that such a link is necessarily established and set the rate of guilty pleas within a broader statistical background. Table 2.3 offers a comparison between rates of guilty pleas in Diplock courts, ordinary Crown Court proceedings in Northern Ireland, and Crown Court proceedings in England and Wales.[101]

The rate in Diplock cases is high when placed alongside the figures for England and Wales (although it is interesting to note that the rates in certain circuits, notably North Eastern and Midland and Oxford, are higher than the average). It is fair to say, however, that the guilty plea rate in Diplock cases is not significantly different from the rate in ordinary trials in Northern Ireland. Accordingly, it has been suggested that the heavy reliance on confessions is not the crucial factor which produces guilty pleas and that other factors 'may include the professional competence of the prosecution service, readiness to engage in plea-bargaining . . . or the reluctance of defence lawyers (perhaps related to the intimacy of the jurisdiction) to contest weak cases'.[102] There is, of course, a major unsatisfactory feature of this argument, namely that it lacks reference to the relationship between confessions and guilty pleas in ordinary criminal trials in Northern Ireland. Statistics on this matter would be essential to answer fully the argument which links confessions to the rate of guilty pleas in Diplock cases.

Whatever the true position, it is tempting to enquire whether factors such as those mentioned operate to equivalent degrees in Diplock and ordinary cases, a question which we address in Chapter Seven. The rate of guilty pleas may be similar in the two contexts, but the motivations behind such pleas may be different. It is possible that the form of trial itself is a significant factor in shaping counsel's pre-trial advice to his or her client and

---

[101] Statistics for 1984–93 in the first two rows of the table are derived from *Commentary on Northern Ireland Crime Statistics*, Tables 4.7 and 4.9. See also note 83 above. The figures in the third row are taken from Lord Chancellor's Department, *Judicial Statistics: England and Wales* (annual), London: HMSO.

[102] Walker and Hogan (1989), 115.

TABLE 2.3 *Guilty plea rates in jury proceedings in Northern Ireland, Diplock proceedings, and jury proceedings in England and Wales, 1984–1993*

Year	1984	1985	1986	1987	1988	1989	1990	1991	1992	1993
Percentage of persons pleading guilty in NI jury proceedings	83%	82%	87%	87%	81%	84%	75%	78%	76%	71%
Percentage of persons pleading guilty in Diplock proceedings	84%	79%	89%	89%	86%	82%	82%	81%	73%	73%
Percentage of persons pleading guilty in jury proceedings in England and Wales	64%	66%	64%	68%	72%	71%	71%	69%	69%	66%

in the plea-bargaining process. On a specific level, is it true as Walsh suggests that a confession is perceived by the defence as a more formidable obstacle in Diplock cases than in jury trials? Or, more generally, the prospect of challenging the entire prosecution case may be more (or less) attractive in a Diplock trial. We interviewed counsel in Diplock trials to investigate whether their approach to such trials differs in these respects from their approach to jury cases. Such a line of inquiry is, we feel, important in gauging the impact of the jury's absence on the general character of the criminal process, an exercise which statistical analysis of outcomes can never fully accomplish.

Of greater concern than the prosecution's reliance on confessions is the manner in which they are obtained. As stated before, the treatment of suspects during interrogation in Northern Ireland was, particularly in the 1970s, an issue which provoked national and international controversy[103] and it was logical to attribute a measure of blame for police and army ill-treatment of detainees to the emergency test of admissibility.[104] As for the courts' use of the residual discretion, its nebulous form in itself carried dangers: as the Bennett Report indicated, 'the uncertainty, despite the standards applied and upheld by the courts, about what is permissible and what is not, short of physical violence, may tempt officers to see how far they can go and what they can get away with'.[105] In the context of a legislative scheme designed to bring more offenders to court and depending so strongly on the inculpatory statements of accused persons, it is understandable that the courts, which (in cases resulting in conviction) place the final legitimizing stamp upon the evidence gathered by the police and presented by the prosecution at trial, should become tainted by any impropriety in the earlier phases of investigation. Thus the Diplock court, itself an integral and controversial facet of that general scheme, has figured much more prominently in the general debate on treatment of suspects than trial by jury has ever done, even though the judge alone makes the decision on admissibility in that context also.

The connection between the way in which confessions are obtained and the general fairness of trials in Diplock courts is most forcefully urged by Korff, who writes:

The 'Diplock' courts convict in the vast majority of cases in which a confession (allegedly) made by the accused in the course of police interrogation is the only evidence of his guilt, as long as there was no evidence that physical ill-treatment (or

---

[103] See Amnesty International (1978); the Bennett Report; Boyle, Hadden, and Hillyard (1975), 48–52 and (1980a), ch 5; Walsh (1983), ch 3.
[104] The point is forcefully made by Boyle: (1982), 160.
[105] Bennett Report, para. 84.

worse) was used to obtain that confession. In doing so, the courts implicitly assume the reliability of confessions obtained as a result of interrogation in which such treatment did not occur ... [I]t is surprising, in view of the evidentiary problems arising out of the private nature of interrogation, that the courts so often hold that it has been established beyond reasonable doubt that nothing untoward has occurred which might have affected the reliability of a confession.[106]

The chief problem with this argument is that it is difficult to substantiate in any systematic fashion. It would be difficult, for example, to make an *ex post facto* assessment of the reliability of those confessions which have been ruled admissible. Even if that were possible, the question would remain whether the court had in such cases been apprised of sufficient information on which to base a decision to exclude. One of the issues we shall consider in Chapter Eight, when we come to analyse judges' approaches to fact-finding, is the way in which they assess confession evidence. It is accepted, however, as stated before, that the trial itself cannot be viewed in total isolation from the other phases of the criminal process. Even if a favourable appraisal were made of the courts' response to confessions, it would not follow that the label of fairness should extend to the criminal process as a whole. In brief, the degree of reproach which can be aimed at Diplock courts for pre-trial failings is not an easily measurable one.

Although complaints of ill-treatment have not completely abated,[107] it is fair to say that the reforms which followed the Bennett Report did have a restraining influence upon police practices during interrogation, and the issue no longer arouses the same concern today as it did in, say, 1977. Concern, however, remains about the secrecy which prevails in the holding centres where suspects are interrogated. International criticism has recently centred around the refusal to grant suspects immediate access to legal advice, and the refusal to introduce audio and video recording of police interviews,[108] and in his first report as independent commissioner for the holding centres Sir Louis Blom-Cooper recommended that serious consideration be given to the possibility of audio and video recording.[109] In general though, criticism of the Diplock courts themselves *vis-à-vis* confessions is now less pronounced than before.

---

[106] (1984), 78.

[107] In November 1991, for example, allegations of assaults by the police in the holding centres where terrorist suspects are taken after arrest came under scrutiny at hearings held in Geneva by the United Nations Committee Against Torture. The Committee was investigating the UK's compliance with the Convention Against Torture. See Dickson (1992b), 602.

[108] See the critical comments made by the United Kingdom's independent expert before the United Nations Subcommission on the Prevention of Discrimination and the Protection of Minorities in August 1992.

[109] *First Annual (1993) Report of the Independent Commissioner for the Holding Centres* (Jan. 1994), 107–12.

(c) Supergrasses

Just as the controversy surrounding the obtaining and admissibility of confessions was becoming less intense, the most difficult period in the history of Diplock courts began. The causal link between the tightening of interrogation procedures and the reliance by the prosecuting authorities on the evidence of informers is difficult to assess with accuracy. Suffice to say that the early 1980s saw the emergence of the 'supergrass' and that this was the era in which public confidence in the Diplock court system reached its nadir, and yet it managed to emerge with some measure of credibility. There is a fairly extensive body of literature on the legal implications of the supergrass issue, as well as on its broader political significance.[110]

Borrowed from Greer's research,[111] the following figures give some indication of the impact of supergrasses on the criminal justice process in Northern Ireland. In a two-year period between November 1981 and November 1983, almost 600 suspects were arrested on the word of at least seven Loyalist and eighteen Republican supergrasses. Fifteen retracted their evidence either before or during the trials in which they were to testify for the prosecution. In the ten trials which proceeded to a conclusion, 120 out of 217 defendants were convicted or pleaded guilty, around 55 per cent. However, in the five cases in which appeals were brought, 67 out of the 74 convictions challenged were overturned, producing an overall conviction rate for the ten trials of 44 per cent. Two other supergrasses came forward after November 1983, but in neither case did the proceedings reach trial. As Greer notes, the broader impact of supergrass trials in the Diplock context far exceeded their numerical significance:

Those tried on the evidence of an alleged accomplice in 1983, 1984 and 1985 accounted for only 12 per cent of the total number of Diplock defendants in this period. Nevertheless, this does not detract from the significance of the supergrass system as a prosecution initiative carefully targeted on the alleged 'godfathers of terrorism.'[112]

The judges, as the triers of facts in these trials, were inevitably thrown into the limelight, since the supergrass strategy depended for its success or failure on the willingness of the courts to convict defendants on supergrass testimony. The trials present a number of points of significance. First of all, the strategy of using supergrasses posed a much more direct challenge to the fairness of the trial system than the use of confession evidence. As we have

---

[110] The main works are as follows: Gifford (1984); Hillyard and Percy-Smith (1984); Boyd (1984); Greer (1986) and (1987); Jackson (1985); and Bonner (1988).

[111] See in particular Greer (1987).

[112] *Ibid.*, 665 (referring to Attorney-General's statement, H.C. Debs., Vol. 94, cols. 187–8).

seen, the courts can become tainted when they are seen to uphold confessions admitted under an emergency framework which deviates from the normal standards of admissibility, and which have been obtained before trial under a regime with a history of abusive techniques. However, the use of confessions to convict persons is not an unusual feature of any trial process. By contrast, when the courts decided the fate of large numbers of defendants on the uncorroborated evidence of former paramilitaries who were in certain cases granted complete or partial immunity, they were seen to connive in a strategy which was much more questionable, both from a moral and a legal point of view.[113] The moral concerns derive from justifying the conviction of some by the grant of immunity to others who may have committed crimes which are just as heinous.[114] The legal concerns derive from the fear that innocent people, or people on the fringes of illegal activity, may be dragged into the net of inculpation on the basis of wide accusations by people with a powerful incentive not to tell the truth about the events they describe.[115] In addition, the large number of defendants involved in these trials (one trial lasted 117 days and involved thirty-eight defendants) gave the impression of 'show trials' designed to convict as many defendants as possible.

The judges did their best to emphasize the separation of the judiciary from the executive and to stress that there was a distinction between the use of uncorroborated accomplice evidence as a method of prosecution and its use as a method of conviction,[116] but their willingness to convict on uncorroborated testimony in three major trials provoked public criticism. In an unofficial report into the trials, Lord Gifford claimed that the judgments could not be relied upon because of the enormous pressures put upon judges in such trials.[117]

The second point of significance is that the wholesale use of accomplice evidence placed demands upon the single judge which brought the absence of the jury into sharp focus. Supergrass trials are not unknown in systems which retain trial by jury, indeed the term 'supergrass' derives from the

---

[113] There was controversy about the actual number of persons convicted on uncorroborated evidence, partly because the issue of whether there is corroboration in a given case is not always clearcut. Contrast the views of Graham (1983) with those of Greer and Hadden (1983); see also Jackson (1985).

[114] Throughout this period there appeared to be a policy not to grant immunity to those who had killed by using a gun or triggering an explosion themselves, but immunity could be granted to those who assisted in acts of murder: see *News Letter*, 28 May 1983, 'No Deal for Killers says Top Detective'. However, this policy was not referred to by the Attorney-General when he made a statement to Parliament about the use of accomplice evidence on 24 Oct. 1983 (see H.C. Debs. Vol. 47, cols. 3–5). The legal basis for granting immunity is unclear: see Smith (1983).

[115] For more discussion of the concerns about supergrass testimony, see Jackson (1988c).

[116] See, for example, *R v Gibney* [1983] 13 NIJB 1, 7–8.

[117] Gifford (1984).

English case of Bertie Smalls who gave evidence in 1973 against a large number of persons allegedly involved in a series of armed robberies between 1968 and 1971.[118] However, they have been rare and one of the reasons for this appears to be that the jury system places an effective restraint on their use. A supergrass strategy depends for its success on being able to try large numbers of defendants together, because there are severe risks in putting supergrasses through the ordeal of giving testimony more than once. It was precisely in order to prevent supergrasses from having to give evidence twice in the same legal proceedings that the prosecution applied for leave to bring a voluntary bill of indictment in two cases during the supergrass period in Northern Ireland, with the result that the supergrasses concerned did not have to give evidence in committal proceedings.[119] But there are limits to juries' ability to cope with trials involving large numbers of defendants. The English Court of Appeal has deprecated long and complex trials before a jury which overload the numbers of indictments and of defendants. In an appeal against convictions arising from one of the longest trials in English history, which lasted 111 days, Lawton LJ commented that the Court did not know how the jury had grappled with a mass of evidence affecting no less than fourteen accused persons.[120] Professional judges do not experience the same level of difficulty when they are the triers of fact. The Northern Ireland Court of Appeal recognized this in the appeal against convictions in the longest supergrass trial in Northern Ireland.[121] The Court of Appeal commented on 'the enormous care and the remarkable and scrupulous mastery of detail that the judge brought to a task with which, as it happens, a jury, no matter how carefully directed, could never have coped and would probably never be asked to cope'.[122] He went on to endorse the difficulties mentioned by Lawton LJ in *Thorne* concerning long trials, but added:

we also believe that a tendency towards unnecessary length and complexity, which he [Lawton LJ] so rightly condemns, is much more likely to confuse a jury than a judge sitting alone, who has the benefit of a complete or partial transcript and his own notes and who will be alert from the beginning to the main issues of fact and law and will not have to wait for a summing up to put them in perspective.[123]

There must nevertheless come a point when the numbers of defendants involved in a trial are going to perplex judges as well as juries, and there may well be other pressures that operate on judges in these trials, as Lord Gifford indicated when he commented that the judges' role as upholders of law and order and their desire to see terrorists brought to justice predisposes

---

118 *R v Turner* (1975) 61 Cr App R 67.
119 See Walsh (1983), 88–90; Gifford (1984), 9.
120 *R v Thorne* (1978) 66 Cr App R 6.
121 *R v Donnelly and Others* [1986] 4 NIJB 33.
122 *Ibid.*, 50–1.
123 *Ibid.*, 52–3.

them to accept the evidence if they possibly can. The point remains, however, that a supergrass strategy can be more easily pursued by professional judges sitting without a jury, because a jury clearly cannot cope with the large numbers of defendants upon which such a strategy depends.

The second reason why the jury system acts as a check on the use of supergrasses is that a jury may simply be less willing to convict. A judge's obligation to direct the jury on the dangers of relying on the uncorroborated evidence of an accomplice does not translate easily to a forum in which law and fact are decided by one person. Reference has already been made to the contrived notion of a judge 'warning himself' of such dangers: in the charged atmosphere of supergrass trials, a decision by a judge to act upon the uncorroborated evidence of an accomplice or an informer raised the question of whether the safeguard provided by the warning was an illusory one in the absence of the jury. Greer notes that in the first three supergrass cases '61 per cent of those convicted were found guilty on the uncorroborated testimony of the accomplice-witnesses concerned while 54 per cent of the convictions in all 10 supergrass trials rested on such evidence'.[124] The limited evidence available concerning jury response to uncorroborated accomplice evidence indicates a much greater reluctance to convict.[125]

The third point raised by the supergrass controversy pertains to the appeals process. The number of successful appeals prompts enquiry as to whether the written judgment is particularly susceptible to review by the appellate body, or whether the series of decisions in supergrass appeals have to be regarded as *sui generis* and reflective of a judicial change of direction in one particular area. An analysis of appeal statistics in general, which do not reveal a markedly greater willingness by the Court of Appeal to overturn convictions in Diplock cases, suggests the latter. Whether or not the judiciary took account of the criticisms made by Lord Gifford and others, a more critical attitude seemed to prevail from late 1983. Greer has commented that the apparent volte-face can be viewed as a triumph of loyalty to the rule of law over loyalty to counter-insurgency policy.[126] It certainly marked the end of the supergrass phenomenon, and there have been no major supergrass trials since 1984.

(d) The abrogation of the right to silence

After the supergrass controversy a period of comparative calm descended on the Diplock system, in terms of both the numbers of cases brought to trial and the level of criticism against the system. For the first time since their

---

[124] Greer (1986), 204.
[125] Gifford (1984), para. 18. See also Greer (1986), 225.   [126] Greer (1987).

inception, the Diplock courts became less identified with any one particular strategy, and in consequence less attention was given to the operation of the courts. The calm was broken, however, when the government introduced a series of emergency measures in 1988 to counter a renewed outbreak of terrorist violence in the summer of that year. These included a number of controversial measures that attracted publicity, including the 'media ban', which prevented the words of those representing or supporting proscribed organizations from being broadcast. The measure which had the most impact on the Diplock courts, however, was the modification of the right of silence under the Criminal Evidence (Northern Ireland) Order 1988. This effected a change which the police had long been advocating, to counter the persistent refusal of certain terrorist suspects to speak when under interrogation.[127]

The Order was chiefly targeted at two particular types of suspect who decline to answer questions while in police custody, namely terrorist suspects and persons suspected of holding money from paramilitary activity. However, it was introduced hurriedly by the Order in Council procedure which, in the absence of specific statutory authorization, cannot be used for legislation specifically concerning emergency matters.[128] Therefore, the Order applies to all criminal suspects in Northern Ireland and is operative in jury trials as well as in Diplock courts. Given the rationale of the legislation, however, it has been of greater significance in the latter context. Further, the dual role of the judge has again come under scrutiny as the effect of the new law has begun to be monitored.

The main provisions of the Order are, briefly, as follows. Article 3 permits the court or jury to draw inferences from the failure of the accused to mention any fact relied on in his or her defence when being questioned by a constable trying to discover whether or by whom the offence was being committed, or on being charged, if the fact was one which in the circumstances the accused could reasonably have been expected to mention. Article 4 relates to an accused's failure to testify at trial, from which a court or jury may draw such inferences as appear proper. Article 5 permits inferences to be drawn from an accused's failure to account for the presence of objects, substances, or marks when asked to account for them by a constable who reasonably believes they are attributable to participation in an offence. Finally, Article 6 in similar fashion allows inferences to be drawn from a failure to account for a person's presence in a place around the time at which the offence for which that person has been arrested is alleged to have been committed.

---

[127] For background to the introduction of the Order, see Jackson (1989).

[128] For a description of the Order in Council procedure, see Hadfield (1989), 130–40 (in particular 134). For criticism of the way in which the Order was introduced, see *Fourteenth Report of the Standing Advisory Commission on Human Rights: Report for 1987–89* (1989), ch 3; Ashworth and Creighton (1990).

The greatest impact of the Order may be expected in future to be on the process of police interrogation, because in addition to the other pressures on suspects at this stage, the additional pressure of being cautioned about a failure to answer questions may induce a number of suspects to speak when they might not otherwise have done so. To date, however, the Order has made its most visible impact on the Diplock trials. As with the use of confessions and supergrasses, the measure depends for its success on the attitude of the courts. The more willing the courts appear to draw inferences from silence, the more likely terrorists will be to change their policy of refusing to answer questions for fear of the consequences. The courts' reaction to the Order was cautious at first (indeed there were press reports that the judiciary opposed the introduction of the Order[129]), and it took some time for cases involving suspects warned under the new cautions about the consequences of failure to answer questions to come to trial. But the courts are now showing a greater willingness to draw inferences under the Order.[130] In the first appeal based on the interpretation of the Order, the Northern Ireland Court of Appeal held that the Order was clearly intended to change the common law and to permit judges (or juries) to draw such inferences as common sense dictated from any failure to testify or to mention in interrogation facts later relied upon, and this approach was subsequently upheld by the House of Lords.[131]

The Criminal Evidence (Northern Ireland) Order has not yet attracted as much criticism to the Diplock system as the supergrass strategy. There has been criticism of the Order, particularly from human rights bodies, but because the Order applies to all criminal suspects the concern has focused not only on Diplock cases but on the application of the Order throughout the entire criminal process of Northern Ireland.[132] When the government announced that it planned to introduce similar provisions for England and Wales in the autumn of 1993, the Order came under greater scrutiny, but again the interest was directed as much to its application in jury cases as to its operation in the non-jury context.[133] In so far as specific concern has been expressed about cases tried by Diplock courts, it has tended to concentrate on the pre-trial phase of the proceedings (particularly on the absence of normal safeguards when suspects are arrested under the emergency legislation) rather than on the trial itself.[134] The danger

---

[129] See McKittrick, 'Ulster Judges Clash with Government', *Independent*, 28 Dec. 1988.
[130] For a description of the cases, see Jackson (1991), (1992b).
[131] *Murray v DPP* [1994] 1 WLR 1. For criticism of this approach, see Jackson (1994b).
[132] See the concerns aired in *Fourteenth Report of the Standing Advisory Commission on Human Rights: Report for 1987–1989* (1989), 12–18 and in Amnesty International (1992).
[133] See Justice (1994).
[134] See Amnesty International (1992), 20–2. For further comment on this, see Doran and Jackson (1994), 100–2.

nevertheless remained at the trial phase, particularly when the Order was first introduced, that an over-zealous application of the Order by the judiciary might have led to the trial process becoming associated with the implementation of security policy to the detriment of due process concerns. Again, the absence of the jury accentuates this danger because the judges, who are supposed to be the custodians of fair procedure, are also made responsible for deciding whether or not to draw inferences from silence. If a jury system were in place instead of a system of trial by judge alone, the judges would have to decide how to direct the jury, but the jury would make the ultimate decision in each case, and the nature of the general verdict would conceal whether or not it drew inferences from the accused's silence.

It was this concern, that judges should appear to deal with the prosecution and the defence on an even-handed basis, that prompted Lord Chief Justice Taylor to object to one of the clauses in the provisions modelled on the Northern Ireland legislation which were put before Parliament by the Government in 1993. One feature of the original legislation was that the trial judge had to warn accused persons about the consequences of silence when they decided not to testify in their trial.[135] The clause was subsequently amended, to address this objection, by changing the judge's responsibility in this regard to one of 'being satisfied' that the accused has been apprised of these consequences, and the Northern Ireland Order was amended likewise.[136] With the passage of the English legislation, the Northern Ireland Order is less likely to be perceived in future as a particular security initiative designed to deal with terrorism and will become a 'normal' feature of the criminal justice system. The difficulty remains, however, that in non-jury trials judges will remain vulnerable to criticism about drawing adverse inferences in particular cases. This in turn may give greater credence to a further line of attack on Diplock courts which has gained some ground in recent years, namely the allegation of miscarriages of justice.

(e) Miscarriages of justice

The allegation that Diplock courts have presided over a number of wrongful convictions represents potentially the most damaging assault on the Diplock system. The point has been made that uncovering particular miscarriages of justice is an effective criticism of any system of criminal procedure because miscarriages of justice highlight inefficiencies in the system, in terms of

---

[135] For comment on the terms of the caution which had to be given by the judge, see *Sixteenth Report of the Standing Advisory Commission on Human Rights: Report for 1990–1991* (1991), para. 7.33; Jackson (1991), 410.

[136] See the amendment to Article 4 of the Order, effected by the Criminal Justice and Public Order Act 1994, Schedule 10, para. 1.

failure to convict offenders, and to meet one of the key due process concerns: the need to safeguard against false convictions.[137] Conversely, the inability on the part of critics to expose any serious miscarriages of justice, whilst not in itself proving their non-existence, constitutes a significant barrier to anyone claiming that a particular procedure is flawed. In his review of the emergency legislation in 1990, Viscount Colville observed that there was little demand on grounds of performance for an end to the system of trial by judge alone in Northern Ireland.[138] In support of this, he drew attention to the report of the Amercian lawyers to the Association of the Bar of the City of New York, which noted that no one had pointed to a single wrongful conviction in the Diplock system.[139]

This claim made in 1987 could not be made today. Since that time a growing number of allegations of miscarriages of justice have been made, although it must be said that there has been nothing like the number of claims made in England and Wales in recent years. The first case to gain publicity concerned the conviction in 1986 of four members of the Ulster Defence Regiment, the Armagh or UDR Four, as they have been known.[140] They were convicted on the evidence of confessions made by each of the four and the evidence of a witness who purported to recognize one of the accused, Latimer, whom she said she saw getting into an army jeep in civilian clothes near the scene of the murder a few minutes before it took place. Her description of what Latimer was wearing tallied with the description of another witness at the scene of the shooting who, however, testified that Latimer was not the man. After a campaign in support of the men, the Northern Ireland Secretary of State referred the case to the Court of Appeal, which quashed the convictions of three of the men on the basis of fresh evidence which took the form of ESDA (electrostatic document analysis) evidence revealing that police notes of the interviews with the men had been re-written, that a request by one of them to see a solicitor had been deleted from the notes, and that false authentications had been added to the notes.[141] All this showed that police officers had lied in court about what the men had said. The Court said that this did not mean the police had concocted the confessions, but that it did cast a doubt about how the confessions were obtained and therefore about their reliability. The Court upheld the conviction of Latimer, the fourth man, however, on the ground that the identification evidence against him still stood and also that he had admitted in court, unlike the others, that he had made a confession in the course of only his second police interview. The judgment of the Court sent out rather confused messages about the guilt or innocence of the three men it released,

---

[137] See Jackson (1994c).

[138] Colville (1990), para. 9.1.

[139] Hellerstein, McKay, and Schlam (1987), 56.

[140] For a brief assessment of the case against the men, see O'Connell (1991).

[141] *R v Latimer, Hegan, Bell, and Allen*, unreported, 29 Jul. 1992.

merely stating that it was a matter of regret that they had served six years in prison in consequence of a verdict upon which the trial judge could not have relied had he known about the untruthful evidence. The Court clearly felt that the blame lay with the police and not with any mistake on the part of the trial judge and to that extent the judgment casts no aspersion on the system of trial by judge alone. Nevertheless, the case was a significant acknowledgement by the Court of Appeal that persons could be wrongly imprisoned for several years after trial within the Diplock system.

The other cases which have caused concern have all arisen out of the trials of several people charged in connection with an incident in West Belfast in 1988, which culminated in the killing of two army corporals by the IRA during the funeral of a man who had been murdered a few days earlier in the course of a gun and bomb attack on a congregation attending another funeral in the area.[142] The aspects of these trials which caused most controversy were the use of film and video evidence on an unprecedented scale to convict people allegedly involved in the incident, and the courts' application of the criminal law on complicity in the circumstances. In one case, for example, a man was convicted of murder on the basis of video evidence which showed that he was one of those active in bringing the corporals into a nearby park but which then clearly showed that despite his confession to the contrary he played no further part in the incident.[143] This case formed the subject of one of a series of television documentary programmes better known for exposing miscarriages of justice within England and Wales.[144] Ironically, however, the aspect of these trials which most damaged the Diplock system was the way that the judges handled matters in their own preserve, namely questions of law, rather than the way they handled the questions of fact. Arguably, the most shocking feature of the trials was the way in which the judges extended the doctrine of common purpose to include persons who had nothing to do with the final shooting of the two corporals. Nevertheless, the cases also raise questions about whether the accused would have fared any better had they been tried by a jury and this in turn relates to the issue of whether judges adopt different approaches to fact-finding, a matter which we discuss in Chapter Eight.

TOWARDS A FRESH PERSPECTIVE

It is too early to say whether the latest attack on the Diplock system, based on particular allegations of injustice rather than on general allegations of

---

[142] See Committee on the Administration of Justice (1992).
[143] *R v Kane, Timmons and Kelly*, unreported, 30 Mar. 1990.
[144] *Rough Justice*, BBC Television, 1 Apr. 1993.

unfairness, will gather momentum. The position at present seems to be that while the assault on the Diplock system has dented its credibility at times, it has fallen short of striking any mortal blow. Some of the most damaging criticisms, for example about the use of confessions and supergrasses, have been met by certain changes of policy and attitude (although in the case of confessions there may be still some way to go before there can be full confidence in the process of police interrogation at Castlereagh holding centre) and the system has managed to survive intact. Yet there remains a public credibility problem, as evidenced by a survey forming part of the British Social Attitudes survey which showed that while 80 per cent of Catholics in Northern Ireland thought that the courts dealt equitably with non-terrorist offences, only 56 per cent felt the courts were fair in dealing with terrorist matters.[145] The reasons for this are unclear. It would seem that there has been no general loss of faith in the fairness of the judiciary and despite recent allegations of miscarriages of justice there does not appear to be widespread disenchantment with the outcome of trials. More likely, to take up an earlier point, the court system has become tainted with what are regarded in certain quarters as unfair security policies such as the use of non-jury courts, the use of supergrasses, and now perhaps the curtailment of the right of silence.

There is another aspect of the debate, however, which has escaped critical scrutiny. Much of the attention has focused on the *output* of the Diplock system and this has inevitably invited comparisons with the jury system in terms of plea rates and acquittal rates. Much less attention, on the other hand, has focused on the *process* of trial by judge alone within the Diplock system. The effect of this has been to concentrate the debate within narrow parameters. Both critics and defenders of the system have assumed that trial by jury is the *ideal* mode of trial in the adversarial system. Much of the debate has therefore focused, as we have seen, on whether the exigencies of the emergency justified the abandonment of jury trial in 1973, and whether it still requires such a drastic curtailment. Critics have denied the need for limiting jury trial so extensively, although even those who have been in the forefront of the demand for the return of jury trial recognize that it may be necessary to abandon it in specific instances, where it is shown that attempts have been made to interfere with a jury.[146] Unfavourable comparisons have then been made with jury trial. Defenders have countered these arguments by reaffirming the continuing need to derogate from trial by jury because of the circumstances of Northern Ireland and also by proclaiming that the Diplock system is producing results which show that the judges are far from prosecution-minded.

---

[145] *British Social Attitudes Survey (Eighth Report)* (1991). See *Independent*, 20 Dec. 1991. For further discussion of the issue of public confidence, see Finn (1991), 115–8.

[146] Greer and White (1986), 66–8.

What is missing here is an evaluation of how the adversarial trial process operates without a jury, and whether in fact its absence creates a different kind of trial altogether from the conventional adversarial trial associated with the jury. The assumption made by Lord Diplock that the adversary trial process would continue undisturbed in the absence of the jury has remained on the part of both critics and defenders of the Diplock system, but it is an assumption that requires to be tested. This is not to denigrate the comparisons that have been made with jury trials but it is argued that such comparisons give an incomplete picture. Only a systematic contextual analysis of the process can hope to explain *why* the outcomes are different.

It is true that particular aspects of the trial process have come under scrutiny. We have seen that critics have drawn attention to the problem for defendants of attacking the weight or reliability of confessions before the same tribunal which determined their admissibility, and the problem of judges warning themselves about the dangers of accomplice evidence. These are specific problems that are thrown up when the rules of evidence are preserved in a non-jury context, but they remain specific problems which do not challenge the suitability of retaining the entire adversary format in the absence of the jury.

Again, the supergrass phenomenon attracted particular odium to the Diplock system as the sheer number of defendants involved in the process seemed to convert ordinary trial procedures into extraordinary spectacles. Although the supergrass phenomenon has disappeared, the Diplock process still presides over fairly large multi-defendant trials which are uncharacteristic of most jury trials. More recently other aspects of Diplock trials have aroused concern. As a result of the right of silence legislation, for example, judges now have the additional burden as triers of fact of deciding whether to draw inferences from an accused's silence. A further source of controversy has been the spectacle of witnesses giving evidence behind screens.[147] This was another by-product of the events leading to the murder of two army corporals in West Belfast in 1988. In the trials that followed, a number of media witnesses were subpoenaed to give evidence of the provenance and authenticity of the video evidence and they were permitted to testify anonymously from behind a curtain which shielded them from the public and the accused.

These are extraordinary features of Diplock trials which have rightly attracted concern, and it is not wholly coincidental that they have been features of trial by judge alone rather than trial by jury. But the focus on these extraordinary features has deflected attention away from more 'ordinary' Diplock trials which have passed by with little comment. Mention was made at the beginning of the chapter of the large number of

---

[147] Marcus (1990); Committee on the Administration of Justice (1992), 33–6.

defendants who have passed through the Diplock system. Despite the publicity that has attended the system in general, only a handful of individual Diplock trials have attracted particular publicity and although the outcomes of the cases have been represented in government statistics and have been analysed by critics, little has been said about how these cases have actually been processed. It is such 'ordinary' cases which form the focus of our study.

3
Two Models of Proof

In Chapter Two we noted that the Diplock courts were introduced as part of a package of emergency measures designed to deal with political violence in Northern Ireland. These measures have been the subject of much controversy and the Diplock courts, which have ultimately been responsible for convicting those who have passed through this security system, have naturally been associated with the measures used. Attention has focused more on how these measures have affected plea rates and conviction rates than on the actual process of trial without jury. In this book we concentrate on the character and practice of this process in order to gauge what happens when the jury is taken away from the conventional trial format, but when the rules of procedure governing the trial are left intact. Before we turn to the trials themselves, however, we need to ask how the common law trial procedure is typically characterized. The epithet which best captures its essence is 'adversarial'. A key question to be addressed therefore is whether this 'adversariness' is affected by the absence of the jury. But first let us examine the basic tenets of the adversarial tradition.

THE MEANING OF 'ADVERSARINESS'

The adversary system of trial is often juxtaposed with non-adversarial or inquisitorial systems which are commonly said to operate in European or continental systems. It is less easy to state precisely the features of the adversary system. Much depends, as Damaska has observed, on the context in which the expression is used.[1] When used to describe a mode of criminal procedure, Damaska explains that the expression is used interchangeably with an old expression of continental origin, 'accusatorial procedure', and here the focus has tended to be on the protection which is offered to the accused and on the position of the accused *vis-à-vis* the state. Adversarial features are linked here with liberal ideology, which contrasts the interests of the state with those of the individual, and which requires a 'balance' between the two interests: that of the state in convicting the guilty, and that of the individual in having the case against him proved.[2] The prosecution

---

[1] Damaska (1983), 24–5.
[2] For discussion of this notion of balance, see Maher (1984); Jackson (1990b).

represents the interests of the state and its function is to accuse the defendant of a specific charge. The evidence is then presented at a public trial in the presence of the defendant.

A classic statement of the core features of an 'accusatorial', as opposed to an 'inquisitorial', system of criminal procedure is to be found in Justice Frankfurter's judgment in *Watts* v *Indiana*.[3] These were defined as 'the requirement of specific charges, their proof beyond reasonable doubt, the protection of the accused from confessions extracted through whatever form of police pressures, the right to a prompt hearing before a magistrate, the right to assistance of counsel, to be supplied by government when circumstances make it necessary, the duty to advise an accused of his constitutional rights', among which is included the privilege against self-incrimination. Although a number of these features are designed to protect accused persons from being wrongfully convicted, they are also designed to protect other individual interests. The privilege against self-incrimination, for example, protects interests such as freedom from state interference and rights of privacy, especially where it is extended to cover pre-trial police inquiries and the production of records and samples which might otherwise be taken from individuals suspected of criminal offences.[4]

The notion that these safeguards apply only in Anglo-American systems is contradicted by the observation of one writer that each of the characteristics mentioned by Justice Frankfurter are met by the German Criminal Procedure Code of 1877, and also by the fact that many of them are enshrined in Article 6 of the European Convention on Human Rights which has been ratified by numerous European countries that are considered to have inquisitorial systems.[5] This suggests that adversary features are not simply a reflection of the central features of the Anglo-American criminal process, but rather a set of standards by which all criminal processes may be judged. At their heart lies a concern for the primacy of individual rights in the legal process.

Of course, the fact that systems have incorporated these characteristics into their rules of procedure does not mean that they live up to the adversarial or accusatorial ideal. For some time now it has been claimed that there are significant inquisitorial features in Anglo-American criminal processes, largely because of their heavy reliance on police interrogation and confessions.[6] We have seen that much of the concern about the Diplock system has stemmed from the over-reliance on confessions, permitted by

---

[3] 338 US 49, 54 (1949).

[4] For discussion of the right against self-incrimination, see Zuckerman (1989), ch 15; Galligan (1988); Easton (1991).

[5] Kunert (1966). The European Court has recently linked Article 6 to the privilege against self-incrimination: see the judgment in *Funke, Cremieux and Miailhe* [1993] 16 EHRR 297, 325–6. [6] Goldstein (1960); Kamisar (1965).

changes in the rules concerning their admissibility. More recently the
encroachment on the right of silence has limited the practical extent of the
principle that no one may be compelled to incriminate themselves. It can
also be argued that the changes dilute the principle that the prosecution
ought to prove the guilt of the accused beyond reasonable doubt, since the
changes enable the defendant's failure to answer questions or testify to be
used by the prosecution as evidence of the accused's guilt.[7] Despite this, it
remains the case that the Diplock trial, as distinct from the criminal process
that leads up to it, contains at least in form the main accusatory features
mentioned by Justice Frankfurter. In particular the absence of the jury,
which represents the main change to the Diplock trial, does not appear to
have changed the formal structure of the trial. This is still essentially
accusatorial because it requires the prosecution to prove the defendant's
guilt, and enables defendants to be represented by counsel.

Another way to view adversariness is as an ideal mode of conflict
resolution and here the focus is not confined to criminal procedure or to the
protection of the accused, but extends to all procedures which have as their
goal the resolution of disputes. The essential characteristic of adversariness
here is the notion of procedure as a contest between two sides brought
before a conflict-resolver. This requires that the parties define the issues in
dispute, and that a neutral third party then resolve these in favour of one
side or the other. Often, again, this notion of adversariness is said to
characterize Anglo-American procedures and a contrast is made with
continental procedures which take the form of a unilateral inquiry into facts
and law. In fact, however, many continental countries have enacted codes of
civil procedure incorporating the notion of conflict-resolution. Conversely,
although many features of Anglo-American criminal procedure are regulated
in terms of a contest (most prominently, the guilty plea and the practice of
plea-bargaining, which permits the parties to negotiate over the charges),
the procedure is not wholly contest-oriented. For example, judges are not
obliged to accept without question a proposed plea to a lesser charge.[8]
Further, they may put to the jury alternative verdicts and defences to those
suggested by the parties.[9] Whether adversarial features should be followed
or not would therefore seem to depend primarily on whether the dispute is
viewed as a conflict between parties, or whether it involves wider issues
which require account to be taken of the public interest.[10] How this
question is determined may depend on a political conception of the role of
government in certain disputes, and conceptions of this role may differ

---

[7] See Jackson (1994b).

[8] See the Report of the Farquharson Committee (1986) on the role of prosecuting counsel.
The report appears in *Archbold*, 4–71–80.

[9] See Chapter Five. See also Pattenden (1990), 55–6; Doran (1991b).

[10] Allen and Kuhns (1989), 558–60.

between continental and Anglo-American countries, with the latter more disposed to favour the reactive liberal ideology of *laissez-faire* government than the former.[11] This may make Anglo-American criminal procedure more inclined to follow the adversarial model of a contest between state and accused resolved by an impartial arbiter, but even here it is interesting to note that once the sentencing stage is reached the judge's role changes from one of resolving conflict between two sides into a problem-solving mode requiring the implementation of sentencing policy.[12]

As for the arbiters in the adversary model of conflict resolution, it does not seem to matter particularly whether they are professional judges or laypersons. It is crucial, however, that the arbiters are, and are seen to be, impartial and independent of the parties so that they are not tainted by association with one side or the other. We saw in the last chapter that the arguments against jury involvement in cases involving the 'troubles' in Northern Ireland hinged on juror intimidation and perverse acquittals which were the result of jurors becoming tainted by association with the defence. When the Diplock procedure was introduced, on the other hand, there were converse fears that 'case-hardening' would make judges increasingly ready to accept the evidence of the police and the security forces in preference to that of the defence. Aside from the context of Northern Ireland, it can be argued that a jury reinforces the image of the criminal process as contest because the jury is truly an outside arbiter and cannot be tinged with any taint of bias in favour of one side or another.[13]

So far the only essential characteristic of adversariness as an expression of an ideal conflict-solving procedure is that of a contest presided over by an impartial and independent arbiter. The aim of the procedure is to resolve the conflict in a manner which is accepted by both sides, and it is often assumed that procedures likely to promote acceptance are those which give process control to the parties, in terms of collecting the evidence and presenting it in court. Accepting a fundamental dichotomy between 'truth' and 'justice', Thibaut and Walker have hypothesized that a system which delegates both process and decision control to a disinterested third party seems most likely to produce a correct view of reality. On the other hand, a system that assigns maximum process control to the disputants but decision control to a third party is most likely to result in a decision which reflects the strength of

---

[11] Damaska (1986), 10–12, 90–2.

[12] Shapland (1981), 143–4. This is not to say that all issues that arise at the sentencing stage are dealt with in a non-adversarial manner. Where disputes occur over facts of an offence, the adversarial model still remains appropriate: see Wasik (1985).

[13] Much will depend on the process that is adopted to select juries. The principle of random selection helps to promote the idea of independence and impartiality, but some procedures are also necessary to remove biased persons from the jury panel. See Buxton (1990).

each party's claims and therefore does most justice to the parties' arguments.[14] The freedom of the disputants to control the statement of their claims is likely to reassure the parties that justice has been done, regardless of the verdict. Other commentators who are less happy about the dichotomy between truth and justice, however, and who are aware of the problems of inequality between the parties, do not consider that conflict-solving procedures require the parties to be responsible for gathering and presenting evidence.[15] Nor, conversely, is it so clear that procedures designed to implement policies must adopt pure 'inquisitorial' methods of truth-finding. Damaska and Thibaut and Walker refer to the example of two state officials, each pursuing a different factual hypothesis and gathering information to support it, and then developing the evidence before a trier of fact, although it is admitted that this is only an option when the subject matter of the proceedings is reducible to two contradictory factual scenarios.[16] One example of this would be in a criminal case where the hypothesis of guilt could be explored by a state prosecutor and the hypothesis of innocence by a state defender. This suggests that although it may be more appropriate for conflict-solving procedures to adopt adversarial methods of proof, and conversely for policy-implementing procedures to adopt inquisitorial methods, there is no necessary connection between the aims of a particular procedure and the mode of proof adopted.

Another way of viewing adversariness therefore is as an ideal model of proof which is able to establish the truth or otherwise of a particular hypothesis, and which can be contrasted with a non-adversarial or inquisitorial model of proof.[17] Again it is often claimed that these contrasting models of proof typify respectively Anglo-American and continental procedures. But they are better viewed as two sets of contrasting features that can be found within the generality of both Anglo-American and continental procedures. As with the other senses of adversariness, the particular composition of the tribunal of fact, judge or jury, may make little difference as to whether a particular mode of proof is characterized as adversarial or not. Before this can be concluded, however, it is necessary to look more closely at the features which typify adversarial and non-adversarial modes of proof. In common with other ideal-type models, it is not claimed that the features are descriptive of any particular system of

---

[14] See Thibaut and Walker (1975) and (1978), who describe this as a distributive form of justice.

[15] Langbein (1985).

[16] Thibaut and Walker (1975), 26–7; Damaska (1986), 163.

[17] Compare the view of Goldstein (1974), 1016–17, who contrasts the *adversary process* as a method of finding facts and implementing norms with the *accusatorial system* which is a procedural model encompassing the adversary process but also certain normative ideals such as keeping the state out of disputes.

proof.[18] Rather, the models represent two extremes, but they may be said to contain enough essential elements of Anglo-American and continental European processes of proof to enable a particular process of proof to be located somewhere along the spectrum between the two extremes.[19] A closer look at the features in these models will help to determine whether the Diplock procedure of trial by judge alone has pushed the trial process in a non-adversarial direction.

THE 'CONTEST MODEL' OF PROOF

The heart of the contrast between adversarial and inquisitorial models of proof is that while one is essentially a contest, the other is essentially an inquiry or inquest.[20] The adversarial model emphasizes the role of contestants and regulates what contestants may or may not do, with much less attention being given to the activities of inquirers. A party must first, of course, prepare its case, and this will involve inquiry, but few controls are exercised over inquiry at this stage. Control only becomes significant when a claim or charge is made. The contest is then announced and rules will govern how the claimant and opponent are to proceed in their preparation for trial. A contrast can therefore be made between preparation or investigation of the case which is relatively unregulated, and preparation for trial which is closely regulated.[21]

Emphasis on the regulation of the parties is important in an ideal model because if each side were allowed to strive self-interestedly to defeat the other, truth-finding could easily become eclipsed. Parties could conceal vital information and resort to unfair tactics, such as intimidating witnesses and other parties. The contest has to ensure that the parties are given an equal opportunity to prepare and present their cases without intimidating each other. This extends beyond the formal equality of each party being subject to the same rules; it also requires substantive equality in the sense that the rules themselves enable the parties to investigate and present their case as effectively as possible. This is sometimes known as the requirement of

---

[18] Scholars have contrasted crime control models with due process models (Packer (1964)), family models with battle models (Griffiths (1970)), and private law litigation models with public law litigation models (Chayes (1976); Galligan (1986), 86–8).

[19] For discussion of the uses of the two models, see Damaska (1973), 562–4, 577.

[20] The following depiction of contest and inquest models owes much to the work of Damaska. See in particular Damaska (1973), (1986), and (1990).

[21] Remedies may be available to prevent one side taking unfair advantage over another during investigation, and exceptionally evidence obtained by unfair or illegal means may be excluded at the trial. English courts have traditionally been reluctant to exclude evidence unfairly or illegally obtained in both civil and criminal cases: see Murphy (1992), 31–40.

'equality of arms' under which the parties have the same access to information which is relevant to the case, and have equal opportunities to present evidence and to contradict the evidence produced by the other.[22] An ideal contest model would therefore put great store by the principle of disclosure of information and by the provision of effective legal representation to prepare and present the case. The use of sporting or game analogies to depict adversary procedure suggests that putting the cards on the table before trial is foreign to the notion of adversariness. But when adversariness is viewed as an ideal mode of proof, it is recognized, as Justice Traynor once wrote, that 'truth is most likely to emerge when each side seeks to take the other by reason rather than by surprise.'[23] Only then can the clash of arms ensue that truth will win out.

Disclosure must first be made by the party seeking to prove the claim or charge, and it requires the precise specification of the claim or charge, and the revelation of all relevant information. Disclosure may, however, be refused when it conflicts with the principle that the parties should be placed on a fair and equal footing to face the trial. Communications between legal representatives and parties, for example, may be privileged in the interests of providing parties with the security of confidential advice. Disclosure may also be denied where it may lead to intimidation of witnesses or where it may enable a party to conceal vital evidence.[24] When proper disclosure has been made by the proponent of the claim or charge, the defendant should be required to disclose the nature of his or her defence. The objection is sometimes raised in criminal proceedings that this interferes with the privilege against self-incrimination, but such a privilege is not incompatible with the disclosure of specific defences.[25] In any event it is more difficult to justify the existence of a privilege against self-incrimination when a defendant has been given full disclosure of the case against him or her.

In the preliminary stages between the announcement of the contest and the trial itself, the role of non-partisan inquirers is limited. There is a role, however, for an independent umpire to ensure that the pre-trial rules of disclosure are enforced, to determine whether there is a sufficiency of proof to make it worthwhile to continue with the case, and to make preliminary

[22] See Jacobs (1980), 99–101.

[23] Traynor (1962), 249. See also Goldstein (1960): 'there can be no question that notice of the facts and legal theories to be litigated is essential to the effective operation of an adversary system' (1180). Cf. Brennan (1963), (1990). This has been recognized by the English courts: 'A disadvantage of the adversarial system may be that the parties are not evenly matched in resources . . . But the inequality of resources is ameliorated by the obligation on the part of the prosecution to make available all material which may be helpful to the defence' (*R v McIlkenny* [1992] 2 All ER 417, 426).

[24] See, for example, Attorney-General's Guidelines for Disclosure of Evidence in Criminal Cases [1982] 1 All ER 734.

[25] See *Williams v Florida* 399 US 78 (1970).

rulings on questions of law.[26] Some form of review may, in addition, be undertaken by one or another party, for example in criminal proceedings a prosecutor may be brought into the case after a decision has been taken to charge to decide whether to continue the prosecution.[27]

The contest culminates in a trial at which the proponent of the claim or charge has the burden of proving what is alleged. As in all contests, there have to be rules of fairness to ensure that each party has an equal opportunity to participate. The proponent must prove its claims to a required standard of proof, the opponent being permitted to show evidence that that standard has not been met. To ensure parity of treatment it is necessary to adopt a standard which allocates the risk of errors being made by the ultimate tribunal of fact as evenly as possible, and this would mean that the claimant has the burden of showing that the evidence for his claim is more probable than not, the preponderance of probability standard.[28] Reasons of policy may, however, dictate that the standard of proof be heavier. The high standard in criminal cases may be justified on the ground that the consequences of a wrongful conviction are worse than the consequences of a wrongful acquittal, but it may also be justified simply on the ground that the greater resources of the state make it reasonable to impose on it a higher standard of proof than on the defendant, who is likely to have fewer resources to present an effective defence.[29]

Other rules are required to ensure that the parties are given an equal opportunity to present their case and contest their opponent's case effectively. These are sometimes known as presentation rules.[30] Because of the importance attached to the parties being able to test each other's evidence, parties are encouraged to produce witnesses who have direct knowledge of the facts.[31] Each witness is then examined by the party calling the witness, who may not ask leading questions, and cross-examined, if desired, by the opposing party. Only relevant evidence may be adduced, to prevent the tribunal of fact becoming confused by a proliferation of issues. A number of rules are also devised to prevent parties admitting prejudicial and unreliable evidence, and to guide triers of fact on the uses to

---

[26] Preliminary hearings are now required in serious fraud cases in England and Wales (sections 9–11 of the Criminal Justice Act 1987) and the Royal Commission on Criminal Justice recommended that in complex cases either party should be able to require a preliminary hearing in front of a judge to secure rulings on the main issues. (See recommendation 139 of the report).

[27] This is the role currently undertaken by the Crown Prosecution Service in England and the Department of the Director of Public Prosecutions in Northern Ireland. See Prosecution of Offences Act 1986; Prosecution of Offences (Northern Ireland) Order 1972.

[28] For discussion of risk distribution within the process of proof, see Zuckerman (1989), 123; Stein (1987).   [29] Ashworth (1979), 414–15.

[30] See, for example, Nijboer (1992).

[31] This is encouraged by means of the hearsay rule, one of the aims of which is to ensure that parties present their best evidence at trial. See Nance (1988).

which certain kinds of evidence should be put.[32] These have the effect of preventing the exposure of certain kinds of evidence to the tribunal of fact, or when exposed to it, by encouraging the tribunal not to use it for prejudicial purposes.

The trial is presided over by a judge whose role is confined by and large to umpiring the contest and ensuring that the parties stick to the rules.[33] Either the judge, or a separate tribunal of fact, a jury, may decide the contest. The tribunal must come to its decision on the evidence presented to it at the contest and not on evidence discovered from any other source. The opportunity for active inquiry during the trial or for generating new evidence of its own initiative is strictly limited, and active intervention is discouraged.[34] Triers of fact may ask for clarification of evidence presented to them and may even attempt to generate new evidence. But two difficulties are commonly pointed out. In a classic article Saltzburg claims that arguably the most important principle in the adversary system is that it permits opposing parties, unencumbered by outside intervention, to present their strongest arguments to the tribunal of fact.[35] In his words:[36]

By disrupting an attorney's preferred order of presentation, a judge's active interrogation may minimise the impact of some witnesses' testimony while maximising the impact of others'. Therefore, the judge's questioning may confer an unintended advantage upon one party that the lawyer could not have obtained otherwise and that the opposing party cannot counteract during trial.

Saltzburg goes on to quote an experienced American judge, Judge Frankel, who was more critical of the adversary process as a model of proof but who argued against judges descending into the trial arena:[37]

The judge views the case from the peak of Olympian ignorance. His intrusions will in too many cases result from partial or skewed insights. He may expose the secrets one side chooses to keep while never becoming aware of the other's. He runs a good chance of pursuing inspirations that better informed counsel have considered, explored and abandoned after fuller study. He risks at a minimum the supplying of more confusion than guidance by his sporadic intrusions.

Active intervention can thus thwart the proof strategies of the parties without any corresponding benefit in terms of truth-finding.

---

[32] Examples include the similar fact rules, and the rules on the character evidence of defendants, which are designed to prevent triers of fact from taking account of the fact that a defendant may have a propensity to commit offences of the type charged, or may be of bad character. See Tapper (1990), chapters 9 and 10.

[33] For discussion of the role of the judge in the adversarial trial, see Frankel (1975); Saltzburg (1978).

[34] See the classic warning of Denning LJ against excessive judicial interventionism in *Jones* v *National Coat Board* (1957) 2 QB 55, discussed in some detail in Chapter Five. See also Doran (1989).   [35] Saltzburg (1978), 55.   [36] *Ibid.*

[37] Frankel (1975), 1042 (footnotes omitted).

The other major problem with judicial intervention is the danger of the judge being seen to develop a commitment to one side or the other. This can lead to a judge appearing to be less than impartial but it is also said that it discourages truth-finding because the parties are in a weak position to challenge any assumptions made by the judge. Psychological insight suggests that it is very difficult for active investigators to suspend judgment and weigh evidence dispassionately.[38] There is a distinct risk that an interventionist judge will favour a particular theory or hypothesis and pursue it relentlessly to the exclusion of others. This problem was highlighted by Fuller in quoting from an American Bar Association Committee statement:[39]

What generally occurs in practice is that at some early point a familiar pattern will seem to emerge from the evidence; an accustomed label is waiting for the case and, without waiting further proofs, this label is promptly assigned to it. It is a mistake to suppose that this premature cataloguing must necessarily result from impatience, prejudice or mental sloth. Often it proceeds from a very understandable desire to bring the hearing into some order and coherence, for without some tentative theory of the case there is no standard of relevance by which testimony may be measured.

This in itself might not be of such concern if it were possible for other participants to challenge the diagnosis. Witnesses may refuse to provide support for that diagnosis. But the problem here is that witnesses may be tempted in their response to read the mind of the judge. Saltzburg says that witnesses often depend on the judge to make their life comfortable and they view the judge as their guardian at trial.[40] Parties may also be reluctant to object lest their objections antagonize the judge or the jury. Even if objection is taken, the damage may have already been done in jury trials where the judge may be considered to be more authoritative than the lawyers for the parties. The judge may direct the jury to disregard the questions and answers but such a direction is unlikely to be effective. In trials by judge alone, the question whether to object may depend on the status and authority of the lawyers objecting *vis-à-vis* the judge, and even if a challenge is made the judge may not be swayed from his or her original diagnosis.

The fact-finding role of the tribunal is therefore limited for the most part to weighing up the evidence adduced by the parties and deciding the issues on the basis of the burden or standard of proof. In addition, some of the rules of evidence will tell the tribunal how to use certain kinds of evidence,[41]

---

[38] Trankell (1972), 25–7.   [39] Fuller (1961), 43.   [40] Saltzburg (1978), 59.
[41] For the view that the law of evidence consists of rules of use rather than rules of exclusion, see McNamara (1985). Juries are frequently directed to use evidence for certain purposes (for example, to go to the credibility of a witness) but not for others (for example, to go to the truth of an issue in dispute). For criticism of this distinction, see Zuckerman (1989), 94–7.

and the tribunal may even have to apply certain rules of weight, such as corroboration rules for dealing with certain kinds of unreliable witness or evidence.[42] This requires the tribunal to take an atomistic view of the evidence whereby probative force is attributed to distinct types of evidence and the final determination is made by aggregating these separate informational units by an additive process, and if necessary disregarding certain items or certain chains of inference if told to do so.[43] The determination is supposed to be less an acceptance of the truth or otherwise of certain facts in issue than a decision that the bits of evidence produced either meet the standard of proof required or do not.

The result is frequently (and if the tribunal of fact is a jury, almost invariably) presented in the form of an enigmatic verdict which indicates neither which facts have been found, nor the reasons for this. This is not to say that the input control has no effect on the output. Although the tribunal cannot realistically ignore evidence it has been told to disregard, the admonitions to ignore evidence or use it for certain purposes only may have an effect on the decision-making process which is frequently conducted in a collective manner.[44] Once the decision of the tribunal is reached, however, it is true that there is little scrutiny of it. As Damaska has put it, input control may be considerable but output control is limited.[45] The reason for this is again linked to the notion of contest. A contest demands a result: a winner and a loser. All the care taken to ensure equal treatment of the parties to the contest would be devalued if the contest could be litigated all over again. The model assumes, provided the contest is fair and the parties are given an equal opportunity to put their case, that truth will emerge. Any appeal based on unfair conduct before or during the contest will therefore be listened to more sympathetically than an appeal based on the incorrectness of the decision reached.

Of course, even if fairness could be guaranteed, there is still the possibility that one party through its legal representative has been less competent than the other.[46] But the problem of one-sidedness is not solved by making it easy to recontest the whole case. It can be argued that if parties knew that the result of the contest was easy to appeal, they would not strive so hard in the first place. Of course, if certain kinds of parties are unable to get competent legal representation, then a problem of unfairness arises and steps must be taken to provide equal access to competent counsel.

---

[42] Corroboration rules are generally diminishing in importance and have been superseded more often by guidelines warning triers of fact to treat certain kinds of evidence with caution. See Law Commission (1991).
[43] For further explanation of this process, see generally Damaska (1988), (1990).
[44] Damaska (1988), 35–6.   [45] *Ibid.*, 36–7.
[46] This is a problem that has concerned the American courts much more than the English courts. But see recently *R v Ensor* [1989] 2 All ER 586; *R v Clinton* [1993] 1 WLR 1181.

Otherwise there must be a presumption of competence, rebuttable only by clear evidence that a party has suffered as a result of incompetent counsel.[47]

To conclude, defects that may arise in particular cases are best remedied by permitting a review of the rules of fairness, rather than by constant scrutiny of the correctness of the decisions reached. Of course, there is only a presumption in any particular case that the decision is correct. Clear evidence to the contrary, particularly if it is fresh evidence, is enough to rebut the presumption and to enable the decision to be reversed on appeal.[48]

THE 'INQUEST MODEL' OF PROOF

The inquest mode of proof shifts the focus away from the contestants towards the inquirers. Even in cases involving private disputes, the aim is to involve a judicial inquirer at as early a stage as possible. Contestants may initially bring their dispute to the inquiry, but it is the inquirer and not the contestants who determines the contours of the dispute within the ambit of the substantive law.[49] This in turn gives inquirers the primary responsibility for gathering, testing, and evaluating the evidence relevant to the dispute.

The contestants are relegated to the role of *objects* of inquiry, instead of being the *subjects* of the action who have charge of their own case. Contestants may suggest that certain lines of inquiry be followed and that certain witnesses be questioned, and they may even be given some freedom in presenting evidence. Lawyers representing the contestants may therefore have a limited role in the process, but they do not have the central role which they occupy in the contest model. Ultimate control rests with the inquirer. In addition, whereas the contest model requires that parties co-operate with other parties only in so far as is deemed necessary to disclose the general nature of their case, the inquest model is much less tolerant of parties who refuse to make full disclosure. Generally speaking, contestants have a duty to disclose everything that is asked of them and to submit to any judicial questioning.

All this conjures up the image of a 'grand inquisitor', free from all control within the domain of his or her investigation. Just as some control was necessary to transform a free-for-all contest into a model of proof, however, so an inquest must also be regulated in the interest of securing accurate outcomes, if it is to be justified as a model of proof. In the contest model there is a danger that one side may dominate the process of proof

---

[47] For discussion see Salzburg (1978), 62–3.

[48] English judges have been reluctant either to reverse jury decisions or to order retrials on the basis of fresh evidence: see O'Connor (1990).

[49] For an overview of German civil procedure, see Langbein (1985).

disproportionately and unfairly. In the inquest model the absence of any competitors means that there is no adversary to dominate. The supreme dominance of the inquirer, though, can easily lead to abuse. Inquirers are judicial appointees, non-partisan and independent of the parties, but they are drawn for the most part from a professional corps of state officials rather than from the public at large. This is not only because of the difficulties of commandeering members of the public for the length of time it takes to complete an investigation; trained investigators are also better able to ferret out the truth. The danger, however, is that such officials may, over time, come to favour certain kinds of litigants over others. One argument against the Diplock procedure, as we have seen, is that judges may become 'case-hardened'. As we have also seen, psychological insight suggests that it is very difficult for active investigators to suspend judgment and weigh evidence dispassionately. There is a distinct risk that one particular hypothesis will be favoured and pursued relentlessly to the exclusion of others.

How is this danger controlled? In the contest model we saw that parties are not greatly impeded in their methods of investigation, but that when the contest is announced their conduct is strictly regulated in order that preparation may be made for trial. Attention is focused throughout on the trial and everything is done to ensure that it is fairly conducted. In the inquest model the notion of a trial is much less important. Rather than the process of proof highlighting one particular event, the trial (which overshadows everything that has gone before and to which everything after relates), the inquest model represents a continuous process of proof with perhaps a number of phases of investigation, each forming part of a continuous whole.[50] Proof is not constituted at the post-investigation trial stage, but throughout the entire process. Like the contest model, there is little control over the actual methods of investigation. Instead of bilateral investigation taking place concurrently and leading up to a trial, however, the emphasis is on several consecutive phases of unilateral investigation, with different investigators at each phase, and with the evidentiary material ripening as each inquirer records the information collected in an investigative file. This file or dossier is handed on at each phase of investigation, with inquirers adding to it as necessary. A decision will be taken at the final phase of the investigation, which may take the form of a formal hearing known as a trial, but which represents the final phase of a cumulative process of inquiry, rather than a contest fought in one episode from start to finish.

Control is exercised by provision for consecutive phases of investigation, each progressively more important and each adding to the dossier which has been built up in preceding phases. Control is also

---

[50] Kerameus (1987), 498.

exercised by providing for a career judiciary in which the judicial tasks of fact-gathering and opinion writing are constantly evaluated and reviewed by peers.[51] However, an essential feature is that even at the more formal final phases, including the hearing before the decision, the inquirer is not impeded by rigid evidentiary rules. These rules are necessary in the contest model to allocate what must be proved by whom and to ensure that the parties contest against each other fairly. In the inquest model, by contrast, such rules would only impede the inquirer in the quest for truth.

Rules on the burden of proof, for example, are essential for a bilateral contest in order to determine who has won the contest. They are less appropriate for unilateral fact-finding where inquirers are themselves required to piece together the evidence and construct a unitary view of what has happened. Their job is less aptly described as considering whether the claimant's version of events matches up to a required standard of proof. Inquirers must themselves form a subjective belief about what has happened, or as it is put in continental procedure, an *intime conviction*.[52] This requires the trier of fact to take a 'holistic' rather than an 'atomistic' view of the evidence. The evidence formally presented in court is treated only as part of the broader informational input which sways the adjudicator's mind, and the final determination is a conviction which arises from the total production of information and not from individual items of evidence.[53]

This need to form a subjective belief about what happened is also incompatible with rules which exclude evidence on generalized grounds of unreliability or which accord low probative weight to particular kinds of evidence. In the contest model such rules are justified on the ground that they prevent parties from basing their case on evidence that cannot be properly tested, and they protect parties from a relatively unaccountable tribunal of fact. In the inquest model they interfere with the duty of judicial inquirers to assess the evidence and they are not required as a mechanism of control because the decision-making of inquirers is subject to review.

A principle of immediacy requires inquirers to insist, wherever possible, on original rather than secondary sources of evidence.[54] There is, however,

---

[51] Langbein (1985), 848–51.

[52] A good illustration of this approach is to be found in the formal warning which the president of the *cour d'assises* in France has to read out to jurors:

The law . . . stipulates that [judges] must search their conscience in good faith and silently and thoughtfully ask themselves what impression the evidence given against the accused and defence's arguments have made upon them. The law asks them only one question which sums up all of their duties 'Are you personally convinced?'

See Article 353 of the French Code of Criminal Procedure, and Pradel (1994), 129.

[53] Damaska (1990), 91.

[54] For discussion of this principle, see Damaska (1973), 517–18.

much less reliance on oral evidence. Unlike the tribunal of fact in the contest model, inquirers in the inquest model do not come 'cold' to the evidence; they are expected to read and digest the dossier and are permitted to base their findings on it. This is because its statements will have been accurately recorded in earlier inquiries, and their credibility may have been vouched for by other inquirers who heard the witness give evidence at first hand. As these officials are independent, statements accredited by them merit much greater weight than out of court statements by competing parties. Although entitled to take the dossier into account, however, each inquirer is equally entitled to recall witnesses if in doubt about their credibility, as it is the mind of each individual inquirer that must be satisfied.

Control in the inquest model and in the contest model is therefore exercised in very different ways. We have seen that the contest model, with its emphasis on the trial, exercises considerable input control to ensure that the tribunal of fact only acts on admissible evidence, but exercises little output control on the actual decision arrived at by the tribunal of fact. The position is reversed in the inquest model. The inquirer has considerable freedom to decide what information to hear, but the information gathered and any conclusions reached are closely scrutinized at later phases of the investigation. There is therefore a shift away from 'presentation' rules towards 'decision' or 'argumentation' rules.[55] This contrast is most striking at the appellate stage of the proof process. In the contest model there is a presumption in favour of the correctness of the decision taken at the trial and it is much easier to challenge decisions on the ground that the procedural rules were not observed than on grounds of inaccuracy. Implicit in the notion of contest is that of a winner and a loser, and of an end result that is final. By contrast, the findings of an inquiry are not so final and more easily reviewed. Although parties are limited in their control over the process of proof, they do have much greater ability to challenge conclusions reached and to reactivate the inquiry in the inquest than in the contest model. There may still be a presumption in favour of the conclusions reached, but the fact that reasons have to be given for decisions means that it is easier to challenge the grounds for those conclusions. This is in contrast, as we have seen, with the contest model where the verdict is unaccompanied, certainly in the case of a jury, by any reasoned explanation. In addition, the methods of inquiry can be scrutinized to ensure that the court adhered to its duty to clarify all the evidence, and did not, for example, neglect to receive evidence exonerating a defendant, or fail to appoint an expert to inquire into a particular matter. In this way the parties are able to exercise some *ex post facto* control over the investigative process and are able in effect to supervise the court's methods of inquiry after the event.[56]

---

[55] Nijboer (1992), 302.
[56] This is known in Germany as the process of *Aufkrungsruge*: see Kunert (1966), 160–3.

LOCATING THE DIPLOCK TRIAL ON THE SPECTRUM

Once again it should be stressed that these models do not claim to mirror the reality of any particular process of proof. They are, however, characterized as encompassing enough of the essential elements of Anglo-American and continental European processes of proof to make it possible to locate a particular process on the spectrum between the two ideals. Certain indicators which highlight the contrast between the models may also be used to discover at what point a particular procedure stands on the contest-inquest or adversarial-inquisitorial spectrum. One key indicator which has been said to lie at the heart of the divergence in character of Anglo-American and European procedures is the role of the judge as passive umpire in the former and as active inquirer in the latter.[57] The extent of intervention by judges in any particular procedure may be reflected in the extent to which judges call and examine witnesses themselves, and the extent to which they direct the course of the trial. Other indicators that could be examined include the extent to which the trial resembles a contest between the various parties, the reliance on oral evidence in trials (and conversely the reliance placed on prior written evidence), the use of rules of evidence to regulate admissibility and to order the inferential process of the triers of fact, and the degree and form of appellate review permitted. A cumulative picture could then be built up of the particular procedure under scrutiny and of its location on the spectrum.

Adopting this approach, this study considers whether a process like the Diplock trial, which substitutes the judge for the jury as trier of fact, is likely to push the criminal process more in the direction of the inquest model of proof. So far, our discussion of ideal models has not suggested that the jury is an essential element of the ideal contest method of proof. However, it would seem that the presence of a jury could be an effective barrier to adopting a pure inquest model since twelve laypersons picked at random from the community are unlikely to be, or to be seen as, an effective court of inquiry.[58] In his famous critique of the Anglo-American trial Jerome Frank argued that the jury results in a distortion of the adversarial model of proof as it encourages the operation of a 'fight theory' rather than a 'truth theory'.[59] Although some of Frank's comments suggest that he was anti-adversarial, in fact what he seemed to object to was not adversariness but

---

[57] Ploscowe (1935).

[58] Of course, juries were originally investigative bodies summoned to swear under oath that their account of the facts of disputes were correct. See Holdsworth (1922), 316–19. Traces of these 'inquisitorial' juries can still be found in the American grand jury which is occasionally used to indict criminal defendants in felony prosecutions.

[59] Frank (1949), 138.

excessive adversariness, which the presence of the jury promoted because it encouraged parties to 'appeal to the crudest emotions and prejudices of the jurors, and jurors are known often to respond to such appeals.'[60]

Against this, it can be argued that the presence of a jury encapsulates the adversarial ideal better than a judicial or specialist tribunal because the jury system ensures that triers of fact come truly cold to the evidence.[61] Moreover, it ensures that the rules governing the admissibility of evidence have real teeth in the sense that it is easier to prevent the jury from hearing inadmissible evidence than to prevent the presiding judge from hearing it, since the judge will already have had to make decisions regarding its admissibility.[62] The absence of the jury may therefore undermine exclusionary rules of evidence such as the hearsay rule and the gradual decrease in importance of these rules in civil cases serves as an example of this.[63]

One response to this is that since the rules of evidence have been claimed to be the 'child of the jury',[64] there is less need for them in non-jury proceedings. Apart from the rather dubious assumption in this argument that judges are better fact-finders and less likely to be affected by prejudicial evidence, many rules of evidence serve the purpose not only of preventing prejudice on the part of the trier of fact but also, as we have seen, of preventing parties from taking unfair advantage over one another either before or during the trial. The rules governing confessions, for example, restrain police abuse of suspects prior to trial and thereby help ensure that only reliable confessions are obtained.

The view of the jury as part of the adversarial ideal, however, may also be opposed by conceding that the rules of evidence are vital to the adversarial mode of proof, but denying that the withdrawal of the jury necessarily undermines them. An example of this may indeed be the Diplock trial where, as explained in the last chapter, the rules of evidence remain intact despite the absence of the jury. This is also true of 'waived' jury trials in the United States.[65] Moreover, the courts have been anxious to uphold the rules of evidence and to maintain a distinction between issues such as the admissibility of confessions which are determined in the *voir dire* and issues of guilt or innocence which are determined in the trial proper, even though

---

[60] Frank (1949), 122.   [61] See Damaska (1986), 137–8.

[62] Of course, it would be possible to have certain issues determined on a pre-trial *voir dire* before a different judge; see Levin and Cohen (1971), 918–19. In practice, however, a number of points of evidence may arise unexpectedly during the course of the trial.

[63] The hearsay rule has been completely abolished in Scottish civil cases under the Civil Evidence (Scotland) Act 1988 and its abolition in England has been recommended by the Law Commission (1993).

[64] This is Thayer's term: see Thayer (1898), 47, 266, 509. For a different view, see Morgan (1937).   [65] See Levin and Cohen (1971), 906.

the same judge may decide both.[66] In *R v Brophy*[67] the defendant was
indicted with a large number of counts including murder, possession of
explosives, and membership of the IRA. The only evidence against him
consisted of confession statements and the trial judge ruled these inadmissible under section 8(2) of the Northern Ireland (Emergency Provisions) Act
1978.[68] During the *voir dire*, however, the accused admitted membership of
the IRA and the trial judge proceeded to admit this evidence in the trial
proper and convicted the accused on the basis of it. One of the reasons given
for distinguishing an earlier authority which ruled that the prosecution
should not be allowed to adduce evidence from the *voir dire* in the trial
proper[69] was that the issues of the admissibility and weight of a confession
are at times intertwined in a non-jury trial as the trial judge 'who comes to
evaluate the creditability of the accused on the general issue of the trial has
in many cases already reached some conclusion on it in the voir dire'.[70] Both
the Court of Appeal and the House of Lords, however, ruled that the trial
judge was wrong to admit the evidence from the *voir dire*. The Lord Chief
Justice of Northern Ireland said that the case involved two cardinal
principles of the criminal law. The first was the common law principle that
a confession should be voluntary and the second was that an accused is not
obliged to incriminate himself. In order to safeguard both principles it is
necessary that defendants be free to challenge the admissibility of a
confession on the *voir dire* without the fear of their testimony being used
against them at a later stage. The fact that the trial was conducted without a
jury made no difference to these principles.

The fact that judges in the trial proper may find it difficult to ignore what
was said on the *voir dire* is no argument for admitting what was said on the
voir dire in the trial proper, if there are good reasons in principle for
excluding such evidence.[71] But the trial judge's candid admission of the
difficulty of ignoring evidence heard by a tribunal of fact is a welcome
expression of the difficulties of giving effect to rules of evidence in a non-
jury trial, and of the fallibility of a trial judge. The idea that judges can
disregard inadmissible evidence or irregularities which occur in the course
of the trial was also questioned in another case. Here, the Crown said at the
outset of the hearing that it would rely on certain witnesses but then closed
its case without calling them, thereby conveying the impression that those
witnesses were unworthy of belief.[72] The Lord Chief Justice said on appeal

---

[66] *R v Corey* [1979] NI 49 (the decision dates from 1973).

[67] [1980] 4 NIJB (Belfast Crown Court), [1981] 2 NIJB (Court of Appeal), [1981] 2 All ER
705 (House of Lords).

[68] This provision is a precursor to section 11 of the Northern Ireland (Emergency
Provisions) Act 1991.   [69] *Wong Kam-Ming v R* [1979] 1 All ER 939.

[70] [1980] 4 NIJB 68.   [71] Jackson (1983a), 13.

[72] *R v Foxford* [1974] NI 181.

that the case perfectly exemplified the difficulty attendant in a procedure where the judge of law was also the judge of fact:[73]

According to one theory, if an irregularity occurs or inadmissible evidence is given and has to be ignored, the trained mind of a judge is less vulnerable to its harmful effects than that of a juror. This may not always be true when one considers that, if there is a jury, the judge assumes the duty of warning them as to what they may take into account, and that the context and significance of an irregularity may fade from the lay mind when it has ceased to be part of the case but stick firmly in the mind of the judge, who is trained to marshal and evaluate evidence.

These difficulties raise the important question of whether the practice of the Diplock trial, as distinct from the rules that govern it, protects the accused to the same extent as a jury trial. Of course, as indicated in the last chapter, it is open to a judge to discharge himself when he hears prejudicial evidence and this option has legislative expression in relation to confessions ruled inadmissible by the judge.[74] There are instances where judges have discharged themselves. In *R v Latimer*,[75] for example, a case which later became known as the case of the UDR Four discussed in the previous chapter, the prosecution again decided not to call a witness whose statement was to form part of the Crown case, and the trial judge discharged himself on the ground that the Crown had raised a doubt in his mind concerning a very important witness. The procedure whereby a judge should discharge himself from a trial is analogous to the procedure in jury trials where a judge decides to discharge a jury on the ground that it has heard prejudicial evidence. However, there is clearly a difference between the tribunal deciding that another has been prejudiced and a tribunal deciding that it may *itself* be prejudiced. For one thing, it requires an acknowledgement, which not all may be willing to make, that one may succumb to prejudice. The danger that tribunals may be judges in their own cause on this point is obviated to some extent by the right of the defence to appeal against the decision of a judge not to discharge himself so that the decision can be scrutinized by another court.[76]

Whether the mechanisms to deal with prejudicial evidence in non-jury trials pose a threat to the protection of accused persons is open to debate. Provided that the rules of evidence continue to be applied, no threat would appear to be posed to the contest model of proof. There is, however, a possibility that although the rules of evidence and procedure still apply, the absence of the jury causes them to be applied in practice less rigorously, with the result that the conduct of the trial is pushed more in the direction of the inquest model, even though in theory the trial remains adversarial. One

---

[73] *R v Foxford* [1974] NI 212.

[74] Section 11 of the Northern Ireland (Emergency Provisions) Act 1991.

[75] [1986] 9 NIJB.   [76] See, for example, *R v Fletcher* [1983] 1 NIJB.

device which is open to judges when they sit without juries, but which would not work in a jury context, is to adopt a practice of not ruling on objections to evidence but instead hearing the evidence. This device seems to have been sanctioned by usage in American bench trials.[77] Another possibility is that rulings on admissibility will be heavily influenced by the judge's view of the guilt of the accused. This is also a danger in jury trials, but the personal responsibility of the judge in non-jury trials to decide the question of guilt may mean that his or her rulings are more inclined to be influenced by this question. One change in practice in Diplock trials (as noted in the last chapter), highlighted by the trial judge in *Brophy*, is that when the trial judge rules a confession admissible on the *voir dire* the witnesses proving the confession are not cross-examined again, nor does the accused give evidence again when the probative value or truth of the confession comes to be evaluated in the trial proper. The defence may elect to cross-examine the same witnesses again on the truth of the confession but this is generally done on the *voir dire*. This means that questions that go to truth are asked on the *voir dire* whether or not they are strictly relevant to the issue on the *voir dire*,[78] with the result, as the trial judge in *Brophy* recognized, that the issues become intertwined. Thus, the issue of the truth of the confession heard on the *voir dire* may affect the decision on admissibility and the decision on admissibility may affect the final decision on the guilt of the accused. If so, then there may be a tendency for confessions which are held to be admissible to be accepted as true unless events later in the trial cast doubt on this.[79]

All this suggests that in applying the indicators to see whether the absence of the jury pushes the trial more in the direction of the inquest model, it is important to look beyond the formal rules of evidence and procedure. Despite the lack of any substantial modification to such rules, the absence of the jury may have altered practices in the following ways: rules of evidence may be less strictly adhered to, more reliance may in practice be placed on written rather than oral evidence, matters contested may be reduced to a minimum and, above all, trial judges may take on a more directorial, or inquisitorial, role in the trial, even though in theory they should still be performing a merely umpireal role. Judges, after all, become the triers of fact, and it may be thought that this additional role would incline them to

---

[77] Levin and Cohen (1971), 908-9.

[78] Although it has been doubted whether an accused can be asked on the *voir dire* if his confession is true (*Wong Kam-Ming* v R), the Lord Chief Justice in *R* v *Brophy* agreed with the dissentient view of Lord Hailsham in *Wong Kam-Ming* that 'whether a confession is true or not *must* often be relevant to, though not at all decisive of, the question whether it has been properly obtained' ([1981] 2 NIJB 30). But it has been argued that such questions may be prejudicial to the accused: see Boyd (1982).

[79] Boyd (1982), 77–8.

take a much more inquisitorial role in the trial. One response to this suggestion is that this could not happen without a change in the rules but, as we noted in Chapter One, there is a body of literature which highlights the gap which often exists in the criminal process between 'the law in the books' and the 'law in action'. If, for example, judges only enforce the rules of evidence at the behest of the parties, then their effect is substantially minimized when parties decide it is not worth invoking them.

More recently, writers such as McBarnet have warned against taking this dichotomy between law and practice too far because when the rules allow certain practices to occur, they legitimate and in a sense become associated with these practices. It is, therefore, often more appropriate to contrast the rhetoric of the law with the rules and practices which operate within the process.[80] In this way it may be argued that although the absence of any major change in the rules of evidence and procedure governing Diplock trials preserves the rhetoric of accusatorial and adversarial principles, these very rules are so malleable that the withdrawal of the jury enables a shift to take place from these principles. McBarnet's dichotomy between the world of rhetoric and the law has itself been criticized on the ground that it rests on a positivist separation between the rules of law and the broader principles which animate it and ignores the Dworkinian view that rhetoric serves as the source of principles which can generate or limit legal rule-making.[81] The *Brophy* case is a good example of accusatorial principles being applied to limit changes in the rules of evidence and procedure in the non-jury trial. Another possibility then is that accusatorial, adversarial principles so infect the culture in which judges operate that although many of the *rules* are malleable enough to resist the application of these principles, the *principles* are strong enough to prevent any significant alteration in the practice of the courts. This may mean that although judges are empowered by the malleable nature of the rules to take a more directorial role than is permitted in adversarial theory, they resist the temptation to do so. The assumption here, however, is that judges are solely motivated by accusatorial and adversarial principles in the criminal trial. When the role of the judge in the criminal trial is examined in Chapter Five, we will see that there are other principles at stake.

It is necessary then to adopt an attitude of 'rule-scepticism' in order to gain an understanding of how procedures are ordered. The rules and principles supposedly embedded in the procedures must in practice be interpreted by the practitioners, judges, and counsel, and the institutional practices which evolve in this process of interpretation must be examined at first hand. This also suggests that an attitude of 'model-scepticism' as well as 'rule-scepticism' should be adopted. The contest and inquest models of

---

[80] McBarnet (1981).   [81] Nelken (1986), 151.

proof have been contrasted in detail in this chapter because these are the models that have been used to characterize Anglo-American and continental legal processes. But there is a danger that over-commitment to these models can obscure the actual dynamics of particular processes. A key feature in the divergent character of these models, for example, is the role of the judge, who assumes an umpireal role in the contest model of proof and an inquisitorial role in the inquest model. Although this suggests that there is no other way of describing the judicial role in legal processes, the reality of practice is that trial judges probably do not conform uniformly and homogeneously to one role or the other. Damaska has contrasted a hierarchical model of officialdom, in which officials are organized into a hierarchy, with a co-ordinate vision, in which judges are organized into a single and more diffuse level of authority.[82] In the latter, official behaviour both in and out of court is more difficult to control and there is much greater scope for deviation from the ideal. The scope for discretion is even greater when single judges hear trials without other judges and are left to develop their own individual judicial style in interaction with the practitioners who appear before them.

THE CHOICE OF PROCEDURE

At this stage of our enquiry it is too early to draw conclusions about whether judges who operate without juries should adopt a more inter-ventionist stance than within the adversarial ideal. This raises difficult questions about the best methods of truth-finding but it also raises other questions about the functions of the criminal trial. Criminal trials are commonly considered to perform valuable symbolic and educational functions, communicating messages about the rule of law and about the deterrence of criminal activity which have nothing to do with truth-finding.[83]

The question of whether the contest or the inquest model of proof is better equipped to lead to the truth cannot, as Damaska has said, be analysed *in vacuo*.[84] In his words the question: 'Truth about what?' must be answered at the outset. Criminal trials involve not only the determination of the accused's conduct and accompanying state of mind but also the gauging of these 'facts' by reference to the relevant legal standard. 'Truth' has one complexion in the first exercise, and an altogether different face in the second. The choice between procedures may also be governed by the nature of the dispute or inquiry. The contest model is particularly suitable where a particular issue has to be determined one way or another; the inquest model

---

[82] Damaska (1975a).
[83] See, for example, Nesson (1985); Goodpaster (1987); Duff (1986).
[84] Damaska (1975b), 1084.

in contrast would seem to be better suited to resolve less focused disputes. Another question that is particularly important in criminal procedure concerns the kind of outcome which is considered desirable. We have seen that accusatorial principles require that any risk of error be allocated in favour of the defendant. Although systems that veer towards the inquest model are perfectly capable of taking account of this probative policy, it may be argued that the contest model can place higher evidentiary barriers to conviction than the inquest model because its rules of evidence can more consistently guide the trier of fact in this probative direction.[85] The choice of procedure may then be governed by the extent to which evidentiary barriers to conviction are valued or tolerated. The choice may also be governed by the extent to which each model is considered better able to safeguard certain other values and policies. This in turn may depend on particular ideological preconceptions, such as the extent to which public officials are trusted, the degree to which it is considered necessary to provide safeguards from abuse within the proof process at the expense of truth-finding, and the need to ensure that the parties are permitted to participate in the proceedings.[86]

Even if agreement could be reached on these issues there may still be disagreement about how best to go about the task of truth-finding. It is now commonly recognized that we have no direct access to the truth or, as it has been put, we have no lines of communication with the Recording Angel.[87] This is particularly so in the context of criminal procedure which involves reconstructing past events. In the absence of self-evident criteria for establishing the truth, we have to construct our own and epistemology is therefore a normative concern.[88] It is agreed that both contest and inquest models have their dangers. Critics of the inquest model commonly point to the danger of inquisitorial judges reaching a conclusion at too early a stage of the proof process;[89] critics of the contest model commonly point to the danger of believing that the truth will somehow emerge from two sides battling the issue out.[90] But we have seen that rules can be developed to prevent the excesses of partisanship in both models and it can be argued that both share the epistemological assumptions of what Twining has called a rationalist model of adjudication.[91] This model involves subscribing to a correspondence theory of truth, by which theories and hypotheses have to be checked against a world of fact independent of human observation. This

---

[85] Damaska (1973).

[86] Damaska has argued that Lockean liberal values, with distrust of the state and freedom from its restraint, are to be found in the ideological matrix of the adversary model, while collectivist values and benevolent paternalism are the principles of the non-adversarial model: (1973), 585.   [87] See Rescher (1980), 135.

[88] Bankowski (1981), 262–3.   [89] Fuller, (1961), 43.

[90] See, for example, Frank (1949), 80.   [91] Twining (1989), (1990).

is done by using the empirical evidence of our sense experience as a foundation and by invoking the classical methods of natural science, induction and deduction, to reach conclusions. Both contest and inquest models assist this by providing for a process of justification of what has been discovered.[92] The contest model permits the parties to justify their case while the inquest model requires the judicial inquirer to justify the case. A further point of affinity is that although atomistic modes of reasoning are often associated with the contest model of proof and holistic modes with the inquest model, in fact as Damaska has observed, both approaches are involved at different stages of each model.[93] The contest model emphasizes atomistic presentation of evidence, followed by a global decision, while the inquest model requires a more holistic treatment of evidence followed by judgment in atomistic form. Viewed in this way the two models have more in common than is often thought and indeed, although argument continues about which model is preferable,[94] they tend to be considered together as ideal models of proof.

Returning to the context of the Diplock trial, however, the question here is not so much which of two models should be adopted, but whether judges should adopt a more interventionist stance within what is still considered to be an adversarial model of proof. There appears to be a consensus that while any particular procedure may have contest and inquest features and may therefore be located somewhere on the spectrum between the extremes, there is a limit to the extent to which features from both models should be mixed.[95] In response to Judge Frankel's suggestion that we should be prepared to enquire whether 'our arts of examining and cross-examining . . . are inescapably preferable to safeguarded interrogation by an informed judicial officer',[96] Uviller has commented that it is 'largely idle to attempt vital organ transplants between dissimilar organisms'.[97] Part of the reason for this is cultural: the contest model is more associated with Anglo-American procedures and the inquest model with continental procedures, and the adoption of institutions in a culture in which they are alien is likely to prove problematic. Although Lord Devlin approved of the ideal of

---

[92] The distinction apparently made by the models between discovery and justification can be criticized: see Bankowski (1981), 12-13; Jackson (1988a), 521–2.

[93] Damaska (1990), 98–9.

[94] Attempts to underpin the debate with empirical evidence have proved difficult: see Thibaut, Walker, and Lind (1972); Damaska (1975b). There has also been debate about the applicability of adversary models of proof to fields such as medicine, science, and history: see Levine (1974); Freedman (1975).

[95] Continental criminal procedures which replaced 'pure' inquisitorial processes in the first half of the nineteenth century are often described as 'mixed', but this would seem to be because these procedures incorporated many 'accusatorial' ideas, and in common law eyes they remain strongly non-adversarial: Damaska (1973), 559.

[96] Frankel (1975), 1053.   [97] Uviller (1975), 1075.

judicial intermediaries operating in pre-trial criminal procedure, he recognized that 'Englishmen would not be soothed by the sound of the *juge d'instruction* rustling in with his dossiers.'[98] As we have seen, however, the current concern about the operation of adversarial procedures in the United Kingdom is prompting much more interest in 'alien' continental procedures, and there may in future be a greater willingness to mix procedures.

The argument against mixing procedures, however, assumes that the two models are mutually exclusive. Although the two models share the same conception of the proof process as a process of justification, they employ quite different means to achieve this. Therefore the more mixed the features of a particular process of proof, the more likely the process will fall short of either ideal. An inquiring judge in a party-dominated contest is likely to impede the proof process because the parties who are given the primary responsibility for marshalling the evidence into a coherent case are less able to do this if they are constantly being interrupted. Conversely, an excessively party-dominated inquiry prevents the inquirer from developing the grounds for justifying his or her conclusions.

The view that deviations from either the contest or inquest ideal are inimical to truth-finding assumes that no other ideal is possible. But this is by no means self-evident. A study of the practice of particular procedures may illustrate not only that deviations from either ideal exist, but that they may be justified in the interests of truth-finding. Our study of the practice in Diplock trials considered whether judges do in fact adopt a more active role in these trials. Whether this is desirable or not should depend on the compatibility of this practice with the best methods of truth-finding and with the other functions of the criminal trial, rather than on its compatibility with some predetermined model of proof. There is a danger that adherence to polarized models of proof which take little account of the vagaries of practice may cloud our judgment here. In the same article in which he warned against adversarial systems employing a figure in the mould of the *juge d'instruction*, Uviller championed the idea that judges in bench trials should take a major role in the interrogation of witnesses and argued that neither 'the inquisitorial spectre nor the prospect of a judicial stumble or two should be allowed to frighten us from an otherwise sensible procedure'.[99] Moreover, as we shall argue in later chapters, the contest and inquest models are not the only models that may be envisaged. In this study, therefore, we will be using the two models as useful reference points rather than as rigid constraints in our task of determining whether the absence of the jury from the Diplock trial changes trial practice.

[98] Devlin (1979), 82.   [99] Uviller (1975), 1069.

4

Inside the Diplock Court

This chapter describes the methods we adopted to study whether the absence of the jury pushes the Diplock trial procedure in the direction of an inquisitorial mode of proof. The point was made in the last chapter that this question cannot be determined merely by looking at the formal changes which have been made to the rules of evidence and procedure. These rules remain substantively the same in both Diplock and jury trials and yet the absence of the jury may have significantly altered the way in which trials are conducted in practice. For example, we have seen that the analytically separate issues of the admissibility of confessions and the weight to be given to those confessions are treated together in Diplock trials, not because of any requirement of the rules of procedure but simply because it has been most convenient to adopt this practice. Counsel have generally followed the practice of questioning witnesses on the *voir dire* on the issues of admissibility and weight because the same tribunal, the judge, decides both matters.

THE RESEARCH DESIGN

The point has been made that when a process has not previously been researched in depth, the research methods used should be exploratory, since methods for the testing of previously defined hypotheses will be unsuitable.[1] Speaking in the context of the sentencing process, Shapland, for example, has said that the methods: 'should be capable of producing an analysis of the complex interaction between participants both in and out of court and of highlighting aspects of the roles of the participants which are crucial to the determination of the end-product . . .'.[2] We have taken this approach in studying the Diplock process of trial by judge alone.

We decided to focus first and foremost on the role of the judge, as it is the added fact-finding responsibility of the judge in Diplock trials which has given rise to the changes of practice. A key question in our study has therefore been to examine whether this change in function has made judges more inclined to take an active role in trial procedures, whether in terms of

---

[1] Shapland (1981), 10.   [2] *Ibid.*

foreclosing certain avenues of enquiry or asking questions of witnesses, or in terms of calling witnesses or asking counsel to elicit certain evidence. At the same time, since judges' fact-finding role is conducted in tandem with, rather than in place of, their traditional umpireal role, we consider whether judges perform their umpireal role so assiduously in Diplock trials. A more active direction of proceedings by judges will inevitably affect the way in which counsel conduct proceedings. Counsel still present and elicit evidence within a formal adversarial setting, but more active participation by judges is likely to constrain the extent to which they are able to question witnesses in the way they would like.

In order to assess the judicial role we adopted a range of different techniques in order to be as conclusive as possible.[3] One obvious approach was to observe the judicial role in practice, and our method of observation will be discussed later. To obtain a fuller picture of judicial practice, however, we also felt it important to interview a number of judges and counsel. This enabled us to discover whether, if judges did perform a more dominant role in Diplock trials, they were conscious of doing so, or whether they deliberately tried to adopt (or to avoid) a more dominant role, and if so for what reasons. We also felt that interviews would throw light on aspects of practice which are not susceptible to observation in the courtroom, for example any out-of-court discussions between judges and counsel. It also seemed to us that direct observation of the dynamics of courtroom interaction might not reveal the full extent to which Diplock procedures were becoming inquisitorial. Clearly the most obvious evidence of a movement towards an inquisitorial procedure would be constituted by an active 'inquisitorial' judge taking a leading fact-finding role. However, even if judges play a relatively passive role in terms of directing the evidence, their views on particular kinds of evidence, witnesses, or strategies are likely to become known to counsel as a result of counsel's continual dealings with them. The fact that judges (unlike juries) are 'repeat players' means that the known views of a judge may play a significant part in counsel's decisions, first whether to contest cases, and secondly whether to contest certain kinds of evidence. Counsel may feel constrained to accept an opponent's evidence in Diplock trials simply because, unlike in jury trials, they know how it is likely to be received. The result may be that, even if trials do not have the appearance of judge-dominated proceedings, they are in reality more akin to a review of evidence already elicited in the form of witness statements or depositions, with the extent of oral examination being reduced.

This 'hidden' influence of judges over counsel may be particularly significant since Northern Ireland is a small jurisdiction where the limited

---

[3] For a brief explanation of the principle of triangulation, which involves the use of a number of methods to study phenomena, see Rose (1982), 309.

size of both the Bar and the bench makes for greater intimacy between judges and counsel. This greater intimacy may also work the other way, to enable senior counsel to exert influence over less senior judges. The judiciary in Northern Ireland is comprised of eleven Supreme Court judges (the Lord Chief Justice, three Lord Justices of Appeal, and seven High Court judges) and thirteen county court judges. All Supreme Court judges, including the Lord Chief Justice himself, and all county court judges (bar one who sits as the Chief Social Security Commissioner for Northern Ireland) preside in the Crown Court and they are all expected to do their share of Diplock judging.[4] Altogether, twenty-two judges were eligible to sit in Diplock cases (ten Supreme Court judges and twelve county court judges) during the period of our research.

Although the size of the Northern Ireland Bar has increased dramatically during the last twenty years (there are now over 320 practising barristers, of whom around thirty are QCs), the numbers who practise in criminal cases in the Crown Court are relatively small. During the period of our research we observed forty-two different counsel (twelve senior and thirty junior) and our investigations suggested that we observed most of the counsel, with a few exceptions, who practised on a regular basis in Belfast Crown Court, where the bulk of Crown Court business is dealt with. The criminal Bar and the bench have a strikingly low female membership. All the Crown Court judges in Northern Ireland are male, as are almost all regular practitioners at the criminal Bar. In the forty-three trials we observed, only one female barrister appeared, and she was led by senior counsel. Although a good number of junior counsel appeared in our cases, there was a small core who appeared regularly. Two particular senior counsel appeared for the prosecution in fourteen of the sixteen trials in which senior counsel prosecuted. One junior counsel appeared in no less than sixteen (37 per cent) of the observed trials. There was more variation on the defence side but even so, one senior counsel appeared in ten (22 per cent) of the observed trials and two junior counsel between them represented at least one defendant in twenty (40 per cent) of the observed trials.

Permission was obtained from the Lord Chief Justice to interview judges and six in-depth interviews were conducted, with three Supreme Court judges and three county court judges. In addition we were able to obtain the views of certain judges who volunteered comments to us when we were observing trials in court. We also held in-depth interviews with ten counsel (four senior and six junior) and, again, a number of others volunteered information to us during trials. Two of the counsel interviewed had experience of judging (practising barristers may sit as part-time deputy

[4] For further details on the composition of the Northern Ireland judiciary, see Dickson (1993), 17–23; Doran and Jackson (1992), 34–5.

county court judges in certain cases) and we were able to ask them about their judicial experience as well as their experience at the Bar.

One key aspect of the inquest model which emerged in the last chapter, apart from the role of the judge and the nature of the trial, was the scope for review of the judgment. Mention has already been made of the obvious fact that in the Diplock procedure there is no judicial summing-up, as there is no jury for whom this is necessary. Although the adversarial rules of evidence and procedure remain unchanged, the absence of the summing-up and the replacement of the general verdict by a written judgment is perhaps the starkest illustration of the shift from input control (where the trier of fact is told how to reach a general verdict but does not have to justify it) towards output control (where the trier of fact personally has to justify the verdict) so that there is *in theory* greater scope for appellate review. Despite this apparent shift, however, it seemed important for us to consider the extent to which the judgment *actually* offers greater scope for appellate review. A close examination of the written judgment in a number of trials has therefore been built into our study.

COURTROOM OBSERVATION

There are comparatively few studies of courtroom procedure, partly because studies of the law in action have rightly recognized that what goes on in actual hearings constitutes only a small part of the way in which cases are processed through the criminal justice system.[5] We have already emphasized that the trial itself cannot be viewed in isolation from other phases of the criminal justice process. As already explained, however, our study was primarily concerned with the trial phase because our aim was to consider the effect of the absence of the jury on the criminal process, and since the jury only appears at trial, it was logical to focus first and foremost on this stage.

Several studies which examined courtroom procedure have tended to be concerned with the way in which defendants, and more latterly victims and witnesses, have been treated, or with the way in which convictions are constructed. They have therefore looked at wider aspects than the trial itself.[6] Atkinson and Drew have criticized studies contrasting courtroom and common sense procedures, on the ground that they have assumed a consensus about how everyday procedures operate and pointed out

---

[5] Atkinson and Drew (1979), 2.

[6] See, for example, Bottoms and McClean (1976); Carlen (1976); McBarnet (1981); Shapland, Willmore, and Duff (1985); Chambers and Millar (1986); McConville, Sanders, and Leng (1991); Jackson, Kilpatrick, and Harvey (1991).

'extraordinary' features of courtroom procedure without dwelling on the supposedly 'ordinary' features:[7]

Thus, courtroom ethnographers notice and report on such things as the ecological environment of the court-room, the special attire worn by some participants, the unusual ways in which talk and bodily activities (e.g standing up and sitting down) and [*sic*] coordinated, etc. But that many features of 'ordinary' conversational practice remain (e.g that one speaker speaks at a time, that speaker change recurs, that speakers exhibit an understanding of what is going on, etc.) is not regarded as worthy of detailed report and analysis. By focusing on the more 'exotic' contextual features, therefore, ethnographers are likely to rely on their unexplicated knowledge (and that of their audience) of how activities in other more mundane settings are organised, and hence to refrain from reporting on anything other than the 'exotic'.

In a similar way there would be a temptation for observers of judicial behaviour in Diplock trials, aware of the supposedly passive role that judges ought 'ordinarily' to take in conventional jury trials, to regard any supposedly inquisitorial features as 'extraordinary', without testing whether these features are actually so extraordinary in the conventional jury trial.

It seemed important to us therefore that some direct comparison should be made with jury trials and that as precise a study as possible be made of the interventions made by judges in both modes of trial. There remained the problem of finding the best method of doing this within the resources available to us. It has been pointed out that while the study of legal texts has received a good deal of attention in recent years, the study of courtroom discourse is relatively new. Bulow-Moller has drawn attention to three categories of studies.[8] First, those based in social psychology involving the connections which are made between linguistic features of witness evidence and social judgment.[9] Secondly, analyses have been made of the cognitive aspects of particular linguistic choices made by questioners. Loftus, for example, has conducted experiments illustrating how the memories of witnesses change according to the way questions are asked ('Did you see a stop sign?', as compared with 'Did you see the stop sign?').[10] Thirdly, and more relevant to our survey, some studies have focused on the way counsel control witnesses by means of different question types.[11] Danet and Bogosch, for example, divided questions into four basic types consisting of (1) declarative questions (asserting that something happened, 'You did, didn't you?'), (2) interrogative yes/no questions, or choice questions ('Did you do it?'), (3) 'interrogative-wh' questions ('who-what-where-when-why?') and (4) 'requestions', or indirect requests for information ('Could you tell us what happened?').[12] The questions range from those which most

---

[7] Atkinson and Drew (1979), 31.   [8] Bulow-Moller (1991), 39.
[9] O'Barr (1982); Erickson, Lind, Johnson, and O'Barr (1978).   [10] Loftus (1980).
[11] Danet and Bogosch (1980); Harris (1984); Walker (1987).
[12] Danet and Bogosch (1980), 43.

contain and control to those which least restrain the witness. On the basis of this classification they set out to test the combativeness of adversary trials, assuming that attorneys must be highly combative for adversary trials to work properly.

This study has been criticized by Dunstan on the ground that it is premature to attempt to assess how well adversary trials work until one has worked out how courtroom interaction in these trials is organized.[13] In other words, asking whether the adversary system works well presupposes that we already know *how* it works. But as Dunstan has said, '[i]t is what participants *do*, as opposed to what they supposedly should do that constitutes courtroom behaviour and hence the adversary system.'[14] Conversation analysts have also criticized the procedure of counting questions by linguistic form without paying regard to the context in which the questions were asked.[15] For example, it has been argued that it is mistaken to study sequences of question and answer in isolation. A question which appears innocuous in form (for example, 'What did you do next?') may in fact be highly coercive if it was not answered in the first place and is being repeated.

The problem from our point of view with most of the studies to date is that they have assumed the traditional structure of the adversary trial with counsel, judge, and jury present, and they have focused on counsel's questioning rather than judicial questioning. In fact, as Bernard Jackson has pointed out, a plurality of discourses takes place in the courtroom apart from questions and answers between counsel and witness (for example, counsel-counsel, counsel-judge, party-counsel and judge-witness).[16] One has to look mainly at the literature about so-called inquisitorial systems to find studies of judicial discourse in courtroom settings.[17] Danet and Bogosch's notion of witness constraint or coercion, however, is a useful starting point, since one of the key indicators (identified in the last chapter) in determining where a particular procedure is to be located on the contest-inquest spectrum is the extent to which judges assume a dominant investigative fact-finding role in the proceedings. Again, though, it is important to consider the context in which witnesses are constrained. Judges have powers to compel witnesses to answer questions put to them by counsel, and in exercising these judges are merely discharging their umpireal role, ensuring that the parties can elicit answers from witnesses, rather than engaging in any independent investigative role.

Over the course of a year we decided to observe as many Diplock and jury trials as we could. We employed a legally qualified research associate to

---

[13] Dunstan (1980).
[14] *Ibid.*, 63.
[15] See, for example, Atkinson and Drew (1979).
[16] Jackson, B.S. (1988), 35.
[17] See, for example, Casanovas (1990).

observe as many judges as possible over this period, and where possible to view the same judges in both Diplock and jury trials. The need to view as many trials as possible meant avoiding lengthy multi-defendant Diplock trials and fraud trials, each of which can last for many months and which may also involve special features (such as the screening of witnesses or the display of large amounts of paperwork) that are not typical of most trials. We sought permission from the Lord Chief Justice to make detailed notes of cases in court, and judges were informed of our research beforehand. This carried the risk that judges would alter their normal judicial practice in the light of her presence. We have no reason to believe that this happened, however. Certain judges were interested in the research but they ignored the presence of our researcher entirely during court proceedings. One judge expressly told her that he was an interventionist and that he doubted whether her presence would have any effect on his conduct of the case.

Obviously, there were limitations in employing a single researcher as much weight had then to be given to that person's individual perceptions.[18] The employment of only one court observer also meant that we were restricted in the number of trials that could be viewed. The advantage of one observer, however, was that it ensured a consistency of approach. Our researcher was able to identify, in respect of each witness in each trial, when judges intervened, the length of each intervention, and the type of intervention involved. Interaction with counsel was also noted, in particular how judges dealt with objections from counsel and what kind of objections they themselves made to counsel's questions. We were unable to take a verbatim record of all testimony but our researcher was able to take an extensive note of the interventions made. In later chapters we shall explain the basis of our classifications in full. Rather than looking at the linguistic form of each utterance we focused on the context of each intervention, as well as the words and the tone used. In the case of judicial questioning this meant that we did not classify each question in isolation but instead classified the entire nature of the intervention which frequently took the form of a sequence of questions.

As we discuss in Chapter Six, the task of making classifications was not unproblematic, and we considered it better for all participants in the research to engage in this task after observation rather than to ask our researcher to categorize interventions during the trial on the basis of *a priori* classifications. The extensive notes taken by the researcher made it possible to do this. It would clearly have been helpful to have had access to a verbatim record of the trial proceedings, but access to trial recordings was forbidden to us.[19] On occasions the notes made by our researcher were

---

[18] For a brief discussion of this difficulty, see Peay (1989), 25.

[19] Baldwin's study of the role of legal representatives during police interviews with suspects had the benefit of full video-recorded material: see Baldwin (1993). In Shapland's research on

supplemented by transcript material. Recordings of trial testimony are normally only transcribed when transcripts are wanted for the purposes of appeal. We obtained permission to have transcriptions specially made for certain key parts of the trials we observed, such as rulings, summings-up and judgments. This was a costly exercise and it would have been beyond our financial resources to request full transcripts of all the trials observed, even if permission were given for this to be done.

THE SAMPLE

We decided to focus our fieldwork on Belfast Crown Court which hears both Diplock and jury trials continuously. Although as we have noted it is possible for Diplock cases to be heard outside Belfast, in practice this has never happened and they have always been heard in Belfast Crumlin Road court-house, first at Belfast City Commission and later at Belfast Crown Court.[20] All full-time judges are required to work for approximately two months per year at Crumlin Road court-house where they are assigned to hear either jury or Diplock trials. The result is that all judges may hear jury cases as well as Diplock cases in Belfast and we anticipated that there would be no shortage of opportunities to view a range of different judges in jury and Diplock trials over the fieldwork period without the need to visit any of the provincial centres to see more jury trials. There are as many as four trials in progress in Crumlin Road court-house at any one time. The large multi-defendant Diplock trials are normally heard in one of the two large courtrooms on the ground floor, and smaller Diplock trials are heard in a more compact courtroom. Jury trials are heard in the other large courtroom and occasionally also in another smaller courtroom.[21]

We observed Diplock trials in both the large and the smaller courtrooms and on occasions it was noticeable that when proceedings were heard in the larger courtrooms, which scattered the various participants over a wide area and imposed a greater distance between them, a more formal atmosphere prevailed. This contrast was exhibited in a particularly striking way in one Diplock trial where proceedings began in a small courtroom but were then moved on the second day to a large courtroom. However, even in the larger courtrooms the key participants tended to huddle around the judge in Diplock cases and it was noticeably more difficult to hear proceedings when

the process between conviction and sentence a verbatim transcript was made by the researcher: Shapland (1981).

[20] For a description of this setting, see Hadden and Wright (1979); Jackson, Kilpatrick, and Harvey (1991), 76–7.

[21] For more detail on how court business is distributed between the various courtrooms in Crumlin Road court-house, see Jackson, Kilpatrick, and Harvey (1991), 99–100.

the jury was absent. It has been observed that the need to retain the public character of the trial, particularly to ensure that it remains audible and comprehensible, imposes limits on how far the formal features of any trial can be dispensed with.[22] The absence of the jury should make no difference to this imperative as defendants and the public are entitled to attend the proceedings. The fact is, however, that courtroom design has often paid little attention to the need for audibility so far as the public and defendants are concerned. In the large Crumlin Road courtrooms bullet-proof glass panels divide the public galleries from the rest of the courtroom. The dock in which defendants sit is also towards the back of these courtrooms, and other research carried out during the fieldwork period revealed that defendants had considerable difficulty in hearing the proceedings.[23] A newspaper report of one of the publicized trials which took place during the fieldwork period, involving a man charged with attacking the funeral of three IRA members shot by the SAS in Gibraltar and killing three people, described how the absence of the jury made the trial barely audible and comprehensible in spite of the imposing setting of the trial in one of the large courtrooms:[24]

You realise that the absence of the jury transforms a criminal trial by relieving lawyers of the need to explain out loud what is going on. The judge and the four barristers sit in a cluster at the front of the court, almost on the same level, conversing with one another in a low, barely audible monotone, checking oral evidence against prepared documents. Clarity, one of the glories of the English jury system, is sacrificed to bureaucratic formalism.

Over the course of 12 months we were able to observe forty-three (40 per cent) of all the trials conducted in Belfast Crown Court. The definition of a trial for our purposes was a hearing in which the evidence of at least one witness was either given or adopted. This excluded the common occurrence of a case being listed for trial but the defendant being re-arraigned and pleading guilty without evidence being heard. However, contested hearings terminated without a decision on guilt by the trier of fact were regarded as trials. Indeed fourteen of our trials (36 per cent), mostly Diplock trials, were aborted for one reason or another. In four cases the Crown offered no further evidence during its case and the trial was abandoned. In four other cases the defendant's plea to some or all of the charges was accepted. In five further cases the defence successfully applied for an application for a direction, which occurs at the end of the prosecution case when the judge is asked to stop the trial by directing the jury (or, if no jury, himself or herself) that there is no case for the defence to answer.[25]

---

[22] Atkinson and Drew (1979), 222.
[23] Jackson, Kilpatrick, and Harvey (1991), 100.
[24] Laurence Marks, *Observer*, 26 Feb. 1989.
[25] See Tapper (1990), 174–5; Jackson (1983a), 16–17, (1983b).

In our observed sample of forty-three trials, twenty-six (60 per cent) were Diplock and seventeen (40 per cent) were jury trials. This almost exactly mirrors the Diplock/jury breakdown for the whole twelve months' fieldwork period, during which there were sixty-two (59 per cent) Diplock trials and forty-four (41 per cent) jury trials. We avoided very long multi-defendant trials that could last many weeks or months and which would therefore have confined our researcher's attention to one particular judge over a long period of time. The result was that we were able to observe sixteen out of the twenty-two judges who heard cases at Belfast Crown Court over the fieldwork period. All but one of the twenty-two who heard cases over this period were full-time judges and, as we have seen, this represented almost the full complement of Northern Ireland judges.

Of the forty-three observed trials, thirty-seven (86 per cent) were heard by county court judges and only six (14 per cent) by Supreme Court judges. This under-representation of Supreme Court judges was caused by our focus on shorter trials; many of the lengthier trials involved murder offences which must be heard by a Supreme Court judge.[26] Another factor here was that Supreme Court judges preside over more serious cases with the result that they were much more likely to hear Diplock cases than jury cases. Since we wanted to observe a roughly even quantity of both Diplock and jury cases it was therefore inevitable that we would be observing more county court judges than Supreme Court judges.

We were less successful in being able to view the same judges presiding in both modes of trial. This was partly because judges are not assigned to hear both Dipock and jury cases in the course of each one-month sitting period, but are assigned to hear either one or the other. Thus, when a judge was observed sitting in one mode of trial, it was necessary to wait for some time before that judge could be observed sitting in the other mode of trial. As stated above, we observed sixteen judges during our fieldwork period. Of these we only managed to view five presiding over both modes of trial. Two of these judges were observed sitting in more than two Diplock and jury trials each. Four of the judges were observed in jury trials only, and the remaining seven in Diplock trials only.

Although our main concern was to view as many judges as possible, and where possible also to view them sitting in both modes of trial, another concern was that the kinds of cases we observed should be common to both Diplock and jury trials. In order to attribute differences in judicial behaviour to the mode of trial, we felt it important to eschew 'unusual' trials with features that in themselves might make judges alter their normal conduct of trials. This was another reason for avoiding trials with a large

---

[26] The Lord Chancellor has issued rules for the hearing of cases by different kinds of judges: see *Northern Ireland Court Business* (1990).

number of defendants and fraud trials, apart from the length of time which these would have involved. Thirty-seven (86 per cent) of the trials observed involved a single defendant, and in the six multi-defendant trials observed, no more than five co-defendants were involved. (These trials tended to involve very serious offences; three of them were murder cases, another was a multiple gang rape and robbery case). We therefore viewed a lower percentage of·multi-defendant trials (14 per cent) than were held over the fieldwork period (24 per cent).

It was also our intention to focus particularly on trials involving deschedulable offences (that is, offences which could be heard in either Diplock or jury trials) or offences (such as robbery) which were heard in one mode or the other depending on the facts of the case (that is, whether or not a firearm was used). Table 4.1 overleaf shows the most serious offence tried in each of the trials observed. In the multi-defendant trials the most serious charge faced by the first named defendant was also the most serious offence charged against the others and this has been used as the indicator in these trials. On this basis only nineteen (44 per cent) of all the trials in our sample related to deschedulable offences, only slightly higher than the percentage of all the trials in this category during the fieldwork period (40 per cent). This meant that the other twenty-four trials were either Diplock trials involving offences which were not capable of being descheduled (mainly charges of possession of firearms or explosives) or jury trials involving non-scheduled offences (mainly sexual offences, theft, deception, and serious road traffic offences). As regards Diplock trials specifically, only 46 per cent of those which we observed involved offences capable of being descheduled. This was slightly at odds with our planned method of selecting trials in the Diplock court which should have resulted in an over- rather than an under-representation of deschedulable offences. One possible explanation for this is that a number of multi-defendant trials involved serious offences such as murder or manslaughter, both deschedulable offences.

Differences between Diplock and jury trials

The difference in the type of offences tried in each mode of trial raises the question of whether there were other features, apart from the type of offence, which marked out the Diplock trials from the jury trials. As we saw in Chapter Two, one of the enduring concerns about Diplock trials has been their over-reliance on confession evidence. In our sample of 'ordinary' Diplock trials, however, there were only four trials out of twenty-six in which the admissibility of either oral or written confessions was contested. (The challenges met with mixed results: in only one trial was the challenge completely successful, although in another a challenge was successful in

TABLE 4.1 *Most serious offence charged in trials*

	No. of trials	Jury	Diplock
Robbery	5	1	4
Explosives/Firearms/Bombing/Arson	11	1	10
Hijacking	2	0	2
Sexual Offences	6	6	0
Property Offences	2	2	0
Assult/Actual Bodily Harm	6	4	2
Intimidation	2	0	2
Murder/Attempted Murder	4	1	3
Withholding Information/Receiving Property for Terrorism	3	0	3
Serious Driving Offences	2	2	0
TOTAL TRIALS	43	17	26

respect of one co-defendant but not the other two.) In two further Diplock trials the police attributed oral statements to the accused which were challenged on the ground that they were never made.

Apart from one trial, where there were two main issues because co-defendants were challenging different aspects of the case, it was easy to identify one main issue in each of the trials. It was less easy to categorize that issue in a precise manner. Table 4.2 shows that we divided the issues raised in the trials into seven broad categories. These were adopted on the ground that, although not legally recognized as distinctive, they were often the categories which counsel in the cases preferred to use in discussing the issues. For example, counsel would describe the cases in which they were involved as identification cases, circumstantial cases, intent cases, or confession cases. The issue we have called 'interpretation of a defendant's actions' involved either a question of legal classification (was the defendant's driving reckless as opposed to careless? Was the defendant guilty of grievous bodily harm as opposed to actual bodily harm?) or a question of factual interpretation (did the defendant's claim to be unemployed deceive the social security officers investigating his entitlement to unemployment benefit?)[27] Circumstantial issues arose where the defendant denied involvement in the offence and the question was whether the forensic evidence or his admitted presence near the scene implicated him. Identification issues were of two kinds: in two cases the identifying witness had picked out the

---

[27] For discussion of the difficult question of distinguishing questions of fact from questions of law, see Jackson (1983).

defendant in an identity parade; another six cases were so-called 'recognition' cases where the witness had earlier seen or known the defendant and the question was whether his recognition of the defendant at the scene of the offence was correct. Usually the defendant claimed that the witness was mistaken, but in one case it was alleged that the witness who had been the victim of a savage attack was deliberately and falsely implicating the defendants involved. Claims of this kind overlapped with the credibility category, where the defence case was that prosecution witnesses, usually police witnesses, were lying about what they saw and heard. The final category involves specific defences, most commonly consent in rape cases, and duress in cases where defendants were allegedly involved in paramilitary activity such as receiving money and property for terrorist purposes, or possession of firearms, or withholding information about paramilitary activity.

The table shows that certain issues were confined to one mode of trial or the other, for example, issues of duress and lack of knowledge or intent in relation to firearms charges were all dealt with in Diplock trials, while defences of consent to rape were all heard in jury trials. Other issues were common to both modes of trial, for example, identification evidence, circumstantial evidence, interpretation of the defendant's actions and confessions. Cases where the defendant denied being present at the scene of the alleged offence, or admitted being present but denied involvement in any offence or the offence charged, were equally divided between each mode of trial.

Another difference between Diplock and jury trials pointed out by some participants was that there tended to be much more expert evidence in the former, particularly forensic evidence. One counsel told us that in his opinion investigation of cases had been transformed over the last ten years by forensic evidence. His view was that blood, fingerprint, and firearms residue evidence previously occurred in fewer than 10 per cent of Crown

TABLE 4.2 *Main issues in trials*

	Total	Jury	Diplock
Circumstantial evidence	2	1	1
Interpretation of defendant's actions	9	5	4
Identification	10	4	6
Specific defence	10	5	5
Confessions	6	2	4
Credibility of accounts	2	0	2
Intent/Knowledge	5	0	5

Court trials, whereas now it was more like 50 per cent of cases. It was inevitable that the police and forensic witnesses would direct their energies towards the more serious kinds of cases, which tended to be Diplock cases: 'One doesn't usually get DNA and fibres in burglary cases. But as one moves up the scale to sexual cases and anything up from theft/burglary, we will now find forensic evidence.'

Table 4.3 shows that there was indeed a much greater tendency for forensic evidence to be adduced in Diplock cases. This was particularly true in offences relating to firearms and explosives. The table records cases where expert evidence was actually adduced during the trial. There were of course certain trials, as we have seen, which were aborted during the prosecution case but where forensic evidence would probably have been adduced had the trial continued. In addition, there were certain trials (mostly Diplock) where evidence was formally admitted or read into the record, with the result that the evidence was not adduced during the trial. The table therefore underestimates the extent to which expert evidence was available in the trials. All the same, there were a number of less serious Diplock cases (such as withholding information, intimidation and hijacking cases) where there was no forensic evidence. It is to be noted that there were only three jury cases in which forensic evidence was adduced (two rape cases and one murder case), but there was a greater tendency for medical evidence to be used in these cases (mostly sexual offences, assault, and bodily harm cases). When one considers expert evidence as a whole, indeed, there was a higher proportion of Diplock trials (eleven out of twenty-six) than jury trials (five out of seventeen) in which no expert evidence was actually adduced. There was also a proportionately greater number of expert witnesses who gave evidence in the jury trials observed (twenty-six in seventeen trials) than in Diplock trials (twenty-six in twenty-six trials).

This raises the question of whether certain types of witness were more prevalent in Diplock or jury trials. We have seen that intimidation of witnesses has been alleged to be a problem in Diplock trials and it might therefore have been expected that there would be a greater proportion of civilian witnesses in jury trials. In fact as Table 4.4 shows there was, on the contrary, a greater proportion of civilian witnesses, including victims, in the

TABLE 4.3 *Expert evidence adduced in trials*

	Total	Jury	Diplock
Medical	16	12	4
Forensic	18	5	13
None	16	5	11

TABLE 4.4 *Types of witnesses in trials*

	Total	Jury	Diplock
Prosecution	433	133	300
Defence	60	29	31
Defendant	28	12	16
Victim	34	11	23
Expert	52	26	26
Police	283	90	193
Other civilian	96	23	73

observed Diplock trials. There was, however, a greater tendency for defendants to give evidence in jury trials (twelve out of a total of twenty-one defendants) than in Diplock trials (fourteen out of thirty-eight defendants).

A final point of difference between Diplock and jury trials which might affect judicial behaviour concerns the counsel who appeared in each mode of trial. An experienced counsel may exercise more influence over a judge than a less experienced counsel. Conversely, judges may be be much more inclined to dominate a less experienced counsel. Several counsel and judges told us that in their view counsel appearing in Diplock trials were much more experienced. Table 4.5 sets out the number of years' experience of the leading counsel for both prosecution and defence in the observed Diplock and jury trials. Where different counsel represented a number of defendants, the figure represents the average number years since call of all the leading defence counsel. Although senior counsel appeared in a similar proportion of Diplock and jury trials, no counsel who appeared in a Diplock trial had less than ten years' experience at the Bar whereas certain counsel who appeared in jury trials had much less experience than this, even though we were concentrating on shorter and therefore less serious Diplock trials. It was also noticeable that there were certain Diplock cases in which counsel had more years of practical experience than the judge in the case and this, as we shall see, occasionally led to friction.

Another question here is the balance of representation between prosecution and defence counsel. Table 4.5 shows little evidence of an imbalance which might have disadvantaged the defence in Diplock cases. Of those, the defence had more years' experience in sixteen Diplock trials, the prosecution were more experienced in seven, and prosecution and defence counsel were equally experienced in the remaining three trials. There was no Diplock case in which senior counsel appeared for the prosecution but did not appear for the defence, but in eight (out of 26) cases senior counsel appeared for the defence only. The picture was different in jury trials, where

Inside the Diplock Court

TABLE 4.5 *Years since call of counsel in each of the Dipock and jury trials*

OFFENCE	Jury (17 trials)		OFFENCE	Diplock (26 trials)	
	CROWN	DEFENCE		CROWN	DEFENCE
Attempted Murder	20	20	Murder/ Attempted Murder	33 33 33	20 33 38
Sexual Offences	13 19 11 20 33 20	15 33 33 19 21 6	Explosives/ Firearms/ Bombing/Arson	13 13 33 13 20 13 13 17 33	15 13 38 17 33 10 33 20 23
Robbery	13	13	Robbery	13 13 13 13	33 15 33 23
Serious Driving	20 20	17 13	Assault/Bodily Harm	10 13	16 33
Assault/Bodily Harm	10 14 13 12	21 12 6 5	Withholding Information/ Receiving Property for Terrorism	13 17 12	13 11 13
Property Offences	20 13	9 4	Intimidation/ Blackmail	40 33	23 21
Arson	11	8	Hijacking	17 12 13	12 15 17

the prosecution were more experienced in terms of years of practice in eleven trials, the defence in four, and the prosecution and defence were equally experienced in the remaining two jury trials. There were three cases in which senior counsel appeared for the prosecution but only junior counsel for the defence. Conversely, there were two cases where senior counsel appeared for the defence but only junior counsel for the prosecution. There were also cases in which the level of experience in terms of years since call was much lower on the defence side. In four cases junior counsel for the defence had less than seven years' experience whereas no counsel for the prosecution had less than ten years' experience. Although the judges spoken to made few complaints about the competence of counsel, there was one jury case where the judge interrupted a relatively inexperienced counsel repeatedly.

Another factor to be considered in evaluating the experience of counsel, apart from years of experience, is the regularity of their appearances, since some counsel appear more regularly than others in criminal cases. We have already seen that there was greater regularity of representation on the prosecution side than on the defence side. This was particularly marked in the Diplock cases we observed. One particular junior counsel prosecuted in almost two-thirds of the thirteen Diplock cases in which junior counsel prosecuted. There was also greater regularity of representation on the defence side in Diplock than in jury cases. One particular senior counsel appeared for the defence in almost half the Diplock cases in which senior counsel appeared for the defence. The balance of representation in terms of regular appearances therefore seemed more even in Diplock than in jury cases. Only one counsel in our sample appeared for prosecution and defence in different trials and these were both in jury cases. One judge we spoke to regretted the fact that there was now much more of a tendency than in the past for counsel to do either prosecution work or defence work but not both.

Apart from the experience of counsel, another question is whether counsel appeared in both modes of trial or only in one. We have seen that judges appeared in both modes of trial and this may serve to reduce the differences in judicial conduct between the two modes of trial more than if special judges were appointed purely to hear Diplock cases. If certain counsel specialized only in Diplock cases, then they might develop practices different from the conduct of counsel in jury trials. In fact, the majority of counsel who appeared regularly in our sample appeared in both Diplock and jury cases. Of the twenty-two counsel who appeared in more than one trial, fifteen appeared in both Diplock and jury cases.

To conclude, there were certain differences between the Diplock and jury trials we observed apart from the absence of the jury, in terms of the type of offence charged, the issues involved, and the experience of counsel, and these may on occasions have influenced judicial conduct to a greater extent than the mode of trial itself. It would, however, be wrong to attribute too much importance to these differences. Despite certain variations in jury cases, the balance of experience between counsel for the prosecution and defence appeared fairly even in Diplock and jury trials, and counsel appeared fairly regularly in both modes of trial.

The way in which judges actually conducted the trials will now be addressed, and here a distinction has to be made, as we have said, between the judge's umpireal role, which exists in both Diplock and jury trials, and the special additional fact-finding role which the judge assumes in Diplock cases.

5

The Umpireal Role of the Judge

In Chapter Three it was explained that the judge's role in the contest model of proof is an umpireal one. This is the general, albeit not universally accepted, view of the role of the judge in the criminal trial. The judge should exhibit both authority and restraint, remain aloof yet attentive, act as umpire but never as player, to borrow terms from the 'sporting theory of justice' by which the adversarial tradition is frequently characterized and at times caricatured.[1] Before we consider the extent to which judges adhered to this role in the Diplock and jury trials we observed, we need to delineate more precisely the limits of the judge's sphere of permissible intervention in the course of the adversarial criminal trial.

THE UMPIREAL ROLE IN THE CRIMINAL TRIAL

There have been surprisingly few judicial definitions of the borderlines of acceptable intervention in criminal trials. On one view, the judge's role should be kept essentially flexible in criminal trials because although the umpireal ideal should be aspired to, judges, as we shall see, have specific responsibilities in criminal trials which may require greater judicial intervention. The one judicial statement which is frequently quoted as encompassing the umpireal ideal is indeed to be found in the context of a civil and not a criminal case:[2]

The judge's part in all this is to hearken to the evidence, only himself asking questions of witnesses when it is necessary to clear up any point that has been overlooked or left obscure; to see that the advocates behave themselves seemly and keep to the rules laid down by law; to exclude irrelevancies and discourage repetition; to make sure by wise intervention that he follows the points the advocates are making and can assess their worth; and at the end to make up his mind where the truth lies.

Lord Denning's statement of the trial judge's function can be viewed as approaching the adversary ideal, stressing that, while not a passive observer,

---

[1] See Pound (1906), 404. See also Frank (1949), 91. The relationship between law and sport continues to attract academic interest: see, for example, Fraser (1993).

[2] *Jones v National Coal Board* [1957] 2 QB 55, 64.

the judge should intervene only to keep the proceedings orderly and to ensure that the rules of evidence and procedure are observed by the parties. It has been generally accepted as applying also to the criminal trial judge. Of course, the closing reference to the ultimate decision on the 'truth' is inapposite as regards the judge's role in a jury trial but adherence to the umpireal role is, if anything, more important in jury trials because of the clear risk that juries may become unduly influenced by judicial intervention. In his article (mentioned in Chapter Three) Saltzburg argued that active judicial interrogation interferes with the independence of the jury.[3] Jurors may not pay enough attention to the weight of the evidence, their views being coloured instead by the judge's approach. We shall see that many of the decisions in this area have been based squarely on the possible prejudicial effect of judicial intervention on the jury.[4]

Even in the absence of this justificatory factor, however, the judicial role is ideally seen as umpireal. We saw in Chapter Three that when a judge adopts an active role in the adversarial trial, this may put truth-finding at risk. It may be added that, apart from the effect on truth-finding, an additional risk of intervention is that it may adversely affect the parties' perception of the fairness of the trial. The English Court of Appeal recognized this recently when it referred to the dangers of intervention in the course of the examination and cross-examination of witnesses:[5]

the judge may be in danger of seeming to enter the arena in the sense that he may appear partial to one side or the other. This may arise from the hostile tone of questioning or implied criticism of counsel who is conducting the examination or cross-examination, or if the judge is impressed by a witness, perhaps suggesting excuses or explanations for a witness's conduct which is open to attack by counsel for the opposite party.

The appearance of partiality may influence the jury's decision and may also affect perceptions about the fairness of the process.

In view of this it is perhaps not surprising that little concession is made in any judicial statements to the possibility that judicial intervention might be more warranted in non-jury trials. In the Diplock context the only reported judicial statement hinting at a different approach which we have found was in a case where the defence alleged on appeal against conviction that interventions by the judge in the trial indicated bias which disabled him from forming a true view of the evidence.[6] In the course of his judgment dismissing the appeal the Lord Chief Justice of Northern Ireland commented:[7] 'In a non-jury trial it is inevitable that the judge as tribunal of fact

---

[3] Saltzburg (1978), 56.
[4] There has been very little work in this country on the influence judges wield over juries, but see Bankowski and Mungham (1976).   [5] *R v Sharp* [1993] 3 All ER 225, 235.
[6] *R v Thompson* [1977] NI 74.   [7] *Ibid.*, 82.

will seek to inform himself on the facts which look like being relevant and he will be more inclined to tidy up as he goes along in situations where, with a jury, he might be more passive.'

There are certain respects, however, in which the umpireal analogy may be a misleading characterization of the judge's role. The umpireal role is often equated with rule application,[8] and the Denning formula expresses the need to ensure that the advocates keep to the 'rules laid down by law'. However, the laws of procedure, and more particularly the law of evidence, are today considered to involve more than the mere application of rules. Traditional exposition assumes that the law of evidence is a series of rule-based exceptions to the principle of freedom of proof, under which the judge admits all evidence adduced by the parties which is logically relevant to the issues in dispute (in a criminal trial, to the charges that are disputed) unless admission is forbidden by a specific rule of evidence.[9] This exposition is based on Thayer's famous two principles:[10] '(1) That nothing is to be received which is not logically probative of some matter requiring to be proved, and (2) that everything which is thus probative should come in, unless a clear ground of policy or law excludes it.' The traditional exposition envisages limited scope for judicial discretion. It is becoming increasingly recognized, however, that the so-called exclusionary rules of evidence do not in fact provide fixed definitions of acceptable or unacceptable practices but rather lay down guidelines for decisions. The concept of relevance also involves more than a yes/no answer to the question of whether the evidence adduced makes the facts in issue more probable. Rulings on relevance instead involve a balancing exercise, weighing the probative weight of the evidence against other collateral reasons for exclusion.[11] It has long been recognized, for example, that the judge may properly exclude evidence even though it may be minimally relevant to the issues and offends no exclusionary rule where its admission would involve a waste of time, or would lead to confusion or prejudice.[12] Thus, as Zuckerman has argued, the question whether a piece of evidence should be admitted requires the judge to consider not only whether the evidence bears a logical relationship to the issues but also whether it makes sufficient contribution to what is already known to justify the time and the conseqences that its reception might involve.[13] The Royal Commission on Criminal Justice urged judges to become more interventionist in this respect by recommending that Rule 403 of the Federal Rules of Evidence be introduced into English law.[14] This rule empowers judges to exclude

---

[8] See, for example, Hart's constant references to games, umpires and scorers in his discussion of rules: Hart (1961), 9, 30–1, 34, 40, 55–8, 62, 136–41.

[9] See Twining (1990), 178–9, 188–9. [10] Thayer (1898), 530.

[11] See Hoffmann (1975), 193, 204–5. [12] Law Commission (1993), 39–40.

[13] Zuckerman (1989), 49–50. [14] Recommendation 181 of the report.

evidence 'if, although relevant, its probative value is substantially outweighed by the danger of unfair prejudice, confusion of the issues or misleading the jury or by considerations of undue delay, waste of time, or needless presentation of cumulative evidence'. In practice, as we shall see, judges already have such powers. What the Commission wanted was for them to be used more robustly and the Lord Chief Justice has supported this by urging judges 'to curb prolixity and repetition and to exclude irrelevance, discursiveness and oppression of witnesses.'[15]

The considerable discretion of the trial judge regarding the admissibility of evidence, therefore, questions the appropriateness of the term 'umpire' as a description of the judge's role, in so far as the job of umpire is viewed as an essentially rule-bound task.[16] When we turn to the specific context of the criminal trial, the term is also misleading in that it suggests that the judge is adjudicating over a private contest between two competing parties. In Chapter Three we identified a number of features of Anglo-American criminal procedure which are not oriented towards the notion of a contest. At the sentencing stage, for example, the judge performs an important policy-implementing task which cannot be seen in terms of resolving conflict. Even during the hearing there are respects in which the judicial role may be viewed as more than one of umpiring a contest between parties. The Denning formula depicts the judicial role as essentially reactive so far as 'hearkening to the evidence' is concerned. Judges may ask clarifying questions and they must follow the evidence but they do not appear to have any active truth-finding obligations. But judges actually have more active responsibilities during the course of criminal trials. Indeed some of these could be said to border on the inquisitorial. As we shall see in Chapter Seven, judges have powers to call witnesses and can play an active part in bringing proceedings to a close before the end of the trial.[17] Further, at the end of the trial they have to sum up the evidence and explain the law, commenting where they see fit on the weight of the evidence.[18] They also have duties to put before the jury any defence or defence issue which has arisen on the evidence even if this has not been specifically raised by defence counsel.[19] The duties in respect of alternative verdicts not argued for by the

---

[15] *R v Whybrow and Saunders* (1994), 144 New Law Journal 124, 129. Some observers, however, consider that judges already exercise these powers to a considerable degree: see Evans (1983), 91.

[16] It has been suggested that this is not an apt characterization of the umpire's role, at least in cricket: see Fraser (1993), ch 5. 'Like a judge, the umpire is vested not only with the interpretation or application of the Laws, but is the sole judge of fair play. Thus he exercises both common law and equitable jurisdiction' (32).

[17] For discussion of these powers, see Pattenden (1990), 102–6, 170–2.

[18] *Ibid.*, 177–212.

[19] One of the authors has described this as the 'invisible burden' on the trial judge, a term that has been approved by the Court of Appeal: see Doran (1991b); *R v Watson* [1992] Crim LR 434.

prosecution are less clear but it has been argued that just as it is the judge's duty to put defences before the jury, so it ought also to be his or her duty to leave to the jury any alternative verdict which it is open to return on the evidence in the case.[20]

These active responsibilities appear to sit uncomfortably with the judge's umpireal role, if that role is viewed merely as one of refereeing a contest. On the one hand, the judge needs to maintain an umpireal position as the trial unfolds, arbitrating on the points of evidence and procedure which arise during the trial. On the other hand, the particular importance of truth-finding in criminal trials seems to dictate that the umpireal role is on occasions set aside in favour of a more directorial stance. Another way of viewing the judge's role in the criminal trial, however, is to see it less as arbitration between private parties but rather as of arbitration between public interests. Zuckerman has argued that there are three important principles of evidence in criminal trials and that it is the responsibility of the trial judge to ensure that these are adhered to.[21] First of all, there is the need to discover the truth, which obligation assumes special significance in the criminal trial because, in Zuckerman's words, 'it represents more than a disinterested wish that verdicts concerning criminal charges should corres-pond with the truth. Rather, it represents the powerful public interest in bringing offenders to justice to protect the community from crime.'[22] As well as this, however, we have already seen that Anglo-American criminal procedure puts a high premium on protecting the individual both before and during trial. Zuckerman argues that two further principles give expression to this interest. The principle of protecting the innocent from conviction finds expression in various rules of evidence such as those requiring judges to direct juries on the high standard of proof required for a conviction (beyond reasonable doubt) and to warn juries about the dangers of relying upon certain types of witnesses and evidence, and the rules excluding evidence of an accused's criminal record and of previous discreditable conduct. Finally, there is the principle of maintaining high standards of fairness throughout the criminal process which is reflected in rules regulating the admissibility of confessions and evidence obtained unfairly. Zuckerman argues that a central feature of the law of criminal evidence is to be found in the interplay between these principles and the continual need to strike a balance between their competing demands. In one respect this balance can be seen as one of public interest over private interest, the community against the individual.[23] However, it can also be viewed as a balance between two conflicting elements of public interest, convicting

---

[20] Doran (1992).   [21] (1989), 6–8.   [22] *Ibid.*, 7.
[23] This was the way in which the Royal Commission on Criminal Procedure represented the balance in 1980. For criticism see Maher (1984); Jackson (1990b).

those guilty of crime and upholding standards of justice for the individual. In this respect the umpireal role in criminal trials involves more than arbitrating between parties; it has an important public aspect as well.

The more active truth-finding responsibilities of the judge in the criminal trial can perhaps be reconciled with an umpireal approach if a broader view is taken of the umpireal role. The umpireal role in the criminal trial may be likened to the kind of role that Ely envisaged for constitutional courts in exercising judicial review.[24] According to Ely, the role of the courts is to guarantee the integrity of the political process. This meant that the courts had to 'keep the machinery of democratic government running as it should' by ensuring that 'the channels of political participation and communication are kept open'.[25] In a similar way it may be argued that the judge's task in the criminal trial is one of guaranteeing the integrity of the criminal process by keeping the channels of participation by prosecution and defence open and by ensuring that the interests of those involved are protected by proper representation. The concern is ultimately about ensuring fair process rather than about ensuring an accurate outcome. A difficulty occurs, however, when the judge acquires the additional role of deciding the outcome of the trial, which is what happens when the jury is withdrawn, for then the judge's concern to find the truth may assume greater dominance during the trial than is otherwise the case. Judges may then be tempted to eschew the umpireal role in favour of a more inquisitorial role. Whether this actually happened in the sample of Diplock trials we observed will be investigated in Chapters Six and Seven. In this chapter we consider how judges managed their umpireal role.

'VAULTING THE BENCH': THE APPELLATE RESPONSE[26]

So far our discussion of the umpireal role has been aimed at defining the sphere of *ideal* judicial intervention in the adversary mode of proof. Another question, however, is how far judges may intervene without incurring the wrath of the Court of Appeal. In our research we came across only one Diplock case where the Court of Appeal quashed a defendant's conviction on grounds which included that of excessive intervention.[27] This case was complicated by the fact that the Crown had indicated in opening the case that it was going to rely on certain witnesses but then closed its case without calling them. Upon the defence submission of no case to answer, it appeared

---

[24] Ely (1980).   [25] *Ibid.*, 76.
[26] Parts of this section are derived from earlier pieces by the authors. See Doran (1989); Jackson and Doran (1990). The term 'vaulting the bench' is borrowed from Uviller (1975), 1067.   [27] R v *Thompson* [1977] NI 74.

that the judge had gone a long way towards accepting completely the leading Crown witnesses, and when the defendant entered the witness box he was closely questioned by the judge. The Court of Appeal emphasized that it was not denying that judges had considerable latitude in questioning an accused person, but held that the overall tenor of the particular questions asked gave the impression that the trial judge had already made up his mind about the conduct of the defendant even though the defence case had not yet been concluded and material evidence was yet to come. It appears that the judge's fault lay not in the close questioning of the accused in itself but in the fact that the questioning revealed that the judge had already made up his mind, so that the defence was effectively denied a fair reception of its case.

Although the Northern Ireland Court of Appeal did not suggest that a radically more interventionist approach was justified in non-jury cases, appellate decisions in England involving appeals from jury cases suggest that greater latitude may in practice be permitted in a non-jury context. Even in the jury context, however, the Court of Appeal has given judges considerable latitude to stray beyond the relatively restricted boundaries of the umpireal ideal. In an early case, for example, the defendant had been cross-examined by the trial judge 'with some severity'.[28] The Court of Appeal, dismissing an application for leave to appeal, disapproved of the course which the judge had taken. However, it accepted that it was proper in principle for the judge, provided defence counsel did not object, to 'put to the defendant when giving evidence the various allegations of the witnesses for the prosecution. . . . So long as they were put colourlessly, no one could object.' The Court added: 'There is no reason why the judge should not from time to time interpose such questions as seem to him fair and proper.' In a later case the defendant, in his evidence in chief, had been subjected to interruptions which were 'injudicial as regards quantity and quality' but which had not prevented the appellant from putting forward his defence.[29] There is also authority for the proposition that discourtesy, even gross discourtesy to counsel, cannot alone be sufficient to justify quashing a conviction.[30] The trial judge had made several interruptions during the cross-examination of prosecution witnesses, implying that defence counsel had wasted time in persistently asking irrelevant questions. On another occasion the Court rejected a submission that the judge had intervened excessively during the giving of evidence although it accepted that he had shown signs of impatience at one of the defence counsel's closing submissions.[31] Apparently the judge had said 'Oh God' and had sighed and

---

[28] *R* v *Cain* (1936) 25 Cr App R 204, 205.
[29] *R* v *Dowell* [1960] Crim LR 436.
[30] *R* v *Ptohopoulos* (1968) 52 Cr App R 47.
[31] *R* v *Leggett, Farmer and Hircock* (1968) 53 Cr App R 51.

groaned throughout the speech. This conduct was held not to justify interference with the verdict, because counsel had not been prevented from developing his case to the jury. It was accepted in principle that witnesses could be called to testify to aspects of the judge's conduct at the original trial which were not reproduced in the 'black and white' of the transcript, but the decision illustrates the extent to which a judge can influence the jury during a trial without sanction by the appellate courts.

There are nevertheless limits to the degree of acceptable intervention. In *R v Hamilton*[32] Lord Parker outlined three situations in which judicial intervention would justify the quashing of a conviction: first, where the jury is invited to disbelieve the evidence for the defence in such strong terms that this cannot be cured by a statement of the common formula that the facts are for the jury alone to decide; secondly, where the interventions are such that it is impossible for defence counsel to do their duty in properly presenting the defence; and thirdly, where the interventions prevent defendants from doing themselves justice and telling their story in their own way. It is noteworthy that these are all extreme illustrations of intervention, and that the bounds of apparently acceptable (if not altogether approved) intervention seem fairly wide. In addition, the nature of the appellate process is such that there are no limits on judicial interventions directed at the prosecution side, including the questioning of prosecution witnesses. There is empirical evidence to suggest that judges can intervene significantly in the questioning of rape complainants.[33]

In so far as the three categories of unacceptable intervention defined by Lord Parker are concerned, not all relevant cases fall easily into one or other of the categories, which overlap to some extent. However, each will be considered briefly in turn. Lord Parker's first category concerns interference with the jury's fact-finding function. This, of course, is not a ground which can be employed where the judge is the tribunal of fact. An early example of judicial interference with the jury's fact-finding process occurred in a case in which the trial judge had asked questions of witnesses which tended to suggest that he himself was satisfied about the defendant's guilt.[34] For instance, he had asked one witness, 'You are very glad you did not employ him [the defendant]?', which received a positive answer, thus conveying to the jury: 'You are pleased you did not engage the man who committed the crime with which the defendant is charged.' The Court of Appeal has also emphasized that where a judge has thought it fit to ask questions which suggest that a witness is not to be believed, he should 'remind the jury that the question of believing or not believing any particular witness is, like all matters of fact, a question for them and not for him'.[35] It should be noted,

---

[32] [1969] Crim LR 486. See also *R v Hulusi and Purvis* (1974) 58 Cr App R 378, 382.
[33] Adler (1982), 673–4.   [34] *R v Rabbitt* (1931) 23 Cr App R 112.
[35] *R v Gilson and Cohen* (1944) 29 Cr App R 174.

however, that this common formula may not always have a curative effect, as it may merely serve to draw attention to the shortcomings in a witness's evidence, at least in the perception of the jury.

This observation is equally valid when applied to the second type of forbidden intrusion. When a judge's conduct is such as to hinder the effective presentation of a case by counsel, the prejudicial effect created may irretrievably damage the fairness of the proceedings. One example concerned a judge whom Lord Denning described as 'the judge who talked too much',[36] and who repeatedly interrupted counsel for the defence both during the presentation of evidence and particularly during his closing speech, apparently convinced that counsel was seeking to raise an unmeritorious defence.[37] Again, though, it is clear that the judicial interruptions must be extreme before a conviction will be overturned. In a more recent case the Court of Appeal said that it was wiser for judges not to interrupt counsel during the conduct of a cross-examination because intervention at a crucial point of cross-examination may have an adverse effect on the trial.[38] However, it added that judges should not be criticized for occasional transgressions. Only when the nature and frequency of the interruptions so hampered counsel in properly conducting the cross-examination could the judge's conduct amount to a material irregularity in the course of the trial.

As for the third category, the Court of Appeal has overturned convictions when the trial judge interrupted so much during the evidence in chief of the defendants that they were prevented from telling their story in their own way.[39] But judges are not discouraged from questioning defendants generally. As the House of Lords has said, the immunity against judicial interrogation is no longer as complete as it was, for the abolition in 1898 of the rule that defendants were not competent witnesses at their trial opened up the possibility that if they did give evidence they would expose themselves to questioning by counsel for the prosecution and in appropriate circumstances by the judge as well.[40] In the recent case of *R v Whybrow and Saunders*[41] the Court of Appeal appeared to lay down clearer guidelines on the legitimate boundaries governing judicial questioning of defendants. The Lord Chief Justice stressed that, of course, judges could intervene to clarify ambiguous answers and to have answers repeated for the purpose of enabling them to make proper notes. But 'it is no part of a judge's duty during examination in chief to cross-examine the defendant, either to understand to what extent he is in agreement with the last witness or to

---

[36] Denning (1980), 58–62.   [37] *R v Clewer* (1953) 37 Cr App R 37.

[38] *R v Sharp* [1993] 3 All ER 225.

[39] See, for example, *R v Hulusi and Purvis* (1974) 58 Cr App R 378.

[40] *Smith v Director of Serious Fraud Office* [1992] 3 All ER 456, 464–5.

[41] (1994) 144 New Law J 124.

make certain that he does mean to say what he has said'.[42] In this case the trial judge had gone far beyond these transgressions. The judge had interrupted the flow of the defendants' narrative during their evidence in chief not simply to clarify what they were saying but to pour scorn upon it. The effect of this, in the Court's view, was that they and their counsel were prevented from presenting their case as they had wished. Later each defendant had been challenged in cross-examination not only by counsel but also, with greater hostility, by the judge who had conveyed by his interventions his disbelief of their story. The Court of Appeal concluded that the defendants were thereby deprived of their right to a fair trial.

All these pronouncements indicate that it is the effect of the interventions, on the presentation of the defence case and on the jury, rather than their effect on the adversarial ideal, that determines whether convictions will be upheld on appeal. It is true that in certain cases counsel have relied on a theoretical line of attack based on the idea that intervention by the judge may render the form of the trial alien to the tenets of the adversary tradition. The Court of Appeal has on occasions accepted the propriety of such submissions and urged conformity with the adversarial ideal. In a significant but unreported case, for example, Cumming-Bruce LJ reiterated the umpireal role of the judge as follows:[43] 'The judge is not an advocate. Under the English and Welsh system of criminal trials he is much more like the umpire at a cricket match. He is certainly not the bowler, whose business is to get the batsman out.' Ultimately, however, the defendant's appeal succeeded because 'the appellant did not have the chance that the adversarial system is designed to afford him of developing his evidence under the lead and guidance of defending counsel.'

In a later case, counsel contended that the effect of the interventions was to substitute an inquisitorial process in the continental style.[44] The Court, however, concluded that the development of the applicants' case had not been deflected from its true course and therefore refused leave to appeal. Purchas LJ summarized the authorities as follows:[45]

(1) Whilst a large number of interruptions must put this court on notice of the possibility of a denial of justice, mere statistics are not of themselves decisive;

(2) The critical aspect of the investigation is the quality of the interventions as they relate to the attitude of the judge as might be observed by the jury and the effect that the interventions have either upon the orderly, proper and lucid deployment of the case for the defendant by his advocate or upon the efficacy of the attack to be made on the defendant's behalf upon vital prosecution witnesses by cross-examination administered by his advocate on his behalf;

(3) In analysing the overall effect of the interventions, quantity and quality cannot be considered in isolation, but will react the one upon the other; but the question

---

[42] (1994) 144 New Law J 24, 129.   [43] *R v Gunning*, unreported, 7 July 1980.
[44] *R v Matthews and Matthews* (1983) 78 Cr App R 23.   [45] *Ibid.*, 32.

which is posed ultimately for this court is '*Might* the case for the defendant as presented to the jury over the trial as a whole, including the adducing and testing of evidence, the submissions of counsel and the summing-up of the judge, be such that the jury's verdict might be unsafe?'

A number of observations may be made about this approach. First it is noticeable how much emphasis the Court put on the risk that a jury might reach the wrong conclusion on the basis of the interventions. This was also emphasized in the *Gunning* case where Cumming-Bruce LJ referred to the danger of putting pointed questions to an accused giving evidence in chief in front of a jury which has the effect of 'blowing the case out of the water' during the stage at which counsel ought to have an opportunity to bring the evidence of the accused to the jury in its most impressive pattern and shape. This again suggests that judges may have considerably more scope to stray beyond the boundaries of the ideal in non-jury cases where the concern about interference with the jury's fact-finding function is absent.

Secondly, the approach illustrates that the Court's ultimate concern is to ensure the safety of convictions rather than to safeguard against any sense of unfairness arising from an interventionist judge. The result is that the Court has not given a clear picture of the extent to which judicial intervention is permissible. Furthermore, its natural reluctance to overturn convictions regarded as safe has meant that it cannot be effective in enforcing standards of judicial conduct in the criminal trial. It may, as we have seen, exhort judges to adopt a particular approach, but since a conviction is only likely to be quashed where intervention was so extreme as to cast doubt on the safety of the conviction, it cannot be a particularly effective monitor of judicial conduct.

The difficulty in mounting a successful appeal on the grounds of judicial intervention is well illustrated in one of the cases in our sample which went to appeal. Defence counsel were very critical of the interventions which the trial judge had made, and invited us to examine the transcript and consider whether or not almost every intervention favoured the prosecution at the expense of the defence. However, when the case was appealed it was argued chiefly on the lack of good identification evidence, which was considered to be a stronger ground of appeal, rather than on the ground of excessive intervention. This was included in the grounds of appeal but at the hearing that issue was raised only towards the end of the defence submission and defence counsel immediately ran into difficulties. He alleged that by asking witnesses as many as seventy questions the judge had set himself upon a certain course of action which in many instances appeared favourable to the Crown and unfavourable to the defence. When pressed by the appellate judges, however, he admitted that he had not been impeded from properly presenting his case and he fell short of alleging any judicial bias. As he put it:

He descended into the arena too enthusiastically. I am slow to use the word bias but there was certainly a trend in the direction of being too favourable to the Crown and less favourable to the defence – an undesirable trait. I accept some responsibility for that. I didn't challenge him at the time. I was very reluctant to become confrontational. But I noticed it and discussed it with my junior. I didn't want to create difficulties by mentioning it. I hoped it would stop.

This argument seemed to have little effect on the judges presiding at the appeal. One of them, interestingly, raised the point that as the trial judge was acting as the tribunal of fact in the case, he was not limited to asking questions merely for clarification. The trial judge was able to take on the role of the jury in such cases and, since jurors are often asked at the end of a cross-examination whether they have any questions, by analogy there was nothing to stop judges as triers of fact from asking questions. The appeal judge added: 'Fortunately, we have been blessed with many silent juries', and he commented that he was not sure how trial judges would deal with jury foremen asking questions for half an hour. At this point another judge intervened to say that he had heard some very good jury questions over the years. This entire exchange was conducted in a rather light-hearted manner (the appeal essentially having been allowed on the issue of identification evidence), and it was clear that the judges were not treating this particular ground of appeal with great seriousness. After the appeal the defence counsel commented: 'If you want to be winning an appeal the Court of Appeal are not really one [sic] to be putting the judge down unnecessarily over something like that. So therefore I could see the case was running all right without putting the intervention of the judge foremost in the grounds of appeal.'

The approach of the appellate courts towards judicial intervention prompts one final observation: between the area of ideal intervention and those situations in which judicial intervention has justified quashing a conviction there is great scope for judicial activity which the Court of Appeal has had to sanction. The decided cases give little indication of the extent to which judges stray into this middle zone. Hence the need to look beyond the decided cases and conduct an empirical analysis of the kinds of intervention in which judges engage in practice. The extent to which judges used their powers to pursue an active fact-finding stance in the cases which we observed will be considered in the following chapters. The remainder of this chapter describes how judges performed their umpireal duties of trial management and enforcement of the rules of evidence and procedure in the sample of trials observed.

UMPIRES IN ACTION: JUDICIAL OBJECTIONS IN TRIALS

The judge's umpireal role involves arbitrating on disputes which arise between parties during the trial, ruling on applications to admit evidence, and on objections to the admission of evidence. As we have indicated, it can also involve a more active intervention to ensure that the parties address the relevant issues in the case, keep to the rules, and behave fairly towards one another. This gives judges, as we have seen, scope for considerable intervention in both modes of trial, but we might expect them to intervene in a more dominant fashion when they are themselves triers of fact. There are particular dangers in jury trials where juries are likely to be influenced by judicial behaviour. By contrast, the judge as trier of fact, in a non-jury trial, may find it hard to resist active intervention. There are various ways of investigating whether more active intervention was evident in the Diplock trials we observed. We shall look at judicial questioning and active fact-finding in later chapters. Here we focus on the extent to which judges disrupted party presentation of the evidence.

(a) Classifying judicial objections

One way of examining the extent to which judges disrupted party presentation is to compare the number of judicial objections to counsel's questioning in the Diplock and jury trials observed. We found that in fact fewer objections were made in the twenty-six Diplock trials (eighty-seven) than in the seventeen jury trials (ninety-one). This, however, is not very revealing. Although more Diplock trials were observed, a number of them were shorter in length than the jury trials, a matter to which we return in Chapter Seven.[46] This also takes no account of the force with which an objection is made. Some objections were made very strongly to counsel. By contrast, some interventions were made in a very mild manner. A tactic adopted by certain judges was to ask opposing counsel whether they had any objection to a line of questioning, perhaps because it was of a leading nature, or because a police witness was being asked to read from notes made about an interview. If counsel made no objection the questioning was allowed to continue. Although we classified this kind of interruption as an objection, the judge was in reality querying the line of questioning rather than taking outright objection to it.

Objections then vary in the force with which they are made. More significantly, perhaps, they also vary considerably in the extent to which they intrude on counsel's presentation of the evidence. Much depends here

---

[46] See Table 7.2 and accompanying text.

on the type of objection raised by the judge, and a number of different types were observed. There were many occasions when judges intervened to require counsel to clarify a line of questioning, either for the benefit of the judge or the jury. Often, however, counsel would then simply re-phrase the question and the objection intruded very little on the questioning. Other interventions which could be more intrusive were designed to ensure that witnesses were given a chance to answer the question. In one example the judge intervened on behalf of an elderly witness who seemed confused about the questions that were being asked:

Counsel: Are you sure about that?
Judge: Give her time to think, Mr X.
Counsel: I will give her plenty of time, Your Honour.
Judge: That was why I was asking because I did not think you were giving her time. Just take your time, Mrs B, and do not rush. Would you like a glass of water? Now can you answer the question, please.

Judges told us that they have a duty to interrupt questioning where a witness is obviously upset or needs time to settle. This kind of intervention was not itself particularly intrusive but repeated interventions can make a judge appear partial towards one side. One such example occurred when a judge constantly interrupted the cross-examination of a medical witness. At one stage the witness protested her long experience as a forensic medical officer examining women and children in abuse cases. Counsel replied by saying 'Yes, yes' in an impatient manner, and the judge objected: 'You are behaving in a grossly unfair manner saying, "Yes, yes". If it is an attempt to influence the jury, it is improper conduct. Please do not do it.' This particular judge told us that it was his duty to intervene to assist witnesses and to prevent words being put into their mouths. The irony here is that in his attempt to prevent the jury being influenced by counsel's view of the witness, the judge himself ran the risk of influencing the jury by indicating a view of the witness.

Judges' objections became even more intrusive when they prevented counsel from eliciting information. We have seen that judges have a duty to ensure that the parties stick to the relevant issues in a case, and on a number of occasions judges in the trials observed queried the relevance of questioning. Often this merely prevented counsel from repeating questions which had already been answered, but sometimes it would provoke argument about the relevance of the line of questioning. In one case counsel was trying to establish the exact steps taken by the police after receiving a report that a robbery had taken place and after an eye-witness had identified the accused as being involved. The police evidence was that they arrived at the accused's home shortly after the robbery and kept surveillance on it for three hours, believing that he had not returned from the robbery. After waiting in vain for his return, they entered the home and found that he was already inside. The defence case was that it would have been impossible for the accused to have committed the robbery and returned to his house before the police arrived, and that in any case the steps taken by the police after the report of the robbery meant that he would have been unable to re-enter his home unobserved by them. In cross-examination defence counsel tried to establish exactly what steps were taken by the police to investigate the accused's movements on the night in question, and whether anyone had seen him returning home. At one stage the following exchange took place:

Judge: No doubt this is all very interesting as a matter of police efficiency but I am required to consider positive evidence, Mr X.

Counsel: That is quite right, Your Honour.

Judge: I mean if there is anything concrete that you have to elicit. So far all I have had is a recitation of hearsay.

Counsel: There is more to it than that. I think I know a little more of it than Your Honour does and until all of the pieces in the jigsaw come together, Your Honour will have to rely on me in doing what I think is right. I am not simply enquiring about police efficiency, important though that may be. . . . At this stage I was about to say that if I can pursue it in this way I could deal with the matter more quickly.

Judge: At the end of the day I have to look at the evidence which so far consists of what the prosecution chooses to place before the court.

Counsel: That is right.

Judge: I have to look at what the evidence is that has been put forward. All we seem to have established so far is that the police seem not to have done certain things which does not prove anything.

Counsel: I want to find out what they did do and did not do. What they did do and did not do may emerge. I am trying to find out what happened at the material time. It may be very important in the matter that Your Honour has to decide. I think that the issue is becoming very clear because one is dealing here with a particularly narrow point of time. I am trying to find out just in fact what was going on in the area at the time and what this witness knows about it. I am not going to take up very much of the court's time and I hope that anything that I ask will not be irrelevant, Your Honour.

Counsel's reference to the judge's understanding of how 'the pieces in the jigsaw' are to be fitted together is a classic expression of one of the chief objections to intrusive judicial behaviour in an adversary framework, identified in Chapter Three. It is the parties and not the judge who are perceived as being responsible for the development of the issues, and a judge's interference comes from an incomplete understanding of the overall picture which counsel wish to construct.

Not surprisingly, counsel particularly disliked judicial interventions on grounds of relevance. One senior counsel mentioned the specific danger that when judges interrupt cross-examination by asking where counsel is going, this can prompt an experienced witness to exercise particular care in choosing words, in anticipation of what that witness believes the judge may be thinking.[47] He gave an example of a case in which forensic evidence was of significance. Firearm residues were found on the hands and clothing of a suspect arrested near the scene of a shooting. He was arrested by soldiers who on the papers did not appear to have taken part in any shootings themselves at the time. Counsel's cross-examination of one of the soldiers was directed at finding out how often they practised shooting in a normal week's duty, because if they had been shooting on a daily basis, they may have carried traces of firearms residue which could have been transferred to the accused. The judge in the case intervened because he could not see the relevance of shooting practice. As counsel put it to us: 'I'm not saying it led the witnesses to deny or tailor their evidence but it could have done and yet one felt under some compulsion to say this is relevant, and it's relevant to X, Y, and Z. The witness for the prosecution is less likely to give evidence that intrisically he feels is going to be helpful to the defence.'

At the same time, counsel admitted that they themselves often had no particular idea where cross-examination might lead. One counsel admitted that cross-examination is often just a fishing expedition and 'what you are doing is pursuing a line of cross-examination in order to try and open a chink which might then develop into something'. Despite this he considered that it was unfair for a judge to cut off questioning at an early stage merely because it did not appear to be leading anywhere:

I know it's difficult. The judge doesn't want to sit there and listen to a whole lot of irrelevant questions. He may think what line of cross-examination is he pursuing here. But the judge knows that sometimes you have to operate in that way because otherwise you're just going to put to the witness what your instructions are and ask him to confirm or deny them.

A final ground of judicial objection to a line of questioning is breach of the rules of evidence. These rules are designed to ensure fairness between the parties but there were examples in our sample of occasions when strict application of the rules of evidence appeared to frustrate counsel's presentation of the evidence. For example, witnesses are required to give evidence and not opinions. In one case involving allegations of buggery, the accused's counsel wanted to find out how the police regarded the allegations when they were interviewing the accused. The judge objected that the police officers' opinion of the allegations was not relevant, but counsel argued that their beliefs were relevant to the way in which the allegations were put to the accused who made admissions during the interview. In the robbery case

---

[47] See Evans (1983), 91.

described above the judge objected to counsel's questioning of the police officers not only on grounds of relevance but also because witnesses were being asked to recite hearsay evidence. The hearsay rule prevents witnesses from relating what other people have told them when the purpose is to establish the truth of what they were told. In the course of questioning another officer, defence counsel asked what steps were taken to seal off the accused's house once it was reported that he had been involved in the robbery. The witness replied that a police inspector was at the house when he arrived there. The judge then interrupted as follows:

Judge: Again this is hearsay evidence and I do not propose to receive it.

Counsel: Well in a way but I do not want to take issue with Your Honour.

Judge: I quite understand the importance of these matters and I am not preventing the defence from getting such information as they think is proper for the defence case. But there are strict limits in relation to hearsay evidence and in a case where matters may be of the utmost importance I would insist on the strict rules being observed so that we get the best evidence and not second-hand evidence.

Counsel: That is ultimately so at the end of the day but in making enquiries of this kind I would have no way of knowing unless I ask . . . I now know that Inspector X was one who was involved at an early stage and I am trying to find out matters of that nature, Your Honour.

Judge: I quite understand all that. Let me remind you that if you do not get the information you require from prosecuting counsel you are at liberty to mention it to the court.

In fact, as counsel mentioned in his closing submission to the judge, he experienced particular difficulties throughout the case in establishing the exact location of police vehicles during the time in question and the precise means used by the police to put a seal around the house were never made clear to the court.

(b) Judicial objections in Diplock and jury trials

There are, broadly speaking, four grounds on which judges may object to counsel's presentation of the evidence: lack of clarity, relevance, fairness, and breach of the rules of evidence or procedure. This calls for some refinement of the suggestion made above that there is likely to be more judicial objection in Diplock trials. Earlier in the chapter we categorized two important judicial concerns in criminal trials: the fairness or umpireal duty and the truth-finding duty. Although these separate concerns can be accommodated together, as a concern for fair presentation by the parties is one means of ensuring an accurate outcome, there is tension between them. This is because fairness is concerned primarily with the trial *process*, while truth-finding is concerned primarily with the trial *outcome*. We can now see how the four kinds of judicial objection address these concerns. The fairness duty is reflected in the need to ensure that counsel act considerately towards the opposing party's witnesses and adhere to the rules of evidence and procedure. The truth-finding duty is reflected in the need to ensure clarity and relevance in the questions counsel ask of witnesses.

These concerns are important in both jury and non-jury trials. One might expect, however, that the absence of the jury would affect the emphasis given to each. In jury trials, judges are not themselves the triers of fact and they may therefore be more anxious to ensure that the parties present their cases fairly and in conformity with the rules of evidence. The fairness concern may consequently be given more emphasis, as an insistence on fair presentation is the means of ensuring that the jury is in a position to arrive at an accurate outcome. Jurors themselves are unable to take any significant active role in fact-finding, although they do ask questions on occasion. Judges may, of course, ask questions on their behalf, but there is the difficulty that the judge is unlikely to know what jurors are thinking and active intervention may be considered unfair intervention on behalf of one party or the other. When judges are themselves the triers of fact, on the other hand, the truth-finding concern may attain greater prominence than the fairness concern. Although fair presentation by the parties remains important in its own right, as a means of assuring the parties that they are given a fair hearing, it is no longer the sole means of ascertaining the truth, as judges may if they choose elicit information for themselves. As a result, judges may be less inclined to enforce the rules of evidence of their own motion, but more inclined to confine parties to what are considered to be strictly relevant questions.

Before discussing how these different kinds of judicial objections were distributed in the Diplock and jury trials observed, two caveats must be made. First, a comparison of this kind is of necessity somewhat crude because of the small number of trials observed and because of the varying duration of the trials. Secondly, it is stressed that it was by no means easy to classify a particular objection as being of one kind or another. To take one example, from a robbery case concerning identification evidence, counsel was cross-examining the witnesses who claimed to have identified the accused when he lifted up his mask briefly from his face. One of the witnesses claimed to have made this identification after he had been hit and was lying on the floor:

Counsel: . . . [I]f you were going to see a person take off the mask from the position you were in looking in the direction that you say you were, you couldn't actually tell this Court that you could see into the kitchen, isn't that right?
Witness: I could see.
Judge: You're putting that forward as an irrefutable proposition . . . If you look at the map. . . . Whether one can see, of course, depends on many features

but the layout of the house as shown on the map makes it quite clear there are certain points one can see from the living room in the kitchen.

Counsel: Would Your Honour kindly let the witness answer?

Judge: No, I will not allow counsel to put to a witness a precision (*sic*) of fact . . . that is not correct. It may be one possible view depending on a combination of circumstances. If it is, you must put it accurately.

Counsel: I'm putting it to the witness, Your Honour, I think it's quite clear what I'm putting to the witness with respect . . .

Judge: You're not putting it with respect, and I'm ruling on it as a proposition of fact, something that is not 100% accurate . . . I expect counsel to be more accurate. You will frame your question accordingly.

The judge was clearly objecting here on the grounds both of clarity and of fairness. When counsel erroneously assumes in his or her question that a proposition of fact is true, then not only is the evidence being misrepresented, but words are also being put into the mouth of the witness. Nevertheless, we classified this as an objection based on lack of clarity as this seemed to be the primary motivation behind it.

Certain rules of evidence can be explained on grounds of relevance and therefore when judges invoke these rules, they are arguably also objecting on relevance grounds. An example of this is the opinion evidence rule already mentioned. Although this rule is underemphasized in conventional evidence textbooks, it was frequently invoked by judges to prevent counsel from commenting on the evidence or from encouraging witnesses to make comment on it. So in one case defence counsel asked a police sergeant, who had supervised the interview of the accused persons, if he had formed a view or given any directions as to whether or not two other people who were not arrested should have been arrested. The judge intervened: 'Whether or not he did or did not is irrelevant. It is not a proper question.' The barrister then dropped the question. Although the ground of this objection may appear to have been relevance, in fact the judge's use of the word 'proper' suggests that he was referring to the opinion evidence rule. This objection was therefore classified as an objection based on the rules of evidence rather than on relevance. In fact the rule is based not only on relevance grounds but also and perhaps more importantly on the fear that if witnesses were asked to draw inferences from the evidence they might usurp the function of the jury whose task alone is to draw inferences from the evidence. This was illustrated in another case where a police witness was describing the actions of three men who were seen walking towards a lorry pulling masks and scarves over their faces as they did so. When the men got to the lorry, the police witness described how they gestured to it to stop and how the police then moved in to arrest them. Crown counsel asked whether he had formed any opinion about the actions of the three men, and before the witness could reply the judge intervened to say 'I suppose that's really a matter for me'. In this example counsel persuaded the judge that there was a legitimate purpose in his question and the witness was permitted to go on and say that he was of the opinion that they were attempting to hijack the vehicle. Although questions of opinion and comment are frequently of limited relevance, because it is generally for the tribunal of fact to draw the necessary inferences, the objection here was made specifically on grounds of the opinion rule and that was how it was classified.

Table 5.1 shows how the different types of judicial objection were distributed between the two modes of trial. The first point to note is that, contrary to what is sometimes assumed in textbooks, the admission of evidence was not regulated entirely or even substantially by the rules of evidence. Objections based on breaches of the rules only accounted for just over a quarter of the objections (49 out of 178) made in the forty-three trials observed. Turning to the differences between the modes of trial, the argument advanced above that one would expect many more relevance objections in Diplock trials is not borne out by the numbers in the table. Nevertheless, two-thirds of the objections in Diplock trials (57 out of 87) were based on truth-finding concerns (relevance and clarity) while just over a half of the objections in jury trials were related to these concerns. Conversely, less than a quarter of the objections in Diplock trials were based on the rules of evidence and procedure whilst almost a third of the objections in jury trials were based on this ground.

Table 5.2 illustrates the extent to which judicial objections in both modes of trial were directed at the prosecution or defence. In Chapter Two the case-hardening argument was raised in the context of a comparison of guilty verdicts against defendants in Diplock and jury trials. An extension of this argument would suggest that judges might be more inclined to object to defence questioning in Diplock trials where they act as the triers of fact than in jury trials where they do not. However, this is not borne out by Table 5.2. Although there were overall almost twice as many objections against the defence as against the prosecution, there were as many objections (indeed slightly more) against the defence in jury trials as in Diplock trials. Looking

TABLE 5.1 *Distribution of the different types of judicial objection*

	Jury (17 trials)		Diplock (26 trials)	
Clarity	35%	(32)	45%	(39)
Relevance	19%	(17)	21%	(18)
Fairness	14%	(13)	11%	(10)
Rules	32%	(29)	23%	(20)
Total	100%	(91)	100%	(87)

TABLE 5.2 *Judicial objections against prosecution and defence*

	Jury				Diplock			
	Crown		Defence		Crown		Defence	
Clarity	33%	(10)	36%	(22)	47%	(14)	44%	(25)
Relevance	23%	(7)	16%	(10)	10%	(3)	26%	(15)
Fairness	13%	(4)	15%	(9)	10%	(3)	12%	(7)
Rules	30%	(9)	33%	(20)	33%	(10)	18%	(10)
Total	100%	(30)	100%	(61)	100%	(30)	100%	(57)

at the specific kind of objections, the table shows that clarity, relevance, and fairness objections were directed more against the defence in both modes of trial, although relevance objections were directed more frequently against the defence in Diplock trials than in jury trials. Objections on grounds of breach of the rules of evidence and procedure were evenly directed against prosecution and defence in Diplock trials but were more frequently directed against the defence in jury trials.

(c) Enforcing the rules of evidence and procedure

The fact that judges enforced the rules of evidence and procedure against the defence more than the prosecution is perhaps surprising in the light of the fact that, as we have seen, many of the rules of evidence are considered to protect the defence rather than the prosecution. Table 5.3 shows more precisely what kind of rules were enforced by judges in both modes of trial.

TABLE 5.3 *Rule-based objections*

	Jury (17 trials)		Diplock (26 trials)	
Leading	3%	(1)	15%	(3)
Opinion/comment	24%	(7)	30%	(6)
Hearsay	45%	(13)	20%	(4)
Character	3%	(1)	5%	(1)
Refreshing memory	7%	(2)	25%	(5)
Authentication	14%	(4)	5%	(1)
Other	3%	(1)	0%	(0)
Total	100%	(29)	100%	(20)

The table shows that judges enforced the rules of evidence in both Diplock and jury trials, although hearsay objections were more prevalent in the latter. This was confirmed by most judges who told us that they thought it was important to enforce the rules of evidence in both modes of trial. There were exceptions. One judge who said he was critical of the rules of evidence took a different view and said that he felt that the Diplock trial liberated him from having to enforce the rules. For example, he said he would never enforce the hearsay rule in Diplock cases: 'To me it stops a witness in full flow, and confuses a witness's account. There is a danger in jury cases that something damaging will be said but this is not a problem in non-jury cases.' By and large, however, most judges appeared to make efforts to enforce the rules of evidence in both modes of trial, although there were indications that certain judges were inclined to take a less strict approach to the rules in the absence of the jury. One example came from a jury case where the judge adopted a different approach towards the evidence in the trial proper from that adopted in the *voir dire*. In this case the defence were contesting the admissibility of a confession in which the accused admitted offences of buggery against a young teenage boy. During the *voir dire* counsel were allowed to ask the interviewing officers whether they believed the boy's allegations against the defendant before they began interviewing him. It emerged later in the trial that the boy had made a number of inconsistent statements in his allegations. Later when the judge admitted the confession counsel, in front of the jury, asked one of the officers whether he had been told that the defendant had raped the boy. The judge objected, the jury were sent out, and defence counsel defended his question by saying that he wanted to know whether the witness had gone into the interview believing in the truth of the boy's allegations. The judge replied: 'It seemed to me that when you asked the question, "Were you told such and such?", you were trying to get in the statement (of the complainant) which raises various questions, is it admissible, is it relevant?' Counsel accepted that the boy's statement was not admissible but suggested that he was able to ask the witness what he believed about the allegations without disclosing the source of the allegations. The judge approved of this approach but later objected again to the disclosure of the boy's allegations. At this stage he said he had permitted a different approach in the *voir dire* because he had read the complainant's statement and reference to it did not therefore matter but he added that it did occur to him that this was not strictly speaking the way to proceed.

Some judges made the point that they applied the rules of evidence evenhandedly against prosecution and defence:

There is a view that the Crown cannot put in hearsay but the defence can ask all sorts of questions of witnesses the answers to which will be hearsay. I think it has to be strictly enforced.

It's quite clear that there isn't any more generous view which one is allowed to take merely because hearsay is in favour of the defence. So whether or not hearsay is objected to, I rule it out. Of course, it's nearly always the defence who want to take advantage of hearsay. If the prosecution try, the defence nearly always objects. Occasionally one gets cases where both sides want it in, or the prosecution recognize it's fairer to the accused for something to be brought out but I'm afraid I don't permit that. Until the rules are changed, they have to be enforced, and this is the same whether there is a jury or not.

These judges clearly took the view that it was important to enforce the rules of evidence, even if their application was difficult to justify in an individual case. This view was not shared by all judges. Another judge had a reputation for bending the rules in favour of the defence in the interests of fairness. One counsel gave an example of a case where there were three or four defendants:

One of the difficulties is that it might depend where you are on the indictment when it comes to whether you're going to give evidence or not. You might say 'I don't think I'll give evidence' but if you're first on the indictment you've got to make up your mind then . . . If you're third on the indictment you can maybe decide whether or not you'll give evidence depending on whether the others give evidence, perhaps against you. But Judge X gave them a chance when they were called and then gave them another chance after somebody else had given their evidence which it seemed to me he didn't necessarily have to do. But he was obviously making sure that they got a chance if they wanted to give evidence then as result of further things said against them.

Variations between judges in the degree of formality insisted on were also noticeable. One judge, for example, apparently took a strict view of the procedure whereby witnesses (usually police officers) may refresh their memory from notes made at the time of an interview. The judge did not openly insist on formality but the formality adopted by counsel indicated that this was an approach which the judge expected. On each occasion when a police officer was about to read from his notes the following exchange occurred:

Witness: May I refer to my notes?
Counsel: Before you do so, can you tell me when these notes were made?
Witness: At the time, Your Honour.
Counsel: And who made these notes?
Witness: I did, Your Honour.
Counsel: And did you read over them and sign them?
Witness: I did.
Counsel: Then you may refer to them.
Judge: Any objection, Mr C?
Defence counsel: No objection, Your Honour.

Other judges did not insist on the same formality. This illustrates that the judge's personality will have an effect on certain aspects of counsel's presentation of the case no matter what the mode of trial. Certain judges have particular expectations as to whether all formalities should be complied with.

(d) Individual judicial approaches

The difference in judicial approach towards the rules of evidence suggests that it is necessary to consider how the judicial objections were distributed between the individual judges who were observed in our sample of trials. Clearly a greater number of interventionist judges in either mode of trial could skew the comparisons between modes of trial quite considerably. Table 5.4 illustrates the number of objections made by individual judges in the trials observed.

The most noticeable point is the considerable variation in the individual propensity to raise objections to counsel's questioning. Certain judges objected much more than others in both Diplock and jury trials. This should not cause particular surprise; other research has confirmed considerable variation in judicial style.[48] Three judges appearing in a total of seven trials

TABLE 5.4 *Number of objections made by individual judges*

| Judge | Jury | | Diplock | | Total |
	No. of trials	Objections	No. of trials	Objections	Objections
1	0	0	4	1	1
2	0	0	1	3	3
3	0	0	2	2	2
4	3	2	3	2	4
5	1	28	1	42	70
6	1	0	0	0	0
7	2	26	0	0	26
8	0	0	2	2	2
9	2	6	3	11	17
10	0	0	1	9	9
11	1	1	1	3	4
12	4	11	0	0	11
13	1	2	4	6	8
14	2	1	0	0	1
15	0	0	1	3	3
16	0	0	3	19	19

[48] See, for example, Peay (1989), 91. For a penetrating portrait of the contrasting judicial personalities and styles of English and continental judges, see Bedford (1961).

(Judges 5, 7, and 16) accounted for almost two-thirds of the total number of objections in both modes of trial. These were the very judges whom counsel told us were the most 'interventionist'. By contrast, a number of judges hardly objected at all to counsel's questioning. Counsel constantly stressed the difference in judicial style: 'There are some judges who just sit back and let the trial run and there are others at the other extreme who are intervening all the time.'

This was borne out by our own observations and by discussions with judges. One judge, for example, played an extremely dominant role throughout every aspect of the proceedings in which he was observed (both in jury and non-jury trials), enforcing complete silence in court when witnesses were being sworn, constantly interrupting to object to the way in which questions were put or evidence adduced by counsel and he clearly had a firm grasp of the evidence in the case. At the other end of the spectrum there was a judge who was by nature much less interventionist, a moderator rather than a director of the proceedings. This judge rarely intervened to insist on the rules of evidence being applied. When he did object to counsel's questions, he did so in the mildest of ways. In one case prosecution counsel asked a defendant whether he or his legal adviser had made a complaint about police conduct during interviews with the police when he had first appeared before the magistrates or when an application was made for bail in the High Court. No such complaint had been made but the judge intervened to question the relevance of this. Crown counsel made the point that bail might be sought on the basis that admissions were being contested. The judge replied that he agreed that there was an opportunity to complain about the way admissions had been obtained during bail applications but he added: 'What weight, if any, should I attach to the failure to mention that?' Counsel replied: 'No complaint was made by the accused until today.' Defence counsel then intervened to say that it was not common to challenge admissions on bail applications because if complaints were made they were often met with a frosty reception by the judge. There followed a lengthy discussion between counsel and in the event the judge allowed counsel to pursue the point 'within reason so that it does not become oppressive'.

(e) The relationship between judge and counsel

This example emphasizes again the limitation of looking merely at the number of objections without considering their impact on counsel's presentation of the evidence. Sometimes counsel could persuade a judge to withdraw an objection and this illustrates the importance of the judge's relationship with counsel. Generally speaking, judges were prepared to listen to counsel and relations seemed reasonably amicable. However, there were occasions when judges appeared particularly exasperated by counsel's conduct of the case and this may have caused the judge to intervene more than he would otherwise have done. One occasion when judges admitted that they found it difficult not to intervene was when a relatively inexperienced counsel was conducting the case. In the words of one judge: 'There's always a temptation to descend into the arena, it is a real temptation, more especially when there are less experienced barristers there. When I intervene it is mainly for the purposes of expedition, I hate questions being asked more than once, the same question, I mean.'

We saw in the last chapter that most counsel in our sample were fairly experienced but one example was cited where the judge was exasperated by a cross-examination conducted by a relatively inexperienced counsel. The case concerned a charge of assault occasioning actual bodily harm and at one point the judge asked counsel whether he was putting it to the victim that he *was* drunk and stumbled and fell back injuring himself or whether he was putting it to him that this is what *could* have happened. At another point the judge cut off counsel's questioning of a witness about an alleged discrepancy between his statement to the police and his evidence in chief. Counsel was putting it to the witness that his statement was inaccurate because in it he referred to seeing the accused with a companion whom he named when in fact at the time of the alleged assault he did not know who the accused's companion was but only found out later. The judge intervened to say that there was nothing wrong with the statement because at the time of making it he did know who the person was. When defence counsel asked to be allowed to clarify the matter with the witness the judge refused saying the evidence was perfectly clear.

The most extreme example of judicial exasperation, however, was to be found in a rape case where some tension arose between the judge and an experienced defence counsel. Counsel was particularly argumentative and often took objections to his opponent's questioning which the judge ruled as having little or no foundation. The judge in turn raised all manner of objections to defence counsel's questioning. Exchanges between counsel and the judge reached boiling point over the questioning of an experienced medical officer who had examined the complainant after the alleged rape. In a cross-examination that took 138 minutes, the judge intervened thirty-four times, objecting to the tone of counsel's questioning, to his interruption of the witness, and to his allegations of deliberate evasion on the part of the witness. At one point counsel asked the witness about her experience of examining women following consensual intercourse. She replied that she often saw women after they had experienced varying degrees of trauma. When asked the question again she replied that she had no reason to examine women on such occasions. When counsel sought to get a more direct answer to the question, the judge intervened as follows:

Judge: I would have thought she has answered that question twice. She said she didn't have experience of that because it doesn't arise very often. If you want to take her up on that.

Counsel: I asked her if she had ever examined women after consensual intercourse – what her experience is. She didn't say she had very little experience. She talks about varying degrees of traumatic experience.

Judge: I'm attempting to allow you to put . . .

Counsel: Your Honour . . .

Judge: Accept the rulings I make . . . Don't become involved in peripheral arguments. Ask questions and follow them up with questions. Dr J gave a clear answer twice. Apparently not as you wanted or expected. Don't harangue the witness about the way she answers questions.

It is clear that the relationship between the judge and counsel can have an important effect on the frequency with which a judge may intervene to interrupt counsel.

THE UMPIREAL ROLE AND THE MODE OF TRIAL

The question remains whether the mode of trial may influence a particular judge to intervene. Table 5.3 does not illustrate a tendency for individual judges to object more frequently in one mode of trial than in the other. Nor does it show any tendency for individual judges to intervene in a particular manner according to the mode of trial. One of the five judges observed in both modes of trial (Judge 5) displayed a greater tendency to object on grounds of fairness and rules of evidence and procedure in the jury trial observed than in the Diplock trial. However, the jury trial concerned was the trial in which the above example of tension between counsel and the judge developed and it cannot therefore be said to be in any sense a typical case.

Nevertheless, there is perhaps a danger of succumbing too readily to what may be described as the 'threat of the available' and of assuming from these figures that the mode of trial has no effect on judicial conduct. It may be asked, for example, whether the strained relations which developed in the above trial would have been so openly displayed in a Diplock trial. It was counsel's openly challenging conduct which seemed to provoke many of the judge's interventions. One senior counsel told us that he was inclined to be much more confrontational with a judge before a jury than in a hearing before a judge alone. As he put it:

. . . there was a judge many years ago, I remember, he was a very difficult judge to win an acquittal in front of because he was very good with juries. I mean he'd been a very skilled advocate at the Bar himself and he could handle juries beautifully, you know, 'did you have a good lunch?' and 'if you have any problems just let me know'.

He was keen to get convictions and I can understand that in a judge, if he thinks that somebody is really guilty. His sympathies are going to be with the prosecution and that's understandable. But the only way of winning with this judge was to have a row with him. When you had a row with him, he went a bit over the top and usually then the jury would be more likely to turn against him and you would get the jury on your side. And it was a tactic, it seems perhaps maybe not in keeping with the best traditions of the law but it was in fact one of the things you were there to do your best for your client and if there had to be a row there had to be a row. Juries love rows, of course. It keeps them going and I've had my share of those and it never does a bit of harm.

This illustrates the dramatic quality of a trial held in the presence of the jury, which lends itself to exaggerated conduct on the part of both counsel and the judge. As a distinguished American scholar wrote some time ago, 'the whole scheme of trial by jury is designed to produce effects tellingly'.[49] The result is that judicial objections may be more vociferously voiced in jury trials and that confrontation between judges and counsel may be more evident in these trials. Conversely, the very presence of the jury appeared to make judges wary of constant intervention precisely because of the effect this may have on the jury. Judges drew our attention to the danger of objecting on grounds of relevance in front of a jury. As two senior judges put it respectively:

A judge can give you a much harder time in a Diplock court. Judges can't really get at counsel in front of a jury because they don't want to influence the jury one way or another.

Judges are justified in being more interventionist in non-jury trials because they do not have to worry about the danger of distortion. Judges do not know how a particular intervention may influence a jury and they therefore need to be very careful about what they say. There is also the danger here that their intervention will damage the communication which counsel must establish with the jury, as it is the jury they are seeking to influence. In a non-jury trial the judge does not have to worry about this. Counsel are seeking to influence him and he is therefore entitled to ask where a particular line of questioning is going and whether it really needs to be pursued.

Some judges said that they felt compelled to let counsel run 'sympathy points', as they put it, before a jury: 'You don't want to be seen to be interrupting counsel and stopping him all the time, or else the jury may say: "This judge is not giving the defence counsel a fair go. Let them run it." Counsel get away with much more in front of a jury.' Another judge also mentioned the difficulty that if a judge did intervene on grounds of relevance in a jury case, an experienced counsel may respond by saying: 'It will soon become apparent to the jury, my Lord . . .' so that the judge may

[49] Green (1930), 398.

be put in the awkward position of having to argue with counsel in front of the jury, which 'is not a happy situation'. We have seen that at least one judge was prepared to argue and to assert his authority over counsel in the presence of the jury. This, however, was a rare example and it concerned an issue of fairness rather than an issue of relevance. Another judge said that if he was concerned about counsel asking irrelevant questions in jury trials, he would send the jury out and ask counsel where their evidence was leading. He gave the example of rape cases where he felt it was particularly important to exclude evidence of sexual history: 'If counsel gets within a foot of this, I send the jury out and ask counsel if he is making an application under Article 4.'[50] Again, however, this is more an issue of fairness and procedure than one of relevance because the procedure requires that the defence must make an application to the judge before they can cross-examine a complainant on sexual history evidence.

By contrast, judges had much greater opportunity in Diplock trials to intrude significantly on counsel's presentation of the case. One Diplock case in our sample contained a good example of the way in which a judge can curtail counsel's cross-examination of witnesses. The case concerned a robbery and the only evidence against the accused was identification evidence by a witness. The judge intervened during cross-examination of this witness to make the point that the witness's attention was more likely to have been directed at the time to the other perpetrator of the robbery, who was carrying a gun and making the threats, rather than to the accused man whom the witness was claiming to identify. Later when counsel attempted to make another point in cross-examination of the witness, the judge shuffled his papers and said 'Yes, yes' and then, 'move on', indicating that there was no need to pursue the point. In later cross-examination of another witness the judge again indicated his impatience by saying 'Yes, yes'. The case was stopped when defence counsel made a successful application that there was no case to answer at the end of the prosecution case. Counsel received a clear impression in this case that there was no point pursuing points on which the judge had already made up his mind. As it happened in this case defence counsel was not in any way disadvantaged by the restriction on his freedom to cross-examine because the judge ruled in his favour, but the danger exists in a non-jury case that a judge may make up his mind and in his impatience to move the case along may prevent counsel from raising new issues which might be pertinent. The extent to which judges did appear to take a view of the evidence during the trial will be discussed in Chapter Seven.

---

[50] Article 4 of the Sexual Offences (NI) Order 1978 is the equivalent of section 2 of the Sexual Offences (Amendment) Act 1976 in England and Wales. The Article requires the defence to seek the leave of the judge before cross-examining a complainant in a rape case on her previous sexual history.

If judges could afford to be less cautious about intervening in Diplock trials, counsel by contrast had to be more cautious in such trials about the lines of questioning they engaged in. There is no point, after all, in exasperating a judge sitting alone because that judge is the trier of fact. Thus even if a judge does not actively intervene to control questioning, counsel's freedom may be effectively curtailed by the fear of alienating the judge.

Earlier in this chapter we saw that judges are given considerable freedom to stray beyond the umpireal ideal in both jury and non-jury trials. The presence of the jury, however, appears to constrain the degree to which judges do this, at least to the extent of disrupting counsel's presentation of the evidence. This seems to be because, although judges have the *power* to disrupt presentation of the evidence, they lack the *authority* to do so because they are ultimately not responsible for truth-finding in the jury trial. So long as judges confine their interventions purely to fairness or umpireal considerations they can assert their full authority, but when they descend into the arena in order to play an active truth-finding role, their authority may at the end of the trial be undermined by the jury which delivers the final verdict. By contrast, in the non-jury context judges have both the power *and* the authority to engage in more active truth-finding. This does not mean that judges have to take such a stance. On one view, a judge's assumption of the fact-finding role can be seen as an extension of the umpireal role. As well as refereeing the contest, they now have to decide who has won. This obviously requires decision-making on the facts, but on the basis of the evidence adduced by the parties in the contest rather than on the basis of any evidence established by the judge. After all, that is the basis on which the jury decides the facts. On another view, however, when judges assume the role of trier of fact, they are in a much more effective position than the jury to adopt an active truth-finding stance throughout the trial and their responsibilities extend beyond simply judging the facts on the evidence presented. At this point the umpireal role becomes inappropriate. Whereas the judicial responsibility in a jury trial can be depicted as umpireal in the sense that the responsibility is to see that the various interests at stake are represented during the trial *process*, in the non-jury trial the responsibility arguably extends to ensuring a fair and accurate *outcome*. The judge becomes a player and not merely an umpire; a player in a different game where the issue is not which party deserves to win but whether the outcome is fair and accurate. We must next consider the extent to which judges went beyond the umpireal role and involved themselves in active questioning during the course of the Diplock trials observed.

6

Judicial Questioning

In the last chapter we examined the classic 'umpireal' role which judges are required to adopt in adversary trials, both with and without a jury. In particular we noted how judges are given considerable scope, under the guise of the umpireal ideal of holding the ring between the parties, to interfere quite intrusively with party presentation and we drew comparisons between Diplock and jury trials. In this chapter we turn away from the umpireal role of checking the excesses of counsel and look at the way in which judges more positively affect the fact-finding process during the trial. As already stated, a good way of examining this is to look at the part played by judges in questioning witnesses.

Judges, of course, do much more than question witnesses. They can compel witnesses (other than defendants) to testify by issuing witness summonses and by requiring them to answer counsel's questions.[1] In one case in our sample the judge had to issue a witness summons to call a reluctant witness to court. In the same case the judge repeated a question asked of another witness who was reluctant to answer, and then interjected: 'You have been asked this question three times, twice by counsel and once by me. I am bound to say that I think you have evaded answering it each time. I want you to be in no doubt about that. I will not ask you again.' As indicated in Chapter Four, this coercive power to require answers to questions is compatible with the umpireal role of ensuring fairness to the parties by requiring witnesses whom the parties wish to attend to come to court and give evidence. It is different when judges of their own motion call or ask to see witnesses, and we shall discuss the extent to which judges did this in the next chapter. It is also different when judges warn defendants at the end of the prosecution case of the consequences of their failure to testify or answer questions, as they were obliged to do in both jury and non-jury trials in Northern Ireland during our sample period when defendants indicated that they did not wish to give evidence.[2] The judge here is doing more than facilitating the parties to call reluctant witnesses. He or she is

---

[1] See *R v Renshaw* (1989), *Times*, 23 June 1989.
[2] Under Article 4 of the Criminal Evidence (Northern Ireland) Order 1988. As noted in Chapter Two, judges are no longer obliged to do this.

entering the arena and exhorting the defendant on behalf of the court to give evidence.[3]

Judges also issue instructions to witnesses. From the transcript of one trial we noted a judge instructing various witnesses not to discuss the case with anyone, to take their time ('It's very important to take this a little bit at a time'), to clarify directions by reference to a map, to describe a gesture they have made so that it appears in the record of the court, to 'Tell the truth', to 'Wait until you hear what is being said to you, then you'll understand the question more easily', to look through a photograph album and 'Point to the door you say you came through'. Although coercive in nature, many of these instructions were compatible with the judge's umpireal role. We have seen that in Lord Denning's statement of the umpireal ideal in *Jones v National Coal Board*,[4] he considered it part of the judge's function to 'clear up any point that has been overlooked or left obscure.' Many of the instructions judges gave witnesses were no more than requests for clarification of what the witness was saying or requests to enable a full and accurate record to be made. Many of them we classified as questions because they were made in the context of a particular question which had just been put by counsel.

Judicial questioning in Diplock and jury trials

(a) Incidence and frequency of questioning

Whether the intervention was interrogative in form or not, by far the most common kind of judicial intervention towards witnesses was of a questioning, inquiring nature. Although questions can be classified in various ways, some within the bounds of the umpireal role and some outside this boundary, as we shall discuss later, if it is the case that judges adopt a more dominant fact-finding role in the course of non-jury trials, then we would expect to see greater questioning overall in these cases than in jury cases. Table 6.1 shows the proportion of witnesses who were questioned by judges in the Diplock and jury trials we observed. There was considerable variation in the proportion of witnesses questioned in both modes of trial. Of the 43 trials there were two (5 per cent) in which there was no judicial questioning of witnesses at any time; at the opposite end of the spectrum there were five trials (12 per cent) in which every witness who gave oral evidence was questioned by the judge. However, the table does not

---

[3] According to the Lord Chief Justice, Lord Taylor, who took objection to this practice, 'a request for the judge to call on the defendant to give evidence tends to introduce an inquisitorial element into the judge's role': see the text of his Tom Sargant memorial lecture in (1994) 144 New Law J 125, 126.   [4] [1957] 2 QB 55, 64.

TABLE 6.1 *Incidence of judicial questioning, by % of witnesses questioned*

% witnesses questioned	Nil–19%		20–79%		80–100%	
Jury (17 trials)	6%	(1)	72%	(12)	22%	(4)
Diplock (26 trials)	11%	(3)	55%	(14)	34%	(9)
Total (43 trials)	10%	(4)	60%	(26)	30%	(13)

show much difference in the levels of questioning between each mode of trial. Judges questioned 80 per cent or more of the witnesses who gave oral evidence in 22 per cent of the jury trials and in 34 per cent of the Diplock trials.[5]

This measure of intervention only shows how many witnesses were asked questions by the judge in each trial. A more sensitive measure is to consider the amount of questioning in terms of length of time rather than in terms of percentage of witnesses questioned. Table 6.2 overleaf shows the frequency with which witnesses were questioned by the judge in each trial as a proportion of the total duration of oral witness evidence. Of course, either of these measures may give a false impression of a particular judge's pattern of intervention. For example, a judge may not question many witnesses in the course of a trial but may question a few key witnesses very thoroughly. That judge's interventions would give a low reading on the first measure and may give a higher reading on the second. Although this was not typical in our sample, a judge in one trial questioned a low percentage of witnesses but intervened many times with one particular witness.

As mentioned before, in two trials there was no judicial questioning. In the rest of the trials the level of intervention varied considerably. At the low extreme, there was a trial in which the judge asked one question for every 49 minutes of the trial given over to the taking of oral evidence, a ratio of 1 : 49. At the high extreme, there was a trial in which the judge asked one question for every 0.7 minutes of the trial given over to the taking of oral evidence, a ratio of 1 : 0.7. In over half (twenty-three) of all the observed trials, the level of judicial intervention was within what we have termed the higher level (that is, where the judge asked an average of at least one

[5] Although this shows that there was a greater tendency for judges to question large numbers of witnesses in Diplock trials, the difference in the level of questioning between the two modes of trial, applying the chi-squared test (Chi-squared = 0.17NS), was not statistically significant. This is a test designed to determine whether the apparent differences in the frequency of a given variable between two groups of a particular size are any greater than would be expected by chance. The value of chi-squared is the standardized measure of the difference between the two groups. Chi-squared results are given where appropriate in notes throughout this chapter. For a brief discussion of this test, see Rose (1982), 79–82. It is difficult to make claims of statistical significance from our study of a small number of trials.

TABLE 6.2 *Frequency of judicial questioning, by ratio of number of questions to duration of oral witness evidence*

Frequency	None[a]		Lower level[b]		Higher level[c]	
Jury (17 trials)	6%	(1)	47%	(8)	47%	(8)
Diplock (26 trials)	4%	(1)	38%	(10)	58%	(15)
Total (43 trials)	5%	(2)	42%	(18)	53%	(23)

[a] No judicial questioning.
[b] Trials in which there was an average of less than one judicial question for every 5 minutes of oral evidence (a ratio of lower than 1 : 5).
[c] Trials in which there was an average of at least one judicial question for every 5 minutes of oral evidence (a ratio of 1 : 5 or higher).

question in every five minutes of oral evidence, a ratio of 1 : 5 or higher). When the trials are divided into Diplock and jury, fifteen out of the twenty-six Diplock trials (58 per cent) and eight out of the seventeen jury trials (47 per cent) fell into this category, thus indicating that on this measure there was, again, little difference in the level of judicial intervention.[6]

These results are based on an examination of the level of questioning in each trial taken in isolation. When we proceeded to consider the frequency with which witnesses were judicially questioned in the total number of Diplock and jury trials, the difference was more pronounced. When this calculation was made, we found that on average in Diplock trials one judicial question was asked in every three minutes of oral evidence, while in jury trials one judicial question was asked only every 5.5 minutes. This indicates that there was almost twice as much questioning in Diplock trials as in jury trials. (This is clearly illustrated by Table 6.6 below which deals with the frequency with which different types of witness were questioned by the judge.)

(b) Questioning by individual judges

Caution must be exercised against reading too much into these figures. The higher level of judicial interventionism in Diplock trials on these measures may not have been attributable to any greater disposition on the part of judges to question more in this mode of trial. In the last chapter we saw that there were considerable differences of judicial style, with certain judges having a reputation among members of the Bar for being much more interventionist than others. Clearly, if one or two interventionist judges

[6] Chi-squared = 0.001NS.

appeared predominantly in one mode of trial, this could swing the balance heavily towards higher levels of intervention in that mode. The somewhat greater amount of intervention in Diplock trials could therefore be explained by the fact that more interventionist judges appeared in these trials.

Table 6.3 shows how the sixteen judges who were observed were distributed in both modes of trial, and the percentage of witnesses questioned by each of them in each trial. Table 6.4 shows the frequency with which individual judges asked questions in the trials over which they presided. The measure adopted again compares the number of questions asked with the total duration of oral witness evidence in the trial (as in Table 6.2 above), but here we have divided the 'lower level' of intervention into two categories to give a more detailed picture of individual judicial intervention. When these two measures of intervention are considered, a high degree of variation can be seen between different judges, but judges who were observed in more than one trial tended to conform to a pattern of intervention. Twelve of the sixteen judges were observed in more than one trial and the majority of them acted in a broadly consistent manner, in the sense that the frequency and duration of their questioning remained fairly constant from trial to trial. Judges who exhibited variations across the entire spectrum of intervention (such as Judges 4 and 14) were exceptions to the rule.

TABLE 6.3 *Incidence of questioning by individual judges, by % of witnesses questioned*

Judge	Jury				Diplock			
	0–20%	20–50%	50–80%	80–100%	0–20%	20–50%	50–80%	80–100%
1						*		***
2								*
3					*	*		
4	*	*	*		*	*		*
5				*				*
6			*					
7			**					
8							*	*
9			*	*		*	**	
10							*	
11				*			*	
12		*	**	*				
13			**					
14		*			*	**	*	
15							*	
16							*	**

(* = trial)

TABLE 6.4 *Frequency of questioning by individual judges, by ratio of number of questions to duration of oral witness evidence*

Judge	Jury			Diplock		
	None[a]	Lower level[b]	Higher level[c]	None[a]	Lower level[b]	Higher level[c]
1						* * * *
2					*	
3				*	*	
4	*	*	*		* *	*
5			*			*
6			*			
7		* *				
8					*	*
9		* *			* *	*
10						*
11			*			*
12		* *	* *			
13		*	*			
14		*		* *	*	*
15						*
16						* * *

(* = trial)

[a] No judicial questioning.

[b] The left hand column contains trials in which there was an average of less than one judicial question for every 20 minutes of oral evidence (a ratio of lower than 1 : 20). The right hand column contains trials in which there was an average of at least one judicial question for every 20 minutes of oral evidence but less than one for every 5 minutes (a ratio of 1 : 20 or higher but lower than 1 : 5).

[c] Trials in which there was an average of at least one judicial question for every 5 minutes of oral evidence (a ratio of 1 : 5 or higher).

It comes as no surprise that there were considerable variations in the levels of questioning between individual judges in the light of our discussion in the last chapter. Most judges acknowledged the dangers of becoming too interventionist: 'The one thing you don't want to become when you're appointed is a litigating judge. You are very conscious of this. It's very bad to become that.' Having said that, judges varied considerably in the degree to which they thought questioning was legitimate. We shall discuss later the different kinds of judicial questioning observed, but there were judges who took a very strict view and thought judges should keep well within the *Jones* boundary: 'You intervene to clarify sometimes because you haven't heard, or to ask them what did you say, did you say "would" or "could"? And also if they use some term which may have two meanings or which may be unclear. But you have to be careful not to get involved in the thing.' At the other extreme, one judge said that he intervened almost always at the end of examination, cross-examination, and re-examination: 'I almost always ask questions either to elaborate on something that has not been brought out adequately by one side or another or to give an indication of my own views about the veracity of a witness.' Most judges seemed to draw a line somewhere between these extremes. They were reluctant interventionists but they felt that they had a duty to take up points which had been overlooked. Non-interventionists agreed that points were sometimes overlooked but they thought this could be remedied by other means:

If something is overlooked, the judge can say to counsel, 'Would you like, do you want to ask about so and so, or do you want to pursue that matter?', putting it that way to them instead of pursuing it himself. The counsel may say, 'No, I don't', or 'Oh yes, thank you, I did want to ask about that.' It would be the better way of doing it.

There was disagreement about whether cross-examination by a judge was ever appropriate. One judge said he adopted an inquisitive approach but added that cross-examining witnesses was not appropriate. Most, however, seemed to think that on occasions it may be necessary to question a witness on a matter of credit. We shall return to different types of questioning later.

A number of counsel thought that there was a tendency for more senior High Court judges to intervene less. In fact, none of the five High Court judges observed were markedly less inclined to intervene than other judges, although we shall see later that they were much less disposed to engage in what we shall call 'inquisitorial' questioning. We observed only half of the High Court complement in our trials. Two of the three High Court judges interviewed said they were cautious about intervening, although the third stated that he was less inhibited about questioning witnesses. Another point to be borne in mind is that although High Court judges are more senior, they are not necessarily more experienced in terms of years of judging, and it was observed that recent appointees to the Bench tended to be more interventionist in practice.[7] One recently appointed judge was relatively non-interventionist throughout one trial until it came to the admission of electrostatic document analysis (ESDA) tests designed to test whether police interview notes were made contemporaneously at the time of the interview. It became apparent that the judge was not familiar with the ESDA procedures and he sought to augment his knowledge by questioning the relevant witnesses at some length.

Another relatively recent appointee seemed much more inclined to be interventionist, often approaching witnesses as a barrister might conduct a consultation with his client, exploring all possible avenues to find out what might or might not be relevant. In one trial this judge began asking questions right from the beginning of the Crown case. He went on to

[7] For discussion of the different qualities required of advocates and judges, see Pannick (1988), 51–2; Pickles (1988), 3–4.

intervene constantly during the examination of the principal Crown witness who testified that he saw three men attempting a hijacking and then later identified the accused as one of the three men by identifying the jacket he was wearing. During the course of this examination which lasted 67 minutes, the judge intervened no less than 32 times for different purposes. Sometimes the questions were purely for clarification, for example what the witness meant by describing the jacket as having a V-shaped inset at the front; others were designed to extract new information, for example whether it was raining on the afternoon of the incident, whether it was possible to see the facial features of the three men, and what kind of view he had of them. Counsel was clearly frustrated by the judge raising many of the issues which he would have raised if he had been given the opportunity. The judge seemed unable to stop himself from asking questions and on occasions even apologized for his interventions. He said to us that he had recently left the Bar after twenty years' practice and found it very difficult not to keep 'diving in'. Other practitioners who did some deputy county court judging also told us they felt it difficult not to intervene: 'I do some deputy judging from time to time and my natural inclination is to intervene if I see a point being missed. My natural inclination, probably being at the Bar is the reason for this, is to jump in whereas I do my best to say no and sit back and wait until he'll get round to it.' Although there seemed to be a tendency for judges less senior in years to be more interventionist, it would seem that after a while judges develop their own distinctive style. One judge who had been on the bench for a number of years compared his approach with that of a very senior judge in this way: 'This question involves personalities as well as judicial attitudes. For example, Judge X had the greatest experience of acting in criminal trials before he became a judge. Yet he is not an interventionist and he would very rarely question a witness. I do as a judge tend to intervene.'

Given the considerable differences in judicial style, the question remains whether judges were more inclined to intervene with questions in Diplock trials. As explained in Chapter Three, we had originally hoped to observe a number of the same judges in both modes of trial but were only able to observe five judges in both modes. There is no evidence in Tables 6.3 and 6.4 that these judges tended to be more interventionist in the Diplock mode of trial. Looking at the other judges, however, there was some evidence of consistently high intervention in Diplock trials. Certain judges whom we did not observe in jury trials were consistently high interveners in Diplock trials. Taking Judges 1 and 16, for example, Table 6.4 illustrates that in the seven trials in which they sat, they questioned witnesses on average more than once every five minutes. It is unfortunate that we did not have the opportunity to observe the same judges in jury trials in order to determine whether it was the form of trial which prompted their interventionism.

Comparisons will become more meaningful when we look at the kinds of questions asked by judges in the respective forms of trial.

Some counsel took the view that, while the degree of intervention in a particular trial was influenced by the style of the individual judge, judges were on the whole more inclined to be interventionist in Diplock trials:

Comparing a judge in the two different spheres one would find that he would be less inclined to intervene in a jury case. There's no doubt about that. I think judges all have styles. But I think that those who intervene will intervene a lot less in jury trials; those who don't intervene won't intervene anyway.

Judges are more inclined to intervene in Diplock cases because they are a jury and they're voicing a problem which they are seeking some enlightenment on.

Other counsel regarded the style of the individual judge as the crucial determining factor: 'I think the level of interventions has got much to do with the judge you have rather than the type of trial whether Diplock or jury.'

Judges also generally took the view that there were no significant differences between the modes of trial. One judge reflected the views of most who were interviewed when he said that the differences were not marked but that there were certain variations in the degree of intervention, depending on whether the case is a criminal jury trial (which represents a situation where judges would be least inclined to intervene) or whether the judge is sitting in a civil trial without a jury (where judges would be inclined to be at their most interventionist). According to him, interventions in non-jury criminal trials and jury civil trials came in the middle of this spectrum. Another judge stressed that any differences between jury and Diplock trials are not the result of any deliberate policy to intervene more in the latter:

I don't see any great difference, certainly not in principle, in the way one would intervene to question a witness in front of a jury or in a trial of one's own. We're all very conscious, certainly I am in Diplock trials, to ensure that so far as possible it is conducted in exactly the same way as it would be if there were a jury present and I think this restrains any tendency there might be to intervene more frequently.

This observation itself calls to mind a central theme of the book, that is whether the adversarial trial structure can be properly maintained in serious criminal cases in the absence of the jury. This judge clearly took the view that the absence of the jury should not *in principle* affect the judge's conduct of the trial. Having said that, however, he and most of his judicial colleagues acknowledged that *in practice* there may be a greater tendency to intervene in Diplock trials simply because they are the tribunal of fact and they have to be clear about the evidence. Judges were acutely aware of the responsibility in these trials of having to justify the verdict themselves and this made some of them aware of the need to pursue things so as to be sure about them in their own minds. As one judge put it: 'I personally would be concerned when I'm saying I'm neither sure nor I'm not sure. I would want to pursue a number of things so as to be sure.'

At the same time it was clear that certain judges took their responsibility to clarify things for the jury very seriously, although one judge said that because it was difficult to know what the jury is thinking judges are unable to intervene very effectively on their behalf. A few counsel thought that judges intervened more in jury trials because of the greater need to clarify matters for the jury: 'Occasionally you see judges ask questions to which they know the answer. They're doing this because they feel that it hasn't been adequately explained to [the jury].' We came across many examples where judges referred to the need to explain technical terms for the benefit of the jury: 'I am sure the jury can understand what is meant by tenderness, laceration and bruising but what about "oedema"?' In the case of other interventions, it was less clear whether the judge intervened for the benefit of the jury or for his own clarification, even though he might suggest the intervention was for the benefit of the jury: 'Just one or two matters which occur to me the jury might wish to know about.' One judge who was inclined to be non-interventionist said that he thought he questioned witnesses more in jury trials:

Speaking for myself, I think I would interrupt with a jury more because I'd be wondering whether a jury are understanding. I mean a judge comes with all the background there—he's read it up in the statements of evidence. But I'm always worried that counsel forget that the jury don't know all the background and therefore you have to be careful that they understand.

Another more interventionist judge made a practice in front of a jury at the end of a witness's evidence, particularly in the case of scientific or medical evidence, of asking two or three questions to summarize a witness's evidence in a succinct way. The reason why he thought this was necessary was because 'if you've had a long rather technical cross-examination, counsel won't particularly want to do that and counsel who has examined in chief isn't really allowed to under the rules because he's really only allowed to ask questions which arise out of cross-examination'.[8]

This emphasis on questioning for the purpose of clarification in jury trials raises the issue of whether there are differences in the kinds of questions asked in the respective forms of trial. Before we turn to examine this question in more detail, however, it remains to be asked whether certain kinds of witnesses were more likely to be questioned than others and whether there were differences in the timing of judicial questions.

---

[8] For the rules on re-examination, see Tapper (1990), 311.

(c) Types of witnesses questioned

Another factor which might explain the greater frequency of questioning in Diplock trials is the possibility that more evidence may require clarification in these hearings. We saw in Chapter Four that more experts gave evidence in the jury trials we observed, but it was the view of certain counsel and judges that there was more complicated forensic evidence in Diplock trials. One judge explicitly stated that judges asked more questions in Diplock trials for this reason: 'One wouldn't normally intervene any more in a Diplock case in theory, but in practice one does because there's generally much more scientific evidence. One's dealing now in explosives and firearms cases and you'd quite often perhaps see a hypothesis that appears to be relevant to you that you might ask a technical witness about.'

Table 6.5 shows the extent to which different kinds of witnesses were subjected to judicial questioning by judges in all trials and in Diplock and jury trials. Although it can be seen that expert witnesses were questioned to a greater extent in Diplock trials, there were other categories of witness who were subjected to an even higher degree of judicial examination.

Altogether 292 witnesses were questioned by judges in the forty-three trials (that is 57 per cent of the 493 witnesses who gave oral evidence). Although, in numerical terms, far more prosecution witnesses were questioned by judges, this amounted to only 56 per cent of all prosecution witnesses, as compared with 84 per cent of defence witnesses. Defendants, victim-witnesses, and defence witnesses were much more likely to be questioned than other witnesses, with defendants being the most likely to be

TABLE 6.5 *Incidence of judicial questioning, by % of witnesses questioned in trials, according to witness type*

Witness type	Percentage of witnesses questioned					
	All trials		Jury		Diplock	
All witnesses	59%	(292)	60%	(98)	57%	(194)
Prosecution	56%	(242)	56%	(74)	56%	(168)
Defence	83%	(50)	83%	(24)	84%	(26)
Defendant	89%	(25)	83%	(10)	94%	(15)
Victim	68%	(23)	82%	(11)	61%	(14)
Expert	67%	(35)	58%	(15)	77%	(20)
Other	55%	(209)	56%	(64)	55%	(145)

questioned. As for differences in the mode of trial, the figures for the incidence of judicial questioning of prosecution and defence witnesses are virtually identical under the two modes of trial. It is interesting to note, however, that defendants and expert witnesses were more likely to be questioned in Diplock trials than in jury trials while victims were more likely to be questioned in jury trials. In view of the small numbers of witnesses in the jury trials observed, it would be dangerous to draw firm conclusions from these differences between the modes of trial. There is, however, a more significant question which will be addressed later, namely whether the kinds of questions put to witnesses differed in the two forms of trial.

While defence witnesses (and defendants in particular) were more likely to be questioned by judges generally, Table 6.6 shows that the questioning of these witnesses was not likely to be any more extensive in terms of the number of questions asked as compared to the total time given over to the taking of their evidence. The ratio for defendants is higher than for any other type of witness, but only slightly so. All types of witnesses had very similar ratios which cluster round the ratio for all witnesses of 1 : 3.6 (that is, roughly one judicial question for every three and a half minutes of oral evidence). When we compare the two modes of trial, Table 6.6 shows that each type of witness (victims excepted) was inclined to be questioned for about twice as long in Diplock trials. Again, however, there was not an appreciable difference between the length of time for which prosecution and defence witnesses were questioned in either mode.

(d) Separate questioning

One remaining issue concerns the timing of judicial questioning. We have seen that judges frequently interrupted to question witnesses during

TABLE 6.6 *Frequency of judicial questioning by ratio of number of questions to duration of oral witness evidence, according to witness type*

Witness type	All trials	Jury	Diplock
All witnesses	1 : 3.6	1 : 5.5	1 : 3.1
Prosecution	1 : 3.7	1 : 5.3	1 : 3.2
Defence	1 : 3.6	1 : 6.0	1 : 2.9
Defendant	1 : 4.1	1 : 6.7	1 : 3.4
Victim	1 : 4.0	1 : 4.4	1 : 3.7
Expert	1 : 4.0	1 : 6.3	1 : 3.0

examination-in-chief and cross-examination. Another interesting point illustrated was that judges often questioned witnesses at the end of counsel's examination. In Chapter Five we noted the Court of Appeal's concern about interventions which make it impossible for counsel to present their case properly. One way of doing this is to take over counsel's questioning of a witness. Some of the judges we spoke to expressly approved of questioning after counsel's questioning was completed: 'I try to restrict my questions to the end because after all counsel if left alone may clarify the unclear word himself or the thing emerges.' One senior judge said that he often made a practice of noting down the points he thought ought to be brought out by counsel in the course of their questioning. These points were usually brought out and there was therefore no need for any intervention. Judges who did ask questions after counsel's questioning said that they always gave counsel the opportunity of re-questioning the witness on the points raised.

As Table 6.7 shows, this judicial practice of questioning witnesses was common but by no means universal: it occurred at least once in fifteen (eight of which were Diplock trials) of the forty-three trials in our sample. Given the relatively small numbers of cases involved, it is not proposed to analyse this form of judicial questioning in detail. It is, however, worth reflecting that it is a fairly regular facet of the trial process which is not given prominent attention in conventional works on the law of evidence and criminal procedure.[9] While it is generally accepted that judges have power to question witnesses, their questioning is not typically viewed as an additional 'layer' to the examination of witnesses by counsel through examination-in-chief, cross-examination, and (less frequently) re-examination.

From a theoretical viewpoint, the phenomenon of separate questioning may be thought to follow a certain logic in the context of jury trial which is absent when the trial is by judge alone. While it is easy to recognize the danger of prejudice inherent in the practice of a judge interrupting the flow of

TABLE 6.7 *Incidence of separate judicial questioning by % of witnesses questioned in this manner*

	None		0–20%		Over 20%	
Jury (17 trials)	59%	(10)	23%	(4)	18%	(3)
Diplock (26 trials)	69%	(18)	23%	(6)	8%	(2)
Total (43 trials)	65%	(28)	23%	(10)	12%	(5)

[9] In *Archbold*, for example, it is stated that 'the judge may . . . question any witness at any stage in the course of the trial' (8–247). There is, however, no recognition of the practice of separate questioning by the judge as a distinctive feature of the trial process.

counsel's examination, it is tempting to argue that the judge's questioning will not have such an intrusive effect in the eyes of the jury if it only follows counsel's questioning. Indeed, the English Court of Appeal has recently suggested that if a judge wishes to ask questions about matters which have not specifically been touched upon, it is generally advisable for him or her to wait until after examination or cross-examination.[10]

When the judge acts as the trier of fact, this risk of prejudice does not arise during the witness's examination by counsel. Indeed, in the Diplock trial one might expect a judge to intervene more readily as soon as a point arises rather than to wait until the examination of the witness by both counsel has come to an end. In the last chapter we saw that the Northern Ireland Court of Appeal recognized this when it said that it is inevitable in a non-jury trial that the judge as tribunal of fact will seek to inform himself on the points that appear relevant and that he will be more inclined to tidy up the evidence as he goes along.[11]

The practice of separate questioning did occur in a greater percentage of jury trials than Diplock trials, and when it occurred in the latter it typically involved fewer witnesses than in jury trials.[12] Moreover, there was some divergence between the two forms of trial in the time spent by judges in separate questioning, judges tending to devote more time to such questioning in jury trials. Also, some of the judges who tended to intervene frequently during witnesses' testimony never questioned them separately. Again the logic of this is self-evident, as the judge who intervenes frequently is less likely to need to clarify matters or explore points at the later stage.

The pattern of separate questioning conformed to that of judicial questioning generally in terms of the types of witness examined. Thus, defendants, defence witnesses generally, victims, and experts were all over-represented. Most categories of witness were more likely to be questioned separately in jury trials than Diplock trials, except for police witnesses and defence witnesses. Defendants in particular were more likely to be questioned separately in Diplock trials. It would be unwise to attempt to draw positive conclusions from these observations given that they are based on a practice followed in only fifteen of our trials. It is, however, worth noting that this is one method whereby judges can perform a significant fact-finding role without interfering with counsel's presentation of the case. An interesting question prompted by the practice is whether it would be preferable, in every situation where a judge sees fit to question a witness, to wait until both counsels' questioning of the witness has concluded. Much may depend here on the type of questioning deployed, and this central issue of the type of questions asked by judges of witnesses is now addressed.

---

[10] *R* v *Sharp* [1993] 3 All ER 225.   [11] *R* v *Thompson* [1977] NI 74.

[12] The difference was not, however, statistically significant according to the chi-squared test (Chi-squared = 0.13NS).

TYPES OF JUDICIAL QUESTIONING

Although examination of the degree of judicial questioning gives some indication of interventionism, a true picture of the extent to which judges adopted a dominant fact-finding role can only be obtained by examining the kinds of questions that were asked. We saw in Chapter Five that when arguments are made to the Court of Appeal about judicial interventionism, some are based simply on a comparison of the numbers of questions asked by the judge and counsel, but it is the kind of interventions and their effect that matter more. We also saw that a certain amount of questioning is compatible with the umpireal role. In his classic statement of the adversary ideal in *Jones*,[13] Lord Denning approved of questions which cleared up any point that may have been overlooked or left obscure. A distinction can therefore be drawn between questioning which keeps within the bounds of the umpireal ideal and questioning which strays beyond. The difficulty lies in locating the dividing line. A distinction has been drawn between questioning which simply clarifies testimony already developed and questioning which elicits new testimony or develops new lines of enquiry.[14] The former may involve asking a witness to repeat an answer which the judge or the jury did not hear, or asking for a fuller explanation of a witness's answer. The latter goes much further. There is a certain ambiguity in Lord Denning's formulation as to whether questioning on 'overlooked points' encompasses eliciting new information, although the words 'clear up' suggest that he was restricting questions purely to points of clarification.

When we started observing judicial questions we found that it was by no means easy to distinguish between those clarifying testimony already developed and those eliciting new testimony. Certain questions were, of course, directed to asking what the witness meant by what he or she had said. So, when witnesses used unfamiliar language judges often intervened to clarify the meaning: 'By signing bail, do you mean somebody has been told to report to the police?' 'Could I ask you what you mean by using the expression "I was afraid of them scallying over", what does "scallying over" mean? It's not a word I have heard before.' Judges were particularly anxious to reduce technical language to lay terms, sometimes for their own understanding and sometimes for the jury: 'So far as the injury to the forefinger is concerned, to reduce it to non-medical terms, what I understand you to be saying is that the top of his left finger was almost completely severed from the rest of his finger hanging on by a flap of skin?'

These questions were clearly clarificatory in nature, but judges would also

---

[13] [1957] 2 QB 55, 64.   [14] Saltzburg (1978), 54.

frequently go beyond merely asking for clarification on the meaning of what had been said and would ask the witness to explain its effect. Judges here wanted clarification of the significance of what was said in the context of the witness's evidence as a whole. There was often a problem in understanding the significance of the evidence where a witness gave inconsistent answers. Judges would frequently intervene in these situations to point out the inconsistencies to the witness, and in pointing these out would elicit new information. One of the robbery trials, for example, turned on the quality of a witness's identification. The judge intervened after lengthy examination and cross-examination to clarify how good a view the witness had got of the defendant. At one stage the witness had suggested that he had got a view lasting one or two minutes; at another 'it was all over in a flash'. The judge tried to pin the witness down and finally elicited the information that the witness had observed the defendant for thirty seconds. He then went on to obtain other information from the witness about the kind of view he was able to get and about the state of the lighting in the street at the time.

In another trial of attempted rape and actual bodily harm the judge appeared anxious from the beginning to ascertain exactly what injuries the complainant was alleging. During examination-in-chief the judge intervened on a number of occasions to require the witness to be more specific:

Witness: Then he suddenly hit me on the nose.
Judge: He hit you on the nose?
Witness: Yes.
Judge: What did he hit you with?
Witness: His hand.
Judge: An open hand or a fist?
Witness: An open hand.

Following counsel's questions the judge then questioned the witness for three or four minutes in order to establish a clearer picture of the injuries she claimed she had received. A medical witness then gave evidence of what injuries the complainant had sustained. Under examination-in-chief counsel tried to show that the doctor's findings were consistent with the blows which the complainant claimed to have received. Throughout the examination, however, the judge sought precise details about both the doctor's report and the complainant's allegations. The judge in effect cross-checked detail by detail the complainant's evidence with the doctor's findings. So, for example, the complainant alleged that she had some difficulty with her hearing after the attack. The doctor said that she had no record of this but that lack of hearing would be consistent with the injuries she had observed. It was clearly important to establish whether the medical evidence corroborated the complainant's story and the judge required that this matter be dealt with fully before cross-examination.

The difficulty here is to decide whether these interventions were clarificatory or were intended to elicit new information. In a sense they do both. They could be described as lying within the *Jones* boundary of clearing up overlooked points, and would therefore appear broadly compatible with the judge's umpireal role. However, a few judges seemed reluctant to intervene in this way, particularly in the case of Crown witnesses. In one trial the defendant pleaded guilty to common assault in respect of one victim but was contesting another assault allegedly carried out with three others, minutes earlier in the same vicinity. The victim claimed he was attacked and thrown into a hedge but, as the judge commented (when granting an application for a direction of no case to answer), there was little elaboration by the victim on how he found himself in the hedge and there was no identification of any of the assailants. The judge said that he had been minded to ask for more elaboration on this but he felt he should not intervene.

One judge said he was very cautious about intervening in Crown testimony:

You have to be very careful because I just don't know what your duties are exactly. If you have a Crown witness who's confused and making a mess of the Crown case because they're upset, emotional, whatever it may be, should you straighten them out or should you let the defence have the benefit of this? If you straighten it out, you're undoubtedly aiding the Crown case, you're taking sides, you're giving the Crown an advantage, and you're being seen to take sides.

Other judges, however, thought that interventions designed to clarify the full effect of a witness's evidence were justified in both jury and non-jury trials even if the effect was to aid one side or the other: 'In the case of forensic witnesses I might very well ask questions that would favour the Crown in the sense that the forensic witness's evidence is being developed by the questions I have asked because something I think has been overlooked.'

Questioning arising out of issues raised by counsel can be distinguished from questioning which effectively opens up totally new lines of enquiry. This latter kind of questioning is broadly similar to the kind of questioning conducted by counsel in eliciting evidence-in-chief from his or her own witness (although, as we shall see, it can be more extensive). We have classified it as 'virtual examination'. The actual form of questioning may not differ significantly from clarificatory questioning based on evidence already elicited. The crucial distinction is that the questioning is in effect more probing, as the judge is drawing out new information rather than merely going over what has been said, with the result that the judge is taken outside the umpireal role of reacting to testimony already elicited into the different realm of inquisitorial questioning.

An example is provided by the examination which the judge conducted in the hijacking case already mentioned (see page 136). A number of questions asked by the judge were purely for clarification but others were quite deliberately designed to extract new information, for example whether it had been raining on the afternoon in question, whether it was possible to see the frontal features of the three men, and what kind of view each witness had of them.

This kind of questioning may not in practice take the case much further than clarificatory questioning which incidentally elicits new information. In this example it is probable that Crown counsel would have elicited this information anyway had he been given the opportunity to do so. Virtual examination, however, can elicit new information which might not otherwise have been elicited and this can have a considerable impact on the parties. In another trial, for example, the defendants were alleged to have worn balaclava helmets while they committed a robbery. In cross-examination of a forensic witness the defence brought out the fact that when the defendants' hair was examined after the robbery no fibres were found. After cross-examination the judge asked what period of time had elapsed between the robbery and the examination, and he elicited from counsel the fact that, at least in the case of two defendants, it had been thirty-six hours. The judge then questioned the forensic witness himself: 'My impression from what you have said (and please correct me if this is not an accurate or a complete statement) is that the position is this, that looking at the balaclava which was produced, that that's a type of material, if one wore the balaclava, that would be likely to shed fibres onto the head of the wearer?' The judge then went on to question the witness hypothetically about the situations when one would expect to find fibres and how long it would take before fibres would disappear. The judge established that if a person's hair is combed immediately after wearing a balaclava, one would expect to find large numbers of fibres on the hair. The exchange continued:

Judge: But if one looks at the situation where there are no fibres found after thirty-six hours?
Witness: Yes?
Judge: Is that something which really results in a neutral situation?
Witness: Yes.
Judge: So far as evidential value is concerned?
Witness: Yes, that's correct, yes. After thirty-six hours I couldn't really come to any conclusion. It may be that the mask had been worn and just through time and natural combing all the fibres had been removed, or it may be that the mask was never worn in the first place.

The effect of this questioning was to render the significance of the absence of fibres neutral, whereas defence counsel had tried to make this significant in his cross-examination of the forensic witness. It is to be noted that this particular judicial questioning went beyond what would conventionally be termed examination-in-chief, as the judge clearly led the witness to some extent (the question: 'Is that something which really results in a neutral situation?' is an example).[15] Thus, as already stated, what we have termed 'virtual examination' includes but ranges beyond examination-in-chief.

Virtual examination usually consists of a lengthy series of questions by the judge, but this is not always the case. One counsel described a robbery case where a witness had identified the defendant as a man with grey hair sticking out of a balaclava and said that he looked about 35 years old. Defence counsel went to some lengths in cross-examination to establish that in her statement to the police she said that she had had a good look at him, that his hair was certainly grey, and that he had wrinkles under his eyes. In fact the defendant was fresh-faced and black-haired. Having established these inconsistencies counsel sat down but the judge went on to ask her just one question: whether the defendant was the man who robbed her, and she said yes. Counsel remarked: 'So the judge asked the one question counsel didn't want to ask because he knew he might get the wrong answer. As a result his good work was destroyed.'

Judges said that they had to be careful about eliciting information not adduced by the Crown in case the evidence turned out to be inadmissible and prejudicial. As one judge put it:

It is the case from time to time that one sees obvious questions not being asked, sometimes because of incompetence on the part of counsel concerned. But having said that, one doesn't do this very often, because if counsel are competent, then you may assume that there is a very good reason for not asking the question and therefore you don't because the risk is that you may open some terrible can of worms because you don't know everything they know.

A more extreme kind of judicial questioning which exceeds the umpireal remit is that which resembles cross-examination. In the context of counsel's conduct of a case, cross-examination has been described as having both a constructive and a destructive function.[16] When it is limited to seeking out positive and favourable evidence to build up a case it is constructive. When cross-examination is designed to discredit or weaken the evidence of a witness or of the case as a whole, its effect is destructive. Of course, these classifications assume cross-examination by counsel, and their application to judicial cross-examination is problematic. When counsel rise to question an opposing party's witness, they are by definition engaging in cross-examination. With the judge, the position is less clear-cut. Judges are not in the position of having to strengthen or weaken a particular case, although

---

[15] For a general discussion of the rules governing examination-in-chief, including the prohibition on leading questions, see Tapper (1990), 269–71.

[16] Stone (1988), chs 8 and 9.

any probing questioning by them may have this effect. We have therefore restricted the classification of judicial cross-examination to situations in which it is clear that judges wish to 'grill' a witness, that is to test the veracity or accuracy of the witness's evidence. Of course, as we have seen, there are other situations where judicial examination has the clear effect of assisting or weakening a party's case. Questioning in these situations may go beyond what is conventionally termed examination-in-chief, for instance when leading questions are asked (see the example involving the forensic witness at page 146 above), but as it is difficult to determine the judge's motivation for such questioning we have classified this not as cross-examination but as virtual examination.

A good example of judicial cross-examination (as we have defined it) was a case where one of the defendants, who were charged with robbery, claimed that he had been asleep in his own home at the time of the offence. The judge began by using the classic cross-examining tactic[17] of getting a witness to commit himself firmly to a particular story:

Judge: Now I just want to be sure that I understand what it is that you are saying to me in relation to this matter about going to sleep. You say you went to bed about half past nine in the evening?
Witness: Yes, that is correct, Your Honour.
Judge: And watched TV for just a few minutes?
Witness: Yes.
Judge: And then you fell asleep?
Witness: Yes.
Judge: And you did not wake up until the police came into your house, is that right?
Witness: Yes, Your Honour.
Judge: Or actually came into the bedroom?
Witness: Yes, Your Honour.
Judge: Well, which is it? Do you understand that I am asking you what is the first thing that you realized? . . . Now did you realize that the police were in the house because someone shook you and woke you or was it because you heard a noise going on downstairs?
Witness: No, the police officer was shining a torch in my eyes, Your Honour.
Judge: And that is when you woke up?
Witness: Yes, that is correct, Your Honour.

Having elicited this account from the defendant, the judge put other inconsistent evidence to him:

Judge: I see. Can you explain to me how it is if that account which you have just given is right that Mrs. P. saw you on the landing looking out of the window at the police?

---

[17] Stone (1988), 115–16.

Witness: I woke up and had to go to the toilet.

Judge: I see and why did you tell me a few minutes ago that you slept between the time that you went to bed between half past nine and the time that the policeman woke you up by shining a torch in your eyes?

Witness: Before that I went into the toilet, you see.

Judge: Thank you very much, Mr D.

In order to test whether the questioning was more probing in Diplock trials, we had to decide where to draw the line between our various categories. We have seen that umpireal questioning may be divided into three broad categories: asking the witness to repeat previous statements or repeating counsel's question, asking the witness to clarify testimony, and clarificatory questions which also elicited new information. Although this third category may have an important impact on the parties, we decided not to draw the line here as this questioning is still clarificatory in nature. Instead we distinguished between umpireal questioning which is purely clarificatory and inquisitorial questioning which takes the form of outright probing for new information, including both 'virtual examination' and 'cross-examination'.

There were nevertheless difficult decisions to be made in particular cases. The problem of distinguishing between clarificatory questions and those extracting new information has already been mentioned. It became clear that these categories could not be determined simply by looking at the form of the questions asked. Likewise, the distinction between clarificatory questions which elicited new information and questions which amounted to virtual examination was based not on question form but on the probing quality of the questioning and on whether it was based on matters raised by counsel. Similarly, the decision to classify questioning as cross-examination was not made by studying the form of the question but by considering the nature of the questioning in the overall context of the witness's examination. Cross-examination, for example, often takes the form of leading questions but many clarificatory questions also take this form. Another way of applying these categories would have been to invoke the notion of constraint put forward by Danet and Bogash (discussed in Chapter Four), but it has already been seen that judges can put questions in a very coercive manner without resorting to cross-examination, for example when they repeat a question which has been put by counsel. It became clear that the only way to make the proper classification was to examine the questioning in the overall context of the intervention and to ask whether new issues were being raised by the judge, whether the witness's evidence was being tested, or whether the judge was merely seeking clarification. Consequently we took the view that it was inappropriate to classify each individual question in isolation.

The above example of cross-examination began by the judge saying to the witness that he wished to understand what the defendant was saying to him.

TABLE 6.8 *Incidence of inquisitorial questioning by judges as a proportion of witnesses judicially questioned in any manner in trials*

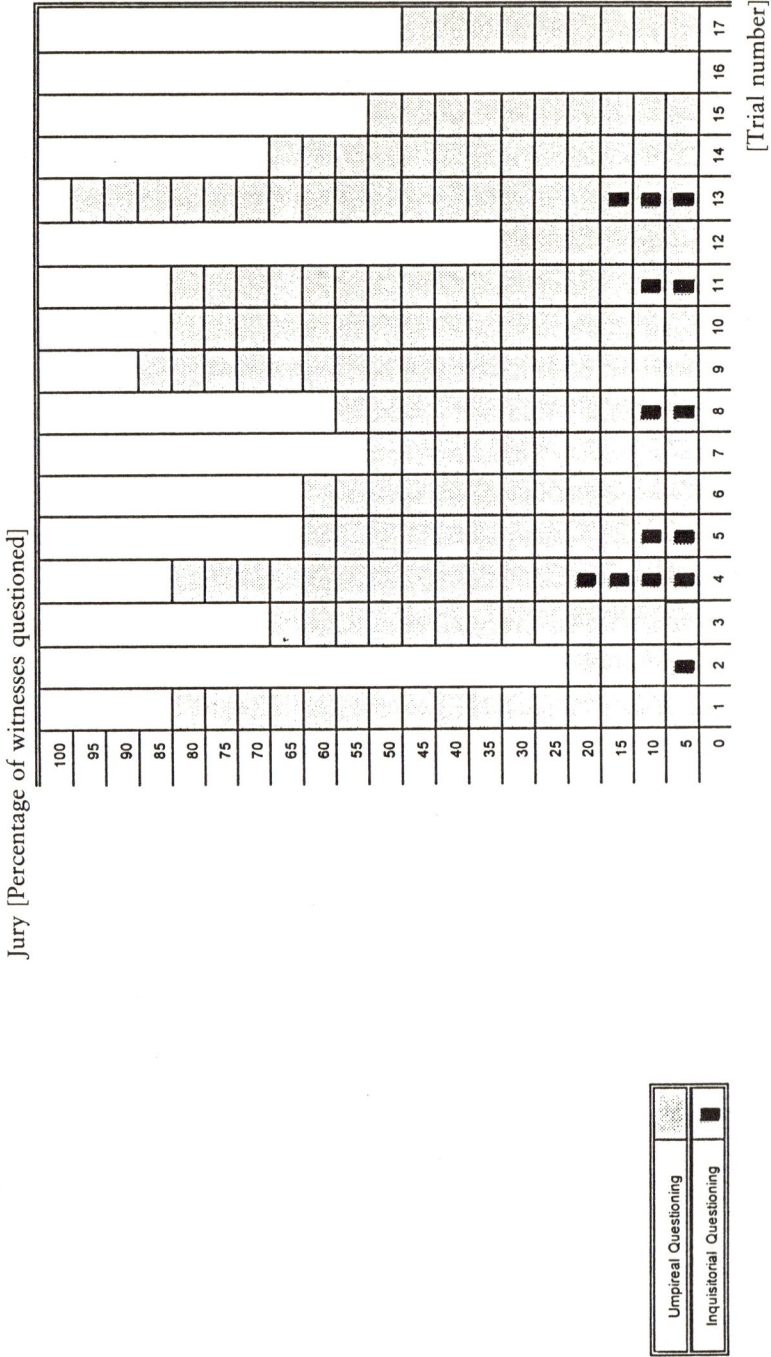

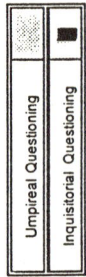

Jury [Percentage of witnesses questioned]

[Trial number]

Umpireal Questioning

Inquisitorial Questioning

Diplock [Percentage of witnesses questioned]

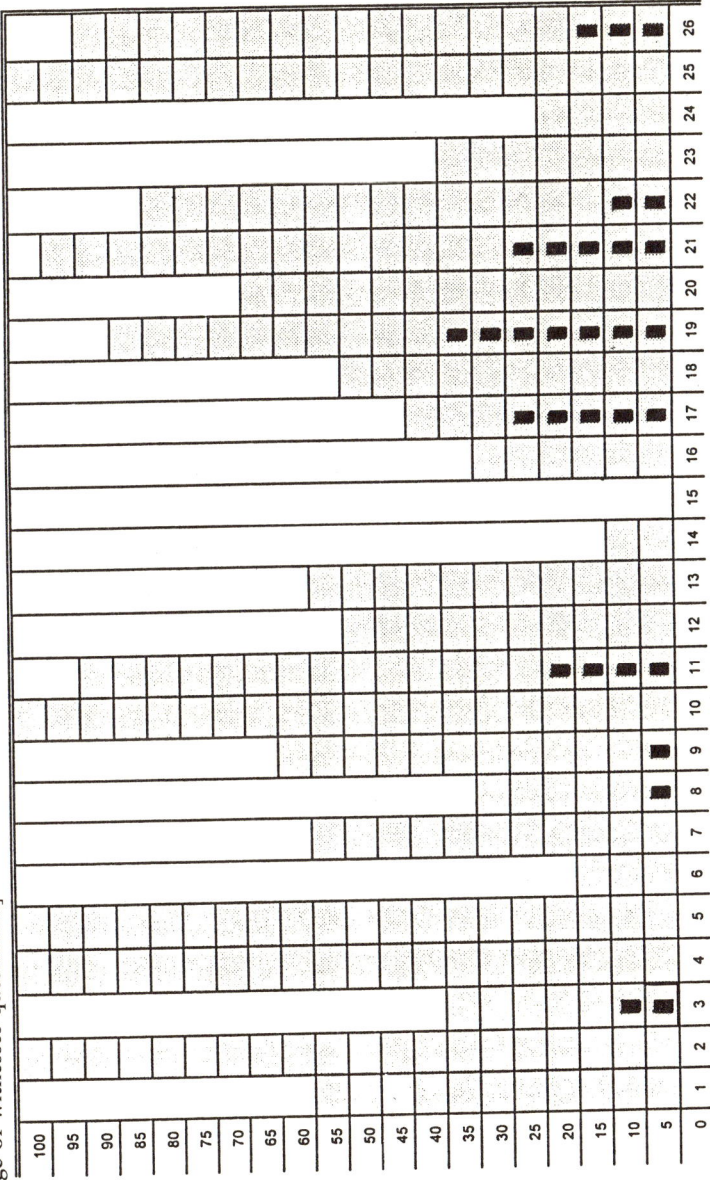

[Trial number]

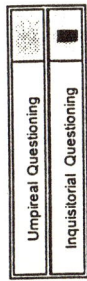

Umpireal Questioning

Inquisitorial Questioning

Much of the questioning that followed seemed merely clarificatory. Only towards the end did it become clear that the judge was in effect testing the witness's account. We could have classified each individual question into a particular category, although in the absence of a verbatim record it would have been difficult to do so. Thus the first eight questions would have been classified as clarificatory and only the final two as cross-examination. But this would have given the misleading impression that the overall effect of the intervention was of a clarificatory nature, which was clearly not the case. We decided therefore that it was more appropriate to classify each judicial intervention as a whole according to the most appropriate category and consequently we classified this intervention as ten cross-examining questions.

INQUISITORIAL QUESTIONING IN DIPLOCK AND JURY TRIALS

Since inquisitorial questioning takes judges clearly beyond the *Jones* boundary of clearing up overlooked points into the different realm of eliciting new information, one would not expect it to occur very frequently. Table 6.8 shows the percentage of witnesses judicially questioned in each mode of trial who were subjected to questioning of an inquisitorial nature. One or more witnesses were questioned in all except two trials, whereas inquisitorial questioning only occurred in approximately one third of the trials (fifteen out of forty-three). In those trials in which inquisitorial questioning occurred, an average of 64 per cent of witnesses were questioned, but only an average of 15 per cent of witnesses were questioned inquisitorially. Thus, inquisitorial questioning was much less frequent than umpireal questioning. This is also illustrated by the fact that while 292 out of the 493 witnesses who testified in all of the trials (59 per cent) were questioned in some way by the judge, only thirty-nine witnesses (7 per cent) were questioned inquisitorially (see Table 6.10 below).

Although inquisitorial questioning was relatively uncommon, one would expect that it would occur more frequently in Diplock trials where the judge assumes the role of fact-finder. However, Table 6.8 shows that in the fifteen trials in which inquisitorial questioning occurred there was little difference in the general incidence of inquisitorial questioning between the two modes of trial. In those trials in which inquisitorial questioning occurred, on average 17 per cent of witnesses were questioned inquisitorially in Diplock cases, while in jury trials the average was 12 per cent.[18]

Table 6.9 shows that nine out of the sixteen judges did engage in this kind of questioning in at least one trial. (These were two of the five High Court judges and seven of the eleven county court judges). In general, however,

---

[18] (Chi-squared = 0.008NS).

TABLE 6.9 *Incidence of inquisitorial questioning by individual judges, by % of witnesses questioned in this manner*

Judge	Jury			Diplock		
	Nil	0–10%	Over 10%	Nil	0–10%	Over 10%
1				***	*	
2				*		
3				*		*
4	***			***		
5			*			*
6	*					
7		*	*			
8				*		*
9	*	*		*	**	
10					*	
11	*			*		
12	**	**				
13	**					
14	*			****		
15				*		
16				*		**

(* = trial)

judges were not inclined to engage in inquisitorial questioning. This disinclination was displayed also by some who otherwise showed a general willingness to intervene (see, for example, the patterns of intervention shown by Judges 1, 4, 11, and 14 in Tables 6.3 and 6.4). However, five judges (Judges 3, 5, 7, 8, and 16) in one or more trials questioned more than 10 per cent of the witnesses inquisitorially. As one would expect, all those five exhibited a consistent tendency to intervene generally (see Tables 6.3 and 6.4).

It will be recalled that in both modes of trial expert witnesses and defence witnesses, especially defendants, were more likely to be judicially questioned than other kinds of witness. As between the two modes of trial, however, the incidence of judicial questioning of prosecution witnesses and defence witnesses was virtually identical, although defendants and expert witnesses were more likely to be questioned in Diplock trials and victims were more likely to be questioned in jury trials (see Table 6.5 above). Table 6.10 shows the extent to which these patterns remained the same when inquisitorial questioning was considered alone.

As with general questioning, defence witnesses, defendants, and experts

TABLE 6.10 *Incidence of inquisitorial questioning by judges, by % of witnesses questioned in this manner, according to witness type (number of witnesses in brackets)*

Witness type	% of witnesses questioned inquisitorially					
	All trials		Jury		Diplock	
All witnesses	7%	(39)	6%	(9)	9%	(30)
Prosecution	5%	(22)	4%	(5)	6%	(17)
Defence	28%	(17)	14%	(4)	42%	(13)
Defendants	29%	(8)	8%	(1)	44%	(7)
Victims	6%	(2)	9%	(1)	4%	(1)
Experts	14%	(7)	4%	(1)	23%	(6)
Other	17%	(22)	13%	(6)	19%	(16)

were more likely to be questioned inquisitorially in both modes of trial. Indeed 29 per cent of defendants were questioned in an inquisitorial fashion as compared with only 7 per cent of witnesses as a whole. There were, however, also differences between the modes of trial. Although the numbers involved were small, especially in jury trials, it can be seen that defence witnesses were more often questioned inquisitorially in Diplock trials than in jury trials.[19] This was particularly the case with defendants. Seven out of the sixteen defendants who testified in Diplock trials were questioned inquisitorially compared with one of the twelve defendants in jury trials. The difference for expert witnesses was also noticeable. Six of the twenty-six experts in Diplock trials, and only one out of the same number in jury trials, were questioned inquisitorially.

Turning to the duration of inquisitorial questioning by judges, it will be recalled that although both defence and prosecution witnesses were generally questioned for almost twice as long in Diplock trials as in jury trials, there was not much variation in the duration of questioning between prosecution and defence witnesses in either mode of trial (see Table 6.6 above). As for inquisitorial questioning, the numbers of witnesses in jury

[19] It was difficult to produce results which are statistically significant in such a small sample of trials (see note 5). Although the difference in the percentage of defence witnesses questioned inquisitorially in each mode of trial again fell short of attaining statistical significance (Chi-squared = 3.4NS), this was more marginal than in the case of the other statistical comparisons made between Diplock and jury trials in this chapter. It is therefore fair to comment that the results in Table 6.10 posited the most marked differences of all the calculations made in this chapter.

trials who were questioned in this way was too small to make meaningful comparisons between them, but there were some noticeable differences between types of witness in Diplock trials. For example, defence witnesses in Diplock trials were questioned inquisitorially for almost three times longer than prosecution witnesses. Moreover, for every one inquisitorial question asked of defendants in Diplock trials there were only seven minutes of oral evidence, whereas for every one inquisitorial question asked of victim witnesses there were forty-four minutes of oral evidence.

JUDICIAL CROSS-EXAMINATION

We have already distinguished between virtual examination (designed to extract new information from a witness) and cross-examination (designed to test the veracity or accuracy of a witness's testimony) as two distinct types of inquisitorial questioning. Cross-examination was less common than virtual examination in the trials we observed. In Table 6.10 we saw that a total of thirty-nine witnesses were questioned inquisitorially in all the trials observed. Only seventeen of these were questioned in a cross-examining manner. Although cross-examination was fairly rare, it occurred in ten trials and this was because (with the exception of one trial where five witnesses were cross-examined by the judge) no more than two witnesses were cross-examined in any one trial. Interestingly, it was conducted by no less than eight (that is half) of the judges in our sample.

Although there was little difference in the incidence of inquisitorial questioning as a whole between the two modes of trial, judicial cross-examination occurred almost exclusively in Diplock trials, in eight (30 per cent) of the Diplock trials observed. In all our jury trials there were only two witnesses who were cross-examined by the judge. We therefore decided to concentrate on the fifteen witnesses who were judicially cross-examined in Diplock trials. The small number of witnesses involved again makes it difficult to draw firm conclusions. Table 6.11 shows the extent to which various types of witness were specifically cross-examined by judges. Almost 25 per cent of defence witnesses and defendants were cross-examined as compared to just over 1 per cent of prosecution witnesses. Judicial cross-examination was therefore heavily weighted towards defence witnesses. A further point, illustrated by Table 6.12, is that these witnesses were inclined to be cross-examined by judges for considerably longer periods of time. Defence witnesses generally were cross-examined for twelve times longer than prosecution witnesses.

We also noted that cross-examination of defendants and defence witnesses, particularly alibi witnesses, was almost invariably conducted in a manner which could be construed as indicating a lack of belief in the witness. In one

TABLE 6.11 *Incidence of judicial cross-examination in Diplock trials, by %
of witnesses questioned in this manner, according to witness type (numbers
of witnesses in brackets)*

Witness type	% of witnesses cross-examined by judge: Diplock trials	
All witnesses	5%	(15)
Prosecution	1%	(4)
Defence	35%	(11)
Defendants	38%	(6)
Victims	0%	(0)
Experts	8%	(2)
Other	3%	(7)

TABLE 6.12 *Frequency of judicial cross-examination in Diplock trials, by
ratio of number of witnesses to duration of oral witness evidence*

Witness type	Frequency of cross-examination by judge: Diplock trials
All witnesses	1 : 23.2
Prosecution	1 : 88.4
Defence	1 : 7.4
Defendants	1 : 8.0
Victims	—
Experts	1 : 12.1

trial the defendant alleged that he had been induced to sign two false
confession statements which the police had made up because his mind was
heavily influenced by incidents of police brutality on the previous night.
When he was asked whether he had any complaints as regards his treatment
by the police on the morning when he made the confessions, he first said no.
The judge intervened to ask whether he was seriously suggesting that he had
been well treated by the police, given his allegations about the fictitious
confessions. The defendant replied that he had misunderstood counsel's
question, which he thought was whether the police had asked him if he had
any complaints. This was just one example of a question asked in a tone
which strongly suggested that the judge was not impressed by the witness.

This was confirmed when the judge cited this in his judgment as an example of the witness altering his evidence as it suited him.

There were fewer examples of judges questioning police officers in a disbelieving manner, although it did happen. In one case defence counsel was suggesting that a police officer's notes did not reflect all the conversations which took place during the interview. In particular it was put to the officer that when the defendant allegedly stated that he 'walked past it when it was alight', he could have been referring to a vehicle other than the bread van which was the subject of the hijacking charge against him. The officer said that he had been told that the defendant was involved in the hijacking of the bread van and he took the defendant to refer to that vehicle. The judge seemed unhappy with this answer: 'You have a number of crimes to clear up. There had been a number of hijackings and petrol bombings. There was mention of an earlier incident about a post office van. Mention of "it" could have been the post office van?' The officer simply repeated that he was involved with the bread van and the judge took the matter no further.

One judge who was not observed in any of our trials told us that there were difficulties about cross-examining police officers because they were used to giving evidence and were often confident witnesses:

If I think a policeman's not telling the truth, I may have a good go at him because I think police witnesses feel over-confident in court; they're used to giving evidence in court, they're accustomed to being believed and I think it's helpful for them to realize when they're being cross-examined [by counsel] that the judge may not be believing what they're saying. If a witness is confident in the witness box, it's very hard to undermine him and if he thinks that the tribunal is siding with him his confidence will remain intact and the cross-examiner will have a hard time.

Although we came across few examples where police officers' evidence was directly challenged by judges in this way, we did observe one trial where a judge's cross-examination of a police officer's identification evidence proved very effective. There had been an armed robbery at a garage involving the theft of a large amount of money. The car used as the get-away vehicle was stopped at a police road-block set up after the robbery. First the car slowed down, in response to a police officer who signalled the witness to stop, but before the car had come to a halt, it speeded up and went through the check-point without stopping. A chase ensued between the get-away car and a police car. After some time the get-away car stopped outside a bungalow in a rural area and three men got out and ran off. Later that night the defendant was arrested and taken to a police station. The police officer at the check-point identified the defendant as the man he had seen in the back of the car at the check-point and as one of the men he later saw running from the vehicle. The officer proved very competent under cross-examination. Defence questioning was directed at the circumstances under which he had been able to view the defendant on both occasions. Defence counsel suggested that at the road-block the witness must have been concentrating on the driver of the car and would not have been able to view the man in the back, but the witness constantly reiterated that as the car had slowed down his attention was drawn to a passenger at the back and he then shone his torch on this person.

The judge then questioned the witness from the standpoint that he seemed an honest but possibly mistaken witness, and he proved more effective than either counsel in getting informative responses on the quality of the sightings. He was concerned about both the witness's sightings, from his position at the check-point and from his position in or near the police car when it stopped near the bungalow. He first established that the witness's evidence was that he had a full frontal view of the person sitting in the back of the car, and then suggested that the officer would have had to exercise some contortion to get this view from his standing position at the check-point. He then established that the witness got only a profile view on the second sighting. The judge also pinned the witness down to admitting a five-second view at the checkpoint and only a two-second view at the bungalow. Only as a result of the judge's questioning was it clearly established that the identification was in fact only of the 'fleeting glance' variety.[20]

Although there were seven examples of judges examining expert witnesses, only two were cross-examined in a testing manner and these were both giving evidence for the defence. One was in the trial mentioned above where the defendant was charged with assisting in the hijacking of a bread van. In this case a medical practitioner and a psychologist both gave evidence of the suggestibility of the defendant, who had admitted his involvement during questioning by the police. The judge had admitted the accused's statements as evidence and the defence then disputed its weight. The judge was concerned about the selectivity with which the defendant had made his admissions, admitting only one of the offences put to him, and even then insisting that he had taken only a minor part in the offence, namely that he had acted as a look-out. When the judge asked the doctor to comment on this, the doctor accepted that it was unlikely that suggestibility alone would lead the accused to confess to one matter and not to others. Although the judge seemed sympathetic to the evidence of suggestibility and eventually acquitted on this ground, he only accepted it after testing the evidence and seeking an explanation for the selected admissions.

We have now considered the extent to which judges in our survey were prepared to engage in inquisitorial questioning, comprising both virtual examination and cross-examination. Finally, we turn briefly to the timing of

---

[20] This terminology derives from the leading decision of *R v Turnbull* [1977] QB 224.

inquisitorial questioning. It may be thought that if such questioning is to take place at all, it is best deferred until counsel's examination of a witness has finished. Although such questioning (especially cross-examination) is intrusive by its very nature, when conducted at this separate stage it is less likely to interfere with counsel's presentation of the evidence. It will be recalled that although separate questioning was a more common occurrence in jury trials than Diplock trials, defence witnesses were more likely to be separately questioned in Diplock trials than in jury trials. When we looked specifically at inquisitorial questioning we found that twenty of the thirty-seven witnesses questioned inquisitorially were separately questioned. In total, 18 per cent of all defence witnesses were separately questioned in an inquisitorial manner, whereas only 2 per cent of all prosecution witnesses were questioned in this way. Recall that the corresponding figures for inquisitorial questioning generally were 28 per cent and 5 per cent (see Table 6.10 above and accompanying text). As regards cross-examination, five of the eight judges who engaged in this confined their cross-examination to separate questioning. Generally, separate questioning was the preferred vehicle for questioning the witness in a probing manner.

Towards an inquisitorial approach to questioning?

We have seen that judges varied considerably in their approach towards judicial questioning. In our discussion of the amount of judicial questioning in Diplock and jury trials we found that there was more judicial questioning in the Diplock trials observed, both in terms of incidence (the numbers of witnesses questioned) and duration. It was, however, difficult to conclude whether this was attributable to the mode of trial, or to a tendency for there to be higher interveners in Diplock trials, or to some other factor. Although some counsel and judges gave a degree of support to the view that there is more judicial questioning in Diplock trials, there were differences of opinion on this. What seemed more significant was the type of questioning engaged in, with a number saying that questioning in Diplock trials tends to be more probing while questioning in jury trials is more clarificatory. When it came to classifying judicial questioning we found it difficult to distinguish between clarificatory questioning and more forceful inquisitorial questioning, because much clarificatory questioning could also be classified as inquisitive. We decided to focus particularly on inquisitorial questioning which clearly strayed beyond the clarificatory and was therefore obviously outside the umpireal boundary. We found that nine out of the sixteen judges observed engaged in this questioning at some time. The number of witnesses thus questioned in both modes of trial, however, was low and remained constant in each mode, although inquisitorial questioning took up more time in Diplock trials. This suggests that judges were inclined in Diplock trials to probe key witnesses in greater depth than in jury trials. The differences between the modes of trial became even more marked when we focused on cross-examination. Almost half of the witnesses who were examined inquisitorially were examined in a cross-examining manner and almost all of these were in Diplock trials.

Thus a number of judges engaged in virtual examination in both modes of trial (although the questioning was much less intense in jury trials), but in the main they only cross-examined in Diplock trials. This was explained to us by one judge as follows:

Where I think perhaps judges do question witnesses more [in Diplock trials] is where you're dealing with witnesses who are vital witnesses whose credibility is in issue. You might then ask a number of questions, many of which may just be going over what already has been done, in order to just see for oneself what it is the witnesses will say in reaction to your questions, which in all probability are simply questions of the sort that you would ask to sum up the evidence for a jury, but perhaps more pointed questions because you are the jury.

Judges were also acutely conscious of the danger of appearing partisan in jury trials. One judge suggested that more intervention is justified in non-jury trials because the danger of distortion (which, as we saw in Chapter Five, is a common concern about judicial intervention) does not arise: 'Judges do not know how a particular intervention may influence a jury.'

Another judge thought that most judges maintain a position of careful neutrality in jury trials because of the danger that they may interfere with either the Crown or the defence case and so cause trouble for themselves. In his view, that trouble did not arise in the absence of a jury and judges then felt freer to intervene. The desire to appear neutral may therefore explain the absence of judicial cross-examination before juries. Nevertheless, judges tended to question defence witnesses much more than prosecution witnesses in both modes of trial. There are several possible explanations for this. One, which is favourable to judges, is that questioning which does not amount to cross-examination often assists the side for whom the witness is called. We have seen that certain judges were reluctant to question Crown witnesses because, in the words of one judge, 'it is no part of the judge's function to intervene on behalf of the prosecution and do the prosecution's job for it.' Another possible explanation is that a number of prosecution witnesses give uncontroversial evidence (for example, mappers and photographers illustrating the scene of the crime), whereas the defence tends more frequently to call vital witnesses. A more sceptical explanation is that judges are generally less willing to accept defence evidence on its face.

In non-jury trials judges probed further and there was a greater tendency for defence (and expert) witnesses to be subjected to virtual examination, and in the case of defence witnesses also to cross-examination. There remains the question of why there was a reluctance to cross-examine prosecution witnesses in Diplock trials where judges felt less compunction to maintain a position of neutrality. One possible explanation is that, although aware that it is not their function to assist the prosecution, judges are more disposed to believe prosecution evidence. This would be consistent with the case-hardening argument which has been put forward by several observers.[21] However, there may be more subtle explanations. It may be that judges felt that the job of cross-examining prosecution witnesses was done well enough by defence counsel; it will be recalled that several judges preferred to cross-examine after rather than during counsel's questioning. Against this, however, certain witnesses (particularly police officers) were, as one judge told us, difficult to cross-examine. That judge said that he did not hesitate to confront police witnesses openly, but judges in our sample were not generally prepared to do this, although we have seen one example of very effective judicial cross-examination of a police officer in an identification case. Another explanation is that cross-examination is avoided because it is the most extreme form of judicial questioning, and the general reluctance on the part of judges to allow Diplock trials to deviate too much from the jury model has been noted above. As the trial reaches its denouement, however, the temptation to probe defence witnesses may be difficult to resist.

The desire to appear neutral in jury trials may also explain the greater incidence of separate questioning in these trials. One judge said that he thought it was more appropriate to intervene at the end of examination and cross-examination in jury trials because constant interruption of counsel created a bad impression on the jury. Separate questioning was also the favoured mode of virtual examination and cross-examination. This may be explained by the fact that judges were mostly reluctant interventionists, only intervening, they said, where they felt it was necessary. Inquisitorial questioning is only necessary where counsel have failed to examine the witness carefully enough, although one judge said that he would occasionally ask a brief question on a matter of credit where the issue was live during counsel's questioning.

Not surprisingly, a number of counsel were not happy about judicial questioning, although there was less hostility to it than to other forms of judicial intervention, and they generally conceded that it frequently unearthed new information. More surprising perhaps was the fact that they seemed to resent virtual examination of witnesses as much as cross-examination. Judges questioned Crown witnesses less than defence witnesses, as we have seen, but some defence counsel complained about

---

[21] For an examination of the case-hardening controversy, see Chapter Two.

what they saw as excessive intervention on behalf of the Crown by certain judges. They believed strongly, as did some judges, that the judicial role should be limited to clarification: 'I think good judges will not intervene, I mean to be a perfect judge, I would say that you should intervene as little as possible and only for the purpose truly of clarifying something.' Others were more philosophical about judicial questioning and reckoned that any difference of view between counsel and judges on judicial questioning was due to their different role in the trial. One counsel, who gave the example mentioned earlier of the judge asking the question counsel did not want asked, said:

The judge is searching for the truth. Your job is to get the defendant off. You don't ask the last question because you want to leave that for comment. The judge may want to know and he may want to ask that. The judge's function is different from that of defence counsel and therefore his line of questioning is going to be different. There's the old saying about how you should never ask a question in cross-examination unless you know what the answer's going to be or you're at least confident about what the answer's going to be. That doesn't apply to the judge; he'll ask questions in order to discover the answers.

Prosecution counsel were generally happier about judicial questioning than defence counsel. One comment typified their attitude:

Well, the judge I suppose has to be guarded about entering into the arena but he's not simply an umpire, you know he's not sitting there watching two opposing sides playing a game. So he's certainly entitled to ask questions. I mean the court has always and rightly had that discretion or exercise of power. It's not something that necessarily happens with any great regularity but they do from time to time and fundamentally I don't know that there's anything particularly wrong about it. It's always open to one side or other to object to it. That happens also.

We observed very little open objection by counsel to judges' questions. The only example we came across was an objection to the way in which a judge interpreted an answer given by a witness he was questioning. The stenographer was called to read out what the witness had said. One counsel said that he would be much more hesitant about objecting to judicial questioning in Diplock trials. This counsel complained about the judge's questioning in one of the observed Diplock trials but said that he had not challenged the judge because this would only have antagonized him: 'I felt I had quite a good case and I didn't want to antagonize him. If I had had a very bad case I wouldn't have minded so much but in any event I don't really want to antagonize the judiciary.' He went on to say that he would have been much more likely to object if it had been a jury trial: 'I would have intervened at an early stage and I would have said, I would have raised the point and he would have been sort of flustered and said that he wasn't and so on but it would have stopped him.'

This again illustrates what we saw in the last chapter, how the absence of the jury restrains the conduct of counsel and also increases judges' discretion to control the trial as they wish. There was considerable variation in judges' exercise of their discretion to question witnesses but some judges seemed to take a more overt fact-finding role in Diplock trials. Although conscious of their continuing umpireal role, they seemed driven by their assumption of the jury's fact-finding function to take a more probing approach than a jury is ever able to do. We next need to consider whether this inquisitorial tendency was reflected in other aspects of judicial conduct in Diplock trials and whether the absence of the jury results in a transition from contest to inquest.

7

From Contest to Inquest?

Before we consider further the respects in which Diplock procedure reflects a shift towards the inquest model of proof, we need to remind ourselves of the essential ingredients of the inquest model, as described in Chapter Three. There we identified the role of the judge as an active inquirer as a crucial indicator. Judges in the inquest model have ultimate responsibility for determining the range of the dispute, gathering the evidence relevant to it, and testing and evaluating the evidence in courts of law. Our study has focused mainly on trial practices, but it is useful at this point to consider that no matter how inquisitorially oriented the trial procedures observed may appear, they are still embedded in an essentially adversarial mould.

PRE-TRIAL PROCEEDINGS

In general, control of the pre-trial phase of criminal proceedings remains in the hands of the parties and the judiciary exercise virtually no powers of pre-trial investigation whatsoever.[1] Magistrates, of course, decide whether to commit defendants to the Crown Court for trial, but their investigative powers ceased long ago and their function at this stage is merely to determine on the basis of the prosecution evidence whether there is a prima-facie case against the defendant which the defendant should meet in the Crown Court.[2] These committal proceedings are normally merely a preliminary review on the papers of the prosecution evidence and are generally not now regarded as a serious opportunity for challenging the prosecution evidence. Indeed, following the recommendation of the Royal Commission on Criminal Justice committal proceedings have been abolished in England and Wales.[3]

When the defendant is committed to the Crown Court for trial the

---

[1] Compare the view of Goldstein, who argues that judicial powers to issue warrants and the like import an inquisitorial dimension to the judicial role: see Goldstein (1974), 1074.

[2] For descriptions of the two types of committal proceedings, see Dickson (1993), 151–3; Jackson, Kilpatrick, and Harvey (1991), 188.

[3] See section 44 of the Criminal Justice and Public Order Act 1994. See generally the report of the *Royal Commission on Criminal Justice* (1993), ch 5, paras. 20–32. For discussion of the relevance of these developments to Northern Ireland, see Doran and Jackson (1994).

defence may move to quash the indictment on a number of limited grounds such as that the Court has no jurisdiction to hear the case.[4] The defence may also ask the judge to stay the prosecution on the ground of abuse of process.[5] In Northern Ireland there is in addition a procedure whereby the judge may quash the indictment by entering a 'No Bill' before the commencement of the trial, if he is satisfied that the witness statements or depositions do not disclose a case sufficient to put the accused on trial.[6] Generally speaking, it would seem that the judge has only a very limited power to intervene in the accused's favour before trial. We shall see, however, that there is nothing to prevent judges from indicating a view to counsel at this stage.

The first formal procedure at the Crown Court is the arraignment, when the charges are put to the defendant who pleads guilty or not guilty to each. The judicial functions at the arraignment are confined to determining whether the defendant's plea is voluntary or not. If the defendant pleads guilty voluntarily, the court will accept the defendant's guilt and the sole remaining question will be sentence. Although disputes over the facts of an offence may arise at the sentencing stage,[7] the defendant's guilt cannot then be questioned.

A certain amount of controversy has centred around the question of whether, and if so to what extent, judges should be involved in what is known as 'plea bargaining'.[8] Discussions may, of course, take place between prosecution and defence in the absence of the judge, and as a result of these the prosecution may seek leave of the judge not to proceed on a particular count in the indictment. It has been suggested that these discussions are more appropriately described as 'charge bargaining'.[9] There are, however, strict rules in England governing the extent to which the trial judge may be involved in discussions with counsel about sentencing. In 1970 the Court of Appeal in England laid down guidelines (known as the *Turner* guidelines[10]) which state (in outline): first, that counsel may tell the client that a plea of guilty is likely to attract a lesser sentence; secondly, that the client must have complete freedom of choice as to whether to plead guilty; thirdly, there must be freedom of access between counsel and the

---

[4] See Valentine (1989), 8.12 and 8.15.
[5] See Pattenden (1990), 32–8; Choo (1993).
[6] Section 2(3) of the Grand Jury (Abolition) Act (NI) 1969. See *R v Adams* [1978] 5 NIJB; Valentine (1989), 7.09.
[7] See *R v Lester* (1975) 63 Cr App R 144; *R v Newton* (1982) 77 Cr App R 13. See also Wasik (1985).
[8] See Baldwin and McConville (1977). For a full discussion of plea bargaining from a number of different perspectives, see the special issue of Law and Society Review: (1979) 3 189–687.
[9] See the report of the *Royal Commission on Criminal Justice*, ch. 7, para. 56.
[10] See *R v Turner* [1970] 2 QB 321.

judge, but both prosecuting and defence counsel must be present at any discussion. The fourth and most crucial element of the guidelines, however, is that when engaging in pre-trial discussion with counsel on sentence, the judge may state that, whether or not an accused pleads guilty, the sentence will or will not take a particular form, but he must not say that he would give one sentence on conviction following a plea of guilty and a more severe one on conviction following a contested trial. The governing rationale is that the defendant's full freedom of choice must not be compromised when deciding how to plead. According to the report of the Royal Commission on Criminal Justice, *Turner* and related judgments have made judges reluctant to discuss sentence with counsel at all and, following 'overwhelming' support for changes to the rules among judges and barristers who responded to its Crown Court study, it recommended a new scheme, which it labelled the 'sentence canvass', which would allow the defendant to obtain an early indication of the maximum sentence he would receive on pleading guilty.[11]

We gained the impression in our discussions with counsel and judges that access to the judge is less formalized in Northern Ireland than in larger and more fragmented jurisdictions. The point is not that practitioners in Northern Ireland ride roughshod over the procedural rules which have been developed in this area. Rather it is an almost inevitable consequence of the intimacy of the jurisdiction that judges and counsel will be less reluctant to discuss matters that might be resolved by an exchange of views.[12]

It was clear that judges did get involved in plea discussions with counsel. Certain judges told us that they were quite prepared to give counsel indications of sentence. As one judge put it:

I think sentencing is discussed more than in England. You know what's the likely sentence and I must say I take a liberal view of it. You've got to be careful but you've got to get through the work, so long as you don't get a situation of plea bargaining where you say this is going to be five years and counsel says, 'Come on, what about four?' You can't have an auction. But I don't see why a judge can't look at the papers although at the trial it may come out for worse or for better for the defence. I mean mitigation may appear which doesn't appear in the papers. I just say on the papers, on a fight it looks like 12 years, on a plea it looks like 7 years or whatever. I'm prepared to say that.

The Northern Ireland Court of Appeal has confirmed that a less rigorous approach is taken in Northern Ireland towards the *Turner* guidelines. In *R v McNeill* the Court made a number of observations on the proper scope of pre-trial discussions between judge and counsel on the issue of sentence:[13]

---

[11] See chapter 7 of the report, paras. 50–2. For criticism see Ashworth (1993); McConville and Mirsky (1994).   [12] Doran and Jackson (1992), 37.
[13] Unreported, 11 Oct. 1993, 2.

It has always been the practice in this jurisdiction that counsel for an accused can go and see the judge in chambers if the judge is agreeable to see him. This has been a practice which in this jurisdiction has been regarded as advantageous to the administration of criminal justice because it has always been clearly understood that any discussion between counsel and the judge in chambers should be strictly confidential.

The Lord Chief Justice went on to indicate that this practice and understanding is clearly and specifically set out in the Code of Conduct for the Bar of Northern Ireland. Section 16.24 of the Code states: 'It has and always has been the practice in Northern Ireland that counsel should have ready access to the Trial Judge but no discussion between counsel and the Judge should take place unless the opposing counsel is present or having had reasonable notice has declined to be present.'

Section 16.26 of the Code states:

In criminal matters counsel for the Defence should only in very exceptional circumstances and with the permission of the Judge inform his client or give him to understand that there has been a discussion of any aspect of the case with the Trial Judge and he must never say or suggest to his client that he knows what is in the Judge's mind or purport to quote what the Judge has said in private. It is essential for counsel at all times to maintain the confidentiality of the relationship between him and the Judge.

In this particular case the judge had indicated to counsel that if the appellant pleaded guilty he would sentence him to six months' imprisonment (the charge was one of wounding with intent, which had been descheduled). It appeared that counsel for the appellant had then communicated this to the client, who had pleaded guilty and was sentenced accordingly. The Attorney-General then referred the case to the Court of Appeal under section 36 of the Criminal Justice Act 1988 on the ground that the sentence was too lenient, and the Court substituted a sentence of two years.[14] The Court, however, suggested that in the circumstances of this case the appropriate course for the appellant would be to appeal against conviction. The appellant did so and the Court quashed the conviction on the ground that the plea had not been voluntarily entered: 'because he was told of the attitude of the judge, he was put under pressure to plead guilty because of his concern that he would receive a higher sentence if he pleaded not guilty and was convicted by the jury.'[15] The Court's judgment closed with the assertion that, in the light of the observations quoted above, the final strand of the *Turner* guidelines does not apply in Northern Ireland.

It is not our present concern to analyse the appropriateness of the procedures endorsed in *McNeill*. On the one hand, they enable counsel to

---

[14] *Attorney-General's Reference (No. 1 of 1993)* [1993] 3 NIJB.
[15] *R v McNeill*, unreported, 11 Oct. 1993, 4.

get a clear picture of what the judge is thinking without the defendant being exposed to the extra pressure of hearing what the judge is recommending. On the other hand, they might be thought to encourage justice behind closed doors, in effect 'paper trials' conducted in the absence of the accused. The English Court of Appeal has expressed grave reservations about a trial judge forbidding counsel from revealing to anyone, including their client and instructing solicitor, the matters which have been discussed in a judge's private room.[16] In the Court's view, 'discussions in the judge's room, with the defendant absent, are an expedient of the last resort', as 'a real sensation of injustice may be engendered in the absent client'.[17]

Any private hearings of this kind, however, must be distinguished from an inquisitorial kind of examination. For one thing, the procedures envisage counsel making the first move to engage in discussion with the judge. The English Court of Appeal has deprecated the habit of judges sending for counsel before the start of a trial,[18] although this is not to say that it does not happen. Then any discussion which does take place is based entirely on the papers in the case, which judges receive before the hearing.[19] Judges have no formal powers of investigation. The defendant is absent and is not able to be questioned. The result is that no more than an impressionistic view can be taken of the evidence. This does not seem to prevent certain judges indicating fairly strong views about the merits of the case either in open court or privately. Recent research in England has shown cases where judges indicated that they would dispose of a case by binding the defendant over whether or not the prosecution decided to proceed.[20] This prompted the prosecution to discontinue proceedings. In our sample there was one example where the judge intimated his view in private to counsel that the prosecution case could not support a conviction. The pressure on prosecution counsel to drop the case at this point must have been very strong; however, the prosecution decided to proceed with the case which was ultimately unsuccessful.

Although pre-trial discussions may not resemble an inquisitorial form of examination, the question remains of whether such discussions or reviews of the evidence were more frequent in Diplock trials. This question was not directly addressed in our research. If the judge who is in a position to advise on sentence is also deciding the case, counsel may be tempted to tease out what the judge thinks about the case to see whether it is worth continuing or contesting. Two important constraints, however, seemed to prevent any regular practice of this kind. First, it assumes a familiarity with the case

---

[16] See *R v Agar* (1989) 90 Cr App R 318.

[17] *Ibid.*, 324–5, *per* Mustill LJ. See also *R v Harper-Taylor* (1988) New Law Journal 80–1.

[18] *R v Llewellyn* (1978) 67 Cr App R 149; *R v Cullen* (1985) 81 Cr App R 17, 19.

[19] For details of when judges (in England and Wales) receive the papers in advance of a case, see Zander and Henderson, (1993), 42–5.   [20] Block, Corbett, and Peay (1993).

which a judge may not have. It has been noted that certain judges took a stricter view of the propriety of out of court exchanges than others. Furthermore none of the judges to whom we spoke suggested that they took a different approach to reading the papers in advance in Diplock cases. At the same time, however, individual judges differed in their approach to reading the papers in Diplock and jury cases generally, some being reluctant to read them in any depth before trial and others trying to read them thoroughly. Even judges who encouraged discussions with counsel and who tried to read the papers beforehand were not necessarily conversant with their contents. As one judge put it:

I get a stack of papers this high for the week ahead. These will be the cases allocated for the whole week. I get a list saying which cases are on which days. But the difficulty is that on Monday people will say what about Friday's case, 'Is that going to be imprisonment come what may?' and you've got to have read the whole bundle in a very cursory manner and then Monday's cases more thoroughly, of course. It's quite a lot to get through and you skim through and you may miss something in them and even when it comes to Monday's cases, there's a fair lump to read and the trouble is that you don't know who's going to plead or not. It's a burden. I sometimes wish we got the papers a little sooner.

The other constraint that seemed to militate against any regular pre-trial review of the evidence was that defence counsel were aware that any approach by them to the judge was in itself an acceptance of strength in the Crown's case. We were told once counsel had approached the judge with a view to pleading it would be unusual for the case then to be contested.

This is not to say that the absence of the jury does not influence counsel's conduct of the case before trial. Comparisons were made in Chapter Two between the plea rates in jury and non-jury cases. In Diplock cases the pressure on defence counsel to advise a client to plead guilty assumes a different dimension than in jury cases, whereas the pressure on prosecution counsel to discontinue proceedings remains fairly constant. We have seen that in one case a judge expressed views about the weakness of the prosecution case and it might seem that this produces a particularly strong effect in a Diplock case where the judge has total control over the outcome. However, even in a jury case the judge has a power to direct an acquittal on an application for a direction after the prosecution has presented its case. Any extra leverage that a judge has in a Diplock case by saying, for instance, that he will acquit is not then significantly greater when he has the power to throw out the case at the end of the prosecution evidence anyway.

By contrast, the pressure on the defence to plead guilty would seem to be much greater when the judge positively indicates to the defence that there is likely to be a conviction. Defence counsel on the whole thought that they tended to plead cases more in trials without a jury. In the words of one defence counsel:

When one looks at the factors that influence pleading a major factor would be whether the case is going to be heard in Diplock rather than in jury trial. It's a major influence (a) on whether you're going to plead and (b) on the extent of your leverage and powers of persuasion in negotiations that take place prior to pleading. In other words, it's a major influence towards making the initial decision to compromise the case. One's more inclined to make the initial decision mentally in a Diplock court than you are when you have a jury trial. Secondly, when you make the decision in a Diplock case, you feel you have less leverage during plea-bargaining or plea-negotiation than you would have in a jury case, because the judge is under less pressure and the Crown are under less pressure to bring the thing home. . . . With the jury things can always go wrong and so the Crown and the judge are under a great deal more pressure and therefore you've got more leverage when you make the decision. So for two reasons you're handicapped in the Diplock system in that regard.

This is an important statement as it identifies two rather different pressures on defence counsel in Diplock cases. First of all, there is a belief that judges would be more inclined to convict if the case were contested. One counsel said that 'a jury will tend to give the defendant the benefit of the doubt where a judge wouldn't'; another that 'in a jury trial there's always a chance of an acquittal even if the defence isn't a very good one'. This brings to mind the case-hardening argument mentioned in Chapter Two. However, another point made by counsel was that in a jury trial the sheer number of persons who must be convinced makes it easier to create a reasonable doubt. These views were qualified by one counsel who said that much depended on the particular judge or jury deciding the case:

I had a case in Downpatrick in the last six months in which the jury convicted of charges which a judge sitting alone would never have convicted of. Jury panels vary in their belief in police evidence from one area to another and from case to case. I think there are very high conviction rates in some areas, for example, North Down is, I think, the top of the UK charts for convictions. Other areas are a world away from that.

We shall discuss the way in which judges and juries approach evidence in the next chapter. For the moment it is enough to note that counsel believed that the mode of trial played an important part in the decision to compromise a case. There were, however, other factors particularly related to the special context of Diplock trials which might explain why differentials in the plea rates between the two modes of trial are not as great as they might otherwise be. Certain counsel suggested that the evidence on paper was weaker in some Diplock cases than in jury trials and that there was therefore more justification to contest these cases. Although, as we have seen, confessions have been a traditional hallmark of Diplock cases, more recently reliance on confession evidence has been less marked and there was a view that some of these cases were weaker. Another point made by counsel was that in the more serious scheduled cases in Northern Ireland, the courts are more reluctant to allow a sentence discount in the event of a guilty plea and there is therefore less incentive for certain defendants to plead guilty.[21] A number of Diplock defendants were also thought to be quite different from the kind of defendants who appear in 'ordinary' cases. Several defence counsel pointed out that the decision on how to plead is ultimately for the defendant to make and that certain Diplock defendants who had resisted the pressures of police interrogation and who had not made a confession were also insistent on exercising their right to plead not guilty. Often this was for the perfectly reasonable explanation that the prosecution case in the absence of a confession was weak. On the other hand, counsel and judges also said that there were certain defendants who would plead not guilty no matter what the strength of the case against them. One judge referred to cases which were contested despite the absence of any real ground for contest as 'fighting pleas'. However, in our (admittedly small) sample of cases, there were no cases that were considered by counsel to be absolutely hopeless from the defence point of view, although as we shall see Diplock cases were often pared down to one very specific issue. The outcome of the trials in our sample is displayed in Table 8.1 (in the next chapter). The precise extent to which Diplock defendants were successful in holding out against the advice of counsel to plead guilty, and the extent to which this factor acts as a counter-balance to any tendency by counsel to advise a guilty plea in Diplock cases, are matters for a separate study, being outside our concern with the trial process. The only conclusion to be drawn here is that the trained and disciplined character of certain Diplock defendants may account for a higher proportion of not guilty pleas in Diplock proceedings than might be expected of other defendants tried without a jury.

As for plea negotiation, here the absence of the jury deprived the defence of using the unpredictability of the jury verdict as a bargaining counter to win concessions from the prosecution, although as we have seen much depended on where the jury trial was being held. Of course, as judges told us, no judge is able to form any definite view of a case merely from reading the prosecution papers but even without approaching a judge, prosecution and defence counsel felt that they generally had a better idea of how a particular judge would respond to a contested case than they could ever have about how a jury would respond. This greater predictability of the outcome of the case places the side against whom the decision is likely to be made in a weaker bargaining position than when the outcome is less certain.

In essence, plea negotiations are always predicated on an implicit

---

[21] For further discussion on the sentencing of those convicted of scheduled offences, see Doran and Jackson (1992), 49–55.

assumption of guilt.[22] In negotiating a case, defence counsel may point to some incentive for the defendant to plead not guilty as a means to persuade the prosecution to drop a more serious charge in favour of a less serious one. But the burden is on the defence to do this. The issue then is not the guilt or innocence of the defendant, but rather one of predicting what will happen if the case is contested. Similarly, in any discussions with the judge, counsel may point to some reason why the defendant may be acquitted in order to obtain a greater discount in sentence than would be awarded if conviction looks certain. As one judge noted:

> At the pre-trial discussion there may well be discussion about the strength and weaknesses of the evidence. These can be seen from the papers. One of the things that may come into it is whether the main prosecution witnesses are prepared to give evidence. If it emerges in a sex case that the complainant is very shaky and doesn't want to give evidence, there may be good reason to take a plea and be lenient and get a conviction rather than risk an acquittal.

The difficulty with a procedure which requires a judge to assume a defendant's guilt in pre-trial discussions and then to determine his guilt or innocence in a trial should the defendant contest his guilt will be discussed later, although as we have said this rarely happens in practice because plea discussions generally result in guilty pleas. For now it is noted that these discussions are a feature of a contest model of proof as they are aimed at enabling counsel to decide on the advisability of contesting the case. Whether they are more common in non-jury cases or not, therefore, they cannot be viewed as a form of inquisitorial procedure prior to the trial.[23] Nonetheless the point that the mode of trial may have a bearing on the nature and course of pre-trial discussions is important in itself. We turn now to the investigative capacity of the fact-finder in the course of the trial proper.

JURORS AND INQUISITORIAL POWERS

If the judge has few opportunities to conduct meaningful inquiries into the case before trial, once the trial opens the position changes and the judge is able to take a more commanding role in the case. The parties, of course, have to present the evidence and the judge acts as umpire of the proceedings,

---

[22] In her study of the way in which cases were disposed of in the Los Angeles County Superior Court, Mather noted that the 'courtroom regulars' tended to presume guilt: see Mather (1979), 45.

[23] Although it is interesting that in an American context Goldstein has argued that judges have assumed supervisory roles over plea-bargaining strikingly similar to those of 'inquisitorial' judges, while lacking the machinery to implement those roles: see Goldstein (1974), 1023.

but we saw in the previous chapter that he or she is also able to influence the outcome by asking questions of witnesses. The central issue in this chapter is whether, when the judge assumes the role of trier of fact, the trial loses its adversarial character, becoming less of a contest between parties and more of an inquiry directed by the judge. Before moving on, however, to the question of whether the assumption of fact-finding responsibilities by the judge leads to a more inquisitive approach, it is worth considering the opportunities afforded to the jury in the conventional trial to engage in activities which may be characterized as inquisitorial in nature. As one might anticipate, juries are much less able to intrude on the development of the criminal trial than judges.

Juries have the responsibility of evaluating the evidence presented to them in the course of the trial, but their powers to direct the course of the trial are extremely limited. They have no powers to determine what charges are appropriate and are dependent on judges putting the appropriate charges to them. This can lead to frustration at times. In one case concerning social security fraud the judge indicated to the jury during the summing-up that they could convict the defendant on the charge of attempting to obtain property by deception, but a misunderstanding arose because this alternative was not expressly provided for in the issue paper which was given to the jury. The jury retired at 12.48 in the afternoon. At 2.56 p.m. they returned but it appeared that they had indicated to the jury keeper that they were not yet ready to return a verdict on the alternative count and would require time for further deliberation. The judge, however, instructed the clerk to ask the jury whether they had returned a verdict and when she did so the foreman answered 'Yes' and the verdict was 'Not Guilty'. The judge asked prosecution counsel if there was anything outstanding against the accused, he was told not and so he discharged the accused.

Although the outcome of the case was the acquittal of the accused, it became clear that there was a matter which the jury wished to have drawn to the attention of the court and the foreman spoke up as follows:

Foreman: There is a point on the form which says First Count. You asked us to consider the Second Count and there is no space provided for the Second Count.

Judge: The issue paper just simply says 'Not Guilty'. It doesn't refer to the attempt at all, gentlemen. As I understand it, the Foreman is saying there is nothing on the form to say anything about the attempt. You will understand, Mr Foreman, that the verdict of Not Guilty and no further comment on the issue paper normally conveys to us that you considered both and decided that Not Guilty is the verdict.

The judge then asked whether counsel had anything to say and the following exchange took place:

Defence counsel:	It would be my submission that the issue paper as returned is conclusive on this matter and that the Defendant should be discharged, there having been only a verdict of Not Guilty recorded against him.
Prosecution counsel:	That should have been the position but it is quite clear from the Foreman's further comments that there is a reservation.
Judge:	What the reservation is I'm not sure that we are entitled to enquire.
Prosecution counsel:	No. Certainly a point has been raised about there being no second count and that's a matter of law on which Your Honour would be entitled to direct the jury.
Judge:	There is no Second Count.
Prosecution counsel:	No, there is no second count because the attempt is contained within the First Count.

The judge concluded by addressing the jury again. He told them that he may have been at fault in not explaining the proper procedures to them if they had wished to enter a verdict of not guilty of the substantive offence but guilty of an attempt. However, he could not let the defendant be penalized by that:

For that reason that verdict having been recorded in uncompromising terms as you have done and signed I'm afraid I can't go behind that. There is a considerable body of case law about what can and can't be done in these circumstances and needless to say I'm perfectly well aware that someone has got some other reservation about that, but, as I say, there are complications here which I would prefer not to go into. Do you understand? I'm sorry but it's terribly important to be scrupulously fair to the defendant in this matter. Not only that but on the strength of that I have already discharged the defendant and I can't bring him back.

The net result was frustration on the part of the tribunal of fact, the jury, which simply could not arise where a single tribunal is responsible for all questions of law and fact. It is also an example of the way in which form can take priority over substance in jury trials where a whole new set of rules come into play governing the relations not only between the prosecution and the defence but also between the judge and the jury. The defendant is entitled to see these formalities adhered to, even on occasions at the risk of injustice being done to the substance of the case. When the judge tries the case in the absence of the jury, on the other hand, the formalities governing judge–jury relations obviously do not apply and questions of substance can take greater priority.

Even when we turn to the jury's own domain of questions of fact, the jury's ability to intervene effectively on these questions during the trial is severely limited, although it does, of course, have the final say on the verdict. It will be recalled from Chapter Three that one of the arguments against judicial intrusion in the contest model was that judges view cases from the peak of 'Olympian ignorance'. Although judges may not always have sufficient time to read the papers in the case before the trial, it was nonetheless clear that some had a good grasp of the case from their reading of the papers. Moreover, judges view cases from a position of control over the proceedings. Juries, by contrast, receive no advance notification of the issues of the case and have no such commanding position during the trial. They may be allowed to view maps and photographs but they are not usually privy to pre-trial witness statements. On occasions judges asked for transcripts of earlier witnesses' evidence so that they could question other witnesses about it. An example of this arose in a rape case where the judge asked for a transcript of the complainant's evidence and then compared this with the evidence of the doctor who had examined the complainant after the alleged rape. The judge invited counsel to look at the transcript but the jury was not given the same opportunity. Of course, as we saw in the previous chapter, judges asked questions for the benefit of the jury but juries were rarely encouraged to ask questions themselves.

Juries then were badly equipped to put forward searching questions which might open up new lines of inquiry. This is not to say that this never happened. In one rape trial where the issue was whether the complainant consented to sexual intercourse which the defendant admitted had taken place, discrepancies emerged between the complainant's description of the alleged rape and other evidence. In her evidence the complainant claimed that she had struggled with the defendant and that this had resulted in considerable disturbance to the room she was in. Police photographs of the state of the room, on the other hand, showed few signs of a struggle. There was some controversy between counsel as to what exactly the photographs showed and whether they were an accurate representation of the state of the room after the alleged incident. Following a lunch-time adjournment the jury asked two questions which were directed at the possibility that the room had been tidied up between the alleged incident and the time the photographs were taken: '(1) Was there evidence that anyone went back to the complainant's house unaccompanied by a police officer between the time she left following the incident and the time the police photographer took the photos the following day? (2) Where did the complainant's change of dress come from?'

The jury had obviously taken note of the fact that someone might have returned to the house to get a change of clothes for the complainant after the incident. On reading out these questions for the court, the judge suggested recalling the woman police officer who had accompanied the complainant after the complaint and who had already given evidence. Crown counsel showed some reluctance to recall the witness because he seemed to believe that the questions could not be answered satisfactorily, whereupon the judge remarked that it was in his discretion to recall the witness. The court adjourned, with counsel agreeing to consult on how the jury's questions could be answered and the judge indicating concern that lengthy investigations might have to be conducted which could hold up the trial. After twenty minutes the court resumed and prosecution counsel informed the court that the officer was available to answer the jury's questions. The jury were called in and the judge himself then questioned the witness, since the prosecution case had already been formally closed and the defence did not wish her to be recalled. She informed the court that she had not entered the room where the alleged rape took place. She stated that she had had a quick glance into the room and confirmed that the room was, at that time, in the same condition as it appeared in the photographs exhibited at the trial.

The example illustrates how the adversary trial can cope with inquiries initiated by the jury. Admittedly, the procedures invoked to deal with the questions were somewhat cumbersome. Counsel had to be consulted and it had to be decided who would question the police officer. Nonetheless, the time taken from the judge reading out the questions to the end of the officer's evidence was only forty-nine minutes and the procedure apparently satisfied the jury about a theory which might have influenced them in their later deliberations had it not been effectively countered by the evidence of the police officer. This example of a jury intervening during the course of a trial was, however, unique in our survey, and even this jury was not satisfied on all the questions which it asked.

Another question asked by this jury at the same time was directed at the medical evidence which they had heard. The doctor who testified in the case had said that there was no evidence of any injury to the complainant's vagina either internally or externally. So far as he was concerned it was free from marks. The complainant's evidence was that she struggled with the defendant the whole time, pushing, 'scrabbing', and shouting at him. The defence invited the jury to conclude that in those circumstances one would expect some mark or indication of injury about the complainant's vagina. However, before this the jury had passed a note to the judge asking whether rape could be committed in the absence of evidence of a sexual assault. The judge seemed to consider that this was a legal question and after consultation with counsel he told the jury that he could not give them any real guidance at that stage but that the definition of the offence of rape would be explained to them in due course.

This illustrates the way in which questions of fact and law are divided artificially during the trial. The jury is supposed first to listen to the evidence and then to be directed on the law, a procedure which certain researchers have criticized as it prevents the jury evaluating the evidence in the light of the legal requirements as they hear it.[24] Hastie, Penrod, and Pennington

---

[24] See Kassin and Wrightsman (1988), 145–6; Heuer and Penrod (1989).

have characterized the ideal juror in the trial as a relatively passive record-keeper who decodes the events of the trial verbatim.[25] Metaphors like 'sponge' or 'tape-recorder' have been used to describe the passive role which the legal system assumes the jury will fill until the deliberations begin.[26] This assumption is rooted in what, as noted in Chapter Three, has been described as a rationalist tradition whereby knowledge is considered to be based on direct sense experience, that objects outside the observer simply imprint their character on the observer. In fact, however, perception is no longer regarded as a passive process of encoding external stimuli. Cognitive scientists now universally recognize that human beings play an active role in the acquisition of information and there is always 'extensive cognitive activity by the perceiver in comprehension and memory tasks.'[27] Jurors do not therefore passively receive information but instead play an active role in making sense of and interpreting it within their existing thought patterns during the trial.

The example also illustrates how easy it is for the judge to misinterpret the jury. Open dialogue between the judge and jury is discouraged, with the result that the jury foreman has to write down any question asked before the judge decides how it should be answered. This written procedure can lead to misunderstandings of communication of the kind observed in the case above involving social security fraud. In the present case the jury's question was prompted by the medical testimony and what the jury probably wanted was not an explanation of the law but an explanation of how rape can occur in the absence of any evidence of sexual assault. In fairness to the judge this matter was dealt with fully in the summing-up when he explained that there were circumstances when it would be possible to obtain penetration without causing injury to the vagina but it seemed that what the jury wanted at the time was medical confirmation of this. Instead they had to wait to have these matters clarified at the summing-up.

Even if juries were better equipped to put questions and procedures were devised to make it easier for them to do so, there would still be a problem in overcoming the reluctance that juries may feel about doing so. The above example of jury intervention was the only case in our sample of trials where a jury asked questions during the course of a trial. Research in Northern Ireland has indicated that jurors are often ignorant about their powers to ask questions or are afraid to do so and this reluctance is confirmed by research conducted for the Royal Commission on Criminal Justice in England.[28] This is hardly surprising given the reluctance on the part of

---

[25] Hastie, Penrod, and Pennington (1983), 18.
[26] See Diamond and Casper (1992), 515.
[27] Hastie, Penrod, and Pennington (1983), 18–19.
[28] See Jackson, Kilpatrick, and Harvey (1991), 126–7; Zander and Henderson (1993), 174–213.

judges to encourage questioning by juries. None of the judges observed in our sample encouraged questioning during the trial, although as we saw in the last chapter they did frequently intervene to clarify matters for the jury's benefit. One of the risks of jury questioning is that the presentation of the evidence at the trial may be disrupted. In the above trial when the judge told the jury in his summing-up that he had not felt able to give the jury any guidance at that stage on their question, one of the reasons he gave was because the defendant was in the witness box. Although the questions arose out of earlier testimony, the jury had been unable to formulate their questions until the lunch-time adjournment by which time the prosecution case had closed and the defendant had begun to give evidence. As we have seen this did not stop the judge recalling the woman police officer to deal with the other questions asked. But the judge was apparently concerned to limit the extent to which the presentation of the evidence was disrupted.

One of the reasons why jury questioning may be disruptive, of course, is because all questions have to be channelled through the foreman who then passes the question to the judge. The opportunities for communication between jurors in court during the trial are extremely limited. In the above trial the questions were formulated during the lunch-time adjournment. In other cases juries were reprimanded when they appeared to be discussing matters between themselves in court during the trial. On one occasion during the judicial questioning of a medical witness the judge stopped his questioning and told certain members of the jury who were having a discussion to keep quiet. The very fact that jurors are only able to consult each other at adjournments allowed by the court, rather than at their own choosing, means that usually they can only formulate questions some time after the evidence which prompted them was adduced. This cumbersome procedure makes it impossible for juries to engage in the kind of cross-examining questions discussed in the previous chapter which certain judges posed, particularly when they were acting as the triers of fact.

Jurors then are in a much weaker position than judges to act as inquisitors. Instead they must rely on judges to ask questions for them. Judges do this, as we have seen, but on the whole they seemed to limit their questioning in jury trials to questions of a clarificatory nature and were unwilling to engage in direct cross-examining questions in this mode of trial. It may thus be argued not only that the jury is badly placed to exercise inquisitorial powers, but also that jury trial is an inappropriate forum for the exercise of such powers, whether by the jury or by the judge. As we noted in Chapter Five, however, aside from the latitude accorded to the judge in the questioning of witnesses, judges in adversarial trials may avail themselves of other powers of an inquisitorial style. We now consider whether judges make use of these and other opportunities to act in an inquisitorial manner and whether they are more willing to do so in the non-jury setting.

JUDICIAL EXERCISE OF INQUISITORIAL POWERS

As described above, judges in the inquest model are charged with four specific responsibilities: determining the range of the dispute or charge, gathering evidence or investigating, testing evidence, and evaluating evidence. In an adversarial setting, the judge has little responsibility for these tasks before the criminal trial, but once the trial starts we have seen that he or she has certain powers in both jury and non-jury trials which are not typically 'umpireal' and which border on the realm of the 'inquisitorial'. Such powers are not necessarily incompatible with the broader view of the judge's umpireal role outlined in Chapter Five, but they are arguably by their very nature of a more inquisitorial hue. In particular, judges may prompt an alteration of the charges if warranted by the evidence, they may call witnesses and ask questions of witnesses and, although not the trier of fact in jury cases, they may withdraw weak cases from the jury. It is true that judicial powers of factual investigation are limited during the trial because the parties present the evidence on the basis of pre-trial investigations. It has been argued that criminal trials are much better suited to the testing of existing theories than to the investigation or discovery of new theories.[29] In the last chapter it was shown that much judicial questioning consisted of clarification and development of lines of inquiry already opened by counsel, rather than developing completely new lines of inquiry, and that when judges did embark on virtual examination of witnesses counsel were often frustrated, as it was evident that judges raised issues which counsel had intended to raise at a later time. Nevertheless it will be seen that the opportunity for investigative discovery can occur as late as the trial itself. Judges often read the papers in the case in advance of the trial. They are not therefore in such a position of 'Olympian ignorance' as may be thought, and are at least in theory in a position to call witnesses themselves and suggest lines of inquiry to counsel.

As a general proposition, however, judges did not use their formal inquisitorial powers extensively in either mode of trial in our sample cases. Perhaps more significant than such formal powers, however, are the judge's opportunities to influence the course of the proceedings informally. We shall now consider in turn the various avenues, both formal and informal, open to the judge to act as inquisitor, assessing in particular whether the absence of the jury invites a more inquisitive judicial approach. First, we shall consider briefly the occasions on which judges played a part in

[29] See Tillers and Schum (1991), 938–9.

fashioning the charges ultimately faced by the accused. Secondly, the exercise of the judicial power to call witnesses and direct the production of evidence will be examined. It will be seen that in our sample this was an area in which judges' informal capacity to influence the course of proceedings was of greater significance than the resort to formal doctrine. Thirdly, perhaps the most striking impact which a judge may have on the trial is to bring the proceedings to an early conclusion. Again, in addition to the legally prescribed judicial powers in this area, it will be seen that views expressed by the judge exerted considerable influence on counsel's decision about whether to persist with a case. Finally, we shall assess the approach of judges towards the closing submissions by counsel. It is arguably at this phase of the trial, the evidence having been presented, that the opportunity for informal inquisition is greatest, particularly when there is no jury to inhibit judge–counsel dialogue. This evokes the theme, developed in the last chapter, that although judges denied that the absence of the jury changes in any way the adversarial structure of the trial, and that it justifies a more frequent exercise of inquisitorial powers, they are in a much better position than a jury to communicate their thoughts to counsel, and because they are the triers of fact in the Diplock trial, they are *in practice* likely to exercise a much more intrusive influence there than in jury trials.

(a) Amending charges

There is no reason why judges should be more inclined in non-jury cases than in jury cases to ensure that the indictment against the accused covers all the charges on which it is open to convict. After all, as we saw in Chapter Five, the judge's role in the criminal trial has an important public interest dimension of ensuring that guilty defendants are convicted in a proper manner. In our sample of cases there were two occasions when judges sought to amend the indictment or put alternative counts to the jury on the basis of the evidence, one in a Diplock case and the other in a jury case. In the Diplock case there was evidence that in the course of a robbery a small piece had fallen off what was apparently a weapon when the victim of the robbery was being hit by one of the intruders in his house. During the course of the trial a witness gave forensic evidence that this item could have come from an imitation firearm instead of a real firearm. In consequence the judge directed that the indictment be amended to indicate the possibility that the defendants had used an imitation firearm in the robbery. The jury case, which involved social security fraud, was discussed above as an example of the jury's misunderstanding about how to register its verdict on the alternative count. The defendant was charged with obtaining property by deception by receiving unemployment benefit while in paid employment (colloquially known as 'doing the double'). Before the jury was directed on the charge, the judge raised the issue (in the absence of the jury) that the social security officers may not have been deceived before the period of time covered in the indictment. After some discussion between the judge and counsel, the judge put the case to the jury on the basis that they could convict either on the substantive offence or alternatively on an attempt to commit the substantive offence (although, as we have seen, the defendant was discharged as a result of a misunderstanding on the part of the jury). Of course, judicial amendment of the charges occurs routinely in both jury and non-jury trials. As we have noted, although this represents a departure from our characterization of the pure contest model, it is not out of step with the broader view of the judge's umpireal role in the criminal trial.

(b) Calling witnesses and directing evidence

There was no example in our sample of the exercise of the judicial power to call a witness whom neither the prosecution nor defence have decided to call; in practice this power is used only in exceptional circumstances.[30] The only occasion on which a judge actually called a witness in the trials observed was the jury trial discussed above when he recalled a police officer to answer questions posed by the jury. However, there were a number of occasions on which judges indicated to counsel that they wished certain evidence to be produced or matters investigated, although there were only two cases where the judge *insisted* on evidence being produced. One of these was the jury case discussed above where the defendant was charged with claiming unemployment benefit while in work. A Department of Employment official claimed that the defendant had been given a document entitled 'Responsibilities of Claimants' in which claimants are told that they must advise the Department of Employment of any work, paid or unpaid, which they have done and that the defendant had acknowledged receipt of this document with his signature. It transpired in the course of his evidence that the form from which the witness was reading was not exactly the same as the one which appeared in the judge and jury's papers. The judge immediately asked the jury to give up their papers and made it clear that he took exception to this irregularity as it might prejudice a fair trial. It became apparent that the document from which the witness was reading was one which she had produced herself. The witness was unable to answer the judge's question as to which version of the form the defendant had been given and had signed. Crown counsel explained that there was no material difference between any of the different versions of the form but the judge was not satisfied and demanded to see the actual document signed, and also required that defence counsel have an opportunity to read the document

---

[30] See *Archbold*, 4–356–7.

before it was read to the jury. After a short adjournment prosecution counsel explained that the original document could not be found and the jury's papers were returned without the relevant exhibit.

Such insistence on formalities is again squarely within the scope of what we have described as the judge's 'umpireal' role. The other example of judicial insistence on evidence being produced also falls within the umpireal domain since the evidence was demanded to facilitate comprehension. At an early stage of this trial the judge was displeased at the absence of any map showing the layout of the premises where a robbery had allegedly occurred. Although this point was first made by defence counsel, at a later point when a photographer was giving evidence of the photographs he had taken of the premises, the judge interrupted him:

Judge:	Perhaps I could interrupt and help you. This illustrates the difficulty which you have already pointed out. Mr C, why isn't there a map of this house?
Prosecution counsel:	I can't give any personal explanation for it, Your Honour.
Judge:	I have no intention of allowing everyone's time to be wasted floundering around when a perfectly normal piece of evidence isn't available. We can spend all day in complete confusion as to the layout of this house with people no doubt doing their best when all this could have been avoided. I expect a map to be prepared for the court not later than the start of the proceedings tomorrow morning.

In view of this it was agreed that the natural order of taking evidence would be interrupted and that evidence of the police activities would be dealt with next rather than the evidence of the victims.

On other occasions judicial interventions went beyond matters of formality and suggested that certain inquiries be made, but here the interventions were much less insistent. This illustrates the fact that judges who exercise their inquisitorial powers prefer to do so informally, apparently in recognition of the fact that although the judge may formally require evidence to be presented, the adversarial structure of the trial requires that it is counsel who present the evidence and not the judge. Interestingly, these informal requests for information all occurred in Diplock trials. In the robbery case where the judge directed that the indictment be changed to include the possibility of an imitation firearm being used, the judge originally asked whether any further evidence was to be adduced about the piece of metal which had come off the weapon. Prosecution counsel said that the only further evidence would be from the crime officer who had collected the item from the floor of the house where the robbery had occurred. Later in the trial, however, counsel asked the forensic witness whether the piece which had fallen off had come from part of an imitation weapon, and she agreed that this looked likely. As the judge's intervention here was prompted by the concern that the indictment might have to be amended, he would probably have made a similar intervention in a jury trial. There were, however, other interventions in the same trial where it was less clear whether the judge would have intervened had the jury been the trier of fact. Towards the end of the trial, for example, before the closing submissions of counsel, the judge said that he was having difficulty with a matter concerning the distances between various locations. The judge admitted that this was a matter which could be worked out from the map but since one of the witnesses who could provide the information was available he suggested that this witness should be recalled to provide the answer. It is unclear whether judges would so vigilantly clear up points at this stage in jury trials. Certainly we did not see this happening, although we did of course see many examples of judges clarifying matters for the jury at the time they arose.

There were also a number of significant interventions in the course of the *voir dire* where the judge presides alone whether the case is ultimately tried by a jury or not. In one case involving petrol bomb attacks on houses, the dominant issue concerned the admissibility of the confessions made by three defendants. The defendants made various allegations of physical violence by the police and after the end of the first *voir dire* the judge suggested that it might be a good idea if the medical report of the examination carried out shortly after the defendant had been charged were made available. The judge explained that on the evidence to date the defendant had not complained to anybody about any maltreatment but he might have complained to the doctor after being charged. He added that if neither the defence nor the prosecution knew the results of the medical examination it might be a good idea if the report were obtained. Crown counsel indicated that the matter would be investigated but in the event no medical evidence was called by either side. During the *voir dire* of the next defendant medical evidence was called but it became clear that the medical witness was not the only member of the medical staff to whom the defendant had spoken. A prison medical officer had also signed the medical report and the judge suggested that he be traced, adding that if the Crown considered it important to call one medical witness it was also important to call the other. This witness was subsequently called and during his examination confusion arose as to whom the defendant might have made allegations of maltreatment. It also became apparent that at some stage the defendant had spoken to a welfare officer who might have made a record of the conversation. The judge suggested that this was another avenue of inquiry that should be followed up.

It is not clear whether interventions like these would have been made in the presence of the jury. The judge did nothing that could have been objected to. Indeed so far as the defence was concerned he seemed to be anxious to determine whether there was any corroboration of the defendant's allegations of maltreatment which, in the event, he rejected. It is uncertain whether the same judge would have displayed such a personal concern to uncover additional evidence if the matter of admissibility was going to be decided by a jury. It is also hard to imagine judges speculating quite so openly about other possible inquiries in the presence of the jury. The judge can always send the jury out of court, of course, but there is a limit to how often it may be thought appropriate to send a jury out in order to speculate on further inquiries which might be undertaken.

The judges in the examples cited above were self-proclaimed interventionists, but there were also examples of less interventionist judges interrupting counsel to seek elaboration on certain matters. One example occurred in a case involving possession of firearms. When counsel made it clear that he did not propose to call the evidence of the forensic witness in the case, the judge intervened to say that he had been minded to ask the previous police witness some questions but had not done so because he had anticipated that the forensic witness would be giving evidence. He told counsel that he particularly wanted to know why the machine gun which was found in the defendant's house was described as 'home-made' when it appeared that the handle of the gun was professionally produced. Although this serves as another example of judicial inquiry, it is also a good example of the continuing dominance of counsel in the presentation of the evidence even in the Diplock context. Although judges receive case papers in advance of the trial, they are not involved in any pre-trial discussions between counsel as to which witnesses will be called and which evidence agreed. Judges will thus be unaware that particular witnesses will not be called because their written evidence has been agreed between the parties.

(c) Halting proceedings

In Chapter Five we argued that judges can take a fairly dominant role in the adversarial trial, both in questioning witnesses and commenting on the evidence, although they have to be more circumspect in jury trials. There are, however, formal limits to the active part which judges can play in drawing proceedings to a close before the trial has run its full course. At the close of the prosecution case, the defence may make an application to the judge for a ruling that the case should be withdrawn on the basis of insufficiency of evidence. At this point the judge's evaluation of the evidence may result in the acquittal of the accused before any defence case is made. The making of an application is the responsibility of defence counsel and it is not up to the judge to take the initiative and suggest that the case ought not to proceed if no submission has been made.[31] As for a request by the

---

[31] See *Archbold*, 7–92.

prosecution that proceedings be discontinued, there has been some dispute as to whether a judge must agree with this course,[32] but in practice judges tend not to override the prosecution's wishes in this matter. Where the judicial capacity to direct a conviction is concerned, such a power would clearly be inappropriate at any point prior to the close of evidence and even then there is considerable doubt as to whether judges are *ever* entitled to direct the jury to convict.[33] If judges were able to influence the outcome of proceedings in these ways the structure of the adversarial trial would be under serious threat, as it is of pivotal significance to an adversarial process that the parties should be free to present their evidence and arguments before the trier of fact exercises any judgment in the case. Moreover, a wide judicial power to direct convictions and acquittals at any stage of the trial would subvert the role of the jury which is responsible for making judgments of fact.

Despite the formal limits on judges' powers to halt proceedings, however, judicial comment on the evidence or the nature of the case may make a substantial impact on counsel's presentation of the case. Counsel can seek an end to the trial at any time. The prosecution may as we have noted request that the trial be discontinued and the defence may, of course, apply at any stage for a re-arraignment to enable the accused to plead guilty to the offences charged. Quite clearly, such decisions might be influenced by the expression of the judge's view of a case, particularly when the judge is the trier of fact. If, for example, the prosecution or defence are already contemplating the possibility of bringing the proceedings to a premature conclusion, then it is not fanciful to suppose that a judicial expression of dissatisfaction with certain aspects of their case might precipitate this decision. We now consider the manner in which the trials in our sample were concluded and the possibility of judicial influence on the closure of proceedings.

Table 7.1 illustrates how the various trials observed were terminated. Diplock trials were more often aborted than jury trials. Over one third (ten out of twenty-six) of the Diplock trials ended early, as opposed to under a quarter (four out of seventeen) of the jury trials. Five of the Diplock trials ended as a result of an application for a direction leading to an acquittal; two as a result of a motion to stop the trial because prejudicial evidence was heard by the judge, necessitating a new trial before a different judge; and

---

[32] See *R* v *Broad* (1979) 68 Cr App R 281. The position has been clarified by a Court of Appeal decision in which it was made clear that a trial judge is not entitled to refuse a prosecution request to offer no evidence where the request is made before the completion of the prosecution case: see *R* v *Grafton* (1993) 96 Cr App R 156. See also *Archbold*, 4–81, 291.

[33] *DPP* v *Stonehouse* [1978] AC 55; *R* v *Thompson* [1984] 1 WLR 962. See Sprack (1992), 146, although note discussion by Griew (1989), 787–8. See also *Archbold*, 4–422–3.

TABLE 7.1 *Disposal of trials*

	Jury		Diplock		Both	
Full trials	76%	(13)	62%	(16)	67%	(29)
Application for a direction	12%	(2)	19%	(5)	16%	(7)
Motion to stop trial	0%	(0)	8%	(2)	5%	(2)
Prosecution discontinuance	12%	(2)	0%	(0)	5%	(2)
Re-arraignment	0%	(0)	11%	(3)	7%	(3)
Total	100%	(17)	100%	(26)	100%	(43)

three as a result of a re-arraignment, involving a late plea of guilty by the accused. In the jury trials, two folded as a result of applications for a direction of no case to answer and the remainder were discontinued by the prosecution. Although the Diplock trials observed ended early more often than the jury trials, no such tendency appeared in the total number of Diplock and jury trials heard in Belfast Crown Court during the sample period. It will be recalled that we avoided long multi-defendant Diplock and jury trials, and it would seem that these trials were more likely to run the full course.

Of course, not all trials that end early do so as a result of the intervention of the judge. In cases which we observed, evidence arose which was not anticipated and in consequence the prosecution or defence decided to bring the trial to an end. In other cases counsel sought to have the case stopped by applying for a direction or for a new trial. Nevertheless, there were plenty of opportunities for judges to make their views known to counsel, especially in Diplock cases, and most counsel said that they were better able to gauge what a judge is thinking in a Diplock case. One counsel said that he could predict the outcome in a Diplock case virtually every time from the attitude of the judge. Nevertheless, there were certain judges who adopted the classic umpireal role of not giving much away so that when they announced their view of the case to counsel they could take counsel by surprise. In one trial, for example, a police officer gave evidence of threats made against him by the accused and testified that he had written up the events in a police car on his way back to the police station. When defence counsel sought to make an application for a direction of no case to answer at the end of the prosecution case, the judge (a non-interventionist by nature) surprised him by saying that there was no need to make the application. Counsel took this to mean that the judge was not entertaining this application; in fact the judge went on to explain that there was no need for counsel to address him because he was going to grant the application anyway. He then asked to have another look at the police officer's notebook and said that he was going to enter a verdict of not guilty on the ground that he did not believe that the notes were written in a police vehicle. The judge added that it was very unfortunate from the prosecution's point of view that the merits of the case could not be ventilated but having reached his conclusion about the notes, he could not do otherwise.

Other judges, as we saw in the previous chapter, were more interventionist while evidence was being elicited. Some had no hesitation in questioning inquisitorially. One judge had a particular habit of commenting on the evidence and on the case as a whole as it unfolded. In the course of the *voir dire* in one case this judge pointed out inconsistencies in the allegations made by the defendant against the interviewing police officers while the defendant was testifying. On one hand, the defendant was alleging that the police had falsified notes containing verbal admissions which were never shown to the defendant; on the other hand, he alleged that the police had shown him the notes which he said contained falsehoods such as the fact that he was implicating one of his co-defendants in order to put pressure on him to confess. The judge commented that the defence case in this regard seemed extremely tenuous.

In the course of the *voir dire* in a different trial, another judge interrupted at the end of the cross-examination of the defendant and said he wished to confer with counsel. There immediately followed a discussion of some length between the judge and counsel in the judge's chambers. When the trial resumed after this adjournment, the judge gave his ruling. The defendant had alleged that he had been hit while being questioned by the police and the judge commented as follows:

I have heard the evidence of the accused and I am bound to say he admits in the witness box telling lies on oath to me about the matter. He didn't seem very set in his own mind as to what did happen that day. He is a young man with a clear record and to that extent I have to take into account that allegations made by him may be true. But on balance having heard his evidence and bearing in mind the inconsistency in it and the lies which he admits telling in the witness box, I am satisfied beyond reasonable doubt that these statements were properly taken.

The interesting point here was that the judge interrupted the *voir dire* before the police had a chance to put their version of events. This was, of course, an example of a judge curtailing a *voir dire* and not a trial proper. We have already seen that certain judges seemed to apply less rigorous standards of procedure on the *voir dire* and there were no examples in our sample of any judge calling counsel into his room during the course of a trial proper and the trial then folding, although as we have seen judges have an opportunity to make their views known to counsel in private before the trial begins. There were, however, examples in Diplock cases where the judge indicated a very clear view in open court. When the judge admitted the confessions in the above trial, the hearing continued and two expert witnesses were called on behalf of the defence to testify as to the defendant's mental capacity. At the close of their evidence the judge immediately observed that in the light of the expert evidence the Crown would have some difficulty in establishing the reliability of the confessions which were the main plank of the prosecution case. After some argument the judge acquitted the defendant.

The stage at which judges are able to exert the most telling influence over the course of the trial is on an application for a direction that the case should be withdrawn at the close of the prosecution evidence. There were examples in Diplock cases where judges stopped the trial at this stage even though the defence had not strictly made out the grounds for granting the application. The strict test a judge must apply on an application, known as the *Galbraith* test, is whether on any possible view of the facts there is evidence upon which a jury could properly come to the conclusion that the defendant is guilty.[34] It is only where no reasonable jury could convict that a judge is justified in granting the application. Certain judges appeared to apply this test strictly. In one case concerning an attempted robbery, for example, the evidence against the accused was that he was stopped by the police in a street near the scene of the crime fifteen minutes after it occurred, sweating and breathing heavily. Witnesses at the scene were unable to identify the defendant in identity parades but the Crown produced forensic evidence linking fibres on the accused's hair with fibres in a black balaclava helmet found with guns and other equipment near the scene of the offence. The evidence was discussed at the application stage and the judge interrupted as follows: 'What's going through my mind is what I would do if there was a jury. I would say, "I'm going to leave it to you but you can stop at any stage." It's not for the judge alone to assess the weight of the evidence but to take the Crown case at its height.'

The application was refused and the court adjourned for the weekend. When the trial resumed the defence called no evidence and closing submissions from the prosecution and defence followed. The one difference for the prosecution was that the defendant's refusal to give evidence was a matter about which the judge, now acting as the tribunal of fact, could draw inferences. The defence reviewed the evidence again in some detail and urged the judge not to draw inferences against the accused as the Criminal Evidence Order should not be used to make a strong case out of a weak case. In his judgment the judge explained the difference between the test to be applied on an application and that which was to be applied at the end of the trial:

[34] [1981] 1 WLR 1039.

On Friday afternoon I directed that there was a prima-facie case and in doing so I bore in mind that at that time the Crown case must be taken at its height. It is now a matter for the court to look at the evidence and draw such inferences from the evidence as seem proper bearing in mind the provisions of Article 4 of the Criminal Evidence Order. I have sought to do so and having done so I am not satisfied that the Crown have established that the identity of one of the robbers has been proved beyond reasonable doubt as being that of the defendant, and in those circumstances bearing in mind all the problems of identification evidence and in particular that the robber was masked at the time I have come to the conclusion that a jury properly directed and bringing in a proper verdict in this case would acquit on both counts.

This formalism reflects the approach which several judges emphasized to us, that the Diplock trial ought so far as possible to follow the practice which would be adopted in jury trials. The judge in this instance took this approach to the extreme of asking how the jury would decide the case.

Other judges adopted a quite different approach. The Northern Ireland courts have indicated that it is permissible to adopt a different standard at the application stage in Diplock cases from the standard normally applied in jury trials, in the sense that the judge may stop a case in Diplock trials not only if he believes no reasonable jury could convict on the evidence, but also if he believes that as the trier of fact he could not possibly see himself convicting in such a case.[35] The justification for this approach is that the judge in Diplock cases acts as both judge and jury, and since it is clear that at common law a jury is entitled to acquit at any stage after the prosecution has closed its case,[36] there is no reason why a judge acting as the trier of fact may not also do so. This is not therefore a radical change of procedure in Diplock cases. The motivation seems rather to avoid trials running on unnecessarily. To adopt this approach, however, which as we have observed not all judges did, is to increase the chances of cases being withdrawn at the application stage, so that the defence is not put to what has been called the tactical burden of deciding whether or not to call evidence,[37] a burden which is more acute for defendants in Northern Ireland since the enactment of the Criminal Evidence Order which puts defendants who refuse to go into the witness box at the risk of inferences being drawn against them.

There were two Diplock cases in our sample where the judge stopped the trial at the application stage apparently because he was simply not satisfied of the defendant's guilt. One of these cases concerned an identification of the accused made by a police officer in the police station as the person he had seen in a car which had been stopped at a check-point after a robbery

---

[35] See *R v Hassan and Others* [1981] 9 NIJB. See Jackson (1983a), 16, 17, 19; (1983b), 199–202.

[36] See *Archbold*, 4–312 (although in practice juries are not apprised of this entitlement).

[37] Tapper (1990), 117.

had taken place in the area. After defence submissions at the application
stage, the judge intervened to say that he did not wish to hear from the
Crown as he could deal with the matter straight away. He went on to give a
judgment indicating that he could not be satisfied beyond reasonable doubt
that the accused had taken part in the robbery because of the weak
identification evidence. Since the leading case of *R v Turnbull*,[38] however,
identification cases are in a rather different category from other cases, and it
may well be that the judge would have adopted the same approach had he
been sitting with a jury. In another case the same judge stopped the trial
when the defendant had admitted possession of firearms and the issue was
whether he had intended to endanger life. The judge interrupted the only
eyewitness called, a police officer, to ask a number of questions about the
organization (the Ulster Resistance Movement) of which the accused
admitted being a member. The organization had been established after the
Anglo-Irish Agreement was signed in 1987 and the judge wanted to know
about its aims and whether it was a violent body. The officer testified that
its members had been found to possess arms, but primarily to deal with a
future 'doomsday situation' when law and order might break down rather
than for immediate resort to violence. During the course of a defence
application for a direction the judge interrupted to ask whether the gun
found had any history of use, and having heard that it did not, he said he
was satisfied that he should find the defendant not guilty on the contested
count. It seemed that the judge was not ruling here in accordance with the
strict rule in *Galbraith*. The result in any event was that the defendant did
not have to go into the witness box to explain himself.

There were limits, however, to the extent to which judges were disposed
to throw weak cases out at the application stage. Much seemed to depend
on the issues involved. There were cases where an assessment could be made
purely on the basis of the prosecution evidence. Other cases involved
specific defences which it was up to the defence to raise. In one case, for
example, the judge had indicated his doubts about the prosecution case and
the defence sought to reinforce these at the application stage by urging the
judge to throw out the case on the basis that no matter what evidence was
called by the defence he could never be satisfied of the prosecution case. The
defendant had been charged with withholding information about the fact
that a car he had used had been hijacked at 8.00 a.m. one morning by men
who claimed to belong to the Ulster Volunteer Force. The defence, which
was brought out during the prosecution case, was that the defendant had
been told not to report the hijacking to the police until at least lunch-time
and that 'if anything happened, he'd get done'. Prosecution counsel said in
answer to the defence application that the Crown did not dispute that the

---

[38] [1977] QB 224.

defendant may have been threatened but the fact remained that he had not reported the offence until the police approached him later in the day. The judge commented that assuming the defence of duress was open to the accused, the issue was one of fact for the jury, adding that this involved him 'in a mental contortion of leaving it to myself as the tribunal of fact'. The judge then refused the application and the defendant had no choice but to go into the witness box. Interestingly, the prosecution lawyer thought the judge would stop the case at the application stage. The judge was certainly unsympathetic to the Crown case. As soon as the defendant had given evidence, he said he could immediately give judgment without going through, as he put it, 'the fiction of rising to consider it', and he acquitted the defendant.

So far we have considered cases where the prosecuction evidence was weak, but judges could also indicate at the application stage that the prosecution case was very strong. If the judge refused an application but gave no indication as to how he would decide the case, then (as we shall see) it could do the defence no harm to rehearse the arguments again after the close of the defence case, and when no evidence was given by the defendant, to urge the judge to draw no inferences from this. If, however, after a full discussion at the application stage it was clear how a judge was thinking, counsel sometimes saw no point in persisting to argue the case. In one particular hijacking case, for example, the accused was approached by a police officer on the basis of descriptions given over the police radio by another officer who had witnessed the offence. After refusing an application for a direction, and when it became clear that the defence was calling no evidence, the judge asked whether counsel had any further submissions to make. Counsel asked him to adopt his earlier submissions and the judge convicted. Whereas in a jury case it would have been necessary for counsel to rehearse the defence arguments before the jury, even if no defence evidence were being called, there was no point in this case in adhering to that formality.

(d) Informal inquiry at closing submissions

When the prosecution and defence have completed their cases, it is customary for counsel to make closing submissions to the trier of fact. Although there were certain judges who insisted on this formality in Diplock trials, others who were more interventionist either proceeded to judgment without hearing submissions at all or engaged in discussion with counsel on issues still troubling them. A clear contrast was evident here with jury trials, where judges can interrupt closing submissions (although in practice they very rarely did) but where juries are required to listen passively. Of the fifteen Diplock trials which ended in judgment, only four proceeded on the basis of the standard procedure. In four others the judge indicated that there was no need for submissions because the judge had decided to acquit, and in the remaining seven trials there was some discussion of the evidence between the judge and counsel. Individual judges adopted fairly consistent approaches throughout, two adopting the standard procedure, three indicating that there was no need for submissions when they were inclined to acquit, and five interrupting submissions significantly.

The opportunity for discussion of the evidence between counsel and the judge which the Diplock trial affords, particularly in the closing stages of the trial, was in the view of some judges the most salient difference between the Diplock and jury trial procedure. One judge said that in his view the most notable difference was the direct communication between the judge and counsel in closing submissions. Another judge said he was not surprised that counsel were able to predict the result in Diplock trials because there is often a rational discussion between the judge and counsel on the weight of the evidence. As he put it:

There's much more rational discussion with counsel in a Diplock trial without a doubt. Counsel can predict the result before judgment because you're saying to counsel, 'Now, Mr Jones, what's the answer here? Here are these six fibres from a pullover of this rather unusual pattern found on this gun. I mean, what do you say about this? And then that's got to be taken in conjunction with the fact that he was running away from the scene of the crime?' With a jury counsel aren't interested in what a judge thinks.

Those judges who interrupted counsel at this stage seemed to adopt different stances. Consistent with the manner they had adopted when questioning witnesses, certain judges took what may be called an inquisitorial approach towards counsel's submissions. Some of the questions sought merely to clarify points which counsel were making. Others went further and queried counsel's interpretation of the evidence, as in the following example from a robbery case where one of the issues concerned the position of the victim at the time he claimed to recognize one of the defendants:

Counsel: If that is so, Your Honour, it would appear that his face could not have been actually looking towards the door . . . through which B purported to see G remove his mask.

Judge: Why do you say that? I would have thought that if what Mr B says he saw was something he did see he would be lying on his right side looking towards the door, which is what Mr B says.

Counsel: Not with his feet pointing towards the fireplace, Your Honour. In fact that would tend to put him, as it were, with his feet pointing away. I mean if one looks at it . . .

Judge: Assuming his body is lying on a straight line, there is no evidence one way or the other is there?

Other judges approached the closing submissions differently, in effect taking them over to state their own views and inviting counsel to comment on them. In one trial the judge launched into a summary of his own views after hearing Crown submissions for less than three minutes. This almost amounted to a judgment in the case except that he prefaced his remarks by telling counsel that they could comment on how his mind was working. The case concerned a horrific attack on a man carried out by a gang. The defendant was present when the man was hit on the head with a stick by someone who was not before the court. The defendant had pleaded guilty to common assault and the issue was whether he had acted in concert with the person who had delivered the blow in which case he would also be guilty of causing grievous bodily harm. The judge indicated that he could not convict him of this because the victim was unclear about the extent of the defendant's involvement. The judge added that this was his view, subject to any points that counsel would make, and the following exchange took place:

Prosecution counsel: In fairness to Mr M [the victim] he is doing his best. He has suffered a vicious attack.

Judge: If one had the person in court and could convict him on the basis of proof beyond reasonable doubt I would have sentenced him without the slightest hesitation. It was a vicious, horrific attack. My difficulties are legal difficulties. I have no sympathy for this sort of person, and every sympathy with Mr M. I have no sympathy whatsoever with the defendant but I cannot find him guilty.

Prosecution counsel: I cannot put the matter any further. I realize there is a gap which cannot be filled due to no fault of Mr M.

Defence counsel: The beating which the man got, which Mr M got, obviously involved a number of people . . . It's an inference which Your Honour could probably draw should Your Honour feel that way inclined. At the same time, it's at least possible that he received that particular injury when he was down on the ground or being kicked by other people. I have really no further submissions in the matter unless there is some specific point which occurs to Your Honour.

Judge: No.

This kind of interaction between the judge and counsel calls to mind the comment by Boyle, Hadden, and Hillyard (quoted in the introduction) that the Diplock trial process had become a 'closed shop' in the hands of a small group of professional lawyers. Of course, discussions like this on the evidence do occur in jury trials on applications for a direction and one counsel told us that it does occur occasionally before a judge sums up to a jury. The role of the summing-up will be discussed in Chapter Nine; the judge has some latitude to expose his thinking to the jury during the summing-up and, as this counsel told us, if a judge is going to give the jury a strong view of the facts, it is only fair for him to put counsel on notice of this and discussion can then occur. Alternatively (and more commonly, as we shall see in Chapter Nine) discussion can occur between the judge and counsel after the summing-up when counsel have an opportunity to make representations to the judge about the content of the summing-up, a practice known as 'requisitioning'. The difference in Diplock trials is that counsel can be given the opportunity to engage in direct discussion with the trier of fact and to argue with him on the facts which he will be deciding.

Whether the discussions that took place in the closing stages of the trial constituted an inquisitorial approach is open to debate. In the above example the judge took the initiative in a highly directorial fashion by stating the clear views he had already reached about the case to counsel. The whole saga could be viewed as a time-saving exercise to prevent counsel putting submissions to him when he had already made up his mind about the case. Indeed it was noticeable that certain judges who considered that the case against the accused was weak would immediately proceed to enter a judgment of not guilty without hearing submissions. This approach would not be acceptable where a judge was proposing to convict, and one way of expediting proceedings in this event is to put his views to counsel.

There were other instances when judges appeared to be swayed by discussion with counsel. In one case where the defendant pleaded duress in response to a charge of unlawfully receiving stolen property, the judge turned to defence counsel after the defendant had given evidence and referred him to inconsistencies between his evidence and the evidence which he had given to the police. The defendant had told the police that he knew who the two men who had threatened him were but that he did not want to name them because he was frightened, whereas he told the court that he had not known their names. The judge added that when a defendant was relying on the defence of duress it was important that there was consistency in his account. Defence counsel countered this point by saying that the defendant had been very forthcoming with the police and that any inconsistency was minor. The issue of the defendant's credibility was then argued between the judge and counsel. The judge was worried that it was very easy for a defendant to doctor his account and claim he was under duress. Counsel tried to turn the issue of the defendant's inconsistency to his advantage by claiming that it showed that the defendant was genuinely in fear. Eventually the trial judge allowed himself to be persuaded by the defence arguments and he did not call on the prosecution to make any submissions.

When discussion of this kind took place between the judge and counsel, the Diplock procedure seemed to be neither adversarial (in the sense of being dominated by counsel) nor inquisitorial (dominated by the judge) but rather deliberation between equals, as one might imagine deliberation between jurors in the juryroom. Of course, this kind of discussion does occur in jury trials when the jury is out of court and judge and counsel discuss points of law or issues in the *voir dire*. The difference is that when this occurs in jury trials, the discussions rarely dominate the entire procedure. The jury is always waiting in the background and even when issues discussed between counsel and the judge resolve the entire trial, as they may when the judge excludes a confession in the *voir dire* which forms the substance of the prosecution case, the judge must then call the jury back and direct them accordingly, explaining why he is directing them in the way that he is. The trial is always concluded by a resounding verdict which announces the end of the contest. When there is no jury, the trial is brought to an end in a less direct way by professional lawyers agreeing that there is nothing further to be discussed.

Not surprisingly, counsel preferred this more amicable and discursive approach towards Diplock procedure to the more authoritarian and inquisitorial approach adopted by other judges. Defence counsel in particular, however, told us that whatever attitude a judge adopted, ultimately they were looking for a result from him, and because of the immense power he exercised in the Diplock setting they felt much more constrained than in jury trials. Two defence counsel described the interaction as follows:

Once you're in court the atmosphere is formal. But I think the term to use is that there is more flexibility in a Diplock court from the point of view of interchange between counsel and the judge . . . I think the judges are more inclined to speak their mind on things when the jury is absent.

I would hesitate to describe either the atmosphere or more particularly the interaction between the judge and counsel in a Diplock trial as informal. Diplock trials are still very formal and as counsel you feel that academically you are being pinned more to the tip of your collar than in a jury case. There's just you and him and you've got to be on your toes, as it were, academically and intellectually . . . All the theatricals and the advocacy tend to get side-lined. It's 'Let's get to the main issue and get it dealt with', be it a legal issue or a factual issue. So that's why I hesitate to use the word 'informal' with regard to Diplock trials. It's not so much a case of informality; it's a case of reading each other's minds in a colder and much more focused way. Whereas, in a jury case it's much more relaxed and you tend to think (about the judge): 'It only takes two of those jurors to get upset about something. I don't care what you think really because after all those people are here and they're going to protect me anyway.'

In earlier chapters we saw that counsel were critical of judges who adopted interventionist approaches towards the presentation of evidence and the questioning of witnesses. This was the case in both jury and non-jury trials. When it came to submissions before the trier of fact, however, counsel made a distinction between the modes of trial and tended to favour a more interventionist approach by the judge in Diplock trials but not in jury trials. Judicial interventions in the course of closing submissions before a jury disrupted the flow of counsel's oratory and were not at all welcome by counsel. By contrast, when judges intervened in Diplock trials as the trier of fact, there was at least the advantage of gaining an indication of the judge's views. Interventions during the course of the trial which made it clear what the judge was thinking were even more welcome:

> If at the end of cross-examination of a witness a fairly damning point has arisen in the mind of the tribunal, and whether through lack of judgment or a different perspective, the defence think that's a matter which is not conclusive, it's helpful at times for the tribunal to say, 'Well, I think you may have problems with that particular piece of evidence as the evidence now stands'. It's alerting you to the fact that before you close your case or decide not to call any evidence, if there's no explanation given or dent put on it in some way, that could be a factor. That's a helpful intervention. That's normally done by way of the tribunal saying, 'That's not conclusive but as my mind is now working that seems to be a point against you. I'm open to argument.' Quite apart from leaving it to you to call evidence, it also puts you on notice that in terms of your final argument, your submissions, you've got to deal with that.

> My attitude to interventions is that I certainly don't like them in jury trials because it would prejudice the jury. In a Diplock trial you're trying to get through to his mind, so if by his interventions he indicates what's in his mind and you feel it's moving in your direction you take advantage of it and allow it to go on.

The upshot is that judicial intrusion in the Diplock setting may serve as a constructive indicator to the parties of the direction in which the mind of the fact-finder is moving. In the jury context, on the other hand, such intrusion may serve only to deflect counsel from the presentational task.

This section has illustrated that the withdrawal of the jury does not necessarily induce judges to resort more often to the formal inquisitorial powers which are available in the conventional trial. Rather, judicial engagement in inquisitorial pursuits more often occurs in informal practices which are facilitated by the jury's absence. Again, this emphasizes the point that the most significant shifts in the trial process may be detected beyond the domain of formal rules and in the realm of informal mores. The next issue is whether the practice of counsel is in turn affected by the greater capacity for judicial inquiry which is afforded by the non-jury context.

Adversarial practices at trial

We have already seen that the pivotal position which judges occupy in trials without jury means that counsel have constantly to take cues from the judge. Judges were on the whole careful not to intrude before the trial began unless approached by counsel, and once the decision to contest was made counsel were left as in jury trials to decide how to conduct the case. The contest model of trial requires the prosecution (or the party initiating the action) to prove all aspects of its case which are disputed by the defence and this is done by calling witnesses to testify to the events on which it is basing its proof. The defence will then cross-examine these witnesses and if a prima-facie case is made out, it may in turn call witnesses who will be cross-examined by the other parties.

Trial manuals pay much attention to the importance of developing a theory of the case and presenting this in the form of a story.[39] The theory of the case is the best explanation of all the information which indicates why the claims made should succeed. The story is the method chosen for presenting the theory. However, advocates cannot present their case solely in the form of a story. Although opening arguments can be presented in this form, advocates must substantiate the claims made in dramatic form by calling up 'actors' or witnesses and relying on a series of 'visual props' such as trial exhibits, documents, maps, photographs, drawings, and the like which go to make up the 'play'. With all of these the advocate has to prepare a number of scenes to substantiate the claims made and the order of these scenes is sometimes called the 'order of proof'.[40]

The ordering of evidence in terms of dramatic scenes would seem to be a necessary task in presenting evidence in the context of the adversarial trial, whether the 'audience' consists of judge and jury or judge alone. In both Diplock and jury trials, the prosecution would typically depict first the scene of the crime to establish the commission of an offence, and then the various scenes of investigation that led up to the incrimination of the accused, ending with the confession if one had been made.[41] But just as we saw in Chapter Five that the presence of the jury imports a more dramatic quality to judge–counsel interaction, so too one would expect the dramatic aspects of the presentation of evidence to be accentuated when the trier of fact is a jury. Jurors, as we have noted, come 'cold' to the contest and every last detail of the case has to be laid out before them. We have also noted that 'sympathy points' are taken in jury trials and, according to one judge, these contributed to an atmosphere of 'forensic razzmatazz'.

By contrast, the dramatic quality of trials may be decreased when they are determined by professional triers. As it has been graphically put: 'If the jury

---

[39] See Inn of Court School of Law (1993), ch 29. For a useful discussion of the key terms associated with advocacy, such as 'theory', 'story', 'situation', 'scenario', 'theme', and 'thelema', and the relationship between them, see Twining (1990), ch 7.

[40] For comment on the theatrical features of the adversary trial, see Goodpaster (1987), 148–9; McEwan (1992), 12–14; Rock (1993), 56–7.

[41] See Jackson (1992a), 44–5.

is taken out of the court-house, the drama is gone. The courtroom is not the same place.'[42] We have seen that when judges sit alone they are in a more powerful position than in jury trials to confine counsel to the key issues and to indicate on which issues they wish to hear argument. This in turn is likely to affect counsel's conduct of the case. We have already seen that counsel may be more inclined to seek an end to Diplock proceedings. There are also a number of respects in which it may be thought that the absence of the jury may affect the adversarial practices in which counsel engage during the trial, and we shall examine these each in turn. First, one might expect counsel to expedite the presentation of their cases. We have seen that judges may be more inclined to curtail counsel's questioning of witnesses in Diplock trials. In general terms, a judge neither requires technical guidance from counsel, nor welcomes non-legal appeals based on sympathy. Secondly, there may also be a greater tendency for counsel to agree evidence, with the result that more written evidence enters the record of the trial. This may be done by counsel actually reading out the statements. Alternatively, the evidence may be formally admitted before the trial in which case the statements are admitted as part of the record of evidence. Clearly the more evidence is agreed, the less adversarial the trial will appear. Thirdly, counsel may also take fewer objections to an opponent's conduct when they are presenting a case before a professional judge who is anxious to confine the trial to the substantive issues.

(a) Expediting the proceedings

Table 7.2 compares the duration of the twenty-nine trials in our sample which ran full course. We saw in the last section that the remaining fourteen trials observed ended early for a variety of reasons and they are excluded from this analysis. The trials varied considerably in duration: the shortest trial lasted twenty minutes and the longest a little less than eight full court days. Trials were classified into very short (less than an hour), short (less than half a day), medium (half a day to two days) and long (over two days). The table shows that there was a marked tendency for Diplock trials to be shorter than jury trials. Almost half of the Diplock trials lasted less than half a day, while only two jury trials came into this category and no jury trial lasted less than an hour.

Caution is needed here because of our avoidance of long Diplock and jury trials during the sample period. Indeed when consideration is given to the length of all the Diplock trials during the sample period which were not ended early, the average length of those trials was greater than that of the Diplock trials in our sample. Less than a quarter of the Diplock trials came

---

[42] Green (1930), 403.

TABLE 7.2 *Duration of full trials*

	Very short	Short	Medium	Long	Total
Jury	0	2	7	4	13
Diplock	5	2	6	3	16

into the short or very short category and almost a half were long. It will be recalled from Chapter Four that many of the long Diplock trials involved a number of defendants and the issues which were contested often involved the admissibility of confessions or detailed forensic evidence. While there was no general tendency for the Diplock trials to be shorter than the jury trials during the sample period, more Diplock than jury trials came into the short or very short category. Almost one in eight Diplock trials lasted less than a hour, while no jury trial was this short.

There is no doubt that certain legal procedures can be dealt with more quickly in the Diplock mode of trial than in jury trials. As stated, there is no formal summing-up in Diplock cases and when judgments were given at the end of Diplock trials they were generally shorter than the summing-up in a jury trial. Generally, there are more formal procedures when the tribunals of law and fact are divided. As one counsel put it:

Quite apart from having to swear a jury the judge has to charge the jury and counsel have to make quite long explanatory speeches to the jury. Also, for example, if you're conducting a *voir dire* in a Diplock court and the judge rules the statement in, you can to a certain extent adopt the *voir dire* into the trial. If that was a jury case, you'd have to go over the whole thing again. Things like that indicate not a more relaxed approach but perhaps a more flexible approach in Diplock trials because of the absence of the jury.

Another factor is the greater time required in jury trials to explain the nature of the case to the jury. Judges had often read the papers in advance of the trial and therefore knew something about the case before it began. According to one counsel: 'The judge is *au fait* with the situation: he knows what everybody is doing with the prosecution and the defence and from that point of view it's perhaps easier to tender witnesses or read certain pieces of the evidence which is much more difficult to do [in front of a jury].' In addition, counsel and judges were usually (although as we have seen not always) well versed in technical matters and there was therefore little need for experts to go into lengthy explanations. As one very experienced counsel told us:

The reason the cases are relatively short (I mean I would think that some Diplock cases wouldn't get done in England) is that both judges and barristers (Crown and defence) are operating in a field with which they're very familiar. They know the general trend and the scientific aspects of the forensic or biological evidence. They don't waste time. Secondly, you don't have to explain to a judge in a murder case what the pathologist did or what his conclusions are. All that's read into the thing and therefore you get down to the nitty gritty issues which are usually based around such things as intent or the admissibility of a statement or something like that. These are the things that occupy us.

(b) Agreeing evidence

There was certainly much more willingness in the Diplock cases we observed to pare the issues down to an absolute minimum. In seven Diplock trials the issues were pared down to one single issue, whereas this only happened in one jury trial. Interestingly, four of the Diplock trials concerned situations where the defendant had already pleaded guilty to lesser counts (for example, possession of firearms or explosives, or causing actual bodily harm) and the contested issue was whether he was also guilty of more serious offences (such as possession of firearms or explosives with intent to endanger life, or causing grievous bodily harm). The remaining three Diplock cases concerned specific defences (automatism or duress) raised by the defence in situations where the defendant admitted the substance of the charge (hijacking or withholding information from the police). The issues in these cases all concerned the state of mind of the defendant (with the exception of the case concerning grievous bodily harm where the issues involved interpretation of the defendant's actions). None of these issues were contested in any of the jury trials and this might suggest that the greater tendency for issues to be pared down in Diplock trials can be attributed less to the mode of trial than to the kinds of cases triable in Diplock trials.

Even so it is extremely unlikely that jury trials involving such issues would have been dealt with so expeditiously. The pattern in the pared down Diplock trials was for prosecution counsel to begin with a short opening, often lasting no more than three or four minutes. Defence counsel would then ask that much of the prosecution evidence be adopted. In one case involving possession of explosives with intent to endanger life the defence asked that all the prosecution evidence be adopted subject to the prosecution tendering one of its police witnesses for cross-examination. Counsel said that it was not necessary to have the prosecution evidence read aloud because it was all contained in the judge's papers. In another case concerning the withholding of information the defence asked that all the prosecution evidence be adopted save for two sentences in the notes of one of the police witnesses. The defence made a reference to the sentences but did not read them out in court. Without any indication given of what the sentences contained, prosecution counsel replied that the matter was of little consequence and it would not call evidence about it. The prosecution case then closed and the defence called the defendant to give details of his defence of duress.

These cases could not have been conducted in this way in a jury trial where the prosecution case would have to be presented to the jury, if only by reading the statements of the key witnesses. This was illustrated in the only jury trial observed in which the defence accepted a good deal of prosecution evidence. In this rape trial the defendant had admitted to the police that he had had sexual intercourse with the complainant and had further admitted that 'Mrs X didn't encourage me in any way but it was a misunderstanding on my part'. The key issue was the state of mind of the defendant at the time of intercourse. He claimed that he had had a fit of nerves. In opening the case before the jury Crown counsel asked that the jury see the statement by the defendant which was not challenged by the defence and he then read the statement to the jury. The complainant then gave evidence and this was followed by DNA evidence, which was not challenged, proving that the defendant had sexual intercourse with the complainant. When the police officers had given evidence as to how the statement was made by the defendant, counsel said that there were a number of other police witnesses but they did not seem to be of any further assistance. After some discussion in the absence of the jury, the prosecution closed its case. Much of the evidence that is usually presented in rape trials (photographic evidence, for example) was not presented. However, it was still necessary to call the key prosecution witnesses, including the complainant, to give evidence orally. Had the case been tried without a jury it would have been possible, as in some Diplock trials observed, which were pared down to a single issue, to adopt almost all of the prosecution evidence. In one Diplock trial, for example, the issue was the defendant's state of mind during an attempted hijacking which the defendant had admitted he had tried to undertake. The prosecution evidence was read into the record and the defence then called medical evidence to the effect that the defendant was in a state of automatism after he had lost his temper with his wife and had rushed out and attempted to drive off in a car that did not belong to him.

Apart from the need to unfold even uncontested evidence more carefully before a jury which is not privy to the prosecution papers in the case, defence counsel said they felt less inclined to contest issues in Diplock cases. This was partly because of the attitude of certain judges whose concern was to move the proceedings along, and partly because defence counsel themselves felt it was a waste of time requiring evidence to be proven which was not disputed:

I might feel more inclined to agree evidence in a Diplock case than in a jury case. In a jury case you tend to put them to their proof because a wheel can always fall off somehow somewhere along the way. You just instinctively put them to their proofs in front of a jury. I can't put my finger on the reason why. Whereas in a Diplock trial you know who you're dealing with, who you're working with, and therefore you know when it's going to be a waste of everyone's time and you'd tend to agree it rather more easily.

It's not that the people you're dealing with are any different in a jury case. It's just that you think the witness may slip somewhere along the way in front of the jury and that somehow the jury might be influenced either against you or for you by something that might happen even if it was in relation to the most formal piece of evidence you could agree. I wouldn't do that in a Diplock case because a judge would attach no weight to it.

One senior counsel, however, denied that he would agree evidence any more in a Diplock case. He said that Crown counsel would occasionally seek his agreement of some evidence before the trial. He said his reaction was always to be careful because as he put it, 'even the most apparently bland evidence can turn up something'. He gave as an example the forensic evidence in a violent robbery case where there was much blood at the scene of the crime and a lot of glass windows had been smashed. The forensic evidence was unable to link the three defendants to the scene of the offence despite the fact that the defendants' clothing was obtained within hours of the event. The prosecution had wanted the defence to agree the forensic report and on the face of it it appeared to be uncontroversial. In fact the forensic evidence proved very significant for the defence case: 'I mean what we wanted to highlight in that case was not just simply that there was no blood found but that in fact in the normal way you would expect to have found blood if the case was as the Crown presented it. Things like that one can bring out.'

(c) Taking objections

The same tendency to be less contentious in Diplock cases was manifest on the question of taking objections. We have already seen that counsel were unwilling to object to judicial questions in Diplock trials. Table 7.3 shows the frequency with which objections were taken by counsel to an opponent's questions in the Diplock and jury trials observed.

TABLE 7.3 *Objections taken by counsel in trials*

No. of objections	None	1–5	Over 5
Jury	6	6	5
Diplock	12	10	4

It can be seen that in almost half the Diplock trials (twelve out of twenty-six) there were no objections taken at all by counsel, while objections were taken in almost two-thirds of the jury trials (eleven out of seventeen). Moreover, frequent objections (more than five) were taken in only a sixth (four out of twenty-six) of Diplock trials as compared with about a third (five out of seventeen) of jury trials. Of course, care is needed in attributing these differences to the mode of trial. It was striking that before one judge (who was observed in three Diplock and three jury trials) no objections were taken by counsel at all. Although this judge was not an interventionist in terms of interrupting counsel and asking questions of witnesses, he complained frequently about time-wasting and he tended to indicate his view of the evidence during Diplock trials.

The personality of the particular judge conducting proceedings may therefore have an important bearing on whether objections are taken. Judges also responded to objections in different ways, some without much discussion ruling formally in favour or against, while others wanted to discuss the point before ruling. Others again were more inclined to let counsel argue the point out and wait for the matter to be resolved by counsel. This difference was particularly discernible when counsel rose to challenge a particular line of questioning adopted by the other side rather than simply challenging one particular question. In one instance defence counsel was cross-examining a police officer on the basis of an allegation made by the accused that the officer had struck the defendant while interviewing him. The Crown objected that the defence should put in exact terms how it was alleged the officer hit the accused. Before defence counsel could reply the judge intervened to say that while the Crown could comment later, the manner of the cross-examination was entirely a matter for the defence. By contrast, in another case the defence objected that Crown counsel in cross-examination of the accused in the *voir dire* was misrepresenting what the accused had said in chief about his involvement in a violent incident which had resulted in the death of certain youths. During the course of the argument which ensued, the judge intervened mildly to state his recollection of what had been said, but he let counsel argue for seven minutes before saying that he had a full note, and agreeing with the defence's recollection. There were other examples in this case where the judge let counsel argue out points and seemed reluctant to rule decisively on them. This occurred in the course of a *voir dire* and it may be that the judge would have found it difficult to maintain such a non-interventionist stance before a jury.

Another important factor is the relationship between counsel and the judge, and the relationship between counsel themselves. We observed very senior counsel before less senior judges and although it was not obvious that more objections were taken in these cases, some senior counsel played a very dominant role in these trials and showed no hesitation in taking objections forcefully. Occasionally relations between counsel became strained and it was noticeable that more objections were then taken. In one Diplock trial relations became very tense between two counsel in front of a judge who seemed to be unable or unwilling to rule on the objections made. Crown counsel became incensed by the defence counsel's manner of cross-examination, which was to question witnesses aggressively and repeatedly on discrepancies between what they had told the police and their evidence in court. On one occasion the Crown objected on the ground that the defence had inferred that the witness was tailoring his description of the accused following his observation of the accused in court. Defence counsel countered this objection by saying that this was not the implication of his questioning. He said he was making the point that the defendant, whom the witness had picked out in an identification parade, did not bear the same description as that given by the witness in his original statement to the police. The Crown denied that this was the main purpose of the defence cross-examination. Feelings began to run high at this point, but the judge said nothing and the matter was not resolved.

These variations in the way in which objections were taken seem to be attributable purely to the personalities of counsel and judges, and the working relationships between them, rather than to the mode of trial. Yet it is doubtful whether the aggressive questioning and the objections which it prompted in this case would have been exhibited with the same intensity in a jury case. Certain counsel made the point that they had to be very careful not to alienate the jury by leaning too hard on eyewitnesses. However, the most acrimonious exchanges during trial occurred before a jury. At one point in a rape trial Crown counsel interjected to make a general complaint about the way in which defence counsel was questioning witnesses: 'With every witness in this case he has insisted in saying, "Is that question so difficult?", as if the witness has something to hide.' The judge referred back to the particular question counsel was asking and said that counsel's objection was justified in this case. Altogether thirty-eight objections were made (sixteen by the Crown and twenty by the defence) in the course of this trial.

Many of these objections were based on the ground that counsel was not questioning witnesses fairly, and this raises the question whether the *kinds* of objections taken differed according to the mode of trial. In Chapter Five we analysed the kinds of objections that can be taken as being of four kinds: clarity, relevance, fairness, and rules of evidence and procedure. Adopting the same classification, Table 7.4 shows the number and kinds of objections taken by counsel in both Diplock and jury trials. It is interesting that while many of the judicial objections referred to in Chapter Five were truth-based (that is based on issues of clarity and relevance), most of the objections

TABLE 7.4 *Different types of judicial objections taken by counsel in trials*

	Jury (17 trials)		Diplock (26 trials)	
Clarity	30%	(28)	31%	(20)
Relevance	7%	(7)	6%	(4)
Fairness	23%	(22)	17%	(11)
Rules	40%	(38)	46%	(29)
Total	100%	(97)	100%	(64)

made by counsel were fairness-based (that is based on infringement of some rule of evidence or procedure or on some other ground of unfairness). Fairness or rule-based objections accounted for approximately two-thirds of all the objections taken in both modes of trial. Although there were more objections of all kinds in the jury trials observed than in the Diplock trials, the kinds of objections did not seem to vary greatly in their distribution according to the mode of trial.

Counsel in general said that they would be more inclined to take objections in jury trials. One view expressed was that 'everyone had to be on their best behaviour before a jury'. Counsel said that they had to be particularly on their guard in jury trials against clever tactics from the opposition. They had to be careful to protect 'their' witnesses in a jury trial, as there is the danger that a jury may get the wrong impression from the tone of counsel's questioning, as in the above case where counsel complained that the impression given was that the witnesses were hiding something. Judges were thought to be less susceptible to theatrical ploys. Apart from concern about the potentially prejudicial impact of witness questioning on the jury, there was also concern about the prejudicial impact that evidence can have on the jury. There was less point in objecting to inadmissible evidence in a trial by judge alone because the judge will already be privy to the inadmissible evidence. Such evidence can usually be kept from a jury, but there was concern that the evidence could often be elicited by clever questioning. To take one example, witnesses may not refer to their previous statements, but can be cross-examined about inconsistencies between an earlier state-ment and the witness's evidence at trial. Without referring to such statements, cross-examining counsel can also imply that the witness is deviating in his evidence from a previous account. In one jury case where defence counsel was accused of making such an implicit allegation, prosecution counsel attempted to put the matter straight by referring to the witness's previous statement in order to show that there was no inconsistency. The defence objected to this and both sides then accused the other of trying to mislead the jury by unfair tactics: the defence was accused of implying that there was an inconsistency when there was none and the prosecution was accused of trying to admit a previous statement in breach of the rules of evidence. In a Diplock case the judge could have seen the statement for himself, even if it was not technically admissible, and this kind of dispute would not have arisen.

There may nonetheless be good reasons in Diplock cases for objecting to inadmissible evidence of which the judge is aware. A judicial ruling that certain evidence is inadmissible means that the judge cannot refer to it in his judgment. One counsel gave a further reason for taking objections in Diplock trials: 'If it's a point of substance one has to take it in a Diplock case, otherwise the Court of Appeal would be slow to let you take such a point in the appeal if the case goes against your client.' There nevertheless seemed to be fewer occasions in Diplock trials when an advantage could be gained from objecting to evidence. Another consideration which counsel considered relevant was that it was easier for judges not to rule on objections in Diplock cases. In Chapter Three we noted that a practice has grown in the United States whereby judges can avoid erroneous rulings simply by not ruling on objections. This was not an established practice in the Diplock cases we observed, but we have seen that certain judges did appear reluctant to make definitive rulings and there was therefore less point in taking objections before them. Certain counsel also admitted that they felt much freer to take objections and to argue them forcefully in jury trials because they could afford to be more confrontational with a judge in a jury trial. As one counsel put it: 'It may be more of an American nature in a Diplock court: "I formally object that the record show", objecting on the spot, although not quite as formal as that. One takes them in a Diplock court but one would argue them more freely in a jury court knowing that all parties are conscious that there's a tribunal of fact that everyone has to go to at the end of the case.'

TOWARDS A NEW MODEL OF PROOF?

Perhaps the main conclusion to be derived from our discussion so far is that it is inappropriate to describe many Diplock trials as purely adversarial or inquisitorial in nature. There was considerable variation in the way in which the trials were conducted. This variation seemed more attributable to the forensic style of the individual judge, and to the chemistry engendered by the working practices between the professional participants in the trial, than to any particular approach required by the mode of trial. Nevertheless this variation in the conduct of Diplock trials did itself seem to be a feature of the absence of the jury. For all its unpredictability, indeed perhaps *because* of its unpredictability, the jury seemed to impose a particular order and consistency on the way in which trial proceedings were conducted. Participants referred to having to be on their best behaviour before the jury, the outside lay element which seemed to some participants to be sitting in judgment on them all. With the jury absent, the shackles would be loosened and the personalities and dispositions of the particular actors could shine through more clearly. Judges who were disposed to be interventionist or non-interventionist could act accordingly. The same applied to counsel. Junior counsel could easily feel dominated by an interventionist judge; but by the same token senior counsel could intrude in a dominating way before a less senior judge.

Yet beyond the importance of the personalities of the actors, the absence of the jury did appear to move the trial proceedings away from a purely party contest. The adversarial structure of the trial was still preserved in the form of party presentation of evidence, but the inquisitorial tendencies of particular judges could more clearly be revealed and the judge then tended to emerge as a player as well as an umpire in the proceedings. This was still a far cry from the role of the judge in the inquest model because the proceedings were formally conducted within the contest mould. However, the judge's assumption of fact-finding responsibilities did alter the nature of the contest.

In a number of trials the contest changed visibly from an all-out forensic battle between prosecution and defence towards a more limited skirmish on key points and an engagement in argument with the judge where the judge chose to raise points himself. In this sense the forensic atmosphere often seemed more akin to the calm and courteous proceedings conducted in the appellate courts than to the more highly charged atmosphere of jury trials. In his study of courtroom interaction in the House of Lords, Paterson described how 'the conventional model of the adversary system in which hired champions joust in the arena with the adjudicator sitting in an elevated position' did not adequately convey the realities of proceedings in an appellate court.[43] Both Law Lords and counsel appearing before them seemed to agree that the real debate was much more between counsel and the bench than between opposing counsel, and one QC in particular was quoted as describing the dialogue between Bar and Bench as 'like a football game: you only play as well as the opponents let you—and by opponents I mean the tribunal'.[44]

There was not the same consensus between the members of the Bar and bench to whom we spoke about the nature of Diplock proceedings. Judges were more inclined to say that the proceedings retained their traditional adversarial structure, although there was some acknowledgement that the added fact-finding responsibilities could induce judges to take a more

[43] (1982), 51. [44] *Ibid.*

interventionist stance. Defence counsel tended to argue that the proceedings had changed in character, away from an all-out contest between counsel and opposing witnesses towards a more restrained and focused contest between the judge and counsel. Even when judges maintained the traditional umpireal stance, counsel believed that trying to convince an individual judge whose characteristics were largely known was quite different from trying to convince an anonymous jury which was largely inscrutable.[45]

Prosecution counsel were less inclined to view Diplock proceedings as a struggle between the Bar and the bench. Instead they appeared to approach the proceedings more as a problem-solving exercise. They spoke much less in adversarial terms and more in terms of solving the problem of the defendant's guilt. To this end they believed that there had to be a strong element of trust between opposing counsel and between counsel and the judge. We have seen that the Northern Ireland Court of Appeal has emphasized the importance of confidentiality in any discussions between counsel and the judge in chambers. Trial proceedings, of course, are conducted in open court but there was a view expressed by prosecution counsel that trust was necessary here as well in order to dispense with the business of the court:

There's always communication between both sides before the trial. We're all friends with each other basically. One of the advantages or disadvantages of having a small bar, we know each other, we know whether someone is honest or not. If someone says to me, 'I'm not going to take issue with points A, B, C, and D', I know I don't have to go through all of it. He's happy to lie in the long grass. It's a way of life. We mostly get rid of our work pretty swiftly compared with England.

One judge also said that Diplock proceedings were more conducive to creating a good working relationship between the judge and counsel in which everyone functions at their best:

My belief, and again it depends on the personality of the judge, is that in a criminal trial, one of the important things for the judge is to create an atmosphere in which everyone functions at their best, that is to say that defence counsel are at ease, and perhaps the defendant is at ease in the witness box. Now this is important in a jury trial as well as a Diplock trial, but it's a great deal easier, I think, to induce it in a Diplock trial by being fairly amiable with counsel. You might make a joke which you wouldn't want to see in a transcript in a jury trial. You would be chary of doing this in front of a jury because the jury wouldn't understand the joke and would not think it relevant to them. I think, particularly in a long trial, or fairly long trial, it's important that people should not be under strain and stress and no doubt defence counsel are. People appearing for the Crown shouldn't be because they shouldn't be that keen to win. The defence are under strain because the man might go down for

---

[45] See Rock (1993), 75–6; Morison and Leith (1992), 152.

life imprisonment or twenty-five years and they have a chance of getting him off—that puts him under considerable pressure and they may not conduct the case as well.

This raises the question of whether the trial proceedings shifted away from the contest model, not so much towards an inquest model (because we have seen that however dominant the judge the proceedings were still conducted on the basis of party presentation) as towards what Shapland has called a 'problem-solving' model. In her study of the procedure between conviction and sentence, Shapland described this as a process in which each participant may be regarded as a provider of particular information required to solve a problem and in which there is open discussion between the participants as to what the solution should be.[46] Defence counsel were not inclined to accept that their role in Diplock proceedings had become any less adversarial, but we have seen that the proceedings generally did at times approach a problem-solving model, particularly at the stage of closing submissions. It is presumably this approach which prompted Boyle, Hadden, and Hillyard's comments (cited in Chapter One) about a 'closed shop' of professionals.

Nevertheless, the Diplock proceedings observed could not fairly be characterized as consistently adopting a problem-solving model. Still less is it possible to claim that when the jury is withdrawn from criminal proceedings trial procedure must necessarily move in a problem-solving direction. Judges may refuse to be openly drawn into the process; counsel may insist on conducting proceedings on as adversarial a basis as possible. There is, however, at least some likelihood that in the absence of the jury, practitioners change the roles which they have traditionally played in the jury context because of the much more dominating influence which a judge can exercise as the trier of fact. Proceedings where practitioners know each other well and have built up a number of informal practices together would probably provide the most fertile ground for the development of a problem-solving model.[47] Even where practitioners are in less regular contact with each other, however, it is perhaps inevitable that court proceedings will take on a more discussion-based or problem-solving mode. In his study of the role of bench trials in Philadelphia in the early 1980s Schulhofer found that judges engaged in a very active role at trial, questioning witnesses and participating in discussion during the closing statements.[48]

The particular direction in which non-jury proceedings will develop clearly depends heavily on the particular context in which they take place. In so far as the proceedings give any appearance of a problem-solving approach, however, there are dangers from the point of view of public perception. When the jury is withdrawn, as in Northern Ireland, to deal

---

[46] Shapland (1981), 144.
[47] Morison and Leith (1992), 153–4.   [48] Schulhofer (1984).

with a particular emergency and when jury trial remains the ideal to which most participants subscribe, then dangers may arise in deviating too much from jury procedures. Apart from this, any deviation from the contest model may give defendants the impression that their interests are being sacrificed for the sake of expediency. This is one of the reasons why the Court of Appeal in England has been so opposed to private discussions in the judge's room.[49] Although the defendant is present during Diplock proceedings, the spectacle of professional lawyers engaging in exclusive debate, albeit for the best of reasons, can blur the formal lines of the trial. One senior judge who was against the idea of debate at the stage of closing submissions felt that there was a great need for justice to be seen to be done to the individual accused:

It is true that in non-jury cases judges have a greater opportunity to interrupt submissions and ask questions. Counsel are after all addressing the judge at this stage and it is only proper that the judge should be able to respond. But it is better practice for the judge to continue to play a recording role at this stage rather than a debating role, making sure what exactly counsel is saying and understanding the argument rather than engaging in debate about the argument. This is as true in dealing with legal submissions as well as factual questions . . . If the judge is seen to be engaging in full-blooded debate with counsel, there is a danger particularly at the closing stage that the defendant will feel that the judge has made up his mind and is prejudiced against him or that he is not taking the issue seriously enough.

As well as affecting perceptions of justice, the choice of procedure also determines the kind of justice dispensed. Referring to the problem-solving model at the sentencing stage, Shapland recognized that there was a danger both that it may exclude the effective participation of the accused and that it may encourage a concept of the offence and the offender negotiated by professionals, 'shrouded in mystique and distant from that of the man in the street'.[50] We have seen that the methods of fact-finding adopted determine the facts that are found. Before we can make an assessment of the ideal role of the judge in non-jury proceedings, we need to probe further into the actual decision-making process and consider how the decisions that are reached are justified.

---

[49] See *R* v *Harper-Taylor* (1988) New Law J 80–1.
[50] Shapland (1981), 155–6.

8
Judging Fact

Although countless volumes have been written on judicial reasoning about the law, less attention has been given to fact-finding in forensic contexts. Some interest was expressed by legal realists in the early part of this century, particularly by Frank who tried to shift the focus of realist attention from 'rule-skepticism' to 'fact-skepticism'.[1] From a different perspective, Wigmore's attempt to develop an interdisciplinary theory of evidence and proof, incorporating the legal, logical, psychological, and scientific aspects of the subject fell largely on deaf ears.[2] In more recent years, however, there has been a burgeoning of interest in theoretical aspects of evidence, particularly in the United States where the mistaken attempt in one case to apply probability theory to the evidence led to a lively debate about the uses of probability theory in legal fact-finding.[3]

Despite this more recent interest in factual reasoning, however, there has been little empirical literature on how judges go about their decision-making tasks, and in particular the task of judging fact.[4] Instead researchers have concentrated more on jury decision-making. Some of this research has compared the verdicts of juries with those of professionals engaged in the case and this has enabled certain inferences to be drawn about judicial decision-making. In Kalven and Zeisel's pathbreaking work *The American Jury,* for example, judges disagreed with the jury verdicts in 24.6 per cent of

[1] Frank (1949).
[2] Twining (1985), 112–14. Wigmore developed his theory in *The Principles of Judicial Proof*, which was published in 1913. Later editions were published in 1931 and under the title *The Science of Judicial Proof* in 1937. See Wigmore (1937).
[3] *People v Collins* 438 P.2d 33 (1968). See Lempert (1986), 441–3. This debate led a growing number of legal scholars to become interested in normative models of decision-making, especially in the United States. See the proceedings of the Symposium on Probability and Inference in the Law of Evidence, published by the Boston University Law Review (1986) and the Cardozo Conference on Decision and Inference in Litigation, published by the Cardozo Law Review (1991). There has been less interest among legal scholars in the United Kingdom although see the exchanges between Williams (1979) and Cohen (1979) in the Criminal Law Review, discussed by Jackson (1980) and Twining (1981). There has been greater appreciation of the importance of fact-finding in forensic contexts. Twining's call for facts to be taken more seriously encouraged the legal professions to place greater emphasis on fact management in vocational training: see Twining (1984); Inn of Court School of Law (1993). There are signs that judges themselves are taking facts more seriously: see Stone (1984), (1986); Stone and McClean (1990).
[4] There have been some studies of the way judges make sentencing decisions: see, for example, Lawrence (1988).

the 3,576 trials examined, with the jury being more lenient than the judge in 19 per cent of the cases and less lenient in 3 per cent of the cases.[5] Baldwin and McConville's study of jury trials in England also found evidence of great disagreement between professionals and juries.[6] In over a third of the acquittals in their sample the judge and one other professional involved in the case expressed doubts about the verdict, and over 5 per cent of those found guilty by a jury were considered by professionals to have been convicted in questionable circumstances. As these studies were designed to provide enlightenment on jury decision-making, a number of them were criticized on the ground that juries were being judged by the standards of professionals.[7] An analysis of the reasons for the disagreements can throw as much light on the decision-making of judges and professionals as on that of lay people. In Kalven and Zeisel's study one important reason suggested for the differences of verdicts was that the jury, unlike the judge, was able as an institution to import its values into the law not so much 'by open revolt in the teeth of the law and the facts' as by what they termed the 'liberation hypothesis'.[8] In their words: 'the jury, in the guise of resolving doubts about the issues of fact, gives reign to its sense of values.'[9] The judge, by contrast, was able to see the stimulus which moved the jury but did not yield to it: 'Somehow the combination of official role, tradition, discipline and repeated experience with the task make of the judge one kind of decider. The perennial amateur, layman jury cannot be so quickly domesticated to official role and tradition; it remains accessible to stimuli which the judge will exclude.'[10] However, Kalven and Zeisel admitted that their primary intention was to give a picture of the jury and that the judge was treated as a 'baseline representing the law', whereas of course on the part of the judge discretion, freedom, and sentiment will also be at work: 'the judge too is human.'[11] They concluded that until an 'equally full and candid story of the judge' was available, we could only have half the knowledge needed.[12]

Almost thirty years later, we still await an 'equally full and candid story of the judge', at least in so far as judicial decisions of fact are concerned. Instead interest in the jury has continued unabated, especially in the United States, so that there is now a large volume of literature on jury and juror decision-making. The focus of much of the research has, however, shifted away from comparisons between jury and other professional verdicts towards simulated jury experiments. There seem to be a number of reasons for this. Many researchers regard the jury as an institution which lends itself

[5] Kalven and Zeisel (1966).   [6] Baldwin and McConville (1979).
[7] See for example the criticisms of Mungham and Bankowski (1976); Freeman (1978).
[8] Kalven and Zeisel (1966), 495.   [9] *Ibid.*   [10] *Ibid.*, 498.
[11] *Ibid.*, 499.   [12] *Ibid.*

perfectly to the examination of individual and group decision-making, issues which go beyond understanding juries for their own sake.[13] The jury's task has the merit of being well defined and therefore readily examinable, whilst also providing examples of many aspects of human-decision making.[14] Jury research has thus shifted away from the evaluation of the performance of juries towards questions about the way in which human beings reason.

In so far as jury research has concentrated on the nature of group decision-making, it would seem to have little relevance to decision-making in single judge trials. That research, however, does draw attention to the ingredient of collective deliberation which is absent in trials by a judge sitting alone. There has been some debate within the Diplock context as to whether a collegiate two- or three-judge trial would be preferable to a single judge trial.[15] The Diplock Commission bluntly rejected the notion of a collegiate bench, not only because there would be problems in finding enough judges, but also on the ground that the idea was alien to the oral adversarial tradition as it would disrupt the flow of examination and cross-examination.[16] In fact, there is a long tradition of judges sitting together in jury cases which only ended in the mid-nineteenth century.[17] The fact that judges try Diplock cases on their own does not mean that they are unable to deliberate with other participants during the trial. In the last chapter we noted the established feature of the closing stages of Diplock trials, in which judges could put issues about which they were unsatisfied to counsel. Ultimately, however, the single judge makes the decision alone. As one judge put it: 'The task is an isolated one. No one can help the judge on this fact-finding responsibility. In other matters, such as questions of law, sentencing or procedure, a judge might consult his brethren. On a matter of fact he is alone. Whether this task would be easier if there were a collegiate court is hard to say.'

Judges agreed that this responsibility was an onerous one. This was not to say that the pressures in a jury trial were any less; it was just that the pressures were different:

in a jury case, you have the pressure of producing at short notice a summing-up which is able to explain to the jury the law and the facts, meshing these together in a comprehensible manner ... The pressure in [Diplock] cases is that I am the trier of fact. Again in the majority of cases this causes no real difficulty because it becomes

---

[13] Lempert (1993).   [14] Hastie (1993).

[15] See for example the Baker Report (1984), paras. 113–21; Jackson (1987).

[16] See Chapter One, pages 9–10.

[17] See Langbein (1983), 31–6. It is also noted that magistrates sit with Crown Court judges in England and Wales when cases are reheard on appeal from magistrates' courts (Supreme Court Act 1981, section 74): see *Archbold*, 2–6, 2–151a. In addition, of course, lay magistrates sit collegially in magistrates' courts in England and Wales.

clear whether the prosecution have made out an overwhelming case or merely a likely case. But sometimes these cases can be complicated.

There is also the added pressure in Diplock cases that judges must give reasons for their decisions. We shall examine both the summing-up and the judgment in the following chapter and we shall return later to the solitary nature of the judge's fact-finding task.

That aspect of jury research which has looked at individual *juror* decision-making may be thought to have more relevance to judicial fact-finding.[18] Research has illustrated that it is easy to exaggerate the effect which group deliberation actually has on the ultimate verdict. Kalven and Zeisel likened the deliberation process to the effect of photographic developer on exposed film: 'it brings out the picture, but the outcome is pre-determined.'[19] This has been confirmed in subsequent research.[20] As noted in the last chapter, the idea that individual jurors can suspend all judgment until the conclusion of the evidence has been discredited, because individual jurors actively process information during the trial (although, of course, a collective judgment is only possible at the conclusion of the evidence). The difference between judges and jurors in this respect is that judges have a better opportunity to bring their thinking to bear on counsel during the trial. This raises the question of how judges and jurors approach their decision-making task.

MODELS OF DECISION-MAKING

Recent research has examined a number of different descriptive models of juror decision-making. Two which have received particular attention are the 'meter' model and the 'story' model.[21] The idea behind the 'meter model' is that after every piece of evidence each juror makes a fresh assessment of the guilt or innocence of the defendant, so that the assessment changes as each piece of evidence is heard. The juror's state of belief can thus be likened to that of a 'mental meter' which continually adjusts as more evidence is heard. One way of viewing this process of adjustment is to invoke Bayesian probability theory. This is named after Reverend Thomas Bayes, who is credited with developing a method of updating prior belief in the

---

[18] See in particular the collection of essays in Hastie (1993).

[19] Kalven and Zeisel (1966), 489.

[20] 'Research studies have shown time and time again that the best predictor of a jury's final decision is the distribution of opinion among jurors at the start of deliberations': Hans and Vidmar (1986), 110. Most of the research has explored criminal cases. Things may be different in the context of civil damage awards: see Diamond and Casper (1992).

[21] See for example Hastie (1993); Lopes (1993).

probability of a particular hypothesis in the light of new evidence. The juror starts with an initial degree of belief in the hypothesis and the meter is determined at this level. Once an item of evidence is adduced, the prior probability or initial degree of belief is combined with this item of evidence to 'update' the belief in the hypothesis. This is done by making a decision about each piece of evidence as to the likelihood of its existence if the defendant is guilty, and the likelihood if innocent. If the former probability is divided by the latter, the 'likelihood ratio' is obtained. This operates to modify the decision-maker's prior belief. So, to take an example used by the late Sir Richard Eggleston, a physician accused of performing an illegal abortion is found to possess the required instruments.[22] This evidence is equally likely to exist whether the accused is innocent or guilty, so the likelihood ratio is one. If the accused is not a physician, the probability that possession of the instruments indicates guilt increases, and this evidence becomes more potent. The probability of such instruments being in the accused's possession if innocent is very remote and the likelihood ratio will be correspondingly large. The (initial) prior assessment of guilt which may have been low is then replaced by a new (posterior) probability which is much higher. The cycle of identifying a new item of evidence and calculating a new posterior probability is repeated until all the information is at hand. The trier must then reach a verdict which requires matching the final probability assessment of the hypothesis with the threshold required for conviction. On a scale of 0 to 1, this must be somewhere close to 1 because of the high standard of proof required in a criminal trial: proof beyond reasonable doubt. If the final meter reading attains this threshold, the defendant is convicted; otherwise he or she is acquitted.

The applicability of Bayes' theorem as a prescriptive model for reasoning about evidence in legal settings has generated considerable debate, both on moral and epistemological grounds.[23] It has been argued that the use of Bayes' theorem conflicts with the presumption of innocence because it encourages triers to begin with some prior belief in the guilt of the accused, and also that it may cause triers to give undue weight to quantifiable data over unquantifiable data.[24] A more fundamental challenge has come from those who have questioned the applicability of conventional probability to trial disputes.[25] There are additional problems with the model as an accurate description of fact-finding in legal settings because there is considerable empirical evidence that human behaviour does not conform to probability theory principles.[26] This is, however, not to deny that there are *similarities* between the Bayesian or 'meter model' and the way in which

---

[22] Eggleston (1991), 275–6.
[23] For discussion of the probabilities debate, see Twining (1981); Tillers and Green (1986).
[24] Tribe (1971).   [25] See Cohen (1977); Callen (1982); Allen (1991).
[26] See Allen (1991); Hastie (1993).

people reason.[27] Moreover, there seems to be a certain resonance between the 'meter model' and the kind of atomistic approach to fact-finding identified in Chapter Three as being required of fact-finders in the contest model of proof.[28]

Others have claimed that instead of making probability assessments on the basis of discrete units of information, jurors take a more holistic approach towards evidence.[29] In the last chapter we saw that advocacy is now associated with story-telling. It is argued that triers of fact as well as advocates use stories to organize the evidence that is presented to them.[30] Pennington and Hastie in particular have developed a 'story' model of decision-making, according to which jurors engage in an active and constructive comprehension process in which evidence is organized, elaborated, and interpreted by them during the course of the trial.[31] This is particularly necessary in trials where the evidence is unwieldy, where it is presented in a disconnected manner by question and answer, and where witnesses do not testify in any particular temporal or causal order. In their opening and closing speeches lawyers themselves present the evidence in story form, but the witness evidence is not presented in a manner which conforms with these stories. We saw in the last chapter that prosecution evidence is presented chronologically in terms of the police investigation, starting with the scene of the crime, moving on to the stories of the victims and witnesses as they came forward during the investigation, and ending with any confession the accused may have made. This is in itself a story which represents the chronology of the police investigation, but not that of the events concerning the alleged offence. Even the simplest of stories, Pennington and Hastie argue, are not stored in the memory in an unembellished form like a tape-recording of the evidence. Instead, listeners achieve comprehension of the story by filling in gaps from their world knowledge. Pennington and Hastie give the example of a simple narrative such as 'Billy went to Johnny's birthday party. When all the children were there, Johnny opened his presents. Later, they sang Happy Birthday and Johnny blew out the candles'.[32] Many listeners will infer spontaneously, and most will agree when asked, that there was a cake at the birthday party. Yet no cake is mentioned and it is not certain that there was one. According to Pennington and Hastie: 'the cake is inferred because we share knowledge about birthday party traditions and about the physical world (the candles had to be on something).'[33]

[27] See Schum and Martin (1982); Schum (1993).
[28] See Chapter Three, page 66.
[29] For discussion of 'atomistic' and 'holistic' approaches towards evidence, see Twining (1900), 238–42, 324–7.
[30] See for example Bennett and Feldman (1981).
[31] Pennington and Hastie (1986), (1991), and (1993).
[32] Pennington and Hastie (1991), 523 (footnote 11).   [33] *Ibid.*

In the context of trial fact-finding, jurors will often have to make inferences about unknown human actions and to do this they will use their knowledge about how people react in certain circumstances. One way of testing the plausibility of a theory or story, then, is by reference to more general beliefs about the world, which are often referred to as 'common sense' generalizations, or the 'stock of knowledge' in a given society.[34] In one of the simulated trials used in Pennington and Hastie's research the defendant had got into a quarrel in a bar with the victim who had threatened the defendant with a razor. Later in the evening they were again at the same bar and they got into a fight which resulted in the defendant fatally stabbing the victim with a knife. The defendant was charged with first degree murder and the issue was whether he had actively stabbed the victim or had merely held his knife out to protect himself. The victim was a large person who was known to be a trouble-maker and his threats against the defendant might cause a juror to infer that the defendant was afraid and that because of this fear he went to collect his knife after the first quarrel in order to protect himself. Not all jurors construct the same story, however, and another juror might believe that confrontations by bullies are challenges to male pride and that anger was a more likely response. General knowledge about the structure of human purposive action leads to organization of the recited events into causal and intentional relations and the story that is accepted will be that which fits best in terms of coverage (the extent to which it accounts for the evidence), coherence (the extent to which it is consistent, plausible, and complete), and uniqueness (the extent to which it stands out from other competing stories). Once a story is constructed, the juror compares this with the various verdict alternatives which are spelt out by the judge, and the juror must then match this story with a verdict alternative. The juror will have to take into account the judge's instructions on the burden and standard of proof at this stage to ensure that the single best story comes up to the standard of proof beyond reasonable doubt. It has been suggested that one way of determining this question is to search for any plausible story consistent with innocence.[35]

JUDICIAL FACT-FINDING IN ACTION

Pennington and Hastie concluded that their research results showed that the story model aptly explains and predicts juror decision-making in criminal trials. We made no systematic attempt to analyse judicial fact-finding along

---

[34] See Twining (1990), 325. For discussion of the different kinds of generalizations and the part they play in arguments about evidence, see Anderson and Twining (1991), 66–9, 367–84.
[35] Allen (1991), 382.

the lines of Pennington and Hastie's research, but it was noticeable that in some cases judges presented the evidence along story lines, both in their judgments and in their summings-up to juries. In one assault case the judge organized the evidence around two rival stories. First an eyewitness gave evidence that he was with the victim walking down an alley-way when two people walked past and the victim was struck suddenly by one of them, the defendant. Against this was the evidence of the defendant, that he saw the victim, who appeared very drunk, stumble and fall. The judge put it to the jury that there was clearly someone describing an event which did not happen and he went on to point out difficulties with both stories. The defence had tried to undermine the eyewitness's story by asking why someone would unleash a blow which was so violent that it made the victim fall over without anything being said. On the other hand, the prosecution had asked why the eyewitness would have made up a story to incriminate the defendant. There was simply no motive for him to tell something that was not true. The judge seemed to think that this was a prime example of the jury having to choose which story to believe, although he did emphasize that the jury, in weighing up the evidence, should remember that the defendant had been under no obligation to give evidence and that it was ultimately for the Crown to prove the offence beyond reasonable doubt.

These credibility issues were mainly approached by judges on the basis of conflicting stories. Another example was in a case where differing accounts were given by the police and the defendant as to what happened in the interview room where it was alleged that the defendant admitted the offence. Some judges said that they found it very difficult to resolve these disputes. According to one judge, one of the most difficult factual issues a judge had to determine was whom to believe when defendants alleged maltreatment by the police. The difficulty seemed to be particularly acute in a number of cases because the judge was unable to accept either the story of the police or that of the defendant as being more likely. The problem, as one judge put it, was that defendants would often make allegations which were bizarre and difficult to believe. The police, on the other hand, had a tendency to claim that they had acted with such complete propriety that it was also difficult to believe everything they said. As he put it:

A lot of their conventional answers, such as 'A man dictated his confession to me without me questioning him in any way', are simply unbelievable. One knows they do it by all sorts of means—sometimes leading questions, sometimes helping the witness. They feel they are circumscribed by the old Judges' Rules which were not conducive to policemen telling the truth and they have continued in their old ways. It is very annoying to listen to people who have no sufficient regard for the truth.

Judges did not articulate very clearly how they resolved these difficulties but from their judgments it seemed that they first adopted a practice (akin to the Pennington and Hastie model) of judging the credibility of the defendants' allegations by reference to their idea of what most people would have done if the allegations were true. So, in one case where serious allegations of violence were made against the police, the defendant's solicitor gave evidence that when he saw the defendant after the interviews, the defendant had told him that he had been hit on a number of occasions and that he had confessed because of the pressure following ten interviews. However, when the solicitor asked whether he was hurt (to decide whether a doctor should examine him), he had replied: 'Nothing serious.' The judge concluded not only that the conduct alleged against the police was serious but also that it was impossible to imagine anyone in the defendant's position saying that it was not. The judge also took into account the fact that the defendant had not made a complaint of violence to any of the medical officers who were available. The judge said that he would have expected a man of the defendant's intelligence, knowledge, and self-assurance to make some allegation of maltreatment to a doctor. Also, the defendant had said in cross-examination that he was angry with a detective, X, during the interview at which a statement was taken from him: 'His explanation for being angry was that X was putting all of the blame on him; that they had all angered him; that he was angry at what had happened. This expression of emotion and the use of the word angry does not suggest to me a man who was either scared of X or who had been seriously assaulted by X.' The judge here minutely matches the defendant's account of events against what the judge thought that someone in the defendant's position would feel and do. When he came to the police accounts, on the other hand, he also doubted some elements of their evidence. For example, the police denied that they had confronted the defendant with a co-defendant who had allegedly implicated him, but the judge felt there was a possibility that this had occurred. It went some way to explaining why the defendant's attitude changed after that point in time. He also thought that the police might well have shouted at the defendant, although officers also denied this. His reason for this was that he found the police to be defensive in response to quite innocuous suggestions, so that 'even if shouting had occurred they would never have admitted it'.

Given these difficulties, the judge frankly admitted in his judgment that he was left uncertain as to what had actually happened. The approach then adopted was to rely on the burden of proof. Since the prosecution bore the burden of proving that the statements had been obtained in a proper way, those conflicts which he had been unable to resolve on the evidence were resolved in favour of the accused. The judge then considered whether the statements could be admitted, taking the defence version of events at its highest. What seemed to count most in this case was his view of the defendant's motivation for making the statements. The judge ultimately admitted the confession. He said he was convinced that the defendant had confessed not because he was assaulted but because of a combination of factors, namely that 'he realized he had been named by everyone that the police had mentioned to him; that he probably had the opportunity of hearing this from [one of the co-defendants] himself, either by talking to him in the cells or by the police producing him to him, and also by the effect on him of successive interviews'. The grudging and limited nature of the admissions also dispelled another of the defendant's allegations, that the police had made up the confession for him to sign. As the judge put it: 'If they were making it up for him they were making up a statement which did not conform with what they believed happened. It was also a very limited statement. . . . Quite apart from that it was also a self-serving statement, mentioning the consumption of magic mushrooms on two occasions and ending with both an apology and an assertion that he did not know what he was doing.'

This illustrates the importance for the fact-finder of gauging motivation when attributing actions to participants. However, not all fact-finding fitted the story-moulding model. Pennington and Hastie conceded that they used in their research case materials that could be considered especially conducive to story construction. For example, they concentrated on criminal cases which almost always involved sequences of goal-directed human activity. Civil cases, on the other hand, may involve causal models other than stories (what caused the mechanical failure in the vehicle which caused the accident?), which may require different approaches to fact-finding. Allen has distinguished between two different approaches, a 'top down' approach which determines whether an episode composed of specified events occurred, and a 'bottom up' approach which can be characterized as the checking of a number of steps to see whether each element has been established.[36] Different disciplines will apply predominantly one or other of these approaches, depending on the task at hand. Standard medical diagnosis, for example, according to Allen, involves considering a relevant set of matters to see if each has been established; if not, an initial diagnosis can be discounted and another considered. Where the investigation involves binary choices testable through a replicable and directly observable experiment, this 'elements' approach is more appropriate. Where, on the other hand, the questions are less well formed and involve imposing an interpretation on the observed 'facts', as often arises in humanities subjects (for example: what were the causes of the French Revolution?) or in the law (for example: did X intend to do Y? Or: did D kill P?), an 'episode' approach is better. The 'elements' approach seems to conform better to the 'meter model' of fact-finding described earlier, as it requires an analysis of the relationship between the evidence and a particular hypothesis or element to be proved. The 'episode' approach conforms to the 'story' model.

[36] Allen (1991).

Although Pennington and Hastie assert that criminal cases commonly involve questions of human activity which are perfect for stories, we saw in Chapter Four that distinctly different issues were litigated in our sample of criminal cases. Many of these involved credibility issues or confession issues which readily lent themselves to story construction. Others involved issues of intent, knowledge, or specific defences where again triers must impose some interpretation on the evidence. However, another common issue in our sample was contested identification or circumstantial evidence placing the defendant at the scene of the offence. Such issues involve less intensive story construction and raise other questions such as the reliability of the eyewitness, or the probability that forensic evidence from the scene of the crime matched that found on the defendant. These issues converged in one case where the defendant was stopped by police in the vicinity of an attempted robbery fifteen minutes after it had taken place. There were a number of identifying witnesses and forensic evidence to link the accused with a sack of guns, gloves, and anoraks found abandoned near the scene of the offence. Fibres were found on the accused's hair which matched those found on a balaclava helmet in the sack. According to the forensic report, it was unlikely that a person chosen at random from the population would have such fibres in their hair. The judge characterized the fact-finding issue as one of determining how far the respective pieces of identification and forensic evidence tied the accused to the scene of the attempted robbery, and he considered each piece of evidence, pointing out on each occasion its weakness. The identifying witnesses were only able to give a sketchy description of the robbers, and although the forensic evidence had seemed quite strong in the report, the forensic witness admitted in the course of evidence that no attempt was made to examine the jersey the accused had been wearing at the time, and that it was conceivable that the fibres found in his hair had come from this jersey rather than from the balaclava.

In another robbery case involving identification evidence the judge listed the *Turnbull* factors for the jury and told them that these should be considered to determine the quality of the identification.[37] Although the case was a recognition case where the identifying witness claimed to know the accused, the judge first emphasized that mistakes of recognition of relations and near friends can be made and continued as follows:

Three people may be mistaken. You may think it decreases the odds when there were three rather than one person recognizing, but it doesn't by any means make it inevitable that it was Mr J. It's a very open question for you. So when you're dealing with this situation you have got to consider many things about the circumstances in which the recognition occurred, the time for making the recognition, how long a time, the range, whether there were any obstructions in the way, the lighting, the sobriety of the person making the recognition, how distinctive is the person being

---

[37] [1977] QB 224.

recognized—has he a very commonplace look or has he a distinctive look, what pressure there is on the witness making the recognition at the time of making the recognition, fear, hysteria—and that might be very applicable in the case of Mrs B.

These cases fall more squarely within the 'meter model' of decision-making than the 'story model'.

Judges appeared to adopt both meter and story models of reasoning in their decision-making. In addition, there were issues to be decided which did not fit in either of these models. It has been pointed out that most debates about evidence, inference, and proof have proceeded on the simplifying, but generally false, assumption that triers of fact in the legal context decide only questions of pure 'fact', which can be clearly distinguished from questions of value and of law.[38] Fact-finding in the criminal process is never a 'pure' exercise of evaluating evidence. As stated before, decision-makers also have to relate the facts to the relevant legal standards.[39] At the end of the inquiry the tribunal of fact must ask whether its findings can be classified within the relevant legal standard.[40] In our sample, some cases involved what in Chapter Four we called 'interpretation of the defendant's action'. Sometimes this involved story construction, determining exactly what the defendant thought or did. Sometimes this involved a question of classification: was the defendant's driving reckless or careless? Was there grievous bodily harm or actual bodily harm? Sometimes both questions were involved, as in one duress case where the defendant claimed he had been pressurized into repairing firearms for the Ulster Defence Association. The judge took the view that the defendant had neither factually nor legally raised the issue of duress. He did not believe the defendant's account of how pressure was applied to him and in any event he refused to accept that his explanation (that he took the weapons to avoid 'hassle') suggested anything resembling a threat to cause death or serious injury.

It is also important to note that the verdict delivered at the end of the trial is more than a descriptive statement of liability (guilty or not guilty); it is also a prescriptive statement of the accused's position *vis-à-vis* the offence for which he or she has been prosecuted.[41] It follows that triers of fact may wish to depart from the strictly factual and legal tasks of determining guilt and consider whether the defendant deserves to suffer the consequences of conviction. Here, there is an important distinction to be made between the position of the juror as trier of fact and the position of the judge as trier of

---

[38] Twining (1986), 391.   [39] Chapter Three, page 77.

[40] Jackson (1983), 88. This task has been given various names: 'classification' (McCormick (1978), 95–7); 'naming' (Wisdom (1951), 187); 'description' (Wilson (1963)); 'disposition' (Morris (1942)); 'denotation' (Williams (1976), 473).

[41] Compare the distinction made by Austin between performative and constative utterances: see Austin (1962), 1–11. The statement 'X is guilty' both *describes* a state of affairs (a constative statement) and *prescribes* a change in X's legal status (a performative utterance).

fact.[42] The judge, as Kalven and Zeisel said, has an official role to play. Judges must classify the facts within the existing legal norms because the judicial task is one of implementing these norms. Jurors, on the other hand, have greater freedom to disregard the law and consider the merits of the individual case. Indeed, defenders of the jury system have emphasized that the advantage of jury trial is that juries are able to do justice, in a way that judges cannot, according to the merits and not just according to law.[43] Whether this is desirable or not depends on whether the purpose of the criminal trial is viewed primarily as implementing the policy of the criminal law, or resolving a conflict between the state and the individual where the central question is not merely whether the defendant broke the law but whether the defendant deserves the censure of conviction. In short, is the goal one of implementing the criminal law (albeit qualified by safeguards for the accused) or one of implementing the principle of judging a defendant on the individual merits of the case?[44]

This brings into question the view expressed in Chapter Three that it does not matter whether the arbiters in conflict-resolution are lay or professional judges.[45] There seems to be an important link between the way in which the criminal process is conceptualized and the choice of lay or professional decision-making. A professional judge must be accountable for his or her decisions to the legal system and ultimately to the community. This means that he or she must apply the standards laid down by the community. A professional judge is therefore better suited to the task of law enforcement. Jurors, on the other hand, are less accountable *to* the community. They are *of* the community themselves and they are therefore in a stronger position to take account of individual merits. In a comparison of the different approaches adopted by lay and professional English magistrates towards sentencing, the more lenient sentencing decisions of lay magistrates was attributed to the different positions which lay and stipendiary magistrates occupy in the court system and in the community.[46] As full-time professionals the stipendiaries saw themselves as responsible to, and held responsible by, the court system and the community. In contrast the lay magistrates viewed '*themselves* as "the public", as representatives rather than delegates', so that although aware of public expectations they had less of an obligation to attend to them.[47]

---

[42] For general comment on the importance of standpoint in decision-making, see Twining and Miers (1991), 64–74, 184–92.   [43] See Devlin (1956), 151–8; Freeman (1981), 90.

[44] See Zuckerman (1986), 495–6. For discussion of the distinction between policy and principle, see Dworkin (1977), 22–3; 90–100.   [45] Chapter Three, page 59.

[46] Diamond (1990).

[47] *Ibid.*, 213. Damaska has also claimed that when power is vested in amateurs, 'verdicts, judgments, or other authoritative determinations, whether rudimentary or collective, are not conceived as pronouncements of an agency independent of the individuals comprising it, and remain highly personal': see Damaska (1986), 24.

This important difference between the roles of the professional trier and the lay trier may account for their different approaches towards decision-making. Jury trial enables defendants through their legal representatives to broaden the scope of the contest beyond purely legal and factual considerations. We have seen that counsel reported that they were able to run 'sympathy points' more easily in jury trials. This does not mean that jurors depart entirely from the facts and the law.[48] Kalven and Zeisel found that jurors gave reign to their sense of values in the guise of resolving doubts about the facts. Judges, on the other hand, were less inclined to yield to equitable considerations. A further point is that judges, unlike jurors, have other tasks in the criminal process and these may influence the approach taken during the trial. One of the judge's tasks is sentencing convicted defendants. One judge said that he thought sentencing decisions could be more difficult to resolve and that it was these decisions, rather than the trial decisions, that gave him 'the wakeful nights' because it was the sentence more than the verdict which really counted, particularly the question of whether someone should go to prison or not. It is unrealistic to think that judges can separate their fact-finding task in the non-jury trial entirely from the decisions that they have to make after the trial. While jurors know that they have to blend any equity they wish to exercise into the verdict itself,[49] judges know that they may have an opportunity of exercising some discretion at the sentencing stage.

JUDICIAL AND LAY APPROACHES TO FACT-FINDING

In Chapter Two we saw that one of the concerns raised about the Diplock process is that judges may become case-hardened over a period of time with the result that they become much more disposed than lay triers to convict defendants. However, we concluded that the debate about case-hardening has proved rather inconclusive and that a more systematic analysis is needed to explain why the outcomes in jury and non-jury cases are different. In particular we argued that a purely statistical approach to this issue could fail to give a true picture of judicial fact-finding. Table 8.1 shows that contrary to the general trend which has shown that the acquittal rate in Diplock cases lags behind that in jury trials, there was in our sample a greater tendency for defendants to be acquitted in Diplock cases. Of course our sample of trials

---

[48] Research provides little evidence that jurors depart entirely from their 'official' fact-finding task. See for example Saks (1976); Hastie, Penrod, and Pennington (1983).

[49] Although juries have a right to add a recommendation of mercy to a verdict of guilty, it is regarded as undesirable for the judge to bring this right to their attention in summing up: see *Archbold*, para. 4–426.

TABLE 8.1 *Outcome of trials*

	Jury (17 trials)	Diplock (26 trials)	Total
Guilty	11	10	21
Not guilty	6	13	19
Mixed[1]	0	1	1
Re-trial	0	2	2

[1] A mixed outcome occurred in multi-defendant trials where not all the accused were convicted.

was very small, but it does illustrate the difficulties about making broad generalizations on the basis of statistics that judges become case-hardened. As we stressed in Chapter Two, there is a need to go beyond the statistics and investigate the approach of individual judges who hear the cases, and the reaction of counsel appearing regularly in Diplock trials, as well as the types of cases involved and the issues contested in these cases.

Proponents of the case-hardening thesis have tended to assume a gradual increase in the conviction rate over time. This argument overlooks the fact that judges retire and are replaced by fresh judges who might be expected at first to display a less case-hardened attitude. There was no particular tendency for recently appointed judges in our sample to acquit more than the others, nor for the most experienced judges to convict more. But a number of defence counsel thought that it was difficult for judges to maintain the same freshness of approach over time. As one counsel put it: 'I don't criticize them because quite honestly even practising on the defence side it's hard not to get case-hardened, it's hard not to get cynical when the same excuse and classic story is presented . . . Constantly one has to nip oneself and say, "Would twelve people who had just freshly walked off the street be just as cynical as I am about this case?"—and that's me defending!'

Other factors at work in the Diplock context, however, counteract these case-hardening tendencies. In the particular context of fact-finding in Diplock trials in Northern Ireland, judges seemed acutely aware of the importance of public accountability. The recommendation by the Diplock Commission to invest judges with the determination of guilt in certain serious criminal cases was an important break with tradition, giving to judges a task which is not legitimately considered to be theirs in the rest of the United Kingdom. In a public lecture in 1992 held under the auspices of the Faculty of Law at the Hebrew University of Jerusalem, the former Lord Chief Justice of Northern Ireland, Lord Lowry, made the point that the justification for dispensing with a jury must be found, if at all, in the performance of the judge, as assessed objectively and by the public.[50] Judges had for a long time had important fact-finding responsibilities in civil and criminal trials. It had long been accepted that civil actions of the greatest importance are satisfactorily tried by judge alone. Moreover, the judge had always had two important decisions to make in criminal trials which involved consideration of the evidence, namely the decision whether to admit an accused's statement and the decision whether the prosecution has made out a sufficiently strong case to be put before a jury. Lord Lowry went on to make the interesting point that since the issue on the *voir dire* and a finding of guilty both require proof beyond reasonable doubt, criminal adjudication on the facts is easier than civil adjudication and this burden of proof therefore constitutes a significant safeguard. We saw in the last section that judges sometimes resolve conflicting stories on the basis of the burden of proof. A further factor which his Lordship went on to stress was the pressure which judges were under in the Diplock context:[51]

... few people who have not themselves undertaken the task can appreciate the grave sense of responsibility, which can only increase in proportion to the gravity of the charge, that the trial judge inevitably feels. I need hardly stress the point that the judge will be aware that he is operating in the glare of publicity and that not only the general public but well-informed and potentially hostile critics will scrutinise his deliberations.

The reference to deliberations is a reference to the reasoned judgment which judges are required to deliver. This was thought by many judges to act as a significant restraint as it meant that judges, unlike juries, were fully accountable for their decisions. We shall examine written judgments in the next chapter.

Another form of scrutiny referred to in the lecture is that foreign courts may have cause to examine the fairness of Diplock proceedings in the course of applications for the extradition of suspects to stand trial in Diplock courts.[52] There are various ways of measuring fairness; one method is to compare the outcome of Diplock cases with the outcome of those cases which have continued to be tried by jury. This is a somewhat crude mechanism, as we have seen, but given the continuing claim made by virtually all participants in the Diplock debate that trial by jury remains the *ideal* method of trial it is not surprising that such a comparison has been made. One judge told us that, although it might not be fair to make comparisons between Diplock and jury cases because the former tended to deal with more serious offences, comparisons were inevitably made between

---

[50] The Lionel Cohen Lecture delivered on 28 April 1992. See Lowry (1992), 130–1.
[51] *Ibid.*, 131.
[52] For discussion of the relevance of fair trial arguments to extradition, see Campbell (1989).

judicial conviction rates and those of juries.[53] We saw in the last chapter that certain judges tried in Diplock trials to conform as closely as possible with the jury trial procedure, and that most believed that their assumption of fact-finding responsibilities did not alter the fundamental umpireal role that they should assume during the trial.

Inevitably, however, the fact that they have to act as judges accountable to the general public, rather than as jurors who may act however they wish, means that their role as triers of fact differs from the role of jurors. Moreover, one of the reasons why they were accorded the responsibility of determining guilt in the first place was because juries were deemed unfit to try emergency cases. By this logic it is undesirable for them to put themselves in the position of a jury, even if it were possible to do so. Instead judges had to develop their own distinctively judicial approach to fact-finding. In the following passage from a judgment delivered in one of the 'supergrass' trials at a time when as we have seen Diplock courts faced their greatest challenge, Lord Lowry made it clear exactly what approach the judges had to follow:[54]

'Amid the clash of arms the laws are silent': so Cicero exclaimed over 2000 years ago. During the greatest conflict of our history Lord Atkin bravely ventured to contradict this assertion. Now, too, peace, order and society itself are under fierce and constant attack and that is why we must remember Lord Atkin's famous dictum: 'In this country, amid the clash of arms the laws are *not* silent. They may be changed, but they speak the same language in war as in peace.' This war is being waged by organisations which style themselves armies and observe military procedures, but it has not invaded, and will not be allowed to invade, the courts. The rule of law has prevailed and will continue to prevail there. We will accept but one standard of proof in criminal cases, namely, proof beyond reasonable doubt. This is a concept difficult enough to describe, but easy for an honest man to recognise, which brings to criminal adjudication, whether by a jury or by another tribunal, a certainty and a finality which can be absent from civil proceedings. It is a statement of the obvious that maintaining the rule of law means deciding cases according to law, and the paramount law in criminal cases is that guilt cannot be established save by proof beyond reasonable doubt.

Later in his lecture Lord Lowry made it clear that this required judges to pay scrupulous attention to the evidence in each case. He referred to a passage in an *Irish Times* article by Mary Holland in 1986 in which she claimed that the Northern Ireland judges had become relatively hardened to the emotions surrounding terrorist trials and contrasted this attitude with the highly charged atmosphere which surrounded such trials in Britain.[55]

---

[53] This issue is discussed in Chapter Two, pages 33–6.
[54] [1983] 13 NIJB, cited by Lord Lowry in his Lionel Cohen Lecture: see Lowry (1992), 118–19.   [55] *Ibid.*, 132.

Lord Lowry drew attention to the fact that the word 'hardened' was given a different nuance here than that which had been used by critics who claimed that the judges were case-hardened. Elsewhere in the lecture he voiced the opinion that the institution of non-jury trial in the tense atmosphere induced by the troubles in Northern Ireland had 'obviated both acquittals and convictions against the weight of the evidence ... caused by the jury's emotional bias.'[56] Other judges stressed to us the importance of adopting a 'judicial' attitude. Judges could not allow sentiment to get the better of them. They were bound by legal principle and 'hard logic and reason'. This is not to say that the fears of some counsel about case-hardened attitudes against the defence were completely ill-founded. It did seem, however, that the special position in which judges find themselves as triers of fact in Northern Ireland impose more significant constraints on any such tendency than may be the case when judges assume fact-finding responsibilities in a less politically charged and less controversial setting.

Nevertheless, however conscious judges seemed of the need to be seen to weigh the evidence carefully, certain biases may creep in at a less conscious level. This is where there seemed to be a consensus, at least among defence counsel, that there were considerable differences between the way in which judges and juries approached certain kinds of cases and issues. Defence counsel said that they would generally favour jury trial over trial by judge alone, but there were certain types of case and certain issues which they would rather have tried by professional judges than lay triers.

Table 8.2 compares the outcome of the Diplock and jury cases in our sample in terms of the most serious offence charged in each case. There does not appear to be any particular disposition towards conviction or acquittal in respect of any particular kind of offence, except that juries convicted in five out of the six sexual offence cases observed (the prosecution offered no further evidence in the sixth case) and judged tended to acquit in the robbery and minor terrorism cases.

There was a view amongst counsel that sexual offences were difficult to defend before a jury. Judges are required in such cases to warn juries against acting on the uncorroborated evidence of complainants. Such warnings have been the object of much criticism and there is certainly an inconsistency in a judge having, on the one hand, to warn the jury that it is *dangerous* to convict solely on the evidence of a complainant of a sexual offence, but on the other hand to tell the jury that they *may* convict without corroboration if the victim's evidence satisfies them beyond a reasonable doubt.[57] In at least two of the sexual offence cases we observed there was no

---

[56] [1983] 13 NIJB, 130.

[57] See Law Commission (1991). Corroboration warnings have been abolished in England and Wales under section 32 of the Criminal Justice and Public Order Act 1994.

TABLE 8.2 *Outcome of trials by most serious offence charged*[1]

	Jury		Diplock	
	Guilty	Not guilty	Guilty	Not guilty
Robbery	1	0	1	3
Explosives, etc	0	1	6	4
Sexual	5	1	0	0
Property	1	1	0	0
Assault	3	1	0	1
Minor terrorism	0	0	1	4
Murder	0	1	2	1
Driving	1	1	0	0

[1] The cases where a re-trial was ordered and the outcome was mixed (see Table 8.1) have been excluded from the table.

solid corroboration but the jury nevertheless convicted. One judge told us that a problem in sexual cases is that there is a feeling of great revulsion, and that in his experience juries tended to convict, although not always. In one case involving alleged buggery on a 13-year-old boy the judge specifically warned the jury to put both sympathy for the young boy, and equally prejudice against the defendant, out of their minds. One counsel referred to a rape case which he was to defend the following day:

I know the situation I'm going to be facing of considerable prejudice against anyone charged with rape . . . I know that's the main problem I have, whether I've a good case or not. I mean this chap says that the intercourse was with consent, that may or may not be, but a lot of the jury will be sitting there saying, 'That criminal over there must be guilty or he wouldn't be in the dock'. Now that is particularly difficult in a rape case because you face all the prejudices. If it was a judge alone I wouldn't have to worry about that because he would deal with it entirely on the evidence. In some cases that would suit me all right. In some cases it wouldn't. Now oddly enough in this case I have tomorrow it would suit me nearly as well not to have a jury at all because I would rather the case was dealt with on a colder, unemotional fashion because there's enough emotion to start with.

Sexual cases were not the only example when defence counsel believed that they might prefer a case to be tried before a professional judge. Although there seems no particular reason why judges should acquit defendants in robbery cases, in our sample such cases invariably concerned identification and forensic evidence, and almost without exception counsel believed that judges were more aware of the dangers of identification evidence than juries. Most said that they would prefer such cases to be tried by judges alone and some said that they would prefer cases turning on forensic evidence to be tried by professional judges. We argued in the last section that these kinds of cases call for a different approach to the evidence, weighing up the probabilities piece by piece rather than constructing a story from the evidence.

Table 8.3 compares the outcome of cases in terms of the main issues in the trials observed. There did not appear to be any tendency for judges or juries to resolve certain kinds of issue in any particular direction, except that juries convicted in all cases where a particular defence was raised. So far as identification cases were concerned, however, the jury convicted in the two cases where the issue was left for them to resolve (the judge withdrew the issue in the other two cases and the jury were directed to acquit). Although judges also convicted in two identification cases, one of these convictions was quashed on appeal.

Certainly judges seemed acutely aware of the dangers of identification evidence. In Chapter Six we saw how in one case the judge took an active stance in eliciting details about the circumstances of an identification, only to grant an application for a direction of no case to answer at the end of the prosecution case. As one defence counsel put it:

In many identification cases the Diplock courts have acquitted and they have acquitted on clear principles of law outlined in *R v Turnbull* where an emotive jury would not . . . I have seen it happening time and time again. I have seen Diplock judges acquit where they virtually tell the defendant that they were involved but the principles of law are such that they are so cautious that they acquit.

There was less agreement among defence counsel about the advantages of judges trying cases which turn on forensic evidence. One counsel's view was that people with no educational achievements are often better at statistics: 'You come across people who frequent bookmakers' shops and they can tell

TABLE 8.3 *Outcome of trials by main issue*

	Jury		Diplock	
	Guilty	Not guilty	Guilty	Not guilty
Circumstantial evidence	0	0	0	1
Interpretation of defendant's actions	1	3	0	1
Identification	2	2	2	2
Specific defence	4	1	1	4
Confessions	0	1	2	2
Credibility of accounts	3	0	1	1
Intent/knowledge	1	0	4	3

you what a triple bet of 6–4, 20–1, 9–2 means within seconds. Forensic sciences often come down to an estimate that there is a 1 in whatever chance of having fibres in the same type of pullover.' Another thought judges had a better grasp of forensic issues: 'Where one is dealing with a forensic exercise which is purely an intellectual, logical, rational exercise in forensics I am much happier having a Diplock judge dealing with that than a jury who may not really listen and not attach a great deal of significance to that and attach significance to something more emotive.'

The view that judges were better at cases involving intellectual exercises caused a number of counsel to say that their experience of Diplock courts had persuaded them that the defence should have a right to elect for a bench trial, as in the United States. However, defence counsel said that they would still normally (nine times out of ten according to one counsel) advise their clients to elect for trial by jury. One reason for this seemed to be that many cases concern credibility issues and on these matters it was thought easier to persuade a jury towards the defence side. This was not necessarily because judges applied a lower standard of proof. Lord Lowry put the importance of proof beyond reasonable doubt at the centre of the approach which judges should take to the evidence. Judges stressed to us, and also throughout their judgments, the importance of the prosecution proving its case beyond reasonable doubt.[58] One senior judge said that even if the defendant was not giving evidence, it was necessary constantly to test the prosecution case to see whether there was an alternative version consistent with innocence: 'In this sense the task is not simply a reactive one of accepting the prosecution version over the defence version or *vice versa*. The judge has to actively consider what other possible versions are consistent with innocence.'

Although counsel thought that many judges did strive to do this, some thought it much easier to raise a reasonable doubt before a jury than a judge. It was not so much that judges set their mind against defendants, but they did scrutinize defence claims very carefully, as we saw in Chapter Six, and when, as one counsel put it, the school of hard logic and reason came face to face with the defence version of events, the latter often came out the worse. Counsel attributed this partly to case-hardening, but part of it also seemed to be explained by an inability to understand how the excuse could be credible:

A point that a judge maybe accepted in a number of cases in his early days, because he has heard the point, alibi, excuse, whatever it is, on a number of occasions, he tends to become case-hardened against it. A jury will not have heard that excuse and perhaps from their own experience in their own house—whether it's a back street, a

---

[58] There seems to be considerable variation in the interpretation of standard of proof instructions: see Fletcher (1968). There is some evidence to suggest that judges in general hold higher standards for conviction than jurors: see Simon and Mahan (1971).

semi-detached or mansion—will know of cases where a dilemma has been put to some member of the public and will know whether it's a valid excuse, rather than someone who has heard it trotted out on a number of occasions. So a jury is fresher to an argument on the excuse, mitigation or whatever than perhaps a case-hardened judge.

It's an odd thing how a jury can be so sensitive at times. I mean, they can really soften the harshness of the law with a common sense approach. A judge is inclined to see things in terms of logic and reason, but life's not an exercise in logic and reason at all, I mean neither is crime or anything like it. There are other factors. A jury will understand those little, illogical stupid things that people do from time to time and a judge will not see it that way. He will be inclined to see it in the cold light of a court. Our everyday behaviour would appear totally ridiculous if you started to analyse it.

These statements suggest that defendants may be disadvantaged by a case-hardening attitude on the part of the judge, but the attitude attributed to judges is not one of rejecting the defence evidence out of hand. Rather, the kind of case-hardening described here is a colder, unemotional attitude towards the evidence. We saw above that this can operate to the benefit of defendants, but clearly it may also work to their disadvantage. The other reason suggested as to why defence explanations may be considered more credible to a jury than to a judge is that judges may simply be unable, because of their personal experience, to understand how an excuse or an explanation could be credible. In the simulated trial used by Pennington and Hastie middle and upper-class jurors were more inclined to find the defendant guilty than lower-class jurors because they could not undersand why the defendant might be carrying a knife other than for the purpose of carrying out an assault on the victim. Lower-class jurors on the other hand found it quite plausible that a man like the defendant would carry a knife wherever he went for his own protection. Although, as we have seen, the composition of the bench in Northern Ireland has been criticized on the ground that it used not to reflect the balance of religious persuasion in the community,[59] one counsel thought that the Northern Ireland judiciary was socially more representative of the community than the judiciary in England.[60] In his view it would not be uncommon to find that ordinary working people were represented in the families of judges, if not in this generation then one or two generations ago. Another counsel said that some judges were better at understanding ordinary people than others and in his view the main difficulty with Diplock trials had nothing to do with the

---

[59] See Chapter Two, page 30.

[60] For discussion of the social composition of the English judiciary, see Griffith (1992), 30–3. No systematic study has been made of the socio-economic background of Northern Ireland judges. Dickson has noted that 'superficially' a similar picture to the English picture emerges: see Dickson (1992), 134.

process but with the attitude of certain judges. He contrasted the attitude of some with that of the late Lord MacDermott, a former Lord Chief Justice of Northern Ireland, who was, in his view, probably the most outstanding judge of his time:

He had a great way of understanding ordinary people and ordinary things, he maintained that kind of interest in it. I mean I remember doing a case, as you know you've got to go into chambers if you're proving a minor settlement in a case, and this wee fellow from Fermanagh, it was some years ago, and he was wearing a big pair of brown boots with yellow laces in them and I remember Lord MacDermott looking at the wee fellow and saying, 'Those are a great pair of boots you've on you, where did you get those boots?' 'I got those in McGinns in West Bellaw.' 'Oh, do they sell boots and shoes there?' 'Yes', and he goes on and he talks about these boots that he has on him and it wasn't just totally patronizing, it didn't sound patronizing to me, I mean he was sort of on the level with the boy, there was an understanding there and he was good with that kind of thing. So it's a personality, it has to do, I think, ultimately with the personality of the judge himself and whether or not he can understand ordinary things or ordinary people and whether or not he can still maintain that freshness.

One case in our sample illustrated how important it is for triers of fact to have a real understanding of what goes on in the communities where arms are hidden. The defendant was a married woman with three children who was charged with possession of explosives in her home with intent to enable others to endanger life. A quantity of arms was found in a 'hide' which had been carefully constructed three or four feet deep below the kitchen floor. The defendant had been living in the house for seven years but in evidence at her trial she denied knowledge of the hide. She told the court that she was separated from her husband but she also said that he had retained a key to the front door, although this was not something that she had initially told the police. Her counsel pointed out that there was a possibility consistent with the defendant's innocence that the hide was constructed and used without her knowledge while she was away on holiday the previous summer. He reminded the judge that the defendant had done nothing to obstruct the police when they were searching her house to find the hide. The case prompted lengthy discussion between counsel and the judge in closing submissions. In his judgment the judge pointed out that the burden of proof was on the prosecution and said that he had asked himself whether there were any circumstances which raised a reasonable doubt as to the case presented by the Crown, but he concluded that he found it impossible to believe that a woman 'as intelligent and as aware as the defendant obviously was, could be unaware that the house in which she had lived had under the kitchen floor a hide of such substantial proportions'.

Of course, it is impossible to gauge whether a jury would have decided this case in any other way but this was an example where a jury might have been in a better position to assess the defendant's explanation, if there were someone of the defendant's background represented on the jury who might have a better understanding of the situation in which she was placed. It is also an example of a case where a jury might show sympathy for the plight of the defendant. The defendant was a young woman with three children with a clean record living alone with no support from her husband whom the police had not been able to find. There was also the consideration which the judge mentioned in sentencing that the defendant may have inherited the problem of the hide from her husband and was therefore put in an appalling predicament. This was not a matter that the defence chose to bring out at her trial because they were relying throughout on the defendant's lack of knowledge of the hide rather than on the predicament she was in, a course which would have involved an assumption that she had knowledge. Although these matters were considered by the judge in sentencing the defendant, he felt that there had to be a deterrent element in the sentence for an offence of this kind so that anyone who put themselves in her position would know 'beyond peradventure that if they were caught they would be dealt with severely.' The defendant was sentenced to nine years' imprisonment.

There is some support for the view that juries give greater credence to defence explanations. According to Kalven and Zeisel's 'liberation hypothesis' judges are much less inclined to 'hunt for doubts' especially in cases where the equities of the case are pressing.[61] Baldwin and McConville found that in the cases where professionals and juries disagreed about acquittals, professionals conceded that there was usually some identifiable factor, particularly a weakness in the prosecution case or a reasonably convincing explanation given by the defendant, which explained the jury verdict.[62] In her comparison of contested magistrates' and Crown Court trials, Vennard found that for the most part acquittals corresponded with a readily identifiable weakness in the prosecution case or an explanation from the defendant which was not manifestly discredited, but that juries were systematically more likely to acquit than magistrates.[63] She suggested that the differences in verdict may be a reflection of the stronger body of evidence which is required by juries from the prosecution in order to be convinced of guilt. In our research counsel seemed to think that the explanation for any greater jury leniency was due less to any discernible difference in the standard of proof required of prosecution evidence than to the greater credence given to defence explanations of the defendant's conduct.

There remains the point that although counsel believed that it was

[61] Kalven and Zeisel (1966), 495.
[62] Baldwin and McConville (1979).
[63] Vennard (1985).

generally more difficult to defend cases before a judge sitting alone, our sample shows no particular tendency for judges to convict more readily in cases involving the kind of credibility issues that some counsel thought worked more to an accused's advantage before a jury. Part of the reason may be that in our sample there were a number of cases involving sexual offences where the jury had little sympathy for the defendant. This emphasizes the point that 'jury equity' may work against, as well as in favour of, the defence. However, it seemed also to be the case that in the Diplock cases counsel were particularly adept in the tactics which they employed to defend cases. The point was stressed that counsel knew the judges well from past experience and therefore knew the best tactics to choose. Although the nature of the offence and the evidence adduced to prove it are matters for the prosecution to decide, defence counsel develop particular expertise in deciding which issues to contest, and how to contest them.

One question, for example, that defence counsel must decide in the course of defending a case is whether the defendant should give evidence. In jury cases, counsel told us when there was an explanation to be put forward, it was always best if possible to put the defendant into the witness box. Juries were always suspicious when defendants did not go into the witness box as they liked to hear the defendant's side of the story for themselves. In Diplock cases, on the other hand, counsel felt less pressure to put defendants into the witness box and there were special risks in doing so. In identification cases, for example, counsel felt that judges could accept more readily that there is no need to put a defendant into the witness box. As one counsel put it: 'In a Diplock identification case I wouldn't be inclined to call the defendant, whereas in front of a jury the jury would wonder why he hadn't been called. The judge knows why he hasn't been called because if the evidence isn't there, it isn't there.'

There are other, and greater, risks in putting defendants into the witness box in Diplock cases. We saw in the last chapter that certain judges cross-examined defendants quite thoroughly. Also, counsel were aware that judgments of credibility against a defendant were very difficult to appeal (a point to which we return in Chapter Nine): 'In a Diplock case quite often you don't call your punter [client] because it gives the judge the opportunity in his judgment to say that he's heard the defendant and he perceives him to be a liar. Once that goes into the transcript, that he's heard the defendant and doesn't believe what he says, it's a difficult case to appeal.' We have seen that legislation now enables judges to draw inferences from the failure of a defendant to give evidence.[64] However, in the sample of cases we observed this did not work to the disadvantage of defendants and certain

[64] See Chapter Two, page 48.

judges expressly stated in their judgments that they were not drawing inferences against the defendant on this account.[65]

There were also differences in the arguments adopted by counsel to contest cases. In the last chapter we saw that counsel felt it necessary in Diplock cases to choose their line of defence very carefully. Consistent with the cold, analytical approach which they ascribed to judges, counsel would try to steer the case if possible towards taking a cold, logical review of the evidence. One analysis of evidence has suggested that it is possible to construct evidence in terms of arguments for and against guilt. Wigmore, for example, devised a chart method for analysing a mixed mass of evidence in order to arrive at a conclusion upon the main facts to be proved.[66] The method required fact-finders to articulate all the components of an argument in the form of propositions and then to chart the relations between these propositions. Although there is no evidence that judges went so far as to adopt the chart method recommended by Wigmore, one judge said that he made it a practice in criminal cases to write down all the essential incriminating evidence on one side of a sheet of paper and the rebutting evidence on the other side. He said that he might begin to do this during the trial. He would then whittle down the points of disagreement and see exactly where battle was joined. This judge thought that the process of writing down the evidence on paper was a very good discipline as it prevented inadmissible evidence filtering through and reduced reliance on instinct and feeling. Another experienced judge said that it was his practice to map out in writing the issues in complicated cases, the charges that were alleged against each defendant, and what evidence had been led on these. The question that was often put before judges was whether there was enough hard evidence to establish proof beyond a reasonable doubt. This meant putting the prosecution to its proof, as it is called, picking holes in the prosecution case rather than attempting to come up with a rival story. If a rival story was put forward, this was done, as we saw in the above case concerning possession of explosives, by proposing an alternative explanation consistent with innocence, rather than on the basis of actual truth. When cases involved the construction of stories this meant that attention was focused on hard evidence that could corroborate the story advanced.

A recent development of the 'story' model of factual reasoning has claimed that triers of fact seek to anchor stories in evidence which is supported by general rules or common-sense presumptions that cannot be

---

[65] For more discussion of the way in which courts have interpreted this legislation, see Jackson (1991), (1993).

[66] (1937). After years of neglect, this analysis has recently become the subject of considerable interest among a number of legal scholars: see Twining (1985); Robertson (1990); Anderson and Twining (1991); Tillers and Schum (1991). For a cogent critique of the chart method, see Twining (1985), 180–3.

contested in a particular case.[67] It seemed that judges often did this. For example, judges said that one of the most difficult questions they had to determine was whether a witness was telling the truth. In assessing credibility one judge said that it was important to look for internal consistency and plausibility, or 'straws in the wind' which may not ring true. It was also necessary to do 'cross-checks with other evidence'. Another judge said that a witness's general demeanour was not a helpful indicator. It was much better to look for 'objective facts' on which to ground the various accounts given and if these were lacking he would be very chary of accepting a witness's story. This was why he was cautious about verbal confessions which were not signed or corroborated in any way:

Policemen are trained to give evidence in court but they rarely come across with absolute integrity, simply because you don't know them well enough. You listen to them for a short period of time, you don't know their background, you don't remember the last time you came across them, so to make an assessment which says, 'I'm sure this man is telling the turth' is an extremely dangerous task to undertake. Equally the accused is nervous, he may lie about a lot of things, but on the question whether he made a verbal confession, whilst you may decide he probably did say it, I don't think I would feel competent about saying he is a liar.

Other judges did not seem to take such a pessimistic view of demeanour evidence. One judge directed us to a passage in a judgment where he had highlighted the particular difficulty of relying on demeanour to assess the credibility of interviewing officers but had then gone on to indicate that he found the evidence of the officers in that case to be very impressive:

The interviewing detective has rarely an independent recollection of the events of interviews that have taken place many months before. Their nature and conduct is blurred on recall not only by time but by many interviews of many suspects since. Recourse therefore to the interview notes is essential for the detective. But it determines the complete ambit of his evidence. It minimises any spontaneity in the giving of his evidence and it reduces perception of his credibility by the judge on the basis of manner and demeanour in the witness-box. Sometimes, however, ironically in the circumstances, a keen cross-examination can give a strong impression of the credibility of a detective's evidence.

Judges agreed that things would be a lot easier for them if there were some authenticating record of what went on in police interview rooms.[68]

The various emphases put by different judges on demeanour evidence

---

[67] Wagenaar, van Koppen, and Crombag (1993).

[68] For details of cases where judges have voiced their concerns about the lack of authentication of police interviews, see Hill and Lee (1993), 92–4. In Chapter Two we noted that the failure to introduce audio and video recording of police interviews with terrorist suspects has been the subject of international criticism. During the period of our research, police interviews with suspects were not tape-recorded. As a result of the Police and Criminal

illustrates the more general point that all judges do not adopt the same approach towards types of evidence. Counsel considered that there were significant differences of approach between judges, and that it was therefore important to know before which judge the case was to be contested. It was also accepted that individual juries could take different approaches towards the evidence. We saw in the last chapter that when calculations were made about pleading guilty, much could depend on where the case was being tried. According to one prosecuting counsel with many years' experience:

There's a basic level of convictions in the east of the province which approximates to Diplock. In the west it doesn't. This is not political. I believe that where you get a middle-class, commercial and better educated, or more sophisticated juror, you'll have a more responsible, a more enlightened approach to the criminal problem and that will result in the appropriate case in a conviction. You see, in the country there's still the view that the law case is to some extent a sort of game. The point about the old Irish jury trials is that they were for such things as assaults, stealing in certain forms but very little by way of murder. But the crime problem was not a very big problem and therefore the community reacted very often by thinking that the guy being tried at all represented a punishment for him and therefore they wouldn't increase that punishment by convicting.

We have seen that counsel have to develop an overall theory of the case they are arguing.[69] One defence counsel said that in each case, the particular mode of trial (judge or jury) would play an important part in the development of this theory, but so also would the *particular* judge or jury before whom he was appearing:

We are so familiar here with the areas of the country and the judges and the types of juries and dealing with prosecution counsel, and everything goes into the computer. I think once you go to court and see what everything is like, it goes into your computer without thinking and I think you then evolve a kind of *modus operandi* to deal with that particular case on that particular day and whether it be a judge or a jury, you take all that into account.

It would be difficult in the light of this to make any conclusive observations about the case-hardening controversy. There were clearly differences in the way in which individual judges and jurors approached the fact-finding task. There were also differences in the way professionals and jurors approached the evidence according to the kind of issues and cases

---

Evidence (Northern Ireland) Order 1989, however, interviews with suspects other than those arrested under the Prevention of Terrorism Act 1989 are now tape-recorded. For comment on the latest position, see Doran and Jackson (1994), 98–100, and see the recommendations of Blom-Cooper, *First Annual (1993) Report of the Independent Commissioner for the Holding Centres* (1994).

[69] See Chapter Seven, page 197.

that were contested and it appears that defendants are not always disadvantaged by having a professional trier of fact. One prosecuting counsel concluded by saying that a defendant's preference for Diplock or jury trial should depend on whether or not he is guilty: 'If I were innocent I would prefer a Diplock situation. If I am innocent the evidence can't be that strong by definition. Whereas if the evidence was strong and I was guilty, I would hope to get some member of the jury who doesn't like the police or something.'

Put simply, this view suggests that a judge should be more likely to come to a 'correct' verdict than should a jury. One problem with this view is that it assumes that an easy distinction can be made between the guilty and the innocent in terms of the legal standards applied. A finding of guilt involves making a number of value judgments, in terms of both the means used to determine the evidence and a decision that that evidence points towards guilt. Another problem with this view is that it takes a professionally-based approach towards the ascription of guilt in the criminal process. Much of the criticism directed at jury research in general has been based on the argument that it is misleading to gauge jury performance by reference to the views of professional participants in the trial process.[70] The 'correctness' of the jury's verdict is to be located rather in the broader conception of the jury's role as a channel for the expression of community-derived values and thus by definition is likely to be irreconcilable with professional expectation.

This dichotomy between the wider, merits-based, approach which a jury can adopt in response to the evidence and the harder, more legalistic, approach of the judge has recurred as an important theme in the present chapter. One point which emerged from our interviews with defence counsel was the strong preference which they had as practitioners for jury trial, despite the fact that many seemed adept at turning cases before a professional judge to their advantage. In the last chapter we saw how the absence of the jury appears to dilute the quality of adversariness between prosecution and defence. The judge played a more intrusive role in the proceedings than in jury trial. One way in which this was evident was in the interventions that he made. Certain counsel, however, seemed less concerned about this than about the fact that *whatever stance the judge took at the trial*, the absence of the jury limited their scope to contest the prosecution case fully and there could be no consideration of the merits of the case other than on the basis of the legal standards to be applied to the accused. This would seem to be an inevitable consequence of allocating the task of determining guilt to professional triers. Indeed this perception of the

---

[70] Freeman (1978).

professional judge's role may offer a new dimension to the case-hardening debate so prevalent in the Diplock context. Perhaps the more pervasive form of case-hardening lies not in judges' readiness to accept the particular lines of prosecution argument, but in the fact that their attention is confined to a logical assessment of the issue of the accused's legal guilt on the offences charged.

Such a stance, while depriving the accused of the opportunity to develop extraneous arguments to persuade the trier of fact of his or her entitlement to an acquittal, does not necessarily operate contrarily to the accused's interests. As one judge indicated: 'To convict, you not only have to be sure of guilt; you also have to be sure on the evidence. In one Diplock case I was sure one of the defendants was guilty but I could not connect guilt with the evidence. There were strands of evidence but not enough to link her with the evidence for sure.' One judge gave us an example of an actual case in which he had acquitted the accused on an explosives charge because of presentational deficiencies in the scientific evidence led by the prosecution, although he said that he was convinced of the accused's guilt. In such a case, if the issues were being presented to a jury defence counsel would undoubtedly exploit the weakness in the prosecution evidence, but it is difficult to envisage that flaws in presentation alone would lead a jury to acquit in circumstances where its members were 'certain' of the accused's involvement in the offence.

Research into lay and professional fact-finding is still in its infancy, but even if specific differences can be discerned in the way in which evidence is approached (as we have suggested is the case), it is another matter altogether to say that one approach is more proper than another. Rather, it would seem that the differences between the lay and professional approaches reflect different views of the purpose of the criminal process. The professional approach places emphasis on the 'rule of law' and values associated with it, such as the need for full proof on the legal charges brought and the exclusion of extra-legal considerations. The lay approach places emphasis upon the need for decision-making to be tuned to take account of community values and of the wider merit of convicting the accused on the charges brought.

THE THREAT OF PREJUDICE

So far we have considered the general approach taken by judges and juries to evidence which is presented in the course of the trial and in accordance with the normal rules of evidence and procedure. The emphasis has been on the role which these decision-makers play in the wider criminal justice system. We now turn to the more specific problem of how the institutional position held by the professional trier of fact bears on the decision-making process. One particular problem in professional trials is that it is more difficult to ensure that the fact-finder is not privy to certain forms of prejudicial information. As observed in Chapter Three, in jury trials the trier of fact comes 'cold' to the evidence, whereas in Diplock trials judges have access to the committal papers which gives them prior knowledge of the case. Further, in jury trials the rules of evidence can be enforced by the trial judge as a physical barrier to the presentation of evidence, but in Diplock trials the judge, as the trier of both fact and law, is invariably exposed to potentially inadmissible material. Thus, although (as observed above) the judge is compelled to confine the contest within narrower boundaries than a lay trier of fact, he or she has access to much more information than a lay trier, which raises another concern for defence counsel about professional triers of fact. We shall now consider in turn the difficulties which arise when judges have some prior knowledge about the case, or become aware of inadmissible evidence in the course of the proceedings.

(a) Prior knowledge

In previous chapters we saw that a number of judges had read the papers before the trial, and in one instance a judge admitted that he had formed a provisional view that the prosecution case was weak. Although this particular view disadvantaged the prosecution rather than the defence, some defence counsel were concerned that first impressions in other cases could swing the case against the defence. In one continental study where a group of professional judges who had read the case file before trial was compared with another group which had refrained from studying the file, it was found that those who had read the file convicted much more often than those who had not read it.[71] In continental procedure, however, judges are required to read the file beforehand and are entitled to be influenced by it.[72] This is not the case in Diplock trials where triers of fact are only permitted to rely on the evidence admitted at the trial. Most counsel thought that judges did make a conscious effort to approach trials with a fresh mind.

We saw in the last chapter that the majority of cases end in a guilty plea, and that in any plea discussions an assumption of guilt tends to apply. One judge said that it is always possible that after negotiations the defendant might not plead and that the case would be contested, but that this was rare. If any difficulty arose, the case could always be transferred to a different judge. Another judge said that if any view was indicated in pre-trial

---

[71] See Wagenaar, van Koppen, and Crombag (1993), 27.
[72] Damaska (1986), 138.

discussions this did not mean that this view would be sustained throughout a contested trial: 'You start afresh as soon as the trial starts because the witnesses may turn out to be hopeless or very good.' This also applied to any view formed about the case from the papers: 'You get these statements of evidence on which the person is returned from trial and they don't swear up to them. I mean, he may say, "I saw A fire the gun", and then it emerges at the trial, "Oh, I didn't actually see it, but B told me he's fired it". I mean you're excluding things all the time from your mind.'

There was some evidence that judges were able to distinguish issues in the *voir dire* from issues in the trial proper and apply a fresh approach towards a confession even if it was admitted in the *voir dire*. In the last chapter we saw that a judge admitted a confession on the *voir dire* but ultimately rejected it in the trial proper on the basis of expert evidence which cast doubt on its reliability. However, there was a view among counsel that, once the trial proper began, judges tended to get the feel of the case sooner than a jury and formed a view fairly quickly. In the last section we saw that certain judges tried to avoid this by writing down the evidence actually admitted at trial, but much seemed to depend on the complexity of the case. One counsel thought that although judges did try to keep an open mind until the trial started, things changed during the trial: 'He will tend to mentally write his judgment in his head before the case ends and will varnish everything to fit that view. I think that's human nature. I think that to honestly say that a judge sits through the whole of a trial wavering one way or another like a jury is to approach naivety.'

In the last chapter we saw that there was a greater tendency for cases to fold in a Diplock trial. As this counsel put it:

The mental exercise which a judge carries out couldn't be the same as for a juror coming in. He gets the feel of a case pretty quickly. If he gets the feel that there's maybe a bit of doubt then he'll get interested and he'll start to look at it and pick at it and either it'll develop into a reasonable doubt or it won't. But if from fairly early on it starts to look pretty hopeless from the defence point of view . . . If you start getting those vibes from a judge . . . then you ask for time to consult again with your client to think about it.

Having looked at the potential prejudice which may arise from a judge's more informed insight into the background of cases, with the danger of prejudgment which such insight entails, we shall now examine the more specific danger which flows from the exposure of the judge to legally inadmissible material.

(b) Inadmissible evidence

A particular problem arises when judges become privy to inadmissible evidence. In Chapters Two and Three we noted that judges have powers to withdraw from cases when they hear inadmissible evidence, although there was doubt about the extent to which these powers were exercised. According to one judge, when a statement was excluded, judges did usually go on and try the case, although it was not common, after a confession was excluded, for the remaining evidence to justify continuing with the case. However, it was not unknown for judges to withdraw from cases when they heard a damning piece of evidence, especially when an application was made by counsel that they should do so. In one assault case in our sample the victim was describing an incident when he was asked by Crown counsel who had been shouting at him. The witness answered 'That fella over there', clearly referring to, although not pointing at, the defendant. It was not part of the prosecution case that the victim could identify the accused as the person who had shouted at him. The defence immediately applied for a new trial on the ground that the witness was making a dock identification and that the defence were as a result facing a trial of a totally different substance to what had been expected. The point was made that if this had happened in a jury trial, the trial judge would probably have had to order a new trial. Although the judge seemed at first reluctant to accept this argument, he did eventually discharge himself from the trial.

In that example the judge heard the damning evidence in the course of the trial. On other occasions judges become privy to inadmissible evidence beforehand. We have seen that judges often read the deposition papers prior to trial. In Chapter Two we noted that a practice seemed at one time to be followed whereby inadmissible material was removed from the papers by means of preliminary editing by a different judge. This practice did not seem to be adopted during our sample period, although counsel had an opportunity of seeking to edit the deposition statements. This could happen when the defendant was being committed for trial, but seemed more often to be done informally after committal. One counsel recollected that in his early years at the Bar it was commonplace for him to be sent to the committal hearings and to be asked to apply for the papers to be edited during these hearings. His view was that solicitors were no longer briefing junior counsel to do this. Instead, editing had become a matter of informal negotiation between counsel later in the proceedings. As one prosecution counsel put it: 'Most of the statements come to us in an unedited state and the defence say, "That oughtn't to be there", and I say, "That's right". Very often they will go away and edit them and bring them back and say. "Do you consent to this being left out?" and we always would. This is after committal, normally before the judge gets them.'

Prosecuting and defence counsel appeared to differ on the importance to be attached to this procedure largely, as we shall see, because of differing perceptions regarding the influence which inadmissible evidence has on a judge's mind. It was unclear how often judges received unedited statements which contained inadmissible evidence. One senior judge told us that the depositions are edited before the judge sees them but that prejudicial evidence still gets in sometimes. Another judge told us that the most common type of inadmissible evidence which is let in inadvertently is an indication that the defendant has been in prison. Other judges, though, pointed out that it was in any event not difficult to work out whether the defendant had a criminal record:

You see you know very soon whether a person has a record or not. If he hasn't, it's usually trumpeted fairly early on—and if the investigating officer isn't asked, you begin to wonder then maybe if he has got a relevant record.

The judge is party to inadmissible evidence and even if he is not he knows by professional experience whether the defendant has a clear record or not simply by virtue of the fact that if his record is clean defence counsel will have this brought out at some stage during the trial, perhaps in the course of cross-examining police officers. So it's a bit like the Sherlock Holmes story of the dog that didn't bark in the night—if no mention is made of the defendant's clear record, it can be assumed that he has not got one.

Despite this judges were on the whole adamant that evidence or suspicion of a defendant's previous record did not affect their reasoning. One judge admitted that one could never be sure about the extent to which one is affected subconsciously by such evidence but that one had to try to disregard it. Others took a stronger view and thought that the record of the defendant did not make a 'whit of difference' to their reasoning. One judge thought that the ultimate proof of this was that even though most Diplock defendants have records, many are still acquitted: 'One can say that in 95 per cent of cases where the defendant has a previous record for a reasonably similar case the defendant is guilty but the knowledge of that is not enough to convict.'

It is hard to believe that any trier of fact, judge or juror, can ignore evidence of an accused's previous record, although that is what jurors are told to do if such evidence is inadvertently admitted during the trial.[73] The question is whether triers of fact permit it to influence their judgment when it should not. Certain judges thought that there was a greater danger that juries would be affected by this kind of evidence. According to one judge, judges, unlike jurors, are bound to compartmentalize knowledge:

[73] For discussion of the problem of inadvertent disclosure of inadmissible evidence of bad character in jury trials, see Munday (1990).

As a judge it is one's duty to compartmentalize knowledge. One's bound to do this also as a barrister—and decide what point should be taken and what should be ignored; in the same way in decision-making a judge has to decide what shall be considered and what ignored and he is perfectly capable of doing this. Judges do this all the time in civil and criminal cases.

Certain counsel were more sceptical about judges' ability to compart-mentalize knowledge in this way: 'I don't think that judges are able to put these things out of their minds. If there's something about a person's antecedents which shouldn't be there then with the best will in the world you can't help but be affected—even if in the trial it's not mentioned at all.' Others were more sanguine:

Judges can put such evidence out of their minds. In my opinion if it influences them in any way it would tend to inflence them towards an acquittal because they will be aware that they have heard it and they will bend over backwards to give the defendant a fair break. In fact in not allowing it to influence them they might allow it to go too far the other way.

There would seem to be two kinds of prejudice which may work against an accused person in the criminal trial.[74] First, there is the risk that the jury may exaggerate or underestimate the probative force of the evidence. Triers of fact may believe, for example, that because the accused committed an offence in the past similar to the one with which he is now charged, he must also be guilty on this occasion.[75] Secondly and more insidiously, triers of fact may take a jaundiced attitude towards the defendant when they learn about a previous conviction with the result that they are more inclined to convict him whatever the state of the evidence. Given our previous argument that judges tend to adopt a 'cold', professional stance in their assessment of evidence, it may be assumed that this would enable them to counteract both these potential sources of prejudice more effectively than juries.[76] First, judges' legal experience should place them in a better position to guard against 'forbidden chains of reasoning' from evidence of bad character. Secondly, the judge's professional role should militate against extra-legal prejudices stemming from an accused's bad character. Judges in our sample appeared to have such dangers at the forefront of their minds.

---

[74] See Lempert (1975), 1027–41; Zuckerman (1989), 231–2.

[75] The LSE Jury Project found that the admission of previous convictions similar to those charged increased the chance of a guilty verdict: see Cornish and Sealy (1973). See also Doob and Kirshenbaum (1972); Hans and Doob (1975); Wissler and Saks (1985).

[76] There is some evidence in Kalven and Zeisel's research that judges were influenced by prior record for a similar crime: see Kalven and Zeisel (1966), 127–30. Laypersons may find it even more difficult to resist being influenced by such information. Damaska has commented that 'more than trained and case-hardened professionals, laymen find it difficult to focus on a specified informational input and disregard data and impressions they would otherwise use in arriving at a decision; they can more easily be swayed by "tacit knowledge" and "sentiment" ': see Damaska (1990), 98–9.

Nevertheless, there are certain kinds of case where it may be extremely difficult for judges not to let an accused's character have some effect on their judgment. A number of cases in our sample involved cases where arms and explosives were found in a house either occupied by defendants or to which defendants had access. The defence in these cases was that the defendant had no knowledge of or no control over the arms. Clearly, in these cases the defence was particularly eager to stress the defendant's previous good record, if the defendant in fact had one, and judges mentioned this as a significant factor in their judgment.

A defendant's character also assumes particular relevance in duress cases, where judges must believe that there is a real possibility that the defendant was genuinely put in fear. It is important in these cases that the defendant should not be tainted by any paramilitary involvement, because duress is no defence where a defendant voluntarily joins a violent organization and then claims he was put under duress to commit acts of violence.[77] So, in a case where the defendant was charged with withholding information from the police when he said that he was told by a gunman to drive to a destination and not to report the matter afterwards, the judge dealt specifically with the defendant's background in judging the credibility of the defence. The fact that the defendant had a virtually clear record and evinced sympathy for the security forces made it more likely that his story was true. The accused's good character was clearly a relevant factor here in assessing the validity of the accused's defence. The question, however, arises as to how a judge would approach this assessment where no evidence of good character had been adduced (with the connotation that the accused is not of good character), or in circumstances where evidence of bad character has inadvertently been revealed to the court. Whereas positive evidence of good character quite properly strengthens the defence in these circumstances, the absence of such evidence must necessarily have an unfavourable bearing on such a defence.

In cases where evidence of bad character is inadvertently uncovered, there remains the option for the defence to apply for the trial to be stopped. This happened in one case in our sample where the defendant was charged with possession of firearms with intent to endanger life. The police had found a home-made machine gun together with three magazines and a 9mm pistol in the accused's home. The defendant denied all knowledge of them. Forensic examination revealed that both weapons were in a serviceable condition although the machine gun was only capable of firing single shots and was prone to jam. A police officer then gave evidence of his interview with the accused. When questioned about whether his home had ever been broken

---

[77] *R* v *Fitzpatrick* [1977] NI 20; *R* v *Sharp* [1987] QB 853; *R* v *Shepherd* (1987) 86 Cr App R 47. See Smith and Hogan (1992), 241–2.

into, the accused had replied to the officer that he did not know, and that for part of the previous year he had been in jail for six weeks for failing to pay maintenance money. No objection was taken by defence counsel to this. The officer went on to say that the accused had said that he was not suggesting that his home *was* broken into during this time but that it would have been empty and the guns could have been left there. The officer then said that he had told the accused that the police could not be expected to believe this, given that he had previous convictions for arms offences. Defence counsel immediately objected to this evidence and after a brief discussion an adjournment was requested. When the hearing resumed, the defence made an application that the trial be stopped on the ground that the evidence indicated that the accused had a criminal record for arms offences. It was argued that it was important that the accused be seen to have a fair trial in these circumstances. The judge appeared to agree with this and suggested also that the Court of Appeal would probably set aside a conviction in such a case. This is an interesting illustration of the importance attached by judges to the possible attitude of the Court of Appeal, a point to which we shall return in Chapter Nine. Although the right of appeal to the Court of Appeal may be an important safeguard in these circumstances, the problem remains that judges may be able to make informed guesses about the record and background of the accused. Unless it is apparent that the judge has seen or heard inadmissible evidence, the defence is not in a position to make an application and the defendant is then at the mercy of the individual judge.

Apart from evidence of an accused's record, another situation which counsel claimed can lead to prejudice is where one co-defendant has implicated another, perhaps in a police interview, in the offence charged. This evidence is technically inadmissible as pure hearsay, but a judge must find such a statement difficult to ignore, and if he believes the confession of the co-defendant he may very well believe that the defendant was also involved. Again counsel differed on the effect that this would have on the judge's ultimate decision. According to one prosecuting counsel:

If he is intellectually honest—I had this experience very recently, and most of them are intellectually honest—he will say, I know the man is guilty, but the evidence just isn't there. And I can think of very few instances where a man we know to be guilty has been convicted if there's not enough evidence. It's not that he puts it out of his mind in one sense, he puts it out of the arithmetic, not out of his mind. In fact I think they bend over backwards sometimes, if they're dealing with someone they know to be guilty.

Another counsel, however, gave the example of a murder trial where the evidence from the police interviews identified a man as one of the defendants. During the trial efforts were made to conceal this by calling this man 'X'. A jury would never have known who X was, but the judge would have gathered this information from the police interviews. As counsel said:

If in that case the evidence against X had been a fingerprint found in the house, that in itself wouldn't convict him because it doesn't fix the time he was in the house as being the time of the crime. So the judge would want corroboration of that. If the defendant refuses to go into the witness box to explain where he was that night that can now be used as corroboration [under the Criminal Evidence Order]. Now it's said that judges are reluctant to use the Order or that they don't like to use it . . . It may well be that without more he wouldn't be prepared to convict in a case like that. But if he also knows because of the interviews that X definitely was such and such a person he might put the prejudicial evidence out of his head and not use it to convict him but it colours his view of how to use the Order. I wouldn't say that a judge would do that either in a devious or a conscious way but everybody's human.

This counsel concluded:

If you were operating on the basis that you were innocent until proven guilty, which you are entitled to do even if you have committed the offence . . . and which we are told the law says, then you would certainly want the tribunal of fact to hear your case not knowing whether you were guilty or not. You wouldn't want the tribunal of fact already to know that you were guilty and then decide whether you were guilty or not on the basis of rules of what was admissible and what was not.

It is very difficult to measure how well judges perform the feat of determining guilt strictly in accordance with admissible evidence. In Chapter Two we saw that the New York Bar Commission reported in 1988 that no one had directed their attention to a single case in which a factually erroneous conviction had occurred. Another measure of fairness, however, also mentioned in the report, was whether there had been convictions of ostensibly guilty persons which were not based on the evidence presented in the case, and on this question it was unable to reach any conclusion. There are certainly features in the process which encourage judges to base their decisions on admissible evidence. When inadmissible evidence is made public during the trial judges have to be scrupulous about avoiding any reliance on it. However, it is impossible to avoid suspicion that judges may be influenced by information, gained either directly through the deposition papers or indirectly through their professional experience, which is never made public during the trial. To avert the suspicion that justice may be done behind closed doors, the trial procedure must be seen to operate scrupulously fairly. We have seen that some judges believed that trial procedure should conform as closely as possible to trial by jury. Yet however formally the rules are applied in the trial, there is no absolute guarantee that the purpose for which those rules were designed, namely to keep prejudicial evidence from the trier of fact, will be achieved. As one counsel summed up the situation:

What seems to be wrong with the Diplock system in practice is that the rules of evidence, for instance on the admissibility of statements, aren't designed to function in a Diplock court . . . We've got rules of evidence which were designed and have developed for the jury system and now we've got a Diplock court grafted on and it doesn't really fit. As a result of that the judges hear a lot of prejudicial evidence and a lot of inadmissible evidence which they are then expected to exclude from their minds when they are deciding on the facts.

One judge explicitly referred in his judgment to the kind of dilemma a judge can face when he is apprised of inadmissible evidence. In this case a number of defendants had been charged with the bombing of a public house and with arson, on the basis of their confession statements. It transpired in the *voir dire* that they had each individually implicated themselves and each other in the incidents, but the trial judge excluded the confession of one of them on the ground that ESDA results had shown that a page of interview notes had been rewritten by the police and no explanation had been given for this. Before acquitting this particular defendant, however, the judge said that he felt he should say something which should rarely be said by a judge: that although he was excluding the defendant's confession, he believed that the defendant was quite probably guilty of the offences with which he was charged, because he accepted the statements of admission made by his co-accused. This example illustrates the fact that judges are prepared to act in accordance with strict rules of evidence and procedure even at the cost of acquitting defendants who may well be guilty. It is therefore a good example of a judge rising above any case-hardened attitude and giving public expression to legal principle. However, it also illustrates the difficulty in which a judge can be placed when he is put in charge of determining questions of both admissibility and guilt. As the tribunal responsible for admissibility he may feel compelled to acquit the defendant, but as the tribunal responsible for convicting the guilty he may feel, as the judge no doubt felt in this case, some anguish about acquitting a person he personally believes is guilty. The judge has an *intime conviction* that the defendant is guilty which would be enough for conviction if he were operating under an inquest model of proof. It is the constraint of proof in the contest model which compels him to acquit. Of course, this kind of dilemma can face a judge in a jury case as well, but the dilemma is less stark when a different tribunal, the jury, is ultimately charged with determining guilt.

Various strategies may be designed to avoid tainting the judge's mind with inadmissible evidence. We have seen, for example, what appeared previously to be common practice, whereby one judge would edit the deposition papers before they were sent to a different trial judge. The defence may seek to have the inadmissible evidence edited out, either formally at committal or informally afterwards. The trial judge may discharge himself from the trial either of his own motion or on an application by counsel, and this decision is subject to appellate review. No doubt other strategies could be devised. One adopted in military summary and court-martial cases in the United States has been to require prosecuting attorneys to exercise restraint in introducing inadmissible evidence, on pain of almost certain reversal if the evidence is introduced.[78] The difficulty with this is that 'self-discipline cannot be enforced by procedural sanctions in all cases unless the courts are willing to impose penalties that are out of proportion to some evidence errors'.[79] Another device suggested is for judges to determine admissibility issues where possible at a preliminary hearing, and for the trial then to proceed before a different judge.[80] This may work well for those problems of admissibility which can be defined before trial. It does not, however, cater for admissibility issues which arise during the trial. It also fails to deal with the problem of other inadmissible evidence learned by the trial judge.

The difficulty with all these devices is that either they do not go far enough in protecting defendants, leaving a lingering suspicion that the trial judge is tainted by the evidence, or they go too far, at the cost of great administrative inconvenience or unjustified acquittal or reversal on appeal. The latter problem of unjustified acquittal or reversal can be avoided by ordering a new trial, but in such a small jurisdiction the new judge may indirectly have knowledge about the earlier trial. All these difficulties increase the importance of another compensatory measure, the requirement for judges to give reasons for each decision to convict, and the accompanying automatic right of appeal against conviction. This ensures that whatever effect inadmissible evidence may have had on the mind of the judge, any conviction must be justified on the basis of admissible evidence, and the reasons given can be scrutinized. This represents a shift away from what we called in Chapter Three 'input control', the *actual* exclusion of evidence from the trier of fact, towards 'output control' exercised through 'reasoned exclusion' whereby judges are obliged to justify findings independently of tainted evidence. It is now time to turn to this final phase of the Diplock trial, the judgment.

---

[78] See Note (1965), 414–15.   [79] *Ibid.*, 415.

[80] See Levin and Cohen (1971), 918–19. The Standing Advisory Committion on Human Rights in Northern Ireland has made this recommendation in relation to confession evidence: see *Tenth Report of the Standing Advisory Commission on Human Rights: Report for 1983–84* (1985), 73; *Fourteenth Report of the Standing Advisory Commission on Human Rights: Report for 1987–89* (1989), 103–4.

9

Judgment and Review

In Chapter Three, one of the distinctions made between contest and inquest models of proof was in the extent to which both information presented to the tribunal of fact and the verdict itself are subject to control. In the typical adversarial trial an extensive network of evidential and procedural rules will closely regulate the presentation of the issues to the fact-finding body, but that body's ultimate decision will take a cursory and inscrutable form. Conversely, the inquest model is based upon limited input control and permits considerable output control, as the decision will be handed down in the form of a fully reasoned judgment.

Although no trial system adheres fully to either ideal model, it has been assumed that any particular system can be located at some point on the spectrum between the two. The features of the trial which we have studied so far, such as the level of judicial interventionism and judicial enforcement of the rules of evidence, differ in an important sense from the issues at the heart of this chapter, which are the formulation of the decision on guilt or innocence and the potential for review of that decision. Although we have detected changes in the judicial approach to intervention and regulation of the trial in Diplock cases, these have been at the level of practice: as we have noted throughout the book, little *formal* alteration has been made to accommodate the single judge. At the closing phase of the trial, however, the principle that the conventional trial structure should remain intact in the jury's absence would be impossible to sustain, even on the purely formal level. Whereas we tend to accept that it would be unreasonable to expect a jury to provide a reasoned argument in support of its verdict, the converse applies in the case of the professional trier of fact, from whom a bare statement of the accused's guilt would appear inadequate in at least two respects.

First, it is one of the attractions of a 'professional' process that the decision can be formulated in reasoned terms which demonstrate that the relevant rules and principles have been adhered to in the decision-making process. As we saw in Chapter Eight, whereas the jury owes its strength to the fact that its members have been drawn *from* the community, a professional judge can and indeed must be accountable *to* the community, in addition to his or her responsibility towards the accused. This notion of accountability partly explains the fact that judges not only give reasons for conviction, as required by statute, but in practice also give reasons for acquitting the accused. As we shall see, this practice is not always in the interests of the accused, but reflects a wider responsibility which extends to the prosecution and to the public: as justification is required of the professional for convicting an accused of a serious offence, so too is some explanation expected when the prosecution has failed to make out its case.

Secondly, moving from general considerations for professional arbiters to the specific context of Diplock courts, although the system has been perceived in official circles as a parallel forum of justice to jury trial, as opposed to a subordinate one, the denial of the right to jury trial necessitated some form of compensatory measure for the accused (as noted in Chapter Two). In addition to the prevailing expectation that judges be accountable, it may be argued that the giving of reasons serves a protective function in relation to the accused's interests.

In the Diplock trial structure, this requirement that the judge give a clearly reasoned judgment in support of conviction has a corollary in the notion of enhanced 'appealability': the more clearly articulated the grounds for a decision, the greater the opportunity to challenge that record on appeal. In addition to the fact that a judgment is *in form* more susceptible to scrutiny, the accountability of the judge and the protection of the accused are reinforced by offering improved access to appellate review through the provision of an automatic right of appeal.[1] As one of the judges in our sample commented:

The big differences are the things the public don't think about. You've got a reasoned judgment and you have a free right of appeal. These are the big things that have made the trials work because it means that the Court of Appeal can pick it over. It's hard to go behind the jury's decision unless there's a misdirection. So from the judge's point of view you have to give a written judgment.

It may be added that the judgment requirement follows the logic of many of our earlier observations that, although the adversarial or contest-oriented character of the trial is not necessarily lost in a non-jury trial, the judge is in reality cast in a more dominant (and often in practice more inquisitive) role. As in a typically inquisitorial process, where the triers of fact are given a freer role to pursue their own lines of inquiry in the course of the trial, such freedom is granted on the understanding that they will be made more accountable for their decision, which will be more readily open to review at appellate level. As Damaska has noted in this context: 'There are few aspects of lower authorities' decision making that are accorded immunity

---

[1] Northern Ireland (Emergency Provisions) Act 1991, section 10(6).

from supervision: fact, law and logic are all fair game for scrutiny and possible correction.'[2] The theory then in the Diplock context (and as we shall see it is one to which many practitioners in the Diplock system subscribe) is that the scope for output control is greater than in the jury context. It is one purpose of the present chapter to analyse the form of giving judgment in Diplock cases in order to assess whether this theory is reflected in reality.

The primary concern of the previous chapter was to examine the approach taken by individual judges to their added fact-finding responsibilities. In order to understand more fully these augmented responsibilities, it was necessary to analyse the written judgments in the cases in our sample, as well as the parallel judicial task in jury trials of summing-up to the jury. In addition, several of the judges interviewed offered insights into their perception of their role at this stage of the trial in the jury's absence. Before we look specifically at these 'raw materials' of our survey, it will be necessary to consider in general the culminating process of decision-making in the criminal trial. First, in the jury context, we shall examine the function of the summing-up and its relation to and influence upon the jury's verdict. Particular note will be made of the features of the summing-up which transcend the mere purpose of elucidation for the jury and which appear to be lessened in their effect in the jury's absence. A section will then be devoted to analysing the guidance which the Court of Appeal in Northern Ireland has offered to judges in Diplock courts on the form of judgment to be adopted. Having then considered the approaches taken by the judges in our sample to the construction of judgments, we shall investigate the claim that the judgment provides a more solid foundation for the launching of an appeal against conviction than the verdict of the jury. In the present book, we have concentrated on the process of determining facts *at trial* and arguably the approach by the appellate courts to the review of decisions in Diplock courts merits a wholly separate study which would extend beyond our remit. In our discussion of the appeals process, therefore, we confine ourselves to a general examination of the scope for review of Diplock decisions rather than a focused analysis of a sample of appellate judgments.

FROM SUMMING-UP TO JUDGMENT

An observer of the system of trial by jury has remarked that 'complicated and insoluble factual disputes have the appearance of being settled with ease when wrapped in the silent garb of a verdict returned in supposed compliance with strict legal rules.'[3] While the prime target of this comment

---

[2] Damaska (1986), 48–9.   [3] Broeder (1954), 417.

is the essentially impenetrable verdict of the jury, which cuts through all legal niceties and factual uncertainty which arise in the course of the trial, criticism is also implicitly levelled at the entire closing phase of the criminal trial. In particular, the reference to the 'supposed compliance' with legal rules calls into question the effectiveness of the judge's summing-up in ensuring the jury's adherence to the relevant rules of evidence and provisions of substantive law in reaching its decision.[4] On this view, the summing-up in the jury trial followed by closed inscrutable deliberations offer no guarantee to defendants that the ultimate verdict is based on the evidence adduced at trial and on the relevant rules of law.

The closed nature of the jury's verdict is, of course, bolstered by the law of contempt, which effectively stultifies research into the modes of reasoning adopted by juries.[5] By a certain irony, and returning to the issue of output control, appellate scrutiny of decisions in jury trials is much less frequently centred upon the decision of the jury itself than upon the *judicial* input into this decision in the form of the summing-up or the judge's general conduct of the trial. Statistical evidence presented to the Royal Commission on Criminal Justice, for example, showed that over 80 per cent of successful appeals were based on misdirections by the judge, defects in the summing-up, or wrong decisions to exclude evidence.[6] In the Diplock context, as we have noted, the judicial summing-up and the verdict are effectively moulded into the reasoned judgment which, in contrast to the decision of the jury, is susceptible to close analysis. The question which has been addressed in previous chapters is the extent to which the adversarial character of the trial has been affected by informal changes in practice. The current issue is rather different. While the formal requirement of the written judgment marks a clear departure from the normal trial structure, the question which presents itself is how significant a difference this creates between the closing phases of the respective forms of trial.

On the one hand, it could be argued that the provision of a reasoned judgment in support of the court's decision clearly offers adequate compensation for the jury's absence. The mystique of the fact-finder's closed deliberations is peeled away and the accused and the public are presented with an open justification of the finding of guilt. One variant of this argument could be used to contend that, *whatever* the composition of the tribunal of fact, reasons ought to be required.[7] On the other hand, an

---

[4] A considerable degree of attention has been focused on the impact of mandatory instructions on the jury: see Charrow and Charrow (1979); Tanford (1990). For an English perspective on the need for simplification of such instructions, see Griew (1989).

[5] Section 8 of the Contempt of Court Act 1981.

[6] See page 169 of the report.

[7] See Maher (1988), 45; Lempert (1992), 51 (footnote 40).

opposing view of the written judgment may be put forward, with reference to a recurrent theme of this study, which is whether the removal of the jury from the criminal process *can* properly be accommodated without a more radical upheaval of existing trial structures than that comtemplated by the Diplock Commission. Contrary to the view that the reasoned judgment offers a ready-made substitute for the judicial summing-up and the jury's verdict, it may be contended that certain aspects of the closing phase of the criminal jury trial are intrinsically incompatible with the merger of the arbiter of law and the tribunal of fact.

First, recalling a point made in the last chapter, there is an important aspect in which Diplock and jury trials diverge at the culmination of the evidence and the submissions of counsel, namely that in Diplock trials the possibility of a decision to acquit founded on extra-legal considerations (or 'jury equity') is removed. Clearly, in the Diplock context, there is no scope for an outcome based on a lay conception of justice which transcends the confines of the evidence presented at trial. Conversely, however, the accused is in theory protected in the Diplock context from what could be termed a 'non-legal conviction'. As we have argued, the judge's focus is a narrower, more 'professional' one than that of the jury. Further, while it is impossible to gauge the extent to which a jury has acted in conformity with the evidence and legal rules as enunciated in the summing-up, the requirement for the judge to deliver a statement of reasons for convicting may have the effect of producing judicial caution in situations where a jury might be less inclined to bow to strict legal doctrine and acquit. Therefore, it can be argued not only that a professional arbiter is inherently more disposed to adhere rigidly to legal constraints than the jury, but also that the reasoned judgment acts as a vehicle for the expression of this difference of approach and serves as the main channel for that accountability which was noted at the outset of the present chapter.

A second area of divergence in the non-jury context stems from the fact that certain rules of evidence and procedure are so closely bound up with the institution of the jury that their effect is diminished in its absence. Even the basic articulation of the burden and standard of proof sits less easily in the context of the written judgment than in the context of a delineation of the issues to the jury. In pressing such fundamental principles upon the jury, one is incorporating into the decision-making process a commitment of the entire criminal justice system to the protection of the innocent from conviction.[8] A statement by the judge, on the other hand, that the required standard has been met, carries none of the solemnity of the message to the jury that it must eliminate all reasonable explanations pointing towards innocence before finding in the prosecution's favour. As we noted in

[8] See Zuckerman (1989), 125–34.

Chapter Eight, judges appeared extremely conscious of the need to apply the correct standard of proof. This, however, does not necessarily meet the point that the expression of the burden and standard of proof and other specific judicial directions in the course of the summing-up fulfils an important symbolic function which is not easily transferable to the single-judge scenario.[9] A related point has been made by Seigel in respect of admonitions to the jury to disregard certain evidence. We have noted earlier that the practical effectiveness of such instructions has been called into question,[10] but Seigel has argued that this may be beside the point: 'admonitions are probably best understood as a part of the ritual associated with the trial process . . . An admonition brings closure, a sense that the system has done its best to make things right. Viewed in this light, the jury's incapacity to abide by the admonition is simply irrelevant.'[11]

The classic example of a direction which is difficult to adapt to the single-judge trial is the corroboration warning which must be given to the jury in respect of the evidence of an accomplice.[12] As one observer remarked, with specific reference to the practice of the courts during the 'supergrass' era (which we discussed in Chapter Two): 'The efficacy of the warning consists in the separation of identity and function between the judge as arbiter of the law and the jury as finders of fact.'[13] One of the counsel in our sample put the point more pithily when he commented:

A lot of it seems to be very artificial . . . because obviously the judge knows from his vast experience what weight to give evidence of a co-defendant who has given evidence against another defendant . . . At the end of the day all evidence has to be weighted and the judge is well aware of the types of evidence that are intrinsically weak. All this stuff about 'I warn myself' is artificial.

The argument here then is not that judges are ill-equipped to make determinations of guilt on the standard of proof beyond reasonable doubt, nor incapable of taking seriously the dangers of relying on uncorroborated accomplice evidence. Indeed, as we have seen in relation to identification evidence,[14] judges tend to apply the *Turnbull* guidelines in a particularly strict manner in Diplock cases. As one judge put it: 'In Diplock judgments, judges tend to apply a stricter standard in identification cases than the *Turnbull* test. Most direct themselves on a *Turnbull* basis, but quite often they would be even more cautious than the warning given. I do think that

---

[9] See Doran (1991a).
[10] See Chapter Eight, footnote 73 and accompanying text.
[11] Seigel (1994), 1022 (footnotes omitted).
[12] For detailed discussion of this warning, see Jackson (1988c).
[13] Gifford (1984), 5.   [14] See Chapter Eight, page 230.

certainly in identification cases the chances of the judge making a mistake are very much less than where there is a jury.'

This view was endorsed by one counsel who suggested that judges 'may be better at applying the guidelines than perhaps a jury.' The difficulty then may be not so much the *ability* of the judge to 'warn himself' on the dangers inherent in certain kinds of evidence and to act accordingly, but the fact that such warnings are specifically tailored to the demands of the separation of function between judge and jury. Thus, when a judge indicates *ex post facto* in the judgment that these matters have been incorporated within his decision-making process, this is less persuasive than when the concerns are voiced in advance of the deliberative process in which guilt is determined, as is the case in the course of the summing-up to the jury.

The final, and arguably most significant, shift in the closing stages of the Diplock trial process stems from the broader function served by the summing-up in the criminal jury trial. The summing-up is a focal point in the adversary trial, when the debate which has been conducted throughout the course of the trial is crystallized, and after which the deliberation on the outcome must take place without further input by the parties or the judge. It has been noted that the force and significance of legal instructions may be diluted in the jury's absence, but it is important to recognize also that the summing-up is the final point at which factual issues are subject to review prior to the jury's retirement. As for judicial instructions on matters of fact, the scope of permissible comment varies throughout different jurisdictions. In Northern Ireland, for example (as in England and Wales), the judge has traditionally enjoyed a broad latitude to comment on the facts of the case,[15] whereas in the United States the judicial role has been perceived as more limited in this regard, the majority of states permitting no comment on the facts.[16] In either case, and whether or not one views the ability to comment as a beneficial aspect of the trial process, it is significant that the judge's putting of the issues to the jury is still an integral part of the argumentative process which has continued throughout the trial. Whereas it is always possible for a judge to form a view of a case at a very early stage of the trial and to gauge all subsequent evidence by way of its impact on that view, the jury cannot form a *collective* opinion until it retires at the end of the evidence, with the judicial summing-up as the final external input into its process of decision-making.

Jurisdictions vary in the extent to which they recognize what could be described as the 'adversarial potential' of this closing phase of the trial. In most common law jurisdictions, the parties are given no formal opportunity to contribute to or to challenge the judge's formulation of the summing-up,

[15] Williams (1963), 303–4; Wolchover (1989), 783–4.
[16] Saltzburg (1978), 22–3; Wolchover (1989), 784–6.

although an indirect influence may be brought to bear through closing speeches to the jury. An American observer has noted that there are strong disincentives to counsel in challenging the judge's presentation of the case to the jury. These include the risk of prejudicing the jury against the objecting party, the fear of appearing to impugn the judge's impartiality, and the fact that the judge's pronouncements may take counsel by surprise, rendering objection more difficult.[17] In England and Wales, it is accepted that the judge may ask counsel (in the jury's absence) for submissions on how he or she should direct the jury on certain aspects of the case. Generally speaking, however, dialogue between judge and counsel after the summing-up is discouraged,[18] although prosecution counsel is under a duty to draw any possible errors of law or fact to the judge's attention at the end of the summing-up.[19] Interestingly, however, the Law Commission has recommended that in all cases involving difficult or controversial points the judge should engage in discussion with counsel in advance of the summing-up (and closing speeches) with a view to clarifying those matters.[20] Although the Law Commission's primary concern was the avoidance of error and unmeritorious appeals, such a procedure would arguably accentuate and strengthen the adversarial character of the culmination of the criminal trial, adversariness here being characterized not simply in terms of debate between counsel but in the novel sense of debate between counsel and the trial judge.

Indeed, as we mentioned briefly in Chapter Seven, in jury trials in Northern Ireland (and in the Republic of Ireland) such protection is built into the summing-up through a procedure whereby counsel may 'requisition' the judge after his address to the jury.[21] When the jury has retired, the judge invites representations from both counsel on the content of the summing-up. If the judge accepts that he or she has made an error or omission or that something has not been explained clearly to the jury, the jury will then be asked to return in order that the matter may be rectified before they become fully engaged in their deliberations. This enlarges the task of summing up to impose a form of joint responsibility on judge and counsel, recognizing that the argumentative basis on which the trial has proceeded should continue until the moment where the issues are finally left to the jury: the issues remain 'up for grabs', so to speak, and the decision which emerges will have

---

[17] Saltzburg (1978), 45.

[18] *R v Cocks* (1976) 63 Cr App R 79; and see *R v Charles* (1979) 68 Cr App R 334.

[19] Code of Conduct of the Bar, Annex H ('Standards Applicable to Criminal Cases'), para. 1.7; and see *R v Donoghue* (1988) 86 Cr App R 267, 271–2. It would seem that defence counsel does not have such a duty: *R v Cocks* (1976) 63 Cr App R 79, 82; *R v Edwards* (1983) 77 Cr App R 5, 7.

[20] Law Commission (1991), paras. 4.19–30.

[21] See Valentine (1989), para. 8.05; Ryan and Magee (1983), 362–3.

been made on the basis of the fullest possible exchange of views as to the merits of the respective cases.

One of the cases in our sample provides a useful example of how the process of requisitioning works in practice. In this case, counsel took objection to the way in which the judge had presented the prosecution evidence. The question for the jury was whether the accused or another person accompanying him had struck the victim, causing actual bodily harm. The victim's evidence implicated the accused, but another witness had cast doubt on this by her uncertainty as to the order in which the two potential assailants had arrived at the location of the assault. The exchange went as follows:

Counsel: Your Honour, three short points. In relation to the third count [assault occasioning actual bodily harm] Your Honour reminded the jury of the evidence of [the victim] as to could [the accused] come up [to the victim] and that he didn't get very far and so on. In my respectful submission Your Honour should have mentioned the evidence of [witness A] in relation to that both men did go into the house at or about that time and that she couldn't say which of them went first or whether they went in side by side.

Judge: I think she said she didn't know which came up the path first, wasn't it, not into the house. Now I may be wrong?

Counsel: In fact, I think maybe that was a question Your Honour asked her?

Judge: Oh yes I asked her as they were coming up the path, mind you I could be wrong.

Counsel: 'I couldn't say who went into the house first . . .', is my note, '. . . or whether they were side by side'.

Judge: Sorry, I've got the wrong place.

Counsel: Your Honour, I asked her . . . it's right at the end of all her evidence. 'I can't say who went into the house first or whether they were side by side.'

Judge: I didn't make a note because I think I thought the answer was not helpful.

Counsel: It wasn't really but it was – all I am saying is that Your Honour has given the account of one witness entirely accurately but has not mentioned other evidence that there was on that point, that's the only other evidence on that point.

Judge: It seems to me just ambiguous evidence, it doesn't really put it much further.

Counsel: On the evidence that Your Honour has reminded the jury it could be [the accused] alone that went into the house at that stage because [the victim] only refers to seeing [the accused] come up whereas there is some other evidence about that suggesting that both went in.

Judge: Yes.

While the judge chose not to act upon two further matters which counsel drew to his attention, he did recall the jury, and gave them a brief further direction on this first point. Ironically, the jury acquitted the accused on this third count, while convicting him on the other counts which he had contested. It would be impossible to gauge the impact of the requisition on this particular decision and it should be remembered that it is entirely in the judge's discretion whether to accept such submissions from counsel. However, the example does illustrate the potential value of a free-ranging discussion on the content of the summing-up at a time when error is still remediable and when the jury has not yet 'settled in' to its private deliberations. Although, as we saw in Chapter Seven, judges often engage in discussion with counsel at the close of the evidence in Diplock cases, such discussion is directed more towards facilitating the judge's decision than to ensuring that the case is presented in a legally correct and factually balanced way to the trier of fact.

One counsel contrasted the position in Diplock and jury cases as follows:

There's no requisitioning in Diplock trials. The judge does not impose his mind formally at a stage where you could requisition but in his judgment after the trial. On occasions a judge will say, 'I want assistance on what is corroboration here, does this amount to corroboration?', before he would theoretically be telling himself yes there is corroboration or there can't be corroboration. And sometimes he would put both parties on notice that he wants argument on that, i.e. he is thinking of using a piece of evidence as corroboration. Perhaps it doesn't amount to requisitioning, but it's pretty close to the same thing. There could also be argument about credibility and weight. In some of the supergrass cases the judges desired arguments on credibility perhaps at the close of the Crown case because it was a live issue that the case shouldn't proceed if he wasn't a credible witness in the absence of corroboration. My recollection is that legally corroboration didn't arise if the witness didn't pass the first test. He had to be credible to begin with. He then decides whether he's with you or against you on the issue of credibility. You then requisition, you tackle his direction to himself, 'Yes, legally I think this could be considered by the tribunal of fact as a credible witness, legally that amounts to corroboration, and I so direct myself'. Then in his judgment he says, 'Yes' or 'I haven't relied on that evidence'. You can say that if he had been directing a jury we would have requisitioned him and if he hadn't accepted the requisition we would have argued that the jury verdict was wrong.'

Yet although this type of address to the judge in a Diplock case is described as 'close to the same thing' as requisitioning, it is arguable that the exchange primarily benefits the trial judge, who is assisted in the final assessment of the evidence. It is fair to say then that although the 'adversarial' nature of the summing-up in a jury trial is not universally exploited, this final address to the jury in whatever form does at least encapsulate the issues on which any conviction is to be based. In a Diplock trial, by contrast, the usual procedure whereby a judge presides over the trial and then gives a reasoned judgment does not allow a corresponding opportunity for the parties to influence the final decision of the trier of fact. The absence of the summing-up essentially leaves an important gap between the closing speeches and the decision of the trier of fact, removing one mechanism of ensuring that the trier of fact acts upon the arguments presented by the parties. In addition, as we have argued in the course of the book, by this stage of Diplock proceedings some of the adversarial traits which characterize trial by jury have already been compromised by a loosening of the evidentiary constraints and a general expansion of the judicial role, thus enhancing the strength of the judge's position.

Having considered the respects in which a Diplock judgment may in theory fail to import the character of the adversarial trial to a single judge context, we shall now examine the form of judgments in Diplock cases, first by reference to the Court of Appeal's prescription and then by reference to the approach adopted by the judges in our sample.

THE FORM OF JUDGMENT IN DIPLOCK CASES

The requirement that a judge deliver a reasoned judgment in support of a conviction in Diplock cases is laid down in section 10(5) of the Northern Ireland (Emergency Provisions) Act 1991, which reads as follows: 'Where the court trying a scheduled offence convicts the accused of that or some other offence, then, without prejudice to its power apart from this subsection to give a judgment, it shall, at the time of conviction or as soon as practicable thereafter, give a judgment stating the reasons for the conviction.'

Two basic observations may immediately be made in relation to this provision. First, there is no requirement that the judgment be given in recorded or written form and, indeed, judgments are only transcribed either in cases of particular importance for reporting purposes or for the purposes of appeal.[22] The second point is that there is no requirement that a judge give reasons for an acquittal.[23] As we shall see, however, judges do in practice offer a reasoned explanation for acquitting an accused, on occasions going so far as to indicate the narrowness of the decision in the accused's favour.

In the absence of any precise statutory guidance on the structure and content of the reasoned judgment,[24] the Northern Ireland Court of Appeal has offered advice on how judges should approach the task. In a 1977

---

[22] As explained in Chapter Four, we received transcripts of the judgments and rulings from the cases in our sample only by special arrangement with the Court Service.

[23] See *R v McClenaghan* [1978] 4 NIJB 3, per McGonigal LJ.

[24] A contrast is to be found in several provisions in the Israel Evidence Ordinance which oblige the judge to reveal the logic behind his or her decision on the credibility of witnesses in both civil and criminal cases: for comment, see Stein (1987), 252–3.

appeal judgment (*R* v *Thompson*), the Lord Chief Justice made the following widely cited observations on the judge's role in giving judgment:

He has no jury to charge and therefore will not err if he does not state every relevant legal proposition and review every fact and argument on either side. His duty is not as in a jury trial to instruct laymen as to every relevant aspect of the law or to give (perhaps at the end of a long trial) a full and balanced picture of the facts for decision by others. His task is to reach conclusions and give reasons to support his view and, preferably, to notice any difficult or unusual points of law in order that if there is an appeal, it may be seen how his view of the law informed his approach to the facts.'[25]

This is a fairly broad prescription, which leaves a considerable degree of latitude to individual judges as to how to express their findings and which recognizes that the judgment need not incorporate a complete record of the legal and factual arguments advanced at trial. The suggestion that it is 'preferable', not essential, that judges should make reference to problematic points of law for appeal purposes is an indication of the Court's reluctance to place rigid demands on judges above and beyond the basic requirement to deliver a judgment.

This reluctance is further illustrated by an earlier appeal in which the Court, referring to the statutory obligation to give reasons, opined: 'We feel that nothing should be said which might suggest an enlargement of that obligation; on the other hand we do not consider that reasons should be required to be detailed. The section of the relevant Act says "reasons", not "detailed reasons" '.[26] Naturally, however, the degree of detail expected will in practice vary according to the nature and complexity of the issues involved. Indeed, in that same case the identification evidence given by the chief prosecution witness contained several contradictions and inconsistencies and the judge's failure to explain these led to the appellant's conviction for murder and robbery being quashed. Thus, although the Court sought to play down the weight of responsibility which the requirement to deliver a judgment places upon the judge, it is clear that in practice gaps in the prosecution case will be exploitable on appeal if not adequately explained in the judgment.

An interesting illustration of the point made in *Thompson* that a judge need not 'state every relevant legal proposition and review every fact and argument' is to be found in the case of *R* v *Thain*.[27] The appellant, a soldier, had been convicted of murder following the fatal shooting of a civilian in Belfast. At trial, the appellant had sought to rely on the defence of self-defence or defence of another, but the judge found as a fact that the appellant had not fired in self-defence: 'Having regard to all the evidence, I simply do not accept the accused's testimony that he believed he was about

[25] *R* v *Thompson* [1977] NI 74, 83.
[26] *R* v *Bennett* [1975] 7 NIJB, per Jones LJ.   [27] [1985] NI 457.

to be shot at and reacted to that danger by shooting in self-defence.' One of the arguments advanced by the appellant at his appeal was that the trial judge had failed to pose, either expressly or by implication, the question of why the appellant *had* fired at the deceased, if not in self-defence, bearing in mind the appellant's testimony (which the judge accepted) that he had not fired at the deceased in order to effect his arrest but had decided to let the deceased go without shooting at him. Counsel for the appellant submitted that it was incumbent on the judge specifically to pose and answer that question and that the obvious explanation was that the appellant *had* in fact fired in self-defence. The terms in which the Court of Appeal dismissed this suggestion are instructive:

With respect, therein may lie the fallacy. Where the trial is conducted and the factual conclusions are reached by the same person, one need not expect every step in the reasoning to be spelled out expressly, nor is the reasoning carried out in sealed compartments with no intercommunication or overlapping, even if the need to arrange a judgment in a logical order may give that impression. It can safely be inferred that, when deliberating on a question of fact with many aspects, even more certainly than when tackling a series of connected legal points, a judge who is himself the tribunal of fact will (a) recognise the issues and (b) view in its entirety a case where one issue is interwoven with another.[28]

As the judge had accepted the appellant's testimony that he had not fired to arrest the deceased and then rejected the appellant's plea of self-defence, the only possible conclusion for the judge was a finding of murder on the basis that the appellant intentionally shot to kill or seriously injure. The judge was not required to set out in express terms how this intention could be reconciled with the appellant's decision not to fire at the accused in order to apprehend him. The judge's refusal to accept the argument based on self-defence was an implicit recognition that these two factors were capable of reconciliation. The Court of Appeal's view is essentially pragmatic: there are limits to the degree of intricacy which one can expect from the fact-finder in giving expression to the reasoning process which has led to a certain conclusion.

A question which is related to the form which the judgment ought to take is whether compliance with the statutory requirement is a prerequisite for a lawful decision. In a number of early cases, judges evidently struggled to meet the demands of this facet of their newly acquired role in Diplock trials. In an appeal heard in 1978, *R v McClenaghan*,[29] a preliminary point was that the judge had at the end of the trial simply announced that he was satisfied beyond reasonable doubt that the accused was guilty, and a week later had given a reasoned judgment in open court without prior notification to the Crown or the defence. The Northern Ireland Court of

---

[28] *Ibid.*, 478, per Lord Lowry LCJ.   [29] [1978] 4 NIJB.

Appeal held that, while the judge had not acted in compliance with the statutory provision, his failure was not such as to justify the ordering of a new trial. The Court reviewed three earlier cases[30] in which similar points had arisen. In the first, the judge had 'launched into' sentencing the accused at the conclusion of the evidence and without giving counsel any opportunity to address him and had then given a reasoned judgment the following day without notification to the defence. The verdict was set aside and a re-trial ordered: the judge had not acted in compliance with the statutory provision and counsel had been precluded from making submissions to the court before sentence. As the Court of Appeal in *McClenaghan* noted, this latter point appeared particularly influential and it is not clear that a new trial would have been ordered if the only defect had been the failure to comply with the Act. The second case was one in which the judge had simply stated that he was satisfied and convicted the accused of the charges against them without giving reasons at any time. A new trial was ordered: apparently there were disputed issues of fact in the case which would have rendered review of the judge's decision impossible in the absence of reasons for the conclusions reached. In the third case also, no reasons were given at any time but the appeal was dismissed on the ground that if reasons had been given, the decision would have been unchallengeable on the evidence against the accused. In these circumstances, the absence of a judgment was not fatal.

The Court of Appeal then made the following instructive reflections on the status of the reasoned judgment:

The effect of those decisions appears to be that while non-compliance with the Act is an irregularity, it does not as a matter of course give a right to an accused to have the verdict set aside and a new trial ordered. The failure to give a reasoned judgment is not an irregularity in the course of the trial which in itself makes a trial a nullity or renders the verdict suspect. It is a post-verdict requirement and does not affect a trial otherwise valid up to that point . . . An appellate Court must . . . consider the evidence and decide whether the evidence is such that the accused is obviously guilty and the verdict arrived at one which if a reasoned judgment had been given could not be attacked, and if in fact the verdict is the only verdict which a Court could properly reach on the evidence.[31]

In the present case, the Court decided, while not condoning the failure to comply with the section, that the only proper verdict which could have been reached was one of guilty and accordingly the appeal was dismissed. There is certainly a measure of economic sense in the Court's attitude to the judge's failure to meet the statutory requirement, but it could be argued that

---

[30] *R v Brenda Murray* (1977); *R v Campbell and Quinn*; *R v McDaid* (1977). The cases are unreported and the only source of information available to the Court was the Registrar's note.

[31] [1978] 4 NIJB 7, per McGonigal LJ.

the perception of the judgment as being 'post-verdict' is objectionable in principle. Whereas in jury trials the summing-up occupies a central position in the decision-making process, in the Diplock context the judgment provides an even more tangible basis for the verdict. Reasons may formally be delivered after the verdict is known, but it is difficult to characterize them otherwise than as an integral *part* of the decision-making process. It will be seen that the depiction of the judgment as a post-verdict requirement sits particularly uneasily with the practice adopted by one judge who would construct the judgment in the course of an informed exchange of views with counsel at the close of the evidence. Further, the view is inconsistent with that taken by the Court of Appeal on other occasions when, as we shall see later in this chapter, it has likened defective and erroneous findings by the judge to misdirections of fact by the trial judge to the jury. The Court in *McClenaghan* conceded that the judgment requirement is 'in ease of an accused and he must be given the opportunity to consider and if he wishes to appeal the verdict and the reasoning on which it is based.'[32] Arguably, however, the Court's view that the absence of a judgment does not necessarily nullify a verdict underplayed the centrality of the judgment's role in the context of a professional process of justice. In any event, after over twenty years of Diplock court practice, it is now unlikely that the judicial lapses which occurred in *McClenaghan* and those earlier cases would be repeated.

Finally, it is fair to say that although we have identified the requirement for a reasoned judgment as one of the few formal modifications of the criminal process in the absence of the jury, it has not been perceived by the judiciary as involving any far-reaching extension of the judge's role at trial. This is, of course, very much in keeping with a recurrent theme of the present book. The transition to trial by judge alone was accomplished without detailed consideration of the new demands which would be made of the tribunal, leaving judges to develop the new system in something of a practical vacuum. Just as we have observed that judges adopt different styles in questioning witnesses, so also they have varying approaches to the formulation of judgment.

JUDICIAL RATIONALIZATION OF THE VERDICT

As noted above, it is natural that the length, content, and structure of judgments will vary depending on the complexity and seriousness of the issues in a case. One county court judge gave an indication of the differing pressures on judges according to the gravity of the offence involved:

---

[32] *Ibid.*, 9.

[The judgment] is nearly always given from notes that have been prepared, if not written out in full. You get the major judgments in murder cases. The High Court judgments that can run up to ninety pages. But in the run of the mill, maybe it's a robbery that hasn't been descheduled, you have something prepared but it may not be fully written out. But you have headings, so you know what you're going to cover. They're seldom given off the cuff.

A High Court judge gave an interesting insight into his approach to constructing the judgment. He suggested that he would never reach any definitive conclusion about a case until the end of the trial. His practice then was to map out the issues in writing, particularly in complex cases: the charges alleged against each accused and the evidence led on these charges. This record would then form the basis of the judgment. This judge stressed that he would always make up his mind about a case before he began writing the judgment, but that he knew of one judge who did not make up his mind until after he had actually embarked on writing the judgment. He added that the writing of judgments is a burdensome task which takes up much time.

In Chapter Eight, we presented a statistical breakdown of the outcomes of the cases in our sample.[33] Of the twenty-six Diplock cases observed, eleven resulted in a finding of guilt (three of these cases involving the rearraignment of the accused and a plea of guilty after some evidence had been presented), in thirteen the accused was acquitted outright, and in the remaining two a new trial was ordered. Therefore, a fully reasoned judgment was only required by the legislation in eight of our cases. As noted before, however, judges as a matter of practice offer reasons for acquittal and in some instances judges devoted considerable attention to the task of formulating the basis on which the prosecution had failed to make out its case. We shall consider the significance and desirability of the giving of reasons for acquittal. First, however, let us consider the approaches which judges in our sample took to the process of judgment. Although again the limited numbers of cases involved prompt the need to sound a cautionary note, some interesting stylistic variations emerged from the cases observed.

As stated in Chapter Seven, the structure of the Diplock trial offers greater opportunity for the judge to engage in debate with counsel at the stage of closing submissions, although it was noted that this practice can create a perception of the criminal process as 'closed' to all but the professional participants. One judge in particular actively exploited the channels of communication which present themselves in the jury's absence. Rather than attempting to maintain a strict separation between the closing addresses by the parties and the giving of judgment, he would formulate a 'judgment in action', offering the parties the opportunity to

---

[33] See Table 8.1 and accompanying text.

challenge the view which he had reached provisionally at the close of the evidence. In one case, for example, discussed in Chapter Seven,[34] this judge set the discussion in motion as follows: 'You can comment upon how my mind is working. When I first read the papers I considered this to be a very weak Crown case bearing in mind the charges.' The charges were causing grievous bodily harm with intent and inflicting grievous bodily harm (contrary to sections 18 and 20 respectively of the Offences Against the Person Act 1861). He then outlined the difficulties in the prosecution case with regard to establishing the accused's responsibility for that degree of harm to the victim. Following some exchanges with both counsel, the judge went on to find the defendant (who had pleaded guilty to common assault) guilty of assault occasioning actual bodily harm and the case proceeded almost immediately to sentence. This judge took a similar approach in another case, considered in some detail in Chapter Eight,[35] in which the accused who had a clear record faced a charge of withholding information and relied on the defence of duress. On that occasion the judge did not give such a clear picture of how his mind was working at the close of the evidence, but a fairly detailed discussion of applicability of the defence of duress in the circumstances took place between him and defence counsel and this discussion culminated in a brief ruling acquitting the accused.

Towards the conclusion of Chapter Seven, we referred to a 'problem-solving' model, whereby the judge would direct discussion with the parties aimed at reaching the appropriate outcome in the case. This particular judge was the prime adherent to this problem-solving approach. The first of the two cases just discussed offers a perfect illustration: the accused had played some role in the incident leading to the victim's injuries and at the close of the case the question remained of how that role could most accurately be reflected in the outcome. Referring back to the spectrum between the contest and inquest models, a trial in which such an approach is adopted does not lean obviously to either extreme: the judge does not act as inquisitor as such, in that a degree of latitude is accorded to the parties as to the course which the discussion should take, but it is the judge and not the parties who retains ultimate control of this course. Thus, typically, the discussion of duress in the second case was preceded by the judge's exhortation: 'Well let's come to the essence of the matter.'

So far, we have stressed the problems of perception which may be created by concluding the trial in closed, professional discourse. Related to this objection is the fact that a judge who reveals how his mind is working runs the risk of appearing to have prejudged the issues. Moreover, it could be argued that this approach reduces the process of judgment to a degree of

---

[34] Chapter Seven, page 193.   [35] Chapter Eight, page 246.

informality which sits uneasily with the principle that the decision to convict must be accompanied by a reasoned justification. On the other hand, the ability of the parties to influence the fact-finder right up to the point of the decision being made has benefits. As we have noted, one of the problems with the transition to non-jury trial is that it is difficult to guard against the danger of the professional being influenced by matters of which the jury would have been ignorant. Further, the jury is precluded from reaching a collective decision until it retires at the close of the case: until that point, the opportunity to influence its decision remains open. In the next section, we shall consider whether the 'judgment in action' could be turned to the advantage of the trial process as a whole.

Although the other judges in our sample gave judgment in a more formal manner and in detachment from the rest of the trial, there were still notable stylistic variations in their approach. Broadly speaking, two approaches to the construction of the judgment could be identified. Some judges tended to begin by stating their conclusion and then proceeding to justify it by reviewing the evidence and explaining its conformity with the standard of proof beyond reasonable doubt on the charges against the accused. Other judges set out their judgments as though detailing the process of deliberation which had led to the decision. This form of judgment would build a conclusion of guilt from the expressly stated premise of the presumption of innocence.

The first approach may be illustrated by two cases of different levels of seriousness tried respectively before a county court judge and a High Court judge. In the first case, in which the accused was charged with possession of explosives, the judge began his judgment as follows: 'I find you guilty . . . of being an aider and abettor in count 1, count 3 and guilty on count 5 of the bill of indictment. You may sit down while I read my judgment.' He went on to give details of the various counts against the accused, noting that a co-defendant had pleaded guilty, and then setting out in chronological order the evidence which linked the accused to possession of the explosives, and the arguments made in the accused's favour by his counsel. The main area of contention was whether the accused had willingly assisted in the storing of the materials by two other men in the house of the co-defendant, with whom he had moved in. The accused claimed that he had no control over the substances and that he did not assent to them being in the house. The judge concluded his judgment with a brief statement of his assessment of the evidence:

I accept from the evidence that when [the accused] arrived at the house he probably had no knowledge of what was going on but I am equally satisfied that as he acquired knowledge he rendered assistance to the two men in the ways that I have indicated. He may not at first have been a willing participant in this matter but I am quite satisfied that he became an active participant as time passed and that he performed positive acts to assist the two men in making the house freely available in their activities. Accordingly, I am satisfied beyond a reasonable doubt that the second named defendant is guilty . . .

The second example of this approach occurred in a case in which the accused was convicted of attempted murder, possession of firearms with intent, and membership of a proscribed organization. The judgment began: 'my decision is to find you guilty of the three offences with which you are charged. I am required by law to give a reason for my decision. You may be seated while I do that.' Following a brief outline of the charges, the judge then continued: 'The Crown evidence has satisfied me beyond reasonable doubt as to the facts which I am about to recite and where elsewhere in this judgment I express myself as satisfied about a particular matter I mean unless I expressly state the contrary that I am satisfied about that matter beyond all reasonable doubt. Now to the facts that I am satisfied about.' The judgment then dealt in meticulous detail with the evidence against the accused, consisting mainly of statements by the accused to the interviewing officers, and forensic evidence linking the accused to the car used in the attack which formed the subject of the charges. The next phase of the judgment was a piece-by-piece deconstruction of the defence case, involving the acceptance of the more damning of two accounts given by the accused of his level of involvement in the incident, and the rejection of two alibi witnesses called on behalf of the defence at trial. The judgment was concluded by a statement of the judge's reasons for his earlier ruling against the defence at the *voir dire*.

The contrasting style of judgment, one which almost replicates a process of deliberation building towards the outcome as opposed to a statement of justification of a stated decision, is well illustrated by two cases involving possession of firearms and explosives which were heard by the same judge. Having outlined the charges against the accused, the judge approached the issues in the manner of a summing-up to the jury, tailored to the merged tribunal of law and fact. Thus, in one of the cases, he began:

I remind myself that the starting point for the consideration of any of these offences by a court of law must be the presumption of innocence in favour of the defendant. This is particularly the case where the defendant has put his character in issue and has virtually a clear record apart from a minor motoring offence but, in addition, as in this case, bears a good character as has been established by the evidence of three substantial witnesses who attended the hearing to give evidence on his behalf . . . In order to rebut this presumption of innocence the Crown must prove the defendant's guilt in respect of each of the offences and that proof must be proof of each offence and of each element of each offence beyond a reasonable doubt.

In the other case, the judge stressed the nature of the burden of proof even more forcefully: 'If at the end of the case I entertain a reasonable doubt in respect of any or all of the offences or in respect of any element in the offences then the defendant is entitled to an acquittal.'

In each case the judge proceeded to analyse each item of evidence presented in the course of the trial, stating the facts as he found proven and the inferences which he was prepared to draw from those facts. Only towards the conclusion of the judgment would the judge make a formal pronouncement of guilt. An even more formally structured approach was adopted by a Lord Justice of Appeal in one of the cases in our sample in which the accused, charged with possession of firearms with intent to enable others to endanger life, had put forward a defence of duress. Having analysed the defendant's evidence with reference to the law on duress, the judge set out his decision as follows in a series of findings dismissing the defence:

I have carefully considered all that [the defendant] said in relation to his meeting with the UDA man . . . (assuming that everything occurred as he says, which I do not accept) and my conclusions are:

1. That what was said, or implied, was not a real threat.
2. That there was no threat of serious injury or death.
3. That what was said did not (viewed objectively) compel [the defendant] to act as he did.
4. That (assuming [the defendant's] actions were in response to what was said) [the defendant] took the weapons to avoid 'hassle' a common colloquial expression whose meaning falls short of causing death or serious injury.
5. That if [the defendant] felt constrained to act as he did this was due to his own apprehension (and there is no evidence that the UDA man knew of [the defendant's] experiences or anxieties).

Accordingly, having regard to all the evidence, I am satisfied beyond reasonable doubt that [the defendant] was not acting under duress and was guilty of possessing the Colt pistol with the necessary intent – namely to enable others to endanger life.

This approach to the process of judgment is far removed from the 'judgment in action' described above, and the logical sequence of findings set out at the conclusion also presents the most extreme contrast to the bald nature of the jury's verdict. The various ways of presenting justification for the accused's guilt which we have identified also evoke the two contrasting styles of juries' deliberations which were noted by Hastie, Penrod, and Pennington in their important study of the psychology of jury decision-making.[36] First, some of the mock juries in their survey would engage in 'verdict-driven' deliberations, whereby the discussion would begin with a ballot to gauge the 'position' of individual jurors as regards the evidence, and the deliberations would proceed 'with many statements of verdict preferences and frequent polling'. 'Evidence-driven' deliberations, on the

---

[36] (1983).

other hand, would be less focused at the outset on the verdict to be reached than on 'story construction and the review of evidence' and it would only be towards the conclusion of the deliberations that the discussion would centre on the classification of the verdict.[37] The judgments which we have described could be categorized in similar fashion. 'Verdict-driven' judgments could depict those in which the judge states a conclusion and proceeds to justify it and, to a lesser extent perhaps, the judgment in action where the judge states his position and directs the discussion towards the appropriate verdict. 'Evidence-driven' judgments are those in which the judge engages in a reconstruction and analysis of the evidence and gradually builds towards the verdict.

It would be wrong to read too much into the different approaches adopted by judges to the process of judgment. It is important to stress again that the number of cases in our survey which culminated in a judgment in support of the accused's guilt was not sufficiently large to make a definitive categorization of judicial approaches to rationalizing the verdict. Further, the broad categorization described above does not imply any qualitative preference for one technique over the other. What we have illustrated, however, is that there is considerable stylistic variation in judges' formulation of their judgments which transcends the nature and seriousness of the issues in a case. As noted above, this variation in itself reflects one of our central themes, namely that the removal of the jury from the criminal process in Diplock cases left judges uncertain as to how the trial ought ideally to be conducted. The lack of specific guidance to judges on this matter, and the maintenance of the basic adversarial structure of the criminal trial, have as we have seen left judges to forge distinctive approaches to their role in the course of the proceedings, but the institution of the jury has often formed an influential backdrop to judicial mores. In this section, we have illustrated a wide diversity in judges' approaches to the specific task of formulating the judgment. At one extreme, a judge was prepared to eschew completely the norms of jury trial and embarked on a highly individualistic method of arguing towards an appropriate outcome. Some judges prepared their judgments more formally but appeared free of 'jury-thinking' in announcing a decision and then going on to justify the conclusion in terms of their own reaction to the evidence. Other judges adhered more closely to the decision-making structure associated with jury trial by assimilating the judgment to the summing-up and infusing their own views of the evidence as they built towards a conclusion. It is interesting to note that one judge, when acquitting an accused, even went so far as expressly to adopt a jury-like stance: 'I have to remind myself in this case that this is a non-jury trial, but the same legal principles apply as regards the

---

[37] *Ibid.*, 163.

burden of proof as in any other case and I have to act as both judge and jury
and I must be satisfied in my own mind that the evidence is such that a
jury, properly directed, would be sure beyond a reasonable doubt of your
guilt.'

Each of the approaches to the process of judgment have both advantages
and disadvantages. When a judge gives an indication of his lines of thought,
the parties are offered a channel of communication with the fact-finder
which enables them directly to influence the decision-making process, but
(as noted) the informality of the method adopted by one judge in our sample
deprives the judgment of the quality of a fully reasoned decision. The
formally prepared judgment does not suffer in this respect, but it renders
the decision unchallengeable in the course of the trial and accentuates the
strength of the position occupied by the professional trier in the jury's
absence. Moreover, judges who are not influenced by notional jury
constraints when delivering judgment may be applauded for confronting
directly the changed nature of the trial, but (again in keeping with an
important theme of the book) there is a lack of specific guidance as to how
judges should approach this new aspect of their role. Lastly, judges who
conform to the expectations of jury trial may be given credit for seeking to
minimize any disadvantage which might be seen to ensue from the jury's
absence, but arguably they fail to confront the reality that in the Diplock
context the jury has departed and that the process of decision-making has
thus ineradicably been changed.

In the next section we shall seek to draw upon these varying approaches
to the judgment with a view to suggesting a possible alternative. Briefly,
however, let us turn to examine the practice which judges have adopted of
giving reasons for acquitting the accused. This is a good example of how the
formal contours of the trial process may be modified in practice without
express prescription. As we suggested before, the fact that judges do offer
reasons for acquitting an accused may be attributable to a wider
accountability to the community which accompanies their specific responsibility to the accused at trial. In fact, the practice of giving reasons for
acquittal provides one of the clearest illustrations of the distinctiveness of
the 'professional' approach to the trying of cases and the commitment
of judges to the notion of legal guilt.

In a case in which the sole issue was whether the accused's admitted
possession of explosives was accompanied by an intention to endanger life,
the judge's comments after having acquitted the accused of the more serious
charge offer a classic reflection on the necessity to divorce the concept of
legal guilt from the 'merits' of the case, or more specifically the merits of the
individual accused: 'the events which have brought you to the dock have
been well ventilated here before the court and are contained in this book of
evidence, and you have escaped being found guilty of a very serious offence I

may say, by the skin of your teeth, but having heard the evidence that was given it seemed to me that it had to follow the finding of Not Guilty.'

In another case, when a judge ruled out a confession by one of three accused persons due to possible irregularities at his interview by the police, he went on to remark:

I would like to say at this stage something that I think should rarely be said by a judge, that I am excluding that oral admission and that written confession even though I believe that [the accused] is quite probably guilty of the offences with which he is charged and I do that because I have ruled in statements of admission in respect of his co-accused . . . and I feel that this is an appropriate case in which I should state my views on the balance of probabilities but, as has already happened, I have ruled the statements of admission and the oral confessions inadmissible, there being no evidence against [the accused]. He is being acquitted of the charges against him.

Although this case differs from the first in that there was no possibility of legal guilt being established without the statements, it does illustrate again this gulf between the judge's personal assessment, of the case and of the accused, and the legal barriers which stand in the way of conviction.

The most obvious attraction of the provision of reasons for acquitting an accused is that, in contrast to the simple jury verdict of not guilty, a clear explanation is given of why the prosecution failed to establish the case against the accused. In the case mentioned above, for example, where the judge adopted a jury-like standpoint in acquitting the accused, he gave a very full account of how he had assessed the accused's defence of duress, and weighed the evidential significance both of his good character and of the fact that he had changed his evidence in court. Similarly, in the hijacking case in which the judge admitted the accused's statement in evidence but then went on to acquit, the judge clearly stated why the prosecution case had failed to come up to proof:

nothing in the admissions points to a detailed knowledge of the alleged crime. On the contrary the circumstances are extremely vague . . . I have to be wary of sinister accused men doctoring details of admissions to delude a Court as to their true state of knowledge. Nevertheless I do not regard this young man, particularly having seen him in the witness box, having heard the powerful medical evidence as to his mental capacity, and bearing in mind his clear record, that he is such an individual.

There is, however, a strong argument of principle against the giving of reasons for acquittal. This is that any express reflection on the character of an accused person who is acquitted may overshadow the fact of his innocence. In those cases where a judge expresses grave reservations about exonerating the accused, the true outcome of the case is less a verdict of not guilty than a finding of 'not quite guilty'. There is an interesting parallel here with judges whose professional instincts prompt them on occasions to express displeasure at the not guilty verdict of the jury in trials over which they have presided, a form of judicial behaviour which has attracted criticism.[38] Perhaps it is an inevitable consequence of the transition to a professionally oriented system of justice that no decision, including a decision to acquit, be left unsupported like a jury's verdict.[39] The next question is whether the process of justifying a finding of guilt ought to become even more demonstrative than at present.

TOWARDS AN ADVERSARIAL STYLE OF JUDGMENT?

We have seen then that judges adopt different approaches towards the process of judgment, derived not merely from the nature of the cases tried but also from the personality of individual judges. While it is most common for judges to deliver a judgment which is fully detached from the submissions of counsel, one judge in particular gave an indication of his view of a case to counsel at the close of the evidence and invited submissions before reading his final conclusion. This was described as a 'judgment in action' because the decision has been reached through a deliberative process in which the fact-finder has subjected his provisional views to debate and remained open to further argument right to the verge of delivering a final view. As we noted in Chapter Seven, another judge expressed reservations about this approach to judgment and argued that there was a danger of giving the defendant the impression that the judge had made up his mind or was not taking the issue seriously enough. The main strength of this objection, however, lies in the undesirability of a judge's views being conveyed in such an informal manner, rather than in any failing of principle in a judge indicating to the parties how his mind is working. Moreover, one could also object to the formal detached process of judgment on the ground that it does not offer the parties an adequate opportunity to influence the fact-finder's reasoning until a stage at which it is too late.

It may, therefore, be contended that elements of both these approaches to the process of judgment could be combined, to allow a more argumentative style of judgment to be adopted but constraining this within a more formal framework. Rather than requiring the judge to deliver a verdict and judgment 'package', there is some attraction in the idea that he or she should be obliged at the close of the evidence to issue a provisional statement of reasons for his conclusion. Counsel would then be permitted to study and challenge those reasons in advance of the judge's final decision on

---

[38] Pattenden (1990), 227–8.

[39] In certain jurisdictions, notably Israel, this notion is carried through to its logical conclusion whereby judgments acquitting the accused are subject to appeal by the prosecution: see Harnon and Stein (1993), 1184.

guilt or innocence. The statement would be aimed at justifying the conclusion that the accused is guilty of the offence charged, and also at rebutting any explanations consistent with the innocence of the accused. The statement could be followed by an exchange of views between counsel and between judge and counsel, an adversarial-style debate on the strength of the judge's preliminary conclusions. In particular, the defence would be given the opportunity to question the judge's approach to the evidence. After this phase of the process, the judge would make a final pronouncement on the accused's liability. In the event of conviction, the final judgment would justify rejection of any defence response to the preliminary statement. In this way, the judge's freer rein over the evidence at trial would be counterbalanced by greater latitude for the defence to challenge the results of his inquiry. This process would fit in neatly with the realities of Diplock trials and the new kind of adversariness reflected in the views of defence counsel in Diplock trials, mentioned in Chapter Seven, whereby the judge is cast in a kind of adversary role *vis-à-vis* the parties.

A possible objection to such a procedure is that it is contrary to principle for the decision-maker to reveal how his or her mind is working in advance of the final decision: the appearance of prejudgment is unsavoury. In the present context, however, such an objection does not hold great force. First, if at the end of the evidence the judge is minded to acquit the accused, the matter would stop there and an acquittal would follow: it would admittedly be difficult to justify in principle a process in which an express inclination towards acquittal could be reversed through the persuasion of prosecution counsel. In the event of a provisional finding of guilt, however, the accused would surely benefit from the opportunity of a final attempt at instilling in the mind of the fact-finder a reasonable doubt as to culpability. Moreover, this would challenge the judge to justify in a more overt way a finding of guilt beyond reasonable doubt, the elimination of doubt being expressly subject to an argumentative process. Interestingly, a similar approach was adopted by some judges in Schulhofer's study of bench trials in Philadelphia: one judge would sum up his own analysis to counsel and ask them to refute it and others would specifically direct counsel to the issues which they found most troublesome.[40] As we have argued, however, unless conducted in a formal manner the deliberations would not be fully effective in isolating the core elements of the dispute as to the accused's guilt.

Another possible objection is that the prospect of challenge to a provisional judgment followed by open debate between the judge and counsel may be seen as an affront to the judge's authority. This raises the question of whether, in the words of one commentator, 'the interests of justice are better served by uncritical devotion and respect for the ideal of

40 (1984), 1104.

judicial infallibility or by open, public critical debate'.[41] In any event, however, it would be up to the judge to indicate that he or she was offering a *provisional* rather than a final judgment. An analogy is to be found in the practice in jury trials of requisitioning the judge after the summing-up. Obviously the context is different, but the practice illustrates how the opportunity for reasoned argument may be maximized following delineation of the issues by the judge but prior to the ultimate decision on guilt or innocence. A similar procedure could be adapted to suit the context of the non-jury trial. The guilt of the accused would have to be justified through a process of argument and debate in which the accused's representative would play an active part in challenging any assumptions which the fact-finder had formed in advance of or during the trial. In the course of the present work we have sought primarily to describe the practice of the single-judge trial rather than to prescribe rules and procedures to govern its operation. Arising from our study, however, are certain aspects of practice which cause us to return to the fundamental question which we raised in Chapter One: is a thorough rethinking of the entire adversarial trial process necessary when the jury is removed from its centre? Arguably, the requirement that a judge deliver a reasoned judgment in support of a conviction should have been designed in a more imaginative fashion. Of course, the judgment delivered at trial does not necessarily offer the final word on the accused's guilt; review may fall to the Court of Appeal, and it is to the Diplock appeals structure that we now turn.

The 'appealability' of Diplock judgments[42]

As indicated above, a detailed investigation of the appeals system would involve too great a departure from our central concern with the trial process to be attempted here. Of the Diplock cases in our own survey, only four proceeded to full appeal, three against both conviction and sentence and the other against sentence alone. The appeal against sentence and one of the appeals against conviction were successful.[43] One of the appeals which failed does, however, provide a useful illustration of the way in which the grounds of appeal on matters of fact may be formulated. This was the case analysed in Chapter Eight in which a woman was convicted of possession of a quantity of explosives found under the floor of her kitchen. The grounds of appeal were framed as follows:

---

[41] Fraser (1993), 52.

[42] This section is derived in part from an earlier work by the authors: see Jackson and Doran (1992b).

[43] From the jury cases in our sample, three appeals were lodged, each against both conviction and sentence. One was abandoned, one refused leave, and the other successful.

1. That the case against the appellant depended upon circumstantial evidence of possession and that since the evidence admitted of the alternative that the appellant's husband was exclusively guilty of possession the circumstantial evidence was insufficiently unequivocal to justify a conviction.

2. That having regard to the material before the court to the effect that the police accepted that there were a number of alternatives, viz., that the appellant's husband, himself or them both were guilty of possession, the conviction cannot be supported.

3. That the learned trial judge did not attach any or sufficient weight to the fact that when the security forces entered the appellant's home for the purpose of conducting a search she behaved in a friendly and co-operative manner and gave no involuntary indication of guilt.

4. That the learned trial judge attached no or insufficient weight to the absence of any forensic connection (e.g. fibres, finger prints etc.) between the appellant, the hide, or its contents.

5. That the learned trial judge did not attach any or sufficient weight to the appellant's denial on oath in the witness box, that she had no [sic] knowledge of the hide or its contents.

6. That the prosecution had failed to discharge the burden of proving beyond reasonable doubt that the appellant was guilty of possession as charged.

In the event, the Court of Appeal accepted the judge's conclusion that the appellant must have known that the explosives had been hidden beneath the kitchen floor, but the grounds of appeal at least illustrate the *potential* to present a detailed challenge to the judge's reasoning in a way that would not be possible in relation to the jury's verdict.

As we have said, one of the underlying features of the Diplock trial process is an implicit recognition, by the provision of an automatic right of appeal, that the sense of finality of the trial judge's verdict is not so strong as that of the jury verdict. The right to appeal, coupled with the provision of the reasoned judgment, makes the judge's decision more vulnerable to correction by the Court of Appeal: the emphasis is as we have noted, therefore, on greater 'output control'. As stated in Chapter Two, the automatic right of appeal has on occasions been cited in support of the argument against three-judge courts being used in emergency cases. It has been contended that the accused would have nothing further to gain, as he or she is already given direct access to three appellate judges.[44] It is proposed now to examine more closely this theory of enhanced 'appeal-ability'.

In one of the 'supergrass' appeals, *R v Donnelly*,[45] the then Lord Chief Justice commented: 'experience in Northern Ireland has shown how much greater in a Diplock trial are the appellant's opportunities of persuading the Court to interfere than when the appeal is from the sphinx-like verdict of a

---

[44] See Chapter Two, note 50 and accompanying text.   [45] [1986] 4 NIJB.

properly directed jury, which does not have to give reasons for its verdict.'[46] The proposition that the more the fact-finder is called upon to justify a finding, the more susceptible to challenge that decision becomes, was also unquestioned by several of the judges and counsel in our survey. One judge commented: 'It is not enough to go on hunch and say the defendant is guilty—there is the pressure to justify the findings of fact to the satisfaction of the Court of Appeal and the Court of Appeal has been zealous, perhaps too zealous, in scrutinizing judgments to see if they are correctly reasoned.' He went on to say that he could think of only one judge who had escaped a 'bruising reversal' of his judgment in the Court of Appeal. Another judge gave the following account of the different kinds of task facing the appellant in challenging the factual findings of judges and juries:

It's very difficult to lodge appeals on fact in jury cases. In a judge case, however, you have, let us say, a transcript of a scientist's evidence and the judge has found the facts connecting gloves or a pullover with a weapon and he says on those facts the accused was wearing these gloves or that pullover, then it's much easier for the appellant to argue that the judge was not justified in drawing that inference than when a jury has brought in a verdict of guilty and you don't know exactly why. The judge may say, 'I reject witness A (an identifying witness) altogether and I find for certain on the fibres', whereas in a jury case for all you know the jury may have accepted witness A and rejected the fibres. You can see exactly with a judge where he has made mistakes – perhaps in recording what the witness has said, in missing a point and so on. In a jury case, you can't tell whether a jury missed a point or was muddled over the facts or whatever.

One counsel echoed this point from an appellant's perspective when he remarked, 'At least with a Diplock case you have a judgment which you can try and impugn'.

Implicit in such views is a belief that the Court of Appeal serves as a form of redress for the perceived disadvantage which the accused in a Diplock case may suffer as a result of the loss of the jury. It is important to emphasize, however, in accordance with a point that has been made throughout this book, that just as the transition to non-jury trial was largely unaccompanied by formal changes to evidential and procedural rules at trial, so too did the jury-oriented appellate structure remain intact. Thus, although the accused's *right* to appeal has been strengthened in the Diplock context, the Court of Appeal in Northern Ireland has been left to develop its own approach to handling appeals from the decision of a single judge. We have observed in previous chapters that in the jury's absence the judge in practice assumes an altogether different and more powerful role in the course of the trial, but it does not follow that appellate courts will adopt

---

[46] [1986] 4 NIJB, 70.

a markedly different approach to trial review in order to serve as a counterweight to the judge's expanding role at trial.

In fact, the argument that the written judgment offers enhanced appeal opportunities needs to be qualified in several respects. In the first place, the Court is not always ideally placed to challenge the judge's findings of fact due to its inherent limitations as a court of review rather than a court of rehearing. Therefore, on one view, it is just as difficult for the Court to take issue with the lower court's findings of fact as in jury appeals, as it does not have the benefit of receiving witnesses' testimony first-hand and seeing their demeanour in court. As one judge in our survey put it:

But of course it's very easy to say I didn't believe a word the accused said and there's very little the Court of Appeal can do about that. You've assessed the accused as a liar and the authorities support the view that the jury or the tribunal of fact is the only person who is in a good position to assess credibility and obviously this is so and it is difficult to criticize a judge who has made an assessment of credibility.

The same judge did, however, stress the point that at least in a Diplock appeal the Court *can* review a credibility judgment, an exercise which is virtually impossible with a jury verdict. On the other hand, it might be contended that interference with a judge's finding of fact may be even more difficult *because* it is almost invariably supported by reasoned argument and is therefore less easily dismissed as contrary to the evidence.

Just as the Court of Appeal has traditionally been portrayed as poorly equipped to review the factual basis of the trial court's decisions, so too it has been seen as ideally placed to correct errors of law at trial. The written judgment would appear to offer the Court an even firmer platform for challenging the way in which the legal issues were handled at trial. Arguably, however, an error of law is just as easily detectable in a jury trial (particularly in the course of the judicial summing-up) as it is from the judgment in a Diplock trial. Indeed, one defence counsel in our survey suggested that the Court of Appeal is less inclined to challenge a judge's legal error in the Diplock context:

The Court of Appeal has been slower to correct a misstatement of law in a Diplock case than in a jury case. In a jury case, if the jury is told something that is legally defective on an issue of relevance, clearly the worst that can happen is a retrial. If in a Diplock case the judge makes an error of such a gross nature that the Court of Appeal feels that the judge knows full well where the burden of proof lies and that it was just a slip of the tongue, they might say, 'Well, he might have said that but he could not have meant it and he would never have applied that standard.' Whereas if he had made this slip to a jury, that would be dangerous. That has happened on occasions. They also say that whereas with a jury one has to be fairly comprehensive, with a judge addressing himself alone, he doesn't have to dot every 'i' or cross every 't' with the same diligence. That's what they say. We often argue differently. The argument used, not often with success, is that Diplock courts were founded on the premise, you're not going to get a jury but as a partial replacement of that, you're going to have reasons why you're convicted. If the reasons that one has been convicted on are unsound they should be quashed. But there has been a tendency when there's been a fairly gross misstatement to say that that's a slip of the tongue, something the judge could not have meant, because no lawyer from first year university could have said that.

The upshot of these arguments is that the notion of enhanced 'appealability', although in theory presenting the accused with a significant extra layer of protection in compensation for the loss of the jury, may not in practice operate so potently in the accused's favour.

Critics of the Diplock system have argued that the statistical evidence fails to bear out the widely held belief that the Court of Appeal is prepared to adopt a more critical stance with respect to the decisions of judges in Diplock trials. Greer and White, for example, drawing upon figures given by the Attorney-General in a Commons written answer in 1985, argued that the appeal facilities were not operating as impressively as one might have expected:

Only 1,444 appeals against conviction and sentence in scheduled offence cases, 16 per cent of the total number of defendants, were lodged between 1973 and 1984. Of these 49 per cent were withdrawn so only eight per cent of the defendants tried by the Diplock courts had their convictions and/or sentences reviewed by the Northern Ireland Court of Appeal. Of this number a mere 28 per cent of the appeals against conviction and 51 per cent of those against sentence were successful. Therefore, between 1973 and 1984 only two per cent of defendants in scheduled offence cases had their convictions quashed and only four per cent had their sentences altered on appeal.[47]

There are certain respects in which this opinion might be challenged. One preliminary question to be resolved is whether the rate of success on appeal is, as Greer and White contended, low. The conclusion was drawn on the basis of the numbers of all Diplock accused, whether or not an appeal had been pursued, and no comparative statistics from jury appeals were analysed. If one sets the number of successful appeals against the total number of defendants who have appeared before Diplock courts, one does not gain a true impression of the appellate body's willingness to intervene. It is more revealing to consider the number of appeals against conviction actually heard to a conclusion and to assess the success of these in both Diplock and jury cases. This method is adopted in the following table.[48]

---

[47] Greer and White (1986), 11.

[48] Table 9.1 is derived from Northern Ireland Court Service, *Northern Ireland Judicial Statistics* 1993 (1994), Part A (The Court of Appeal), Table 5A, supplemented by figures provided by the Court Service for the years 1987–92 (an equivalent table does not appear in the previous annual statistical bulletins).

Table 9.1 *Appeal rates in jury and Diplock cases, 1987–1993*

Appeals against jury convictions							
	1987	1988	1989	1990	1991	1992	1993
Total appeals against conviction	14	12	12	10	16	7	14
Appeal abandoned	9	5	5	2	5	5	4
Appeal allowed	1	1	2	3	3	2	4
Appeal dismissed	4	6	5	5	8	0	6
Appeals allowed as % of appeals heard to conclusion	20%	14%	29%	38%	27%	100%	40%

Appeals against Diplock convictions							
	1987	1988	1989	1990	1991	1992	1993
Total appeals against conviction	34	31	44	18	39	23	42
Appeal abandoned	8	4	20	8	17	8	22
Appeal allowed	2	4	3	1	7	4	2
Appeal dismissed	24	23	21	9	15	11	18
Appeals allowed as % of appeals heard to conclusion	8%	15%	13%	10%	32%	27%	10%

These statistics invite a number of comments. First, a greater number of appeals are brought against conviction in Diplock cases than in jury cases. Secondly, and in keeping with the Greer and White view, the success rate is indeed fairly low even when our more restrictive framework is adopted. Thirdly, and contrary to what one might expect, the success rate in appeals heard to a conclusion is actually lower than that in jury appeals (the respective overall rates derived from the above figures for the period 1987–93 are 16% and 32%).

It is emphasized, however, that although the statistical analysis does demonstrate, at the very least, that the automatic right of appeal has not had a dramatic impact on the rate of success of appeals in Diplock cases, it does not necessarily justify the conclusion that the Diplock appeals process is defective. It could, for example, be argued that a low rate of success on appeal and the relatively low rate of appeals lodged or actually pursued were a reflection of the success of the Diplock trial system. The lower the number of convictions overturned and the fact that the automatic right of appeal is not routinely exercised might be presented as a vindication of judges' first instance decision-making. As stressed in Chapter Two, however, it is important to look behind the statistical picture in order to gain a comprehensive understanding of the workings of the Diplock process. If we study the figures in isolation, for example, they do not reveal whether successful appeals in Diplock cases were based on issues of law or issues of fact. Moreover, recalling a point made in Chapter Eight, if judges in Diplock cases tend to take a more focused approach than juries to the task of matching the evidence to the notion of legal guilt, then it might be expected that the tightly-knit reasoning process involved would be more difficult to challenge on appeal. The point here is not simply that judges have the opportunity to construct judgments that are 'appeal-proof', but that inherent in a legalistic approach to the issue of guilt is the likelihood that fewer loose ends will be left untied in the process of judgment than in the event of a jury's bare determination of guilt. A more specific point, referred to in Chapter Seven, is that judges are on occasions influenced by the abiding presence of the Court of Appeal in making decisions in the course of the trial. The example given was of a judge who withdrew from a case in which inadmissible character evidence had been leaked at trial and stated as one reason for taking this course that the Court of Appeal would probably set aside a conviction if he were to proceed to hear the case.

If judges at trial act in conformity with norms which they believe the Court of Appeal would uphold (and it must be recalled that many of the judges who hear Diplock cases at first instance also sit in an appellate capacity), this could have some impact on the rate of successful appeals. Such factors, although admittedly indeterminate, must at least be taken into account in an assessment of the appeals process. A more concrete explanation for the relatively low rate of success may, however, be found in an examination of the stated approach of the Court to Diplock appeals, which reveals a deference to the first-instance fact-finder similar to that which is customary in the jury context. On those occasions when the Court has sought to articulate principles for review, it has tended to draw upon its experience in jury appeals and also the principles which guide an appellate court in reviewing the decisions of a single judge in a civil case. In *Thain*,[49] a Diplock appeal discussed earlier in this chapter, the Court drew upon the principles stated in the civil case of *Northern Ireland Railways* v *Tweed*[50] which may be summarized as follows:

1. The judge's finding on primary facts can rarely be disturbed if there is evidence to support it.
2. The appellate court is in as good a position as the judge to draw inferences from documents and from facts which are clear but even here must give weight to his conclusions.

[49] [1985] NI 457.   [50] [1982] 15 NIJB 10–11.

3. The judge can be more readily reversed if he has misdirected himself in law or if he has misunderstood or misused the facts and may have thereby reached a wrong conclusion. For this purpose his judgment may be analysed in a way which is not possible with a jury's verdict.

4. The appellate court should not resort to conjecture or to its own estimate of the probabilities of a balanced situation as a means of rejecting the trial judge's conclusions.

In *R v Donnelly*,[51] the Court added to these principles other dicta of the English Court of Appeal in jury appeals (subject to modification to render them applicable to a non-jury situation). First, the Court cited the suggestion in *R v Thorne*[52] (relating to accomplice cases) that the Court should 'examine the villain's evidence with care to see whether there were any weaknesses in it which the jury may have overlooked or not assessed properly'. The Court then approved the following comment in *R v Turnbull*: 'On matters of credibility this Court will only interfere in three circumstances: first if the jury has been misdirected as to how to assess the evidence; secondly if there has been no direction at all when there should have been one; and thirdly if on the whole of the evidence the jury must have taken a perverse view of a witness, but this is rare.'[53] Further, in *R v Gibson and Lewis*,[54] the Court compared a defective and erroneous finding in a judgment with a misdirection of fact to the jury, the test for determining whether the conviction was safe and satisfactory being 'whether the jury would inevitably have convicted if the summing-up had not contained the misdirection'.

In this way, the Court of Appeal has adopted a practical solution to the novel difficulties which the written judgment presents to the appellate body. It may be argued, however, that there are certain anomalous elements in its approach. The analogy with civil appeals is a tempting one, but it is also somewhat misleading in that the judge's responsibility in a Diplock case is of a different order to that in a civil dispute. Although the Court has stressed the difference in the respective burdens and standards of proof, one might also argue that the appellate body ought to be more ready to interfere with the judge's findings in the criminal context in order to protect the accused. In the civil context, deference to the trial judge not only makes economic sense, but it also accords with the notion of procedural equality which underpins the civil process: not only are plaintiffs and defendants afforded equal access to evidence in advance of trial, but they proceed in the knowledge that a finding in favour of either side will attract the same measure of protection on appeal. Such an argument obviously does not

---

[51] [1986] 4 NIJB 70.   [52] (1978) 66 Cr App R 6, 16, per Lawton LJ.
[53] [1977] QB 224, 231, per Lord Widgery LCJ.
[54] Unreported, 19 Dec. 1986.

translate to the criminal process, where only a finding of guilt is subject to being reopened, due to the much higher premium attached to the risk of convicting the innocent than to that of acquitting the guilty. Moreover, to attempt to gauge the impact of a misdirection on the minds of a jury is not an exercise which is easily translated to the single-judge situation.

It has been argued in the course of this book that one consequence of the removal of the jury has been to place the judge at trial in a more powerful position *vis-à-vis* the parties. In this section, we have suggested that the requirement that the judge deliver a reasoned judgment in support of conviction and the provision of an automatic right of appeal have not caused the Court of Appeal to adopt an overtly more protective role. Generally speaking, it has not taken a markedly more robust approach to the findings of fact of the court of trial than it adopts in jury appeals. A notable exception to this trend occurred in the Court's handling of the 'supergrass' appeals in the mid-eighties, which as we saw in Chapter Two effectively precipitated the end of that particular security strategy. In those cases, the Court conducted a painstaking analysis of the trial judges' assessment of the credibility of the accomplice witnesses and was prepared to enter the domain of fact in a most direct fashion. However, such interventionism has not been typical of the Court's generally cautious approach to Diplock and jury cases alike.

There is an argument that in Diplock appeals the Court should generally be encouraged to jettison conventional appellate approaches to the findings of lower tribunals, and to be more prepared to take issue with the judge's findings, even to the extent of assuming a more investigative role itself.[55] In the context of trial by jury, it is understandable that the Court of Appeal has been wary of intruding readily on the jury's fact-finding province. As we have noted, one of the attractions of employing the jury in a fact-finding capacity is that it imports a lay element into the decision-making process; faith in the value of lay participation might be undermined if the Court of Appeal were to interfere too readily with its factual assessment. Although the Royal Commission on Criminal Justice advocated a greater prepared-ness by the Court to overturn convictions, even in the absence of any new information, in cases where it has serious doubts about the correctness of the jury's verdict,[56] it stopped short of suggesting that the Court's role should become more investigative. In the context of trial by judge alone, however, there is arguably less need for the Court to be so protective of the inviolability of the trial court's findings of fact and any objection to the Court itself rehearing witnesses and calling other witnesses is patently less strong. As stated above, the automatic right of appeal appears to signal a

---

[55] See Jackson and Doran (1992b), 284–5.
[56] See pages 170–2 of the report.

more appellant-oriented appeals process, but the success of such a process rests ultimately on the power and the willingness of the Court of Appeal to take a more vigorous approach to the review of judges' decisions.

It may therefore be argued that in the Diplock context the Court of Appeal's general role should be redefined to encourage it to undertake a re-evaluation of the evidence presented at trial and the reasoning of the trial judge based on his or her assessment of that evidence. It is not suggested that the Court should conduct a complete rehearing of the evidence, but simply that it should be more prepared to recall witnesses, rehear evidence and receive new evidence of its own motion or at the behest of the appellant. Although the findings of fact of the trial judge should be given due regard, they need not be viewed as almost fully shielded from reconsideration. The Court of Appeal would then be better equipped to fulfil the tasks of providing a forum of accountability for the trial judge and of acting as a residual protector of the accused's interests in the absence of the jury. It would, however, be beyond the scope of the present book to develop such ideas at length. We have been primarily concerned with an evaluation of practice in Diplock trials and, although the role of the Court of Appeal is, as we have seen, highly significant within the general Diplock process, it is to the trial which we return in our final chapter.

At the beginning of this chapter, we argued that the stress upon the opportunity for control of the output of a professional decision-making body is justified both in terms of compensating the accused for the loss of the jury, and in terms of making the judge accountable to the community as well as to the parties. Such accountability is promoted by the requirement that a reasoned judgment be delivered in support of conviction, but it may only be enforced by an overseeing body which is prepared to take issue with the judge's conclusions. The formal structure of decision-making in Diplock trials bears some of the hallmarks of an inquest-oriented model, with the strengthened appeal procedure evoking the image of a typically hierarchical system of authority which is not commonly associated with the Anglo-American adversary tradition. In the present chapter, however, it has been argued that these formal changes to the conventional trial process have not in practice made a significant difference to the accused's capacity to challenge a finding of guilt which has been made against him.

In Chapter Three we contrasted two models of proof, the inquest and the contest, and in subsequent chapters we considered where the Diplock process may be located between the two. We have emphasized that the Diplock system was introduced on the assumption that the removal of the jury could be accomplished without any significant changes to the adversary trial structure. As we have found, however, in practice the professional trial takes on a character different from that of its jury counterpart. At the close of the trial and beyond, the Diplock process has at the formal level been endowed with more overtly inquest-oriented characteristics. By a certain irony, however, despite this formal shift the practical impact on the appeals process has been limited as the Court of Appeal has tended to adhere to the norms of the jury trial in its review of judges' decisions.

We return then to the question which has occupied us throughout the present work, namely whether the transition to non-jury trial ought to have been preceded by a more fundamental reassessment of the entire trial process. In this chapter we have touched upon alternative approaches to judgment and appeals which might counter criticism of the professional trial by those from a jury-oriented tradition. The primary aim of the present book, however, has been to describe and assess practice in non-jury trials. In the final chapter, we consider what general lessons may be reached from the results of our study, first in the specific context of the criminal justice process in Northern Ireland, and then in the context of the wider jury debate to which essentially this book is devoted.

10

The Future of Judging Without Jury

Responses evoked by the expression 'judging without jury' will vary according to the perspective of the audience. In the specific context of Northern Ireland, the term will evoke for both lawyer and layperson the removal of the jury from the trial of serious criminal cases arising from the troubles and its replacement with the Diplock process. The debate on the respective merits of these forms of trial feeds into the wider debate on the suitability of the general emergency regime which has run in parallel to Northern Ireland's 'ordinary' criminal process.[1] The Diplock court system is often represented as the epitome of this regime, but it is only one aspect of a much larger legislative and administrative programme.

Stepping beyond the particular context of Northern Ireland, lawyers educated in the common law tradition might take the reference to the jury's absence as a pointer to the debate on the wisdom or otherwise of the jury's gradual diminution in influence within the sphere of the administration of criminal justice. The rarity of the civil jury in the United Kingdom and Ireland, and the handing over of an increasing number of cases to the magistrates from the Crown Court, would doubtless be prominent in the discussion. The North American lawyer's mind might turn to the bench trial and the capacity of the accused in the majority of cases to eschew the privilege of jury trial and entrust his or her fate to the professional judge. For the lawyer from a civil law culture, the opportunity to contrast the workings of trial with and without jury may provoke reflection upon the advantages of incorporating more lay judging into continental procedures.[2] Finally, for the comparativist and theorist, there is an invitation to consider whether the conceptual models used to compare the professional trial with trial by jury, principally the contest model and the inquest model, are

---

[1] See Dickson (1992b).

[2] Certain European countries are considering the introduction of a greater lay element into their procedural systems. The new Spanish Constitution imposes a duty on the legislature to introduce jury trial: see Munday (1993). Italy is considering the introduction of lay justices: see Davies, 'Lay justice: one of our best exports?', *Times*, 28 June 1994. Japan is considering the restoration of jury trial: Lempert (1992).

helpful either in explaining the working practices of the trial process or in idealizing the range of procedural choice in such a process.

It is hoped that this book contains at least some material of interest to those engaged in each of these debates. The authors recognize the following ambitions and limitations in this study. First, although the book focuses on forty-three trials conducted in the Crown Court in Northern Ireland, twenty-six Diplock and seventeen jury trials, it is intended to present more than a simple analysis of the mechanics and dynamics of the court process in those trials observed. For one thing, the number of cases analysed is small. More importantly, the trials provided a platform for a broader discussion, rather than a framework to contain and restrict analysis. On the other hand, the book does not provide an answer to the major question underlying the comparison of the professional trial and its lay counterpart, namely which forum has the greater benefits or strength. On a more positive note, we believe that our description of the dynamics at work in Diplock and jury trials is relevant to the various debates identified above. Primarily, the study enables reflections to be made about the Diplock process of trial by judge alone in Northern Ireland. Our aim has been to analyse the workings of the Diplock trial and to make contrasts with trial by jury with as few preconceptions as possible about either mode of trial. However, in view of the controversy surrounding the emergency regime in which the Diplock trial has existed, some evaluation of this method of trial is appropriate. Secondly, although there are risks in extrapolating too much from one specific context, particularly when it has been at the centre of political strife, we believe that our analysis does offer some wider lessons for the operation of trials without jury throughout the common law world. There are those who see trials by professional judges as a *via medea* between the expensive full-scale jury trial and the alternative of the guilty plea,[3] but we would suggest that some fundamental rethinking needs to take place before these trials can be viewed as an acceptable substitute for trial by jury. Finally, we believe that the study poses a challenge to some of the theoretical constructs used to describe trial processes in both the common law and civil law world. The remaining sections deal in turn with each of these issues.

REFLECTIONS ON THE DIPLOCK CONTEXT

In this book we have sought to ascertain whether the judge's assumption of fact-finding responsibilities in Diplock trials changes the nature of the adversarial trial by jury. We contrasted two ideal models of proof, the contest model and the inquest model, which have long been used to

---

[3] See Langbein (1979), 269.

characterize Anglo-American and continental European legal processes, and considered whether the absence of the jury caused judges to deviate from the umpireal role associated with the former model towards the inquisitorial role associated with the latter. We found that judges have scope in both jury and non-jury criminal trials to exercise a more intrusive influence over the proceedings than is compatible with the umpireal ideal. There was, however, no clear evidence from our survey that judges necessarily acted in a more inquisitorial manner when sitting in the absence of the jury. The general, although not universal, view expressed by the judges who spoke to us was that it was inappropriate to deviate from the umpireal role required in adversarial proceedings. Judges were mindful of the fact that in Northern Ireland jury trials continue alongside trials by a judge alone, and that since jury trial is still considered to be the ideal mode of criminal trial, deviations from this ideal should be kept to a minimum. This illustrates the fact that ideological influences play an important part in shaping judicial behaviour in court. Since justice is itself considered to be epitomized by jury trial, it is not surprising that judges should try to adhere to the umpireal role associated with these proceedings. This is especially likely when, as in Northern Ireland, jury trial continues to be a prominent feature of the criminal justice system.

The counsel who appeared in Diplock trials were also heavily steeped in a 'jury culture', as counsel as well as judges in Northern Ireland regularly appear in both jury and Diplock proceedings. Counsel clearly directed very different arguments towards judges and juries but there were no marked differences in the way in which they chose to present the evidence in the two modes of trial. This may have been attributable as much to a 'Diplock influence' on jury trials as to a 'jury influence' on Diplock trials. Although, for example, counsel tended to agree more evidence in Diplock trials, this did occur in some jury trials. We have seen that in a small jurisdiction such as Northern Ireland informal working practices between counsel, and between counsel and judges, are inevitable, but the existence of an entirely professional mode of trial such as the Diplock trial is likely in itself to encourage informal working arrangements which smooth the paths of all the practitioners concerned and these may have spilled over into the conduct of jury trials.

There were not then dramatic differences between the professional conduct of Diplock and jury trials, but there was in both jury and Diplock proceedings considerable variation in the degree of active intervention by individual judges, with some acquiring a reputation for being 'interventionist' or 'non-interventionist' no matter what the mode of trial. A minority of judges confessed to interventionist tendencies which deviated from their proper umpireal role, but most seemed to believe that their interventions were compatible with this role. There was some disagreement, however, about the extent to which it was appropriate for judges to engage in particular kinds of questioning such as cross-examination and even questioning designed to clarify the full effect of a witness's testimony. This illustrates that there is considerable uncertainty about the proper boundaries of the judicial role in criminal trials in general, and it can be argued that these boundaries need to be clarified. In its concern to improve the efficiency of trial management, the Royal Commission on Criminal Justice urged judges to take a more interventionist approach towards trial proceedings,[4] but little thought was given to whether this was compatible with the umpireal ideal.

Although judges were not generally ideologically disposed to adopt a different role in non-jury proceedings, almost all the judges we spoke to admitted that there were occasions when the fact-finding function which they assumed in Diplock proceedings meant that they might take a more probing approach than if they were presiding over a jury trial. It was noticeable that judges in Diplock trials took a more inquiring approach towards defence witnesses. The absence of the jury seemed to free judges from the careful detachment which they felt had to be preserved in jury trials and at the same time prompted them as the triers of fact to play a more intrusive role. Judges also accepted that, unlike jurors, they were able to engage in direct discussion with counsel on questions of fact. Closing submissions were in many cases transformed from formal speeches to personal dialogue between judge and counsel. Counsel in turn generally said that a judge who played an intrusive role affected their own conduct of the proceedings. Although the adversarial structure of the trial remained in so far as the prosecution and defence still presented their cases to the court, the contest itself changed at times from an all-out forensic struggle between prosecution and defence towards a more focused skirmish on particular contested issues, with the judge himself occasionally entering into the fray of argument, particularly in the closing stages. At times this gave the impression of a 'problem-solving' model of proof. In Chapter Nine we saw that one judge in particular adhered to this approach even to the extent of formulating his judgment in the course of a deliberative exchange with counsel.

More significant perhaps than any change in the way in which the proceedings were conducted was the fact that whatever stance the judge took at trial, the substitution of the judge for the jury effected a change in the nature of the arguments raised against the prosecution case. Such arguments tended to abandon broader sympathy points in favour of a closer and more focused analysis of the weight of the evidence. This prompted us to suggest that judges *did* adopt an approach towards the evidence which

---

[4] See ch 8, para. 2 of the report.

could be described as 'case-hardened', not in the commonly understood sense of being prosecution-minded, but in the sense of confining their consideration to the issue of legal guilt on the offences charged. This did not necessarily disadvantage accused persons. Indeed we saw that judges were scrupulous in applying a strict legal standard of proof to the evidence and there were certain kinds of cases and certain kinds of evidence which counsel admitted they would prefer to be tried by professionals. The fact remained, however, that the scope of the contest was more restricted and there could be no consideration of the merits of conviction other than on the basis of the legal standards to be applied to the defendant. In jury trials, by contrast, counsel were given greater freedom within more relaxed standards of relevance to build up a rounded picture of a defendant or a witness which then enabled them to appeal to the merits of the case. Of course, judges may question the relevance of certain lines of inquiry in jury trials, but they seemed to have greater inhibition about doing so. In sum, even when conducted within an ostensibly similar set of formal rules and procedures, the professional trial and the lay trial will almost inevitably differ in practice. To confine the lay tribunal's attention purely to the issue of legal guilt, or to expect of judges a merits-based approach which transcends the evidence, would be to controvert the essential nature of those respective institutions. In the next section we shall consider more fully the implications of the removal of the lay element from the decision-making process.

In our introductory chapter we noted that 1994 saw a significant step towards the ending of the troubles which have beset Northern Ireland since the late sixties. At the time of writing, however, the Diplock era has not ended. Yet the controversy surrounding the use of non-jury trials will continue, largely because the trials have been associated with an emergency regime which has, by its very nature, symbolized the instability of the Northern Ireland political situation. It would, though, be facile to suppose that the political context within which the courts operate provides the sole impetus for discontentment about trial without jury. Let us suppose that Northern Ireland's troubles had subsided totally, without any question of a reprise, that non-jury courts had been preserved as the norm for the trial of any offences of a political nature, and that the Diplock system had maintained a record in respect of miscarriages of justice which compared favourably with that of the criminal justice system in England and Wales. Even then, it is by no means certain that criticism of the non-jury process would significantly decline. On the contrary, the demand for a return to trial by jury for all serious criminal cases would be likely to intensify due to the less pressing justification for its continued disuse.[5] This demand would

---

[5] The experience of the Special Criminal Court in Dublin, however, is that it has become accepted as a relatively permanent fixture in the administration of justice in the Republic of Ireland: see Robinson (1980), 4.

be largely attributable to the enduring appeal of the lay element of the jury, an appeal which (as discussed in Chapter One) has remained remarkably strong in the face of considerable pressure. However, there are at least two further related factors which would keep the non-jury issue live. First, picking up on a constant theme of this book to which we shall return at the end, the process of trial without jury continues to be conducted in the same environment as jury trials and within jury-styled perameters. Secondly, this lack of attention to the changed nature of the process has left a vacuum in which the professional trial is disabled from affording the accused a qualitatively equivalent opportunity to influence the trial's outcome. This disablement might be described as an 'adversarial deficit'.

AN ADVERSARIAL DEFICIT?

The cardinal lesson to be drawn from the study of the Diplock system is that the absence of the jury does not lead ineluctably to the abandonment by triers of fact of the traditional umpireal role and the adoption of an active case management approach which substantially increases the guilty plea and conviction rate. Much depends on the context in which the professional trial operates and a number of factors seem to be relevant to the issue of whether the trial will uphold the due process values associated with traditional jury trial. First of all, there is the question of whether trial by judge alone is considered of equal importance to jury trial. Diplock proceedings involve the most serious offences and they must therefore attempt to match the standards of jury proceedings. Other kinds of professional trial, of course, may determine less serious cases. Secondly, ideological considerations, together with societal and institutional pressures, motivate judges and counsel to adopt a particular stance. In the Diplock context we have seen that judges have to perform their fact-finding functions in the full glare of publicity, and this extra pressure has made them particularly anxious to be seen to uphold the 'rule of law' and the principle of proof beyond reasonable doubt. However, the temptation to pursue policies which are less advantageous to the accused might be much stronger in a regime which is under less constant scrutiny. Judges are, of course, required to be independent, but they can never be totally independent of the environment in which they work and any pressure to increase quantitative output at the expense of qualititative output could work to the disadvantage of defendants.[6] Another important consideration here is the degree to which

---

[6] The proposal to employ justices' clerks in English magistrates' courts on fixed term contracts with performance-related pay was criticized, for example, on the ground that it threatened the independence of the justices' clerk in giving advice to magistrates: see 'Justices' clerks opposed to Government "reforms" ', (1993) 143 New Law Journal, 1322.

practitioners arc steeped in a jury culture. When practitioners appear regularly in both jury and non-jury proceedings, the influences of jury trial are reinforced in their day-to-day practice. A third factor derives from the institutional practices which have taken hold in the working environment of the criminal courts. As we have noted, the intimacy of the Northern Ireland jurisdiction promotes the evolution of informal working practices among judges and counsel which would not be possible in a larger jursdiction. Moreover, when judges are permitted to read the prosecution papers before trial they can get a feel of the case before it is formally presented in court. Finally, there are the personalities of the individual actors and working relationships between them. A dominant judge may be inclined to adopt an inquisitorial approach, particularly before inexperienced counsel. Conversely, experienced practitioners may dominate proceedings before a relatively passive judge.

All these factors show that there is room for significant variation in the way in which non-jury proceedings are conducted. Whatever attempts are made, however, to base such proceedings on the model of the jury trial, the accused necessarily suffers an 'adversarial deficit' when tried in a totally professional environment. In Chapter Three we discussed various meanings of adversariness. The first definition associated adversariness with a liberal ideology in which the individual is entitled to have the case against him or her proved. This has tended to be associated with Anglo-American procedures, although we noted that many of the features identified as adversarial are found in European procedures. Although adversariness is often associated with giving primacy to individual rights, there has been considerable imprecision about what 'adversarial rights' are. One way of clarifying 'adversariness' is to view it as a set of processual characteristics which enable individuals both to invoke legal procedures to uphold their legal rights and interests and also to participate in any procedures which affect their rights and interests, in order that they may influence the outcome of the proceedings.

It is our argument that even when constraints are placed on judges to adopt an umpireal role in proceedings where they are charged with the task of determining guilt, the defendant suffers an adversarial deficit in at least two respects. The first concerns the nature of the fact-finding function which the tribunal is required to discharge. On one view, when judicial triers assume fact-finding responsibilities their role is no different from that of jurors. Essentially this role is to determine whether the prosecution has proved the guilt of the accused. On a different view, guilt is not the only issue to be decided. Criminal proceedings are taken on behalf of the community, and decisions must therefore be taken either by the community or by persons acting on its behalf. When lay triers are the decision-makers they act *as* the community and they can afford to take a more wide-ranging view of both the merits of the proceedings and the merits of convicting the defendant as charged. Professional triers cannot take such a wide-ranging view of the case. They are accountable first to the legal system and ultimately to the community for their decisions and this requires them to apply the criminal law to the accused strictly on the basis of the evidence relevant to the specific charge brought. The nature of the proceedings therefore shifts away from the resolution of a dispute between the state and the individual towards a more tightly controlled forum for determining the defendant's guilt. The chief reason why defence counsel seemed to prefer jury to Diplock proceedings was that the former gave them more freedom to develop their case. Although professional proceedings may remain adversarial in form, the parties themselves are granted less scope to determine the ambit of the dispute.

The second respect in which the accused suffers an adversarial deficit is derived from the position occupied by the professional trier in the proceedings. Whatever stance individual professional triers assume, we have seen that they exercise a more pervasive influence over the proceedings than lay triers could ever achieve. It could not, of course, be argued that the parties to *any* type of dispute would thereby necessarily suffer an adversarial deficit. In civil proceedings, for example, the parties decide on the ambit of the dispute, and they are put on an equal procedural footing to influence the professional trier deciding the case. In criminal proceedings, however, the parties are not in a position of equality. The prosecution is invariably in a much stronger position than the defence and procedures have to be designed to protect the accused. Where procedural control of the action is vested in the parties, as in the common law world, this requires that high evidentiary barriers be erected to enable the defendant to confront and challenge the prosecution case at trial where all admissible evidence is presented freshly before a tribunal unversed in the details of the case.

One problem with this, however, is that it is easier to keep information away from lay triers than from professional triers, and there are greater opportunities for a professional tribunal to reach conclusions about the case which are not based strictly on admissible evidence adduced at trial. Juries generally come to the trial ignorant about the details of the case whereas professional triers may have some inside information. This need not always follow, of course. Jurors may have some knowledge of cases which have provoked widespread media attention and, conversely, judges may on occasions be unable to read any papers in advance of the trial and therefore have little idea of what the case is about. Once the case starts, however, professionals are much better placed than lay triers to pick up background about the case which may not be apparent to lay minds. As noted in Chapter Eight, for example, judges can very quickly work out whether a defendant is of good or bad character. Apart from this, judges can easily become privy to inadmissible evidence during the trial. It may be that judges are better placed than lay triers to prevent themselves being influenced by this inadmissible evidence. This is not because they are endowed with a superhuman ability to exclude such evidence from their minds, but rather because the judicial fact-finder must confine the scope of his or her inquiries within legal boundaries. Nevertheless, we saw in Chapter Eight that there are several ways in which inadmissible evidence may affect the judge's fact-finding inquiries.

A further problem is that proceedings which are structured to enable the defence to mount a full contest to the prosecution case may become skewed by the intrusion of a professional trier, who inevitably exercises a greater influence over the conduct of the case than a lay tribunal. The result is that counsel may be less contest-oriented in their approach to the case. Professional triers have an opportunity to make their views known even before the contest has begun. Once the case has started they can indicate, either explicitly or implicitly, how they view it. Of course, counsel may resist such signals, but there is little point in doing so if it is clear that the judge's mind is veering in a particular direction. Moreover, counsel must maintain a working relationship with the judge which is likely to last beyond the individual case at hand. The point is not just that judges may consciously try to influence counsel's approach to the case, but that judges and counsel may with time get to know each other so well that counsel has a very clear idea how the case will be received, which may in turn influence his or her conduct of the case. It is not likely that a jury's reaction can be gauged so readily. Jurors are less able to communicate their views to counsel during the trial and even if this opportunity were given, since the jury consists of twelve individuals, they are unlikely to speak with one voice. This may suggest that a collegiate bench would be preferable to trial by a single judge because it may be less easy for a collegiate bench to come to a view about a case at an early stage of the proceedings. Much, however, would depend on the composition of such a bench, as less experienced judges might find it difficult to withstand the forcefully expressed views of their more senior colleagues.[7]

It is stressed again that the fact that defendants are subject to an adversarial deficit in non-jury proceedings does not mean that they must always be disadvantaged in such proceedings. Defendants may have a better chance of contesting certain issues successfully before a judge. Moreover, the fact that counsel have a much less clear idea of how jurors are thinking about the case may not always be an advantage. It prevents counsel from responding to the real concerns of the jury and it may encourage counsel to contest a case which has no hope of succeeding. It does not therefore follow

---

[7] This difficulty is referred to in the Baker Report (1984), 35–6.

that the outcome of jury trials will always be more favourable to defendants. The point is rather that the process is rendered less adversarial by the pressures on the defendant not to contest the prosecution case fully on the merits, as is the norm in the context of jury trial.

Although it appears inevitable that defendants suffer an adversarial deficit in non-jury proceedings, we have nevertheless seen that judges have considerable discretion in the conduct of such proceedings. There are at least two ways in which the deficit which we have identified could be redressed. First, judges could consciously try to follow the umpireal role demanded of them in the jury trial. This is the strategy which seems to have been most favoured in Diplock trials. It has the advantage of deviating as little as possible from the conventional role of judges in jury trials and of maintaining the semblance of the jury ideal. One problem, however, as we have seen, is that it is by no means clear exactly what the conventional umpireal role *does* demand of judges. Apart from this, such a strategy makes no concession to the fact that the structure of the trial is irredeemably altered when the jury is withdrawn, and a professional trier of fact is placed in a very different position from that of his or her lay counterpart. Both the responsibility that is given to the professional trier to determine guilt on behalf of the community and the position of strength that he or she occupies in the trial make it inevitable that a more dominant influence will be exerted over the parties than could possibly be exerted by a jury. Even if the judge's freedom were curbed by explicitly reinforcing the umpireal role, it is unlikely that this would remedy the adversarial deficit. The deficit is inherent in the assumption by a judge of fact-finding responsibilites, *whether or not* this prompts individual judges to adopt a more active stance during the trial. Ironically, the dominance of the judicial position may be *reinforced* by a reluctance to intervene. The intrusive judge will at least make his or her feelings known and counsel may get a chance to counter them. The passive judge on the other hand need not disclose his or her line of thought and counsel will not get a chance to contest it before judgment is delivered.

The alternative and more satisfactory method of countering the deficit would commence with an open recognition that the judge's assumption of fact-finding responsibilities has changed the nature of the proceedings. The aim would be to consider how best adversarial values could be accomodated within the new structure. We saw in the last chapter that this has to some extent been recognized in the requirement of the professional trier to justify the conclusions. If the transfer of fact-finding responsibilities from lay triers to professional triers inevitably dilutes the quality of the adversarial struggle between prosecution and defence and casts the trier of fact in a much more dominant position, then it seems natural to require the trier of fact to account fully for any decision reached against the accused. In the last chapter, however, we found that in contrast to the summing-up, the judgment is generally constructed in private by the judge, and that there is limited opportunity for counsel to influence its form. Moreover, even when an automatic right of appeal is given to the defendant, the Court of Appeal is reluctant to dispute the validity of the judge's findings of fact. It follows that the judgment alone is not sufficient to meet the adversarial deficit which defendants experience as a result of the judge's dominance of the trial. The defendant may be able to challenge the prosecution case but the judgment requirement does nothing to enable the defence to challenge the views of the person who really matters in the forum which counts, the trial.

For this reason, we suggested in Chapter Nine that judges should be required to make a provisional statement of their conclusions which could be challenged by the parties in advance of the final determination. It was argued that such an approach to the process of decision-making would import an element of adversariness which is lacking in present procedures. In this way, the judge's position of strength would be offset by the opportunity for the defence to challenge fully at trial the line of reasoning followed by the decision-maker. It was also argued that a recognition of the changing shape of the trial in the jury's absence should be accompanied by a recognition that appellate courts need not be bound by those constraints which inhibit the review of juries' findings of fact. However, it has not been our intention in this book to construct an ideal model of decision-making for a non-jury trial system. Rather, our observations have prompted us to argue that there is a *need* for such an exercise to be conducted. It should be recognized that trial by a professional judge is a distinct mode of proceeding rather than perpetuating the fiction that a jury-oriented process is easily adapted to a jury-less tribunal. Such an observation is valid not only in the specific context of the Diplock court system in Northern Ireland, but also in the broader context of the debate on the future of trial by jury within the adversary tradition.

RETHINKING THE ROLE OF JUDGES AND JURIES

Our analysis throughout has been rooted in the trial process itself. However, it would be wrong to ignore the deep malaise current in the criminal justice systems of a number of countries. The establishment of two Royal Commissions within less than fifteen years of each other has reflected this discontent in England and Wales. These were established to address particular miscarriages of justice which had come to light, but there has also been a more general public concern about the way in which criminal cases are dealt with, and an increased feeling on the part of defendants and other interested parties such as victims that matters are concluded over their heads.[8] One reason for this is the growing 'professionalization' of criminal justice. The increased opportunity for representation by trained legal professionals has placed accused persons in a much stronger position to argue the merits of their case.[9] But increasing professionalization, with the police, lawyers, and the criminal justice agencies dominating the criminal justice system, has created the risk of justice becoming out of tune with both the demands of the community and the interests of lay participants, including the defendant.[10] The gradual waning of the jury's influence has led in many common law jurisdictions including England and Wales to substantial numbers of cases being concluded on the basis of professional advice and negotiation which is not subject to any open scrutiny.

This loss of confidence has caused many to suggest radical solutions. Some have found attraction in the idea of moving towards a more informal system of justice.[11] Others have looked for solutions beyond their immediate jurisdiction, with many in the common law world seeking to draw lessons from the so-called inquisitorial system of justice in continental Europe, and Europeans looking increasingly towards the common law world. Although the Royal Commission on Criminal Justice was reluctant to delve deeply into comparative experience, it did make certain recommendations which on its own admission would move the system in a more inquisitorial direction. It has not been part of our task to offer solutions to the complex question of loss of confidence. However, our study of the dynamics of judge and jury trials in Northern Ireland suggests that we need to rethink some of the concepts associated with our systems of criminal justice before we can consider solutions.

Running throughout the present book has been a series of contrasts. Our main concern has been to examine those features which distinguish trial by a professional judge from conventional trial by jury. On a more specific level, we have sought to contrast the approaches adopted by different judges to the determination of issues in the jury's absence. In this process we have referred to certain theoretical categories which have been employed to characterize legal procedures. Particular reference has been made to the dichotomies developed by Damaska in the course of his work on the comparative law of procedure: the distinction between conflict resolution and policy implementation as two different purposes of adjudication, the distinction between coordinate and hierarchical structures of judicial authority and, most particularly, the distinction between contest and

---

[8] Langbein (1978). The concerns of defendants were voiced in Baldwin and McConville (1977), ch 5. See also Justice (1993a); (1993b). For the concerns of victims, see Shapland, Willmore, and Duff (1985).

[9] It took a long time for defendants to secure adequate legal representation in the English criminal courts: see Abel-Smith and Stevens (1967), ch 6.

[10] See Shapland (1994); McConville, Hodgson, Bridges and Pavlovic (1994).

[11] See Matthews (1988).

inquest models of proof. The first of these helped to illustrate how the distinctively merits-approach of lay adjudicators to a case is far better suited to a procedure which aims at conflict resolution than the one intended to implement policy. Jury trial also helps to reinforce the coordinate ideals of common law adjudication because it illustrates the greater priority given to the application of community norms and the greater tolerance for inconsistent decision-making which is less susceptible to review by a superior authority. Trial without jury, on the other hand, inevitably shifts the focus towards more technical standards of decision-making and greater accountability on the decision-maker.

However, as stressed in Chapter Three, reliance upon generalized distinctions and ideal-type models has its risks, as it can conceal alternative perspectives, and also fail to catch the full complexity of real life processes.[12] For these reasons perhaps, the distinction between contest and inquest models of proof turned out to be less illuminating in the context of our study than anticipated, even though this distinction is the one most commonly invoked to contrast different legal procedures. The point was made in Chapter Three that Anglo-American systems cannot adequately be characterized as 'adversarial' or contest-based, and that continental systems do not conform purely to 'inquisitorial' or inquest-based methods of procedure. Nevertheless, it has generally been assumed that, beyond the level of description, these terms are useful ways of idealizing the essential attributes of Anglo-American and European legal procedures. In our study, however, even this assumption proved questionable.

Indeed, as the study progressed it became apparent that the contest and inquest models of proof were not always capable of encapsulating the full dynamics of practice in either the jury or the non-jury trials we observed. We saw that the crucial dynamic between counsel and judge in both modes of trial made it difficult to describe either process as party-driven (contest-oriented) or judge-driven (inquest-oriented). This was particularly the case in certain Diplock trials where the dialogue which developed between counsel and judge reflected a problem-solving model of proof rather than a contest or inquest model. But even in jury trials, where the judge is typically described as an umpireal moderator, judges on occasions played an important facilitative role in teasing out the truth. In Chapter Five we suggested that the wider responsibilities of judges in criminal trials can still be reconciled with the notion of an umpireal role, but the considerable

---

[12] 'Dichotomies provide only two-dimensional slices through reality: they give us black and white and—depending upon their degree of refinement—"innumerable shades of grey" . . . But they do not give us the "reds and greens and blues" ': Markovits (1989), 1340–1. As an example, Markovits notes that one of the problems with the dichotomy between policy-implementation and conflict-resolution is that these notions are not 'truly antithetical' because some policies may aim for a multitude of goals which are themselves in conflict (1337).

variation in judicial style which we observed and the lack of clarity about the extent to which judges should intervene in the course of the criminal trial questions the usefulness of continuing to describe this role as purely 'umpireal' in nature.

Nor is it so clear that either of the traditional models *should* necessarily dominate our conceptions of proof in the forensic process and govern our choice of procedure. The point has been made that the two models may epistemologically have more in common than is usually thought. In particular we suggested that both subscribed to what has been called a rationalist theory of evidence.[13] Challenges have been made to the assumptions which underlie this theory[14] and, more specifically, to the contest and inquest models of proof on which it is based.[15] Both models assume that witnesses' perceptions are crystallized at the time of events and that information about the past does not change much as it is reported and repeated, with the result that the formal stages of proof are able to provide first-hand accounts of the events in question.[16] In addition, as emphasized in Chapter Eight, the kind of 'atomistic' or individuated approach towards the presentation and justification of evidence which both models encourage does not reflect the way in which triers of fact actually approach many of the factual issues in criminal cases. A further assumption is that triers of fact do not need to engage in the cut and thrust of argumentative debate with the parties before reaching their conclusion. If, however, evidence is a process by which fact-finders come to conclusions, rather than a set of individual items from which conclusions may be deduced, then arguably the process of reasoning used by fact-finders to reach conclusions ought to be subjected to as much argument as the evidence actually adduced by the parties. Nor is it so clear that either model promotes satisfaction of the important requirement that all interested parties must be able to participate meaningfully in the process. We have suggested that concepts such as 'adversariness' can be reconceptionalized to give expression to this goal, but this does not entail a commitment to the traditional contest and inquest models and indeed may be regarded as a call for a loosening of the theoretical constraints which these models impose.

What does this mean then for judge and jury trials, the focus of our study? One way to facilitate greater participation by interested parties is by shifting the focus of attention from the trial towards the pre-trial process. The absence of the jury enables this shift to take place. This is already happening in civil cases where the withdrawal of the jury has made it possible to move

---

[13] See Chapter Three, pages 78–9.
[14] See, for example, Jackson, B.S. (1988); Nicolson (1994); Seigel (1994).
[15] See, for example, Jackson (1988a); MacCrimmon (1990).
[16] See MacCrimmon (1990), 381.

the emphasis away from the continuous trial.[17] So long as the jury remains a force in criminal procedure, the focal point of adversarial protection is the contested trial where the jury arbitrates between the prosecution and defence. Attempts to involve professional judges more in pre-trial and appellate procedures can be met with the objection that judges are not best equipped to fulfil the fact-finding function. But when jury trial is withdrawn or waived there is less reason why the focal point of adversarial protection should remain at the trial itself. The professional triers who take the jury's place may move into areas where they have hitherto feared to tread and take a more active fact-finding role in both pre-trial procedure and appellate review. As the substitution of professionals for lay triers shifts the process away from conflict resolution more towards the pure determination of guilt, so indeed there is less justification for permitting the parties to negotiate over the guilt of the accused, and more justification for subjecting the guilty plea to greater judicial scrutiny. An open professional trial with proper adversarial protections for the accused may be considered a better way of disposing of criminal cases than a plea negotiated between professionals outside court, which at present accounts for the vast majority of disposals. It could be argued that the choice facing accused persons should not be whether to waive the right to a trial, but whether to waive the right to *jury* trial. Every defendant who chose to waive this right would appear for a trial at which the prosecution would first outline the evidence on the charges brought and the judge would have to be satisfied of the guilt of the accused before the question of sentence was considered. Accused persons who admitted their guilt would have to submit themselves to questioning by the judge. Questions of cost could no doubt be raised against such a procedure. However, many trials would end up substantially abbreviated because there would be no true contest to the charges ('slow pleas' as they have been called in the United States[18]), and in addition there might be a number of genuine contests which defendants preferred to have heard in the (much less expensive) bench trial. At any rate such a system would provide a more accountable form of justice to both the community and the accused. There would no doubt be sentencing incentives to those who waived jury trial, if only because those who were admitting their guilt would be entitled to have this fact reflected in their sentence. But the accused would at least have the protection that an accountable trier of fact had been publicly satisfied that a finding of guilt should be made.

---

[17] One contributor to the W. G. Hart Workshop on 'Dispute Resolution: Civil Justice and its Alternatives' noted that the two striking features of the English trial—'its climactic nature as a drama played out in one continuous session' and 'the extent to which the proceedings are oral'—have each undergone substantial change: see Hoffmann (1993), 297, 304.

[18] See Maher (1979), 2, 149–50.

Such ideas, with their obvious inquisitorial connotations, may not appeal to those with a deep scepticism about merging elements of adversarial and inquisitorial procedures. As noted in Chapter Three, it has been argued that it is 'idle to attempt vital organ transplants between dissimilar organisms.'[19] Our response to this, however, would be that the absence of lay participants from the criminal process affects the procedure in any event because professional triers of fact exercise a dominance over the procedure which could never be matched by the lay tribunal. The judge's dominance derives from the strength of the judicial role and not just from the extent of an individual's propensity to intervene. Before a jury a picture of guilt is built up slowly, piece by piece, with an opportunity at each stage for the defence to challenge the emerging picture. No matter how hard a professional trier may try to simulate the conditions of jury trial, the trial can no longer be perceived purely as a two-way contest between prosecution and defence. Although the trial may not necessarily assume an overtly inquisitorial character, as particular judges may not enter the arena with enthusiasm, the adversary context must change to incorporate a tripartite channel of communication.

Viewed in this light, the 'transplant' analogy is less pertinent. Rather, the issue is how adversarial protections may be infused into a process which has *already* undergone fundamental change. Our argument for a revised approach to non-jury trials does not stem from a belief that there are particular facets of inquisitorial procedure which are intrinsically preferable to those of adversarial procedure, nor indeed that the inquest model of proof is better than the contest model. It stems rather from a need to recognize the changed context of practice and from a need to attune existing models of proof to current conceptions of truth-finding and fair process generally. Such rethinking need not be restricted to the non-jury trial, but may also have ramifications for the process of trial by jury itself. It has, for example, been suggested that one of the strengths of jury trial, in addition to the 'freshness' of the lay mind, is that the fact-finding body remains fully open to persuasion by the parties right up until the point of its retirement to deliberate as a collective unit. It may be, however, that this theoretical opportunity for the parties to maximize their influence on the decision-making process is not fully exploited in practice. In Chapter Nine, for example, we noted that not all jurisdictions which employ jury trial offer the parties a real opportunity to influence the judge's final presentation of the issues to the jury. A call for greater party participation at this stage of the process need not be perceived in terms of enhancing the trial's contest orientation, nor in terms of curtailing the judge's more

---

[19] Uviller (1975), 1075. See Chapter Three, note 97 and accompanying text.

inquisitive abilities. Rather, it may be viewed as transcending the contest-inquest dichotomy and as striving towards a process which gives greater prominence to the concerns of truth-finding and fairness than to conformity with a model which has traditionally been associated with the Anglo-American trial.

Another aspect of jury trial procedure which invites closer attention is the ability of the jury to engage more actively in the trial process as the evidence unfolds. We demonstrated in Chapter Seven that jurors are neither ideally placed nor generally encouraged to ask questions in the course of the trial. Judges frequently question witnesses on their behalf, whether at the request of the jury or otherwise. The possibility could also be explored of opening a more formal channel of communication through which the jury could take a more active truth-finding role. It is remarkable that so many defences of the institution of the jury are based on its claim to primacy as a fact-finder, yet pay scant attention to the reality of the conventional jury trial in which there is an almost complete barrier between those who ultimately determine the facts and those who provide the basis for this determination. The fear has been expressed that juror participation may result in a greater risk of prejudice to the accused, and in a risk of proceedings getting out of hand,[20] but equally there are risks attached to the non-participation of the jury. It may be better that any possible ignorance and prejudice on the part of the jury are exposed during the trial than that they be allowed to fester silently until they are unleashed behind the closed doors of the deliberation room.[21]

There is then an argument for a revised approach to both jury and non-jury trials. But it is not our view that jury trials are an anachronism of a bygone age which should be abandoned in favour of professional trials. Admittedly, if presented with the task of devising an ideal criminal process from the mythical state of the original position, behind what Rawls termed the 'veil of ignorance', it is unlikely that one's rational inclination would lead towards the adoption of a system of trial by jury as we currently know it.[22] Yet we have argued that there is an important connection between adversarial protection and the present system of trial by jury, and that such protection ought not readily to be sacrificed even if one is prepared to sacrifice the institution of the jury itself. It is an inescapable fact that jury trial is in many jurisdictions being confined to increasingly limited classes of offences. In our view, this development ought to be accompanied by a vigorous search for feasible alternative modes of trial and disposition,

[20] See the Morris Committee (1965), para. 283.

[21] For further argument in favour of more meaningful dialogue between presenters of evidence and triers of fact, see Jackson (1988), (1990); Allen (1994). For further discussion of the prejudice which can be caused by jury passivity, see Jackson (1995).

[22] See Rawls (1972), ch 4 (but for Rawls' more recent views, see Rawls (1993)).

within which the adversarial protection afforded by the jury is preserved. The professional trial is worth considering as one alternative, but only if the changed context in which such a trial takes place is recognized. Reason might not lead one to the choice of the present system of jury trial from behind the veil of ignorance. Yet it is even more unthinkable that one would be attracted to a process whose rules, practices, and procedures are predicated on the existence of a lay fact-finding tribunal but from which that tribunal has been extracted. Such, however, is the formal character of the present day non-jury trial in the common law world and, more specifically, in Northern Ireland.

Procedural choices in the realm of criminal justice are not of course taken from a position of ignorance. The real backdrop to such decisions is the long history of the jury standing at the pinnacle of the criminal justice process. When considering alternative decision-making mechanisms, it is right to aspire to a system which will preserve the degree of adversarial protection which the jury accords to an accused person. This does not, however, mean that the best means of securing justice is to import procedural characteristics from jury trial to the new environment from which the jury is absent. It is at this point that we need to free ourselves from the grip of jury-thinking. Trial without jury need not remain transfixed as at present by the jury's spectre.

Bibliography

Abel-Smith, B., and Stevens, R. (1967). *Lawyers and the Courts: A Sociological Study of the English Legal System, 1750–1965*, London: Heinemann.

Adler, Z. (1982). 'Rape – the Intention of Parliament and the Practice of the Courts', Modern Law Review 45: 664–75.

Allen, R.J. (1991). 'The Nature of Juridical Proof', Cardozo Law Review 13: 373–422.

—— (1992). 'Introductory Remarks: Reform of Evidence Conference'. Vancouver, 12–14 Aug. 1992. (Unpublished.)

—— (1994). 'Factual Ambiguity and a Theory of Evidence', Northwestern University Law Review 88: 604–40.

Allen, R.J., and Kuhns, R.B. (1989). *An Analytical Approach to Evidence*, Boston: Little, Brown.

Amnesty International (1978). *Report of an Amnesty International Mission to Northern Ireland, 28 Nov. – 6 Dec. 1977*, London: Amnesty International.

—— (1992). *Fair trial concerns in Northern Ireland: the right of silence*, London: Amnesty International.

Anderson, T., and Twining, W.L. (1991). *Analysis of Evidence*, London: Weidenfeld and Nicolson.

Andrews, J.A. (ed.) (1982). *Human Rights in Criminal Procedure: A Comparative Study*, The Hague: Nijhoff.

Archbold: Pleading, Evidence and Practice in Criminal Cases (1994) (general ed., Richardson, P.J.). London: Sweet and Maxwell. (Cited in the text as '*Archbold*'.)

Ashworth, A. (1979). 'Concepts of Criminal Justice', Criminal Law Review 412–27.

—— (1993). 'Plea, Venue and Discontinuance', Criminal Law Review 830–40.

Ashworth, A., and Creighton, P. (1990). 'The Right of Silence in Northern Ireland', in Hayes and O'Higgins (eds.).

Atkinson, J.M., and Drew, P. (1979). *Order in Court: the Organisation of Verbal Interaction in Judicial Settings*, London: Macmillan.

Austin, J.L. (1961). *How to do Things with Words*, Oxford: Oxford University Press.

Baldwin, J. (1993). *The Role of Legal Representatives at the Police Station*, London: HMSO.

Baldwin, J. and McConville, M. (1977). *Negotiated Justice*, London: Martin Robertson.

—— (1979). *Jury Trials*, Oxford: Clarendon Press.

Bankowski, Z. (1981). 'The value of truth: fact scepticism revisited', Legal Studies 1: 257–66.

—— (1988). 'The Jury and Reality', in Findlay and Duff (eds.).

Bankowski, Z., and Mungham, G. (1976). *Images of Law*, London: Routledge & Kegan Paul.

Bankowski, Z., Hutton, N., and McManus, J. (1987). *Lay Justice?*, Edinburgh: T. & T. Clark.

Bardon, J. (1992). *A History of Ulster*, Belfast: Blackstaff.

Bedford, S. (1961). *The Faces of Justice*, London: Collins.

Bennett, W.L., and Feldman, M. (1981). *Reconstructing Reality in the Courtroom*, London: Tavistock.

Berman, H.J. (ed.) (1961). *Talks in American Law* (revised edition, 1971). New York: Vintage Books.

Binder, D., and Bergman, P. (1984). *Fact Investigation*, Minn.: St. Paul.

Block, B. , Corbett, C., and Peay, J. (1993). 'Ordered and Directed Acquittals in the Crown Court: A Time of Change?', Criminal Law Review 95–106.

Blom-Cooper, L. (1991). 'Public Confidence and the Criminal Process'. Northern Ireland Criminal Justice Conference, Oct. 1991. (Unpublished.)

Bonner, D. (1984). 'The Baker Review of the Northern Ireland (Emergency Provisions) Act 1978'. Public Law 348–64.

—— (1985). *Emergency Powers in Peacetime*, London: Sweet & Maxwell.

—— (1988). 'Combating Terrorism: Supergrass Trials in Northern Ireland', Modern Law Review 51: 23–53.

Bottoms, A.E., and McClean, J.D. (1976). *Defendants in the Criminal Process*, London: Routledge & Kegan Paul.

Boyd, A. (1984). *The Informers: A Chilling Account of the Supergrasses in Northern Ireland*, Dublin: Mercier Press.

Boyd, D. (1982). 'Justice on the *Voir Dire*: Two Cheers for *R v Brophy*', Northern Ireland Legal Quarterly 33: 70–84.

Boyle, K. (1982). 'Human Rights and the Northern Ireland Emergency', in Andrews (ed.).

Boyle, K., Hadden, T., and Hillyard, P. (1973). *Justice in Northern Ireland: A Study in Social Confidence*, London: Cobden Trust.

—— (1975). *Law and State: The Case of Northern Ireland*, London: Martin Robertson.

—— (1980a). *Ten Years On in Northern Ireland: The Legal Control of Political Violence*, London: Cobden Trust.

—— (1980b). 'How Fair are the Ulster Trials?', New Society, 13 Nov. 1980, 320–2.

Brennan, W. (1963). 'The Criminal Process: Sporting Event or Quest for Truth?', Washington University Law Quarterly 61: 279.

—— (1990). 'The Criminal Process: Sporting Event or Quest for Truth? A Progress Report', Washington University Law Quarterly 88: 1–18.

Broeder, D.W. (1954). 'The Functions of the Jury: Fact or Fictions?', University of Chicago Law Review 27: 386.

Buckland, P. (1981). *A History of Northern Ireland*, Dublin: Gill and Macmillan.

Bulow-Moller, A.M. (1991). 'Trial Evidence: Overt and Covert Communication in Court', International Journal of Applied Linguistics 1: 38–60.

Buxton, R. (1990). 'Challenging and Discharging Jurors', Criminal Law Review 225–35.

Byrne, R. (1984). 'The Director of Public Prosecutions' Power to Refer Cases to the Special Criminal Court – Judicial Reviewability', Dublin University Law Journal 6: 177–84.

Callen, C. (1982). 'Notes on Grand Illusion: Some Limits on the Use of Bayesian Theory in Evidence Law', Indiana Law Journal 57: 1–44.

Campbell, C. (1989). 'Extradition to Northern Ireland: Prospects and Problems', Modern Law Review 52: 585–621.

Carlen, P. (1976). *Magistrates' Justice*, London: Martin Robertson.

Casanovas, P. (1990). 'Towards a Sociopragmatics of Legal Discourses and Decision-Making in a Spanish Court'. Paper delivered at Law and Semiotics Conference, Onati. (Unpublished.)

Chambers, G., and Miller, A. (1986). *Prosecuting Sexual Assault*, Edinburgh: HMSO.

Chambliss, W., and Seidman, R. (1971). *Law, Order and Power*, London: Addison-Wesley.

Chan, T.F., Duff, P., Findlay, M., and Howarth, C. (1990). *The Jury in Hong Kong*, Hong Kong: City Polytechnic of Hong Kong Law Department.

Charrow, R.P., and Charrow, V.R. (1979). 'Making Legal Language Understandable: A Psycholinguistic Study of Jury Instructions', Columbia Law Review 79: 1306–74.

Chayes, A. (1976). 'The Role of the Judge in Public Law Litigation', Harvard Law Review 89: 1281–1316.

Choo, A.L-T. (1993). *Abuse of Process and Judicial Stays of Criminal Proceedings*, Oxford: Oxford University Press.

Clark, R. (1990). *Comparative and Private International Law: Essays in Honour of John Merryman*, Berlin: Duncker and Humblot.

Cohen, L.J. (1977). *The Probable and the Provable*, Oxford: Clarendon Press.

—— (1980). 'The Logic of Proof', Criminal Law Review 91–103.

Committee on the Administration of Justice (1992). *The Casement Trials: A Case Study on the Right to a Fair Trial in Northern Ireland* (CAJ Pamphlet No. 19), Belfast: Committee on the Administration of Justice.

Cornish, W.R. (1968). *The Jury*, London: Penguin.

Cornish, W.R., and Sealy, A.P. (1973). 'Juries and the Rules of Evidence: LSE. Jury Project', Criminal Law Review 208–23.

Damaska, M. (1973). 'Evidentiary Barriers to Conviction and Two Models of Criminal Procedure: A Comparative Study', University of Pennsylvania Law Review 121: 507–89.

—— (1975a). 'Structures of Authority and Comparative Criminal Procedure', Yale Law Journal 84: 480–544.

—— (1975b). 'Presentation of Evidence and Factfinding Precision', University of Pennsylvania Law Review 123: 1083–106.

—— (1983). 'Adversary System', in Kadish (ed.).

—— (1986). *The Faces of Justice and State Authority*, New Haven: Yale University Press.

—— (1988). 'Reflections on the Character of Evidence in Continental and Anglo-American Systems'. (Unpublished.)

—— (1990). 'Atomistic and Holistic Evaluation of Evidence', in Clark (ed.).

—— (1992). 'Of Hearsay and its Analogues', Minnesota Law Review 76: 425–58.

Danet, P., and Bogosch, P. (1980). 'Fixed Fight or Free-For-All? An Empirical Study of Combativeness in the Adversary System of Justice', British Journal of Law and Society 7: 36–60.

Davies, G., Lloyd-Bostock, S., McMurran, M., and Wilson, C. (eds.) (1995). *Psychology, Law and Criminal Justice: Developments in Research and Practice*, Berlin: de Gruyter.

Denning, Lord (1980). *The Due Process of Law*, London: Butterworths.

Dennis, I.H. (ed.) (1986). *Criminal Law and Justice*, London: Sweet & Maxwell.

Darbyshire, P. (1991). 'The Lamp That Shows That Freedom Lives: Is it Worth the Candle?', Criminal Law Review 740–52.

Devlin, P. (1956). *Trial by Jury*, London: Stevens.

—— (1979). *The Judge*, Oxford: Oxford University Press.

Diamond, S.S. (1990). 'Revising Images of Public Punitiveness: Sentencing by Lay and Professional English Magistrates', Law and Social Inquiry 191–218.

Diamond, S.S., and Casper, J.D. (1992). 'Blindfolding the Jury to Verdict Consequences: Damages, Experts and the Civil Jury', Law and Society Review 26: 513–63.

Dickson, B. (1989). 'The Contribution of Lord Diplock to the General Law of Contract', Oxford Journal of Legal Studies 9: 441–62.

—— (1992a). 'Northern Ireland's Troubles and the Judges', in Hadfield (ed.).

—— (1992b). 'Northern Ireland's Emergency Legislation – the Wrong Medicine?', Public Law 592–624.

—— (1993). *The Legal System of Northern Ireland* (3rd edition.), Belfast: SLS.

Doob, A.N., and Kirschenbaum, H.M. (1972). 'Some Empirical Evidence on the Effect of s.12 of the Canada Evidence Act Upon an Accused', Criminal Law Quarterly 15: 88–96.

Doran, S. (1989). 'Descent to Avernus', New Law Journal 139: 1147–48, 1160.

—— (1991a). 'The Symbolic Function of the Summing-Up in the Criminal Trial: Can the Diplock Judgment Compensate?' Northern Ireland Legal Quarterly 42: 365–73.

—— (1991b). 'Alternative Defences: the "invisible burden" on the trial judge', Criminal Law Review 878–91.

—— (1992). 'Alternative Offences: Let the Jury Choose', Criminal Law Review 843–53.

Doran, S., and Jackson, J.D. (1992). 'The Judicial Role in Northern Ireland', in Munro and Wasik (eds.).

—— (1994). 'The Relevance to Northern Ireland of the Report of the Royal Commission on Criminal Justice', in *Nineteenth Report of the Standing Advisory Commission on Human Rights: Report for 1993–94*, London: HMSO.

Duff, A. (1986). *Trials and Punishments*, Cambridge: Cambridge University Press.

Duff, A., and Simmonds, N. (1984). *Philosophy and the Criminal Law*, Wiesbaden: Steiner Verlag.

Dunstan, R. (1980). 'Context for Coercion: Analyzing Properties of Courtroom Questions', British Journal of Law and Society 7: 61–77.

Dworkin, R. (1977). *Taking Rights Seriously*, London: Duckworth.

Easton, S. (1991). *The Right of Silence*, Aldershot: Dartmouth.

Eggleston, R. (1991). 'Similar Facts and Bayes' Theorem', Jurimetrics Journal 31: 275–87.

Ely, J.H. (1980). *Democracy and Distrust: A Theory of Judicial Review*, Cambridge, Mass.: Harvard University Press.

Enright, S., and Morton, J. (1990). *Taking Liberties: The Criminal Jury in the 1990s*, London: Weidenfeld and Nicolson.

Ericson, R., and Baranek, P.M. (1982). *Ordering of Justice: A Study of Accused Persons as Dependants in the Criminal Process*, Toronto: Toronto University Press.

Erickson, B., Lind, A., Johnson, B., and O'Barr, W. (1978). 'Speech Style and Impression Formation in a Court Setting: The Effect of "Powerful" and "Powerless' Speech", Journal of Experimental Psychology 14: 266–79.

Evans, K. (1983). *Advocacy at the Bar*, London: Blackstone.

Findlay, M., and Duff, P. (eds.) (1988). *The Jury Under Attack*, London: Butterworths.

Finn, J.E. (1991). *Constitutions in Crisis: Political Violence and the Rule of Law*, New York: Oxford University Press.

Fletcher, G. (1968). 'Two Kinds of Legal Rules: A Comparative Study of Burden-of-Persuasion Practices in Criminal Cases', Yale Law Journal 77: 880–935.

Flew, A. (ed.) (1951). *Essays on Law and Language*, Oxford: Blackwell.

Frank, J. (1949). *Courts on Trial: Myth and Reality in American Justice* (reprinted 1973), Princeton, New Jersey: Princeton University Press.

Frankel, M. (1975). 'The Search for Truth: An Umpireal View', University of Pennsylvania Law Review 123: 1031–59.

Fraser, D. (1993). *Cricket and the Law*, Sydney: Institute of Criminology, Sydney University Law School.

Freedman, M. (1975). 'Judge Frankel's Search for Truth', University of Pennsylvania Law Review 123: 1060–6.

Freeman, M. (1978). 'The Social Construction of Truth: Some Thoughts on Jury Trials and Current Research into Juries', Preston Polytechnic Law Review 1: 3–17.

—— (1981). 'The Jury on Trial', Current Legal Problems 34: 65–111.

Fuller, L. (1961). 'The Adversary System', in Berman (ed.).

Galligan, D. (1986). *Discretionary Powers: A Legal Study of Official Discretion*, Oxford: Clarendon Press.

—— (1988). 'The Right to Silence Reconsidered', Current Legal Problems 41: 69–92.

Gearty, C. (1993). 'The European Court of Human Rights and the Protection of Civil Liberties: An Overview', Cambridge Law Journal 52: 89–127.

Goldstein, A. (1960). 'The State and the Accused: Balance of Advantage in Criminal Procedure', Yale Law Journal 69: 1149–99.

—— (1974). 'Reflections on Two Models: Inquisitorial Themes in American Criminal Procedure', Stanford Law Review 26: 1009–25.

Goodpaster, G. (1987). 'On the Theory of the American Adversary Trial', Journal of Criminal Law and Criminology 78: 118–54.

Gifford, T. (1984). *Supergrasses: The Use of Accomplice Evidence in Northern Ireland*, London: Cobden Trust.

Graham, E. (1983). 'A Vital Weapon in the Anti-terrorist Arsenal', Fortnight, Oct. 1983, 10.

Grant, E. (1985). 'The Use of "Supergrass" Evidence in Northern Ireland 1982–1985', New Law Journal 135: 1125–7.

Green, L. (1930). *Judge and Jury*, Kansas: Vernon.

Greer, D.S. (1973). 'Admissibility of Confessions and the Common Law in Times of Emergency', Northern Ireland Legal Quarterly 24: 199–210.

—— (1980). 'The Admissibility of Confessions Under the Northern Ireland (Emergency Provisions) Act', Northern Ireland Legal Quarterly 31: 205–38.

Greer, S.C. (1986). 'Supergrasses and the Legal System in Britain and Northern Ireland', Law Quarterly Review 102: 198–249.

—— (1987). 'The Rise and Fall of the Northern Ireland Supergrass System', Criminal Law Review 663–70.

—— (1994). 'Miscarriages of Criminal Justice Reconsidered', Modern Law Review 57: 58–74.

Greer, S.C., and Hadden, T. (1983). 'Supergrasses on Trial', New Society, 24 Nov. 1983, 330–1.

Greer, S.C. and Morgan, R. (eds.) (1990). *The Right to Silence Debate*, Bristol: Bristol Centre for Criminal Justice.

Greer, S.C., and White, A. (1986). *Abolishing the Diplock Courts: The Case for Restoring Jury Trial to Scheduled Offences in Northern Ireland*, London: Cobden Trust.

—— (1988a). 'Restoring Jury Trial to Terrorist Offences in Northern Ireland', in Findlay and Duff (eds.).

—— (1988b). 'A Return to Trial by Jury', in Jennings (ed.).

Griew, E. (1989). 'Summing Up the Law', Criminal Law Review 768–80.

Griffith, J.A.G. (1992). *The Politics of the Judiciary* (4th edition). London: Fontana.

Griffiths, J. (1970). 'Ideology in Criminal Procedure *or* a Third "Model" of the Criminal Process', Yale Law Journal 79: 359–417.

Hadden, T., and Wright, S. (1979). 'A terrorist trial in Crumlin Road', New Society, 28 June 1979, 770–1.

Hadfield, B. (1989). *The Constitution of Northern Ireland*, Belfast: SLS.

—— (ed.) (1992). *Northern Ireland: Politics and the Constitution*, Buckingham: Open University Press.

Hans, V.P., and Doob, A.N. (1975). 'Section 12 of the Canada Evidence Act and the Deliberations of Simulated Juries', Criminal Law Quarterly 18: 235–53.

Hans, V.P., and Vidmar, N. (1986). *Judging the Jury*, New York: Plenum.

Harcup, T. (1983). 'Supergrasses in Northern Ireland', Legal Action Group Bulletin, Dec. 1983, 10, 16.

Harnon, E. and Stein, A. (1993). 'Reform Movements in Criminal Procedure and the Protection of Human Rights in Israel', International Review of Penal Law 64: 1177–92.

Hart, H.L.A. (1961). *The Concept of Law*, Oxford: Clarendon Press.

Harris, S. (1984). 'Questions as a Mode of Control in Magistrates' Courts', International Journal of the Sociology of Language 49: 5–27.

Harvey, R. (1981). *Diplock and the Assault on Civil Liberties*, London: Haldane Society.

Hastie, R. (ed.) (1993). *Inside the Juror*, Cambridge: Cambridge University Press.

Hastie, R., Penrod, S.D., and Pennington, N. (1983). *Inside the Jury*, Cambridge: Harvard University Press.

Hayes, J., and O'Higgins, P. (eds.) (1990). *Lessons from Northern Ireland*, Belfast: SLS.

Hellerstein, W.E., McKay, R.B., and Schlam, P.R. (1988). 'Criminal Justice and Human Rights in Northern Ireland: A Report to the Association of the Bar of the City of New York', The Record of the Association of the Bar of the City of New York 93: 110–214.

Heuer, L., and Penrod, S.D. (1989). 'Instructing Jurors', Law and Human Behaviour 13: 409

Hill, C., and Lee, S. (1993). 'Without Fear or Favour? Judges and Human Rights in Northern Ireland', in *Eighteenth Report of the Standing Advisory Commission on Human Rights: Report for 1992–93*, London: HMSO.

Hillyard, P., and Percy-Smith, J. (1984). 'Converting Terrorists: The Use of Supergrasses in Northern Ireland', Journal of Law and Society 11: 335–55.

Hoffmann, L. (1975). 'Similar Facts After *Boardman*', Law Quarterly Review 91: 193–206.

—— (1993). 'Changing Perspectives on Civil Litigation', Modern Law Review 56: 297–306.

Holdsworth, W.S. (1922). *A History of English Law* (3rd edition), London: Sweet & Maxwell.

Howard, A. (ed.) (1965). *Criminal Justice in Our Time*, Charlottesville: University Press of Virginia.

Hunt, P., and Dickson, B. (1993). 'Northern Ireland's Emergency Laws and International Human Rights', Netherlands Quarterly of Human Rights 173.

Hunter, J. (1987). 'How justice is done according to Diplock', The Law Magazine, 27 Nov. 1987, 28–9.

Inn of Court School of Law (1993). *Evidence and Casework Skills* (5th edition), London: Blackstone.

Jacobs, F.G. (1980). *The European Convention on Human Rights*, Oxford: Clarendon Press.

Jackson, B.S. (1988). *Law, Fact and Narrative Coherence*, Merseyside: Deborah Charles Publications.

Jackson, J.D. (1980). 'Probability and Mathematics in Court Fact-Finding', Northern Ireland Legal Quarterly 31: 239–54.

—— (1983a). *Northern Ireland Supplement to Cross on Evidence*, Belfast: SLS.

—— (1983b). 'The Application for a Direction in Northern Ireland', Northern Ireland Legal Quarterly 34: 187–206.

—— (1983c). 'Questions of Fact and Questions of Law', in Twining (ed.).

—— (1985). 'The Use of "Supergrasses" as a Method of Prosecution in Northern Ireland', in *Tenth Report of the Standing Advisory Commission on Human Rights: Report for 1983–1984*, London: HMSO.

—— (1986). 'Three Judge Courts in Northern Ireland', in *Twelfth Report of the Standing Advisory Commission on Human Rights: Report for 1985–1986*, London: HMSO.

—— (1988a). 'Theories of Truth Finding in Criminal Procedure: An Evolutionary Approach', Cardozo Law Review 10: 475–527.

—— (1988b). 'The Northern Ireland (Emergency Provisions) Act 1987', Northern Ireland Legal Quarterly 39: 235–57.

—— (1988c). 'Credibility, Morality and the Corroboration Warning', Cambridge Law Journal 47: 428–54.

—— (1989). 'Recent Developments in Criminal Evidence', Northern Ireland Legal Quarterly 40: 105–30.

—— (1990a). 'Developments in Northern Ireland', in Greer and Morgan (eds.).

—— (1990b). 'Getting Criminal Justice out of Balance', in Livingstone and Morison (eds.).

—— (1990c). 'Jury Confidence in Jury Service: A New Impetus to Jury Research', Social Behaviour 5: 139–53.

—— (1991). 'Curtailing the Right of Silence: lessons from Northern Ireland', Criminal Law Review 404–15.

—— (1992a). 'Law's Truth, Lay Truth and Lawyers' Truth: The Representation of Evidence in Adversary Trials', Law and Critique 3: 29.

—— (1992b). 'The Dangers of Discretion', Legal Action, Nov. 1992, 8–9, 42.

—— (1994a). 'Trial by Jury and Alternative Modes of Trial', in McConville and Bridges (eds.).

—— (1994b). 'The Right of Silence: Judicial Responses to Parliamentary Encroachment', Modern Law Review 57: 270–80.

—— (1994c). 'Due Process', in McCrudden and Chambers (eds.).

—— (1995). 'Juror Decision Making and the Trial Process', in Davies, Lloyd-Bostock, McMurran, and Wilson (eds.).

Jackson, J.D., and Doran, S. (1989). 'The Diplock court: time for re-examination', New Law Journal 139: 464–6.

—— (1990). 'Judicial Fact-Finding in the Diplock Court in Northern Ireland', University of Manchester Faculty of Law Working Paper No. 2.

—— (1992a). 'Diplock and the Presumption Against Jury Trial: a critique', Criminal Law Review 755–66.

—— (1992b). 'The Court of Appeal in Northern Ireland', in *Seventeenth Report of the Standing Advisory Commission on Human Rights: Report for 1992*, London: HMSO.

—— (1993). 'Conventional Trials in Unconventional Times: The Diplock Court Experience', Criminal Law Forum 4: 503–20.

Jackson, J.D., Kilpatrick, R., and Harvey, C. (1991). *Called to Court: A Public View of Criminal Justice in Northern Ireland*, Belfast: SLS.

Jennings, A. (1988). *Justice Under Fire: The Abuse of Civil Liberties in Northern Ireland*, London: Pluto.

Jennings, A., and Wolchover, D. (1984). 'Northern Ireland: Star Chamber versus the Gang of Twelve', New Law Journal 134: 659–61, 687–8.

Jowell, J., and Oliver, D. (eds.) (1989). *The Changing Constitution* (2nd edition), Oxford: Clarendon Press.

Justice (1989). *Miscarriages of Justice* (Chairman of Committee, Sir George Waller), London: Justice.

—— (1993a). *Miscarriages of Justice – A Defendant's Eye View*, London: Justice.

—— (1993b). *Negotiated Justice*, London: Justice.

—— (1994). *Right of Silence Debate: The Northern Ireland Experience*, London: Justice.

Kadish, S.H. (1983). *Encyclopaedia of Crime and Justice*, London: MacMillan.

Kalven, H., and Zeisel, H. (1966). *The American Jury*, Boston: Little, Brown.

Kamisar, Y. (1965). 'Equal Justice in the Gatehouses and Mansions of American Criminal Procedure', in Howard (ed.).

Kassin, S.M., and Wrightsman, L.S. (1988). *The American Jury on Trial: Psychological Perspectives*, New York: Hemisphere.

Kedar, L. (1987). *Power through Discourse*, Norwood: Ablex.

Kerameus, K.D. (1987). 'A Civilian Lawyer Looks at Common Law Procedure', Louisiana Law Review 47: 493–509.

Korff, D. (1984). *The Diplock Courts in Northern Ireland: A Fair Trial?*, Utrecht: Studie en Informatiecentrum Mensenrechten.

Kunert, K. (1966). 'Some Observations on the Origin and Structure of Evidence under the Common Law System and the Civil Law System of "Free Proof" in the German Code of Criminal Procedure', Buffalo Law Review 16: 122–64.

Langbein, J.H. (1979). 'Understanding the Short History of Plea Bargaining', Law and Society Review 13: 261–72.

—— (1983). 'Shaping the 18th Century Criminal Trial: A View from the Ryder Sources', University of Chicago Law Review 50: 1–136.

—— (1985). 'The German Advantage in Civil Procedure', University of Chicago Law Review 52: 823–66.

Law Officers' Department (1974). *Prosecutions in Northern Ireland: A Study of Facts*, London.

Lawrence, J. (1988). 'Making just decisions in magistrates' courts', Social Justice Research 2: 155–76.

Lee, S. (1990). 'Comparative Law: Home Rule(s)', in Plender (ed.).

Lempert, R. (1975). 'Modeling Relevance', Michigan Law Review 75: 1021–57.

—— (1992). 'A Jury for Japan?', American Journal of Comparative Law 40: 37–71.

—— (1993). 'Why do jury research?', in Hastie (ed.).

Levin, A.L., and Cohen, H.K. (1971). 'The Exclusionary Rules in Nonjury Criminal Cases', University of Pennsylvania Law Review 119: 905–32.

Levine, M. (1974). 'Scientific Method and the Adversary Model', American Journal of Psychology 29: 661.

Livingstone, S. (1990). 'Using Law to Change a Society: The Case of Northern Ireland', in Livingstone and Morison (eds.).

Livingstone, S., and Morison, J. (1990). *Law, Society and Change*, Aldershot: Dartmouth.

Loftus, E. (1980). 'Language and Memories in the Judicial System', in Shuy and Shnukal (eds.).

Lopes, L. (1993). 'Two Conceptions of the Juror', in Hastie (ed.).

Lowry, Rt. Hon. Lord (1992). 'National Security and the Rule of Law', Israel Law Review 26: 117–41.

McBarnet, D. (1981). *Conviction*, London: Macmillan.

McCabe, S. (1988). 'Is Jury Research Dead?', in Findlay and Duff (eds.).

McCabe, S., and Purves. P. (1972). *The Jury at Work*, Oxford: Blackwell.

—— (1974). *The Shadow Jury at Work*, Oxford: Blackwell.

McConville, M., and Baldwin, J. (1981). *Courts, Prosecution and Conviction*, Oxford: Clarendon Press.

McConville, M., and Bridges, L. (eds.) (1994). *Criminal Justice in Crisis*, London: Elgar.

McConville, M., Hodgson, J., Bridges, L. and Pavlovic, A. (1994). *Standing Accused: The Organisation and Practices of Criminal Defence Lawyers in Britain*, Oxford: Clarendon Press.

McConville, M., and Mirsky, C. (1994). 'Redefining and Structuring Guilt in Systematic Terms: The Royal Commission's Recommendations Regarding Guilty Pleas', in McConville and Bridges (eds.).

McConville, M., Sanders, A., and Leng, R. (1991). *The Case for the Prosecution*, London: Routledge.

MacCormick, D.N. (1978). *Legal Theory and Legal Reasoning*, Oxford: Clarendon Press.

McCrudden, C. (1989). 'Northern Ireland and the British Constitution', in Jowell and Oliver (eds.).

McCrudden, C., and Chambers, G. (1994). *Individual Rights and the Law in Britain*, Oxford: Oxford University Press.

McEwan, J. (1992). *Evidence and the Adversarial Process*, Oxford: Blackwell.

McNamara, P. (1985). 'The Canons of Evidence: Rules of Exclusion or Rules of Use', Adelaide Law Review 10: 341–64.

Maher, G. (1984). 'Balancing Rights and Interests in the Criminal Process', in Duff and Simonds (eds.).

—— (1988). 'The Verdict of the Jury', in Findlay and Duff (eds.).

—— (1994). 'Reforming the Criminal Process: A Scottish Perspective', in McConville and Bridges (eds.).

Marcus, G. (1990). 'Secret Witnesses', Public Law 207–23.

Mark, R. (1973). *Minority Verdict*, Dimbleby Lecture, London: BBC Publications.

Mather, L.M. (1979). *Plea Bargaining or Trial?* Lexington, Mass.: Lexington Books.

Markovits, I. (1989). 'Playing the Opposites Game: On Mirjan Damaska's *The Faces of Justice and State Authority*', Stanford Law Review 41: 1313–41.

Matthews, R. (ed.) (1988). *Informal Justice?*, London: Sage.

Morgan, E.M. (1937). 'The Jury and the Exclusionary Rules of Evidence', University of Chicago Law Review 4: 247–58.

Morison, J., and Leith, P. (1992). *The Barrister's World and the Nature of Law*, Milton Keynes: Open University Press.

Morris, C. (1942). 'Law and Fact', Harvard Law Review 55: 1303–41.

Moxon, D. (ed.) (1985). *Managing Criminal Justice*, London: HMSO.

Munday, R. (1990). 'Irregular Disclosure of Evidence of Bad Character', Criminal Law Review 92–7.

—— (1993). 'Jury trial, continental style', Legal Studies 13: 204–24.

Munro, C., and Wasik, M. (eds.) (1992). *Sentencing, Judicial Discretion and Training*, London: Sweet & Maxwell.

Murphy, P. (1992). *A Practical Approach to Evidence* (4th edition), London: Blackstone.

Nance, D. (1988). 'The Best Evidence Principle', Iowa Law Review 73: 227–97.

Nelken, D. (1986). 'Criminal Law and Criminal Justice: Some Notes on their Irrelation', in Dennis (ed.).

Nesson, C. (1985). 'The Evidence or the Event? On Judicial Proof and the Acceptability of Verdicts', Harvard Law Review 98: 1357–92.

Nicolson, D. (1994). 'Truth, Reason and Justice: Epistemology and Politics in Evidence Discourse', Modern Law Review 57: 726–44.

Nijboer, J.F. (1992). 'Common Law Tradition in Evidence Scholarship Observed from a Continental Perspective', American Journal of Comparative Law 41: 299–338.

Nobles, R., Schiff, D., and Shaldon, N. (1993). 'The Inevitability of Crisis in Criminal Appeals', International Journal of the Sociology of Law 21: 1–21.

Nokes, G.D. (1956). 'The English Jury and the Law of Evidence', Tulane Law Review 21: 153–72.

Note (1965). 'Improper Evidence in Nonjury Trials: Basis for Reversal?', Harvard Law Review 79: 407–15.

O'Barr, W.M. (1982). *Linguistic Evidence: Language, Power and Strategy in the Court*, New York: Academic Press.

O'Connell, M. (1991). 'The Case of the Armagh Four', New Law Journal 141: 429–31.

O'Connor, P. (1990). 'The Court of Appeal: Re-trials and Tribulations', Criminal Law Review 615–28.

Packer, H.L. (1964). 'Two Models of the Criminal Process', University of Pennsylvania Law Review 113: 1–68.

Pannick, D. (1988). *Judges*, Oxford: Oxford University Press.

Pattenden, R. (1990). *Judicial Discretion and Criminal Litigation* (2nd edition), Oxford: Clarendon Press.

Paterson, A. (1982). *The Law Lords*, London: Macmillan.

Peay, J. (1989). *Tribunals on Trial: A Study of Decision-Making under the Mental Health Act 1983*, Oxford: Clarendon Press.

Pennington, N., and Hastie, R. (1986). 'Evidence evaluation in complex decision making', Journal of Personality and Social Psychology 51: 242–58.

—— (1991). 'A Cognitive Theory of Juror Decision Making: The Story Model', Cardozo Law Review 13: 519–57.

—— (1993). 'The story model for juror decision making', in Hastie (ed.).

Pickles, J. (1988). *Straight From The Bench*, London: Hodder & Stoughton.

Plender, R. (ed.) (1990). *Legal History and Comparative Law: Essays in Honour of Albert Kiralfy*, London: Frans Cass.

Ploscowe, M. (1935). 'The Development of Present Day Criminal Procedures in Europe and America', Harvard Law Review 48: 433–73.

Pound, R. (1906). 'The Causes of Popular Dissatisfaction with the Administration of Justice', in *Report of the Twenty-ninth Annual Meeting of the American Bar Association*, Philadelphia: Dando.

Pradel, J. (1994). 'France', in Van Den Wyngaert (ed.).

Pugh, G.W. (1962). 'Administration of Criminal Justice in France: An Introductory Analysis', Louisiana Law Review 23: 1–28.

Rawls, J. (1972). *A Theory of Justice*, Oxford: Clarendon Press.

—— (1993). *Political Liberalism*, New York: Columbia University Press.

Rescher, N. (1980). *Scepticism*, Oxford: Blackwell.

Robertson, B. (1990). 'John Henry Wigmore and Arthur Allan Thomas: An example of Wigmorian analysis', Victoria University of Wellington Law Review 20: 181–212.

Robinson, M.T.W. (1974). *The Special Criminal Court*, Dublin: Dublin University Press.

—— (1980). 'The Special Criminal Court: Almost Eight Years On', Fortnight, Mar. 1980, 4–6.

Rock, P. (1993). *The Social World of an English Crown Court: Witnesses and Professionals in the Crown Court Centre at Wood Green*, Oxford: Clarendon.

Rose, G. (1982). *Deciphering Sociological Research*, London: MacMillan.

Roshier, B., and Teff, H. (1980). *Law and Society in England*, London: Tavistock.

Rutherford, A. (1993). *Criminal Justice and the Pursuit of Decency*, Oxford: Oxford University Press.

Ryan, E.F., and Magee, P. (1983). *The Irish Criminal Process*, Dublin: Mercier Press.

Saks, M.J. (1976). 'The limits of scientific jury selection: Ethical and empirical', Jurimetrics Journal 17: 3–22.

Saltzburg, S. (1978). 'The Unnecessarily Expanding Role of the American Trial Judge', Virginia Law Review 63: 1–81.

Sanders, A., Bridges, L., Mulvaney, A., and Crozier, G. (1989). *Advice and Assistance at Police Stations*, London: Lord Chancellor's Department.

Schulhofer, S. (1984). 'Is Plea Bargaining Inevitable?', Harvard Law Review 97: 1037–107.

Schum, D.A. (1993). 'Argument structuring and evidence evaluation', in Hastie (ed.).

Schum, D.A., and Martin, A. (1982). 'Formal and empirical research on cascaded inference in jurisprudence', Law and Society Review 17: 105–51.

Seigel, M.L. (1994). 'A Pragmatic Critique of Modern Evidence Scholarship', Northwestern University Law Review 88: 995–1045.

Shapland, J. (1981). *Between Conviction and Sentence: The Process of Mitigation*, London: Routledge & Kegan Paul.

—— (1994). 'Professional justice and the public good: is there a choice?' Inaugural lecture, University of Sheffield, 4 May 1994. (Unpublished.)

Shapland, J., Willmore, J., and Duff, P. (1985). *Victims in the Criminal Justice System*, Aldershot: Gower.

Shuy, R.W., and Shnukal, A. (eds.) (1980). *Language Use and the Uses of Language*, Washington DC: Georgetown University Press.

Simon, R.J., and Mahan, L. (1971). 'Quantifying Burdens of Proof: A View from the Bench, the Jury and the Classroom', Law and Society Review 5: 319–30.

Smith, A.T.H. (1983). 'Immunity from Prosecution', Cambridge Law Journal 42: 299–327.

Smith, J.C., and Hogan, B. (1992). *Criminal Law* (7th edition), London: Butterworths.

Spencer, J.R. (1989). *Jackson's Machinery of Justice*, Cambridge: Cambridge University Press.

Spjut, R. (1987). Review of Greer and White's *Abolishing Diplock Courts* and

Darby's *Intimidation and the Control of Conflict in Northern Ireland*, Journal of Law and Society 14: 495–500.

Sprack, J. (ed.) (1992). *Emmins on Criminal Procedure* (5th edition), London: Blackstone.

Stein, A. (1987). 'Bentham, Wigmore and Freedom of Proof' (Review of Twining's *Theories of Evidence: Bentham and Wigmore*), Israel Law Review 22: 245–76.

Stone, M. (1984). *Proof of Fact in Criminal Trials*, Edinburgh: Green.

—— (1988). *Cross-Examination*, London: Butterworths.

Stone, M., and McClean (1990). *Fact-Finding for Magistrates*, London: Fourmat.

Tanford, J.A. (1990). 'The Law and Psychology of Jury Instructions', Nebraska Law Review 69: 71–111.

Tapper, C. (1990). *Cross on Evidence* (7th edition), London: Butterworths.

Thayer, J.B. (1898). *A Preliminary Treatise on the Law of Evidence*, Boston: Little, Brown (reprinted 1969).

Thibaut, J., and Walker, L. (1975). *Procedural Justice: A Psychological Analysis*, Hillsdale, New Jersey: Erlsbaum.

—— (1978). 'A Theory of Procedure', California Law Review 66: 541–66.

Thibaut, J., Walker, L., and Lind, E.A. (1972). 'Adversary Presentation and Bias in Legal Decision Making', Harvard Law Review 86: 386–401.

Tillers, P., and Green, E. (1986). *Probability and Inference in the Law of Evidence: The Uses and Limits of Bayesianism*, Dordrecht: Kluwer.

Tillers, P., and Schum, D.A. (1991). 'A Theory of Preliminary Fact Investigation', University of California Davis Law Review 24: 931–1012.

Trankell, A. (1972). *The Reliability of Evidence*, Stockholm: Beckmans.

Traynor, R.J. (1962). 'Ground Lost and Found in Criminal Discovery', New York University Law Review 39: 228–50.

Tribe, L. (1971). 'Trial by Mathematics: Precision and Ritual in Legal Process', Harvard Law Review 84: 1329–93.

Twining, W.L. (1973). 'Emergency Powers and Criminal Process: The Diplock Report', Criminal Law Review 406–17.

—— (1981). 'Debating Probabilities', Liverpool Law Review 2: 51–64.

—— (ed.) (1983). *Facts in Law*, Wiesbaden: Steiner Verlag.

—— (1985). *Theories of Evidence: Bentham and Wigmore*, London: Weidenfeld and Nicolson.

—— (1986). 'The Boston Symposium: A Comment', Boston University Law Review 66: 391–9.

—— (1989). 'Rationality and Scepticism in Judicial Proof: Some Signposts', International Journal of the Semiotics of Law 2: 69–80.

—— (1990). *Rethinking Evidence: Exploratory Essays*, Oxford: Basil Blackwell.

Twining, W.L., and Miers, D. (1992). *How To Do Things With Rules* (3rd edition), London: Weidenfeld and Nicolson.

Uviller, R. (1975). 'The Advocate, The Truth and Judicial Hackles: A Reaction to Judge Frankel's Idea', University of Pennsylvania Law Review 123: 1067–82.

Valentine, B.J.A.C. (1989). *Criminal Procedure in Northern Ireland (and 'PACE' Supplement)*, Belfast: SLS.

Van Den Wyngaert, C. (1993). *Criminal Procedure Systems in the European Community*, London: Butterworths.

Vennard, J. (1985). 'The Outcome of Contested Trials', in Moxon (ed.).

Vogler, R. (1989). *A Guide to the French Legal System*, London: Prisoners Abroad.

Wagenaar, W.A., van Koppen,P.J., and Crombag, H.F.M. (1993). *Anchored Narratives: The Psychology of Criminal Evidence*, New York: Harvester Wheatsheaf.

Walker, A.G. (1987). 'Linguistic Manipulation, Power and the Legal Setting', in Kedar (ed.).

Walker, C., and Hogan, G. (1989). *Political Violence and the Law in Ireland*, Manchester: Manchester University Press.

Walsh, D.P.J. (1983). *The Use and Abuse of Emergency Legislation*, London: Cobden Trust.

Wasik, M. (1985). 'Rules of Evidence in the Sentencing Process', Current Legal Problems 38: 187–209.

Wigmore, J.H. (1937). *The Science of Judicial Proof* (3rd edition), Boston: Little, Brown.

Wilberforce, R. (1986). 'Lord Diplock and Administrative Law', Public Law 6–7.

Williams, G. (1963). *The Proof of Guilt* (3rd edition), London: Stevens.

—— (1976). 'Law and Fact', Criminal Law Review 472–83, 532–40.

—— (1979). 'The Mathematics of Proof', Criminal Law Review 297–308, 340–54.

Wilson, W.A. (1963). 'A Note on Fact and Law', Modern Law Review 26: 609–24.

Wisdom, J. (1951). 'Gods', in Flew (ed.).

Wissler, R.L., and Saks, M.J. (1985). 'On the Inefficiency of Limiting Instructions On Individual and Group Decision Making', Law and Human Behaviour 9: 37.

Wolchover, D. (1989). 'Should Judges Sum up on the Facts?', Criminal Law Review 781–92.

Zander, M. (1974). 'Are Too Many Professional Criminals Avoiding Conviction? – A Study of Britain's Two Busiest Courts', Modern Law Review 37: 28–61.

—— (1992). 'The Royal Commission's Crown Court Survey', New Law Journal 142: 1730–4.

Zander, M., and Henderson, P. (1993). *Crown Court Study* (Research Study, Royal Commission on Criminal Justice, No. 19), London: HMSO.

Zuckerman, A.A.S. (1986). 'Law, Fact or Justice?', Boston University Law Review 66: 487–508.

—— (1989). *The Principles of Criminal Evidence*, Oxford: Clarendon Press.

OFFICIAL REPORTS

Report of the Departmental Committee on Jury Service. Cmnd. 2627 (1965), London: HMSO. (The Morris Report.)

Report of the Commission to consider legal procedures to deal with terrorist activities in Northern Ireland. Cmnd. 5185 (1972), London: HMSO. (The Diplock Report).

Report of a Committee to consider, in the context of civil liberties and human rights, measures to deal with terrorism in Northern Ireland. Cmnd. 5847 (1975), London: HMSO. (The Gardiner Report).

The Distribution of Criminal Business Between the Crown Court and Magistrates'

Courts: Report of the Interdepartmental Committee. Cmnd. 6323 (1975), London: HMSO. (The James Report).

Report of the Committee of Inquiry into Police Interrogation Practices in Northern Ireland. Cmnd. 7497 (1979), London: HMSO. (The Bennett Report).

Review of Operation of the Northern Ireland (Emergency Provisions) Act 1978. Cmnd. 9222 (1984), London: HMSO. (The Baker Report).

Report of the Fraud Trials Committee. (1986), London: HMSO. (The Roskill Report).

Law Commission (1991). *Criminal Law: Corroboration of Evidence in Criminal Trials*. Cm. 1620 (Law Com. No. 202), London: HMSO.

Law Commission (1993). *The Hearsay Rule in Civil Proceedings*. Cm. 2321 (Law Com. No. 216), London: HMSO.

The Royal Commission on Criminal Justice: Report. Cm. 2263 (1993), London: HMSO.

In 1973, the Standing Advisory Commission on Human Rights was established under the Northern Ireland Constitution Act 1973 to advise the Secretary of State for Northern Ireland on legislation preventing discrimination. In its annual reports, the Commission has frequently examined aspects of the emergency legislation. Where reference is made in the text to the Commission's annual reports, the full citation is given.

In May 1987, Viscount Colville of Culross QC was appointed by the Secretary of State for Northern Ireland 'to report on the way in which the [emergency] legislation has been applied over the previous year and to draw attention to any of the temporary provisions which might safely be allowed to lapse.' Viscount Colville made three annual reports from 1987 to 1989 on this basis, cited in the text as 'Colville' with relevant year in parenthesis. In September 1989, he was appointed to make an 'enhanced review' of the emergency powers in operation. This report was published as *Review of the Northern Ireland (Emergency Provisions) Acts 1978 and 1987*, Cmnd. 1115 (1990), London: HMSO. (Cited as 'Colville (1990)'.) In 1994, responsibility for conducting the annual review passed to John Rowe QC, whose first report was issued in May 1994 (with a major review to follow in 1995).

In December 1992, Sir Louis Blom-Cooper was appointed by the Secretary of State as Independent Commissioner for the Holding Centres and in January 1994, the *First Annual (1993) Report of the Independent Commissioner for the Holding Centres* was issued. (The title of the report is cited in full in the text.)

Index